## DATE DUE

| | | | |
|---|---|---|---|
| | | | |
| | | | |
| | | | |
| | | | |
| | | | |
| | | | |
| | | | |
| | | | |
| | | | PRINTED IN U.S.A. |

# Children's Literature Review

# Guide to Gale Literary Criticism Series

| For criticism on | Consult these Gale series |
|---|---|
| Authors now living or who died after December 31, 1959 | *CONTEMPORARY LITERARY CRITICISM (CLC)* |
| Authors who died between 1900 and 1959 | *TWENTIETH-CENTURY LITERARY CRITICISM (TCLC)* |
| Authors who died between 1800 and 1899 | *NINETEENTH-CENTURY LITERATURE CRITICISM (NCLC)* |
| Authors who died between 1400 and 1799 | *LITERATURE CRITICISM FROM 1400 TO 1800 (LC)*<br><br>*SHAKESPEAREAN CRITICISM (SC)* |
| Authors who died before 1400 | *CLASSICAL AND MEDIEVAL LITERATURE CRITICISM (CMLC)* |
| Black writers of the past two hundred years | *BLACK LITERATURE CRITICISM (BLC)* |
| Authors of books for children and young adults | *CHILDREN'S LITERATURE REVIEW (CLR)* |
| Dramatists | *DRAMA CRITICISM (DC)* |
| Hispanic writers of the late nineteenth and twentieth centuries | *HISPANIC LITERATURE CRITICISM (HLC)* |
| Poets | *POETRY CRITICISM (PC)* |
| Short story writers | *SHORT STORY CRITICISM (SSC)* |
| Major authors from the Renaissance to the present | *WORLD LITERATURE CRITICISM, 1500 TO THE PRESENT (WLC)* |

ISSN 0362-4145

R

volume 34

# Children's Literature Review

Excerpts from Reviews,
Criticism, and Commentary
on Books for Children
and Young People

**Gerard J. Senick**
Editor

**Sharon R. Gunton**
**Alan Hedblad**
Associate Editors

 *Gale Research Inc.*

An International Thomson Publishing Company

I(T)P

NEW YORK • LONDON • BONN • BOSTON • DETROIT • MADRID
MELBOURNE • MEXICO CITY • PARIS • SINGAPORE • TOKYO
TORONTO • WASHINGTON • ALBANY NY • BELMONT CA • CINCINNATI OH

## STAFF

Gerard J. Senick, *Editor*

Sharon R. Gunton, Alan Hedblad, *Associate Editors*

Thomas Carson, Tina Grant, Kathryn Horste, Zoran Minderović, *Assistant Editors*

Marlene H. Lasky, *Permissions Manager*
Margaret A. Chamberlain, Linda M. Pugliese, *Permissions Specialists*
Susan Brohman, Diane Cooper, Maria Franklin, Pamela A. Hayes, Arlene Johnson, Josephine M. Keene,
Michele Lonoconus, Maureen Puhl, Shalice Shah, Kimberly F. Smilay, Barbara A. Wallace,
*Permissions Associates*
Brandy C. Merritt, Tyra Y. Phillips, *Permissions Assistants*

Victoria B. Cariappa, *Research Manager*
Mary Beth McElmeel, Donna Melnychenko, Tamara C. Nott, Tracie A. Richardson, *Research Associates*
Maria E. Bryson, Eva M. Felts, Shirley Gates, Michele P. Pica, Amy T. Roy, Laurel D. Sprague, Amy Beth Wieczorek,
*Research Assistants*

Mary Beth Trimper, *Production Director*
Catherine Kemp, *Production Assistant*

Cynthia Baldwin, *Art Director*
Barbara J. Yarrow, *Graphic Services Supervisor*
C. J. Jonik, *Desktop Publisher*
Willie Mathis, *Camera Operator*

∞™ This book is printed on acid-free paper that meets the minimum requirements of American National Standard for Information Sciences—Permanence Paper for Printed Library Materials, ANSI Z39.48-1984.

Library of Congress Catalog Card Number 94-29718
ISBN 0-8103-8473-6
ISSN 0362-4145
Printed in the United States of America
Published simultaneously in the United Kingdom
by Gale Research International Limited
(An affiliated company of Gale Research Inc.)

I(T)P™   Gale Research Inc., an International Thomson Publishing Company.
ITP logo is a trademark under license.

10 9 8 7 6 5 4 3 2 1

# Contents

Preface   vii

Acknowledgments   xi

# Preface

Literature for children and young adults has evolved into both a respected branch of creative writing and a successful industry. Currently, books for young readers are considered the most popular segment of publishing, while criticism of juvenile literature is instrumental in recording the literary or artistic development of the creators of children's books as well as the trends and controversies that result from changing values or attitudes about young people and their literature. Designed to provide a permanent, accessible record of this ongoing scholarship, *Children's Literature Review (CLR)* presents parents, teachers, and librarians—those responsible for bringing together children and books—with the opportunity to make informed choices when selecting reading materials for the young. In addition, *CLR* provides researchers of children's literature with easy access to a wide variety of critical information from English-language sources in the field. Users will find balanced overviews of the careers of the authors and illustrators of the books that children and young adults are reading; these entries, which contain excerpts from published criticism in books and periodicals, assist users by sparking ideas for papers and assignments and suggesting supplementary and classroom reading. Ann L. Kalkhoff, president and editor of *Children's Book Review Service Inc.*, writes that "*CLR* has filled a gap in the field of children's books, and it is one series that will never lose its validity or importance."

## Scope of the Series

Each volume of *CLR* profiles the careers of a selection of authors and illustrators of books for children and young adults from preschool through high school. Author lists in each volume reflect these elements:

- an international scope.

- representation of authors of all eras.

- the variety of genres covered by children's and/or YA literature: picture books, fiction, nonfiction, poetry, folklore, and drama.

Although earlier volumes of *CLR* emphasized critical material published after 1960, successive volumes have expanded their coverage to encompass important criticism written before 1960. Since many of the authors included in *CLR* are living and continue to write, their entries are updated periodically. Future volumes will supplement the entries of selected authors covered in earlier volumes and will include criticism on the works of authors new to the series.

## Organization of This Book

An author section consists of the following elements: author heading, author portrait, author introduction, excerpts of criticism (each followed by a bibliographical citation), and illustrations, when available.

- The **Author Heading** consists of the author's name followed by birth and death dates. The portion of the name outside the parentheses denotes the form under which the author is most frequently published. If the majority of the author's works for children were written under a pseudonym, the pseudonym will be listed in the author heading and the real name given on the first line of the author introduction. Also located at the beginning of the introduction are any other pseudonyms used by the author in writing for children and any name variations, including transliterated forms for authors whose languages use nonroman alphabets. Uncertainty as to a birth or death date is indicated by question marks.

- An **Author Portrait** is included when available.

- The **Author Introduction** contains information designed to introduce an author to *CLR* users by presenting an overview of the author's themes and styles, biographical facts that relate to the author's literary career or critical responses to the author's works, and information about major awards and prizes the author has received. The introduction begins by identifying the nationality of the author and by listing the genres in which s/he has written for children and young adults. Introductions also list a group of representative titles for which the author or illustrator being profiled is best known; this section, which begins with the words "major works include," follows the genre line of the introduction. For seminal figures, a section that begins with the words "major works about the author include" follows when appropriate; this section lists important biographies about the author or illustrator that are not excerpted in the entry. The centered heading "Introduction" follows the major works section and announces the body of the text. Where applicable, introductions conclude with references to additional entries in biographical and critical reference series published by Gale Research Inc. These sources include past volumes of *CLR* as well as *Authors & Artists for Young Adults, Classical and Medieval Literature Criticism, Contemporary Authors, Contemporary Authors Autobiography Series, Contemporary Authors Bibliographical Series, Contemporary Literary Criticism, Dictionary of Literary Biography, Drama Criticism, Nineteenth-Century Literature Criticism, Poetry Criticism, Short Story Criticism, Something about the Author, Something about the Author Autobiography Series, Twentieth-Century Literary Criticism,* and *Yesterday's Authors of Books for Children.*

- **Criticism** is located in three sections: **Author's Commentary** (when available), **General Commentary** (when available), and **Title Commentary** (in which commentary on specific titles appears). Centered headings introduce each section, in which criticism is arranged chronologically. Titles by authors being profiled are highlighted in boldface type within the text for easier access by readers.

- The **Author's Commentary** presents background material written by the author or by an interviewer. This commentary may cover a specific work or several works. Author's commentary on more than one work appears after the author introduction, while commentary on an individual book follows the title entry heading.

- The **General Commentary** consists of critical excerpts that consider more than one work by the author or illustrator being profiled. General commentary is preceded by the critic's name in boldface type or, in the case of unsigned criticism, by the title of the journal. *CLR* also features entries that emphasize general criticism on the oeuvre of an author or illustrator. When appropriate, a selection of reviews is included to supplement the general commentary.

- The **Title Commentary** begins with the title entry headings, which precede the criticism on a title and cite publication information on the work being reviewed. Title headings list the title of the work as it appeared in its first English-language edition. The first English-language publication date of each work is listed in parentheses following the title. Differing U. S. and British titles follow the publication date within the parentheses.

Entries in each title commentary section consist of critical excerpts on the author's individual works, arranged chronologically by publication date. The entries generally contain two to seven reviews per title, depending on the stature of the book and the amount of criticism it has generated. The editors select titles that reflect the entire scope of the author's literary contribution, covering each genre and subject. An effort is made to reprint criticism that represents the full range of each title's reception, from the year of its initial publication to current assessments. Thus, the reader is provided with a record of the author's critical history. Publication information (such as publisher names and book prices) and parenthetical numerical references (such as footnotes or page and line references to specific editions of works) have been deleted at the editor's discretion to provide smoother reading of the text.

- Selected excerpts are preceded by **Explanatory Notes,** which provide information on the critic or work of criticism to enhance the reader's understanding of the excerpt.

- A complete **Bibliographical Citation** designed to facilitate the location of the original book or article follows each piece of criticism.

- Numerous **Illustrations** are featured in *CLR*. For entries on illustrators, an effort has been made to include illustrations that reflect the characteristics discussed in the criticism. Entries on authors who do not illustrate their own works may also include photographs and other illustrative material pertinent to their careers.

# Special Features

Entries on authors who are also illustrators will occasionally feature commentary on selected works illustrated but not written by the author being profiled. These works are strongly associated with the illustrator and have received critical acclaim for their art. By including critical comment on works of this type, the editors wish to provide a more complete representation of the author's total career. Criticism on these works has been chosen to stress artistic, rather than literary, contributions. Title entry headings for works illustrated by the author being profiled are arranged chronologically within the entry by date of publication and include notes identifying the author of the illustrated work. In order to provide easier access for users, all titles illustrated by the subject of the entry are boldfaced.

*CLR* also includes entries on prominent illustrators who have contributed to the field of children's literature. These entries are designed to represent the development of the illustrator as an artist rather than as a literary stylist. The illustrator's section is organized like that of an author, with two exceptions: the introduction presents an overview of the illustrator's styles and techniques rather than outlining his or her literary background, and the commentary written by the illustrator on his or her works is called "illustrator's commentary" rather than "author's commentary." Title entry headings are followed by explanatory notes identifying the author of the illustrated work. All titles of books containing illustrations by the artist being profiled as well as individual illustrations from these books are highlighted in boldface type.

# Other Features

- The **Acknowledgments,** which immediately follow the preface, list the sources from which material has been reprinted in the volume. It does not, however, list every book or periodical consulted for the volume.

- The **Cumulative Index to Authors** lists all of the authors who have appeared in *CLR* with cross-references to the various literary criticism series and the biographical and autobiographical series published by Gale Research Inc. A full listing of the series titles appears before the first page of the indexes of this volume.

- The **Cumulative Nationality Index** lists authors alphabetically under their respective nationalities. Author names are followed by the volume number(s) in which they appear. Authors who have changed citizenship or whose current citizenship is not reflected in biographical sources appear under both their original nationality and that of their current residence.

■ The **Cumulative Title Index** lists titles covered in *CLR* followed by the volume and page number where criticism begins.

# A Note to the Reader

*CLR* is one of several critical references sources in the Literature Criticism Series published by Gale Research Inc. When writing papers, students who quote directly from any volume in the Literature Criticism Series may use the following general forms to footnote reprinted criticism. The first example pertains to material drawn from periodicals, the second to material reprinted from books.

[1]T. S. Eliot, "John Donne," *The Nation and the Athenaeum,* 33 (9 June 1923), 321-32; excerpted and reprinted in *Literature Criticism from 1400 to 1800,* Vol. 10, ed. James E. Person, Jr. (Detroit: Gale Research, 1989), pp. 28-9.

[1]Henry Brooke, *Leslie Brooke and Johnny Crow* (Frederick Warne, 1982); excerpted and reprinted in *Children's Literature Review,* Vol. 20, ed. Gerard J. Senick (Detroit: Gale Research, 1990), p. 47.

# Suggestions Are Welcome

In response to various suggestions, several features have been added to *CLR* since the beginning of the series, including author entries on retellers of traditional literature as well as those who have been the first to record oral tales and other folklore; entries on prominent illustrators featuring commentary on their styles and techniques; entries on authors whose works are considered controversial; occasional entries devoted to criticism on a single work or a series of works; sections in author introductions that list major works by the author or illustrator being profiled; explanatory notes that provide information on the critic or work of criticism to enhance the usefulness of the excerpt; more extensive illustrative material, such as holographs of manuscript pages and photographs of people and places pertinent to the authors' careers; a cumulative nationality index for easy access to authors by nationality; and occasional guest essays written specifically for *CLR* by prominent critics on subjects of their choice.

Readers who wish to suggest authors to appear in future volumes, or who have other suggestions, are cordially invited to write the editor.

# Acknowledgments

The editors wish to thank the copyright holders of the excerpted criticism included in this volume, the permissions managers of many book and magazine publishing companies for assisting us in securing reprint rights, and Anthony Bogucki for assistance with copyright research. We are also grateful to the staffs of the Detroit Public Library, the Library of Congress, the University of Detroit Mercy Library, Wayne State University Purdy/Kresge Library Complex, and the University of Michigan Libraries for making their resources available to us. Following is a list of the copyright holders who have granted us permission to reprint material in this volume of *CLR*. Every effort has been made to trace copyright, but if omissions have been made, please let us know.

**COPYRIGHTED EXCERPTS IN *CLR*, VOLUME 34, WERE REPRINTED FROM THE FOLLOWING PERIODICALS:**

*The ALAN Review,* v. 13, Winter, 1986. Reprinted by permission of the publisher.—*Americana,* v. 18, November-December, 1990. Reprinted by permission of the publisher.—*Appraisal: Children's Science Books,* v. 12, Spring, 1979; v. 13, Spring, 1980; v. 13, Fall, 1980; v. 14, September, 1981; v. 15, Winter, 1982; v. 16, Winter, 1983; v. 16, Fall, 1983; v. 17, Fall, 1984; v. 21, Winter, 1988; v. 22, Winter-Spring, 1989; v. 22, Autumn, 1989; v. 23, Spring, 1990; v. 23, Autumn, 1990; v. 25, Spring, 1992. Copyright © 1979, 1980, 1981, 1982, 1983, 1984, 1988, 1989, 1990, 1992 by the Children's Science Book Review Committee. All reprinted by permission of the publisher.—*Best Sellers,* v. 37, December, 1977. Copyright © 1977 Helen Dwight Reid Educational Foundation. Reprinted by permission of the publisher.—*The Book Report,* v. 2, January-February, 1984; v. 11, May-June, 1992. © copyright 1984, 1992 by Linworth Publishing Co. Both reprinted by permission of the publisher.—*Book World—The Washington Post,* August 14, 1983; May 11, 1986; November 6, 1988. © 1983, 1986, 1988, *The Washington Post.* All reprinted by permission of the publisher.—*Bookbird,* n. 4, December 15, 1965. Renewed 1993. Reprinted by permission of the publisher.—*Booklist,* v. 73, February 14, 1977; v. 74, November 1, 1977; v. 75, September 15, 1978; v. 76, October 1, 1979; v. 77, December 15, 1980; v. 77, June 1, 1981; v. 78, September 1, 1981; v. 78, December 15, 1981; v. 78, March 1, 1982; v. 79, September 15, 1982; v. 79, October 1, 1982; v. 79, May 15, 1983; v. 80, October 1, 1983; v. 80, May 1, 1984; v. 81, April 15, 1985; v. 81, May 15, 1985; v. 83, February 15, 1987; v. 83, April 1, 1987; v. 83, June 1, 1987; v. 84, November 15, 1987; v. 84, February 1, 1988; v. 84, March 1, 1988; v. 85, October 15, 1988; v. 85, March 1, 1989; v. 85, July, 1989; v. 86, February 15, 1990; v. 86, March 1, 1990; v. 87, February 15, 1991; v, 87, August, 1991; v. 88, November 1, 1991; v. 89, October 15, 1992; v. 89, December 1, 1992; v. 89, January 15, 1993; v. 89, March 1, 1993; v. 89, April 1, 1993. Copyright © 1977, 1978, 1979, 1980, 1981, 1982, 1983, 1984, 1985, 1987, 1988, 1989, 1990, 1991, 1992, 1993 by the American Library Association. All reprinted by permission of the publisher.—*Books for Keeps,* n. 36, January, 1986; n. 48, January, 1988; n. 53, November, 1988; n. 56, May, 1989; n. 59, November, 1989; n. 63, July, 1990; n. 66, January, 1991; n. 73, March, 1992; n. 75, July, 1992. © School Bookshop Association 1986, 1988, 1989, 1990, 1991, 1992. All reprinted by permission of the publisher.—*Books for Young People,* v. 2, October, 1988 for a review of "Jingle Bells" by Peter Carver. All rights reserved. Reprinted by permission of the publisher and the author.—*Books for your Children,* v. 6, Autumn, 1970; v. 26, Summer, 1991. © *Books for Your Children* 1970, 1991. Both reprinted by permission of the publisher.—*Books in Canada,* v. 16, December, 1987 for a review of "The Wheels on the Bus" by Mary Ainslie Smith; v. XX, April, 1991 for a review of "Frank and Zelda" by Anne Denoon. Both reprinted by permission of the respective authors.—*British Book News Children's Books,* Winter, 1986, Summer, 1986. © The British Council, 1986. Both reprinted by permission of the publisher.—*British Book News,* Children's Supplement, Autumn, 1981; Autumn, 1982. © *British Book News,* 1981, 1982. Both courtesy of *British Book News.*—*Bulletin of the Center for Children's Books,* v. 20, July-August, 1967; v. 23, July-August, 1970; v. 24, November, 1970; v. 26, February, 1973; v. 33, October, 1979; v. 34, October, 1980; v. 34, November, 1980; v. 35, November, 1981; v. 35, March, 1982; v. 35, April, 1982; v. 35, July-August, 1982; v. 36, April, 1983; v. 37, October, 1983; v. 37, December, 1983; v. 37, July-August, 1984; v. 38, October, 1984; v. 38, May, 1985; v. 38,

author.—Cameron, Eleanor. From *The Green and Burning Tree: On the Writing and Enjoyment of Children's Books*. Atlantic-Little, Brown, 1969. Copyright © 1962, 1966, 1969 by Eleanor Cameron. All rights reserved. Reprinted by permission of Little, Brown and Company in association with The Atlantic Monthly Press.—Canemaker, John. From *The Animated Raggedy Ann & Andy: An Intimate Look at the Art of Animation: Its History, Techniques, and Artists*. Bobbs-Merrill, 1977. Copyright © 1977 by Macmillan Publishing Company. All rights reserved. Reprinted with the permission of Macmillan Publishing Company.—Eyre, Frank. From *British Children's Books in the Twentieth Century*. Revised edition. Longman Books, 1971, Dutton, 1973. Copyright © 1971 by Frank Eyre. All rights reserved. Reprinted by permission of the publisher, E. P. Dutton, a division of Penguin Books USA Inc. In Canada by Penguin Books Ltd.—Farjeon, Annabel. From *Morning Has Broken: A Biography of Eleanor Farjeon*. Julia MacRae, 1986. © Annabel Farjeon 1986. All rights reserved. Reprinted by permission of the publisher.—Fisher, Margery. From *Margery Fisher Recommends Classics for Children & Young People*. Thimble Press, 1986. Copyright © 1986 Margery Fisher. Reprinted by permission of the publisher.—Fisher, Margery. From *Who's Who in Children's Books: A Treasury of the Familiar Characters of Childhood*. Weidenfeld & Nicolson, 1975. Copyright © 1975 by Margery Fisher. All rights reserved. Reprinted by permission of the publisher.—Godden, Rumer. From "Tea with Eleanor Farjeon," in *A Book for Eleanor Farjeon: A Tribute to Her Life and Work, 1881-1965*. Henry Z. Walck, Incorporated, 1966. © 1966 Hamish Hamilton Ltd. Reprinted by permission of the publisher.—Lewis, Naomi. From an introduction to *A Book for Eleanor Farjeon: A Tribute to Her Life and Work, 1881-1965*. Henry Z. Walck, Incorporated, 1966. © 1966 Hamish Hamilton Ltd. Reprinted by permission of the publisher.—Moss, Elaine. From *Children's Books of the Year: 1974*. Hamish Hamilton, 1975. © Elaine Moss 1975. All rights reserved. Reprinted by permission of the author.—Sebesta, Sam Leaton and William J. Iverson. From *Literature for Thursday's Child*. Science Research Associates, 1975. © 1975, Science Research Associates, Inc. All rights reserved. Reprinted by permission of the authors.—Sutherland, Zena, and May Hill Arbuthnot. From *Children and Books*. Seventh edition. Scott, Foresman, 1986. Copyright © 1986, 1981, 1977, 1972, 1964, 1957, 1947 Scott, Foresman and Company. All rights reserved. Reprinted by permission of the publisher.—Townsend, John Rowe. From *Written for Children: An Outline of English-Language Children's Literature*. Third revised edition. J. B. Lippincott, 1987, Penguin Books, 1987. Copyright © 1965, 1974, 1983, 1987 by John Rowe Townsend. All rights reserved. Reprinted by permission of HarperCollins Publishers, Inc. In Canada by the author.—Viguers, Ruth Hill. From "Poetry," in *A Critical History of Children's Literature*. By Cornelia Meigs and others, edited by Cornelia Meigs. Macmillan, 1953. Copyright, 1953, by Macmillan Publishing Company. Renewed 1981 by Charles H. Eaton. All rights reserved. Reprinted by permission of the publisher.—Waggoner, Diana. From *The Hills of Faraway: Guide to Fantasy*. Atheneum, 1978. Copyright © 1978 by Diana Waggoner. All rights reserved. Reprinted with the permission of Atheneum Publishers, an imprint of Macmillan Publishing Company.

**PERMISSION TO REPRODUCE ILLUSTRATIONS APPEARING IN *CLR*, VOLUME 34, WAS RECEIVED FROM THE FOLLOWING SOURCES:**

Illustrations from *The Little Bookroom: Eleanor Farjeon's Short Stories for Children Chosen By Herself*, by Eleanor Farjeon. Oxford University Press, 1956. Copyright © 1955 by Eleanor Farjeon. Illustrations by Edward Ardizzone. Reprinted by permission of Oxford University Press./ Illustrations by Johnny Gruelle from *The Animated Raggedy Ann & Andy*, by John Canemaker. Copyright © 1977 by The Bobbs-Merrill Company, Inc. Reprinted by permission of Macmillan Publishing Company, a division of Macmillan, Inc./Illustration by Johnny Gruelle from *Raggedy Ann & Andy Giant Treasury*, by Johnny Gruelle, retold by Nancy Golden. Copyright © 1924, 1925, 1929, 1930, 1946, 1961, 1984 The Bobbs-Merrill Company, Inc. Reprinted by permission of Macmillan Publishing Company, a division of Macmillan, Inc./ Illustration by Johnny Gruelle from his *Raggedy Ann Stories*. The Bobbs-Merrill Company, Inc., 1960. Reprinted by permission of Macmillan Publishing Company, a division of Macmillan, Inc./ Illustration by John B. Gruelle from *The Complete Fairy Tales of the Brothers Grimm*, translated by Jack Zipes. Bantam, 1987. Copyright © 1987 by Jack Zipes. Reprinted by permission of Bantam Books, a division of Bantam Doubleday Dell Publishing Group, Inc./ Illustration by Charles Keeping from his *Through the Window*. Reprinted by permission of Oxford University Press./ Illustration by Charles Keeping from his *Charley, Charlotte, and the Golden Canary*. Reprinted by permission of Oxford University Press./ Illustration by Charles Keeping from *The God Beneath the Sea*, by Leon Garfield and Edward Blishen. Longman Young Books, 1970. Illustrations copyright © 1970 by Charles Keeping. Reprinted by permission of the Estate of Charles Keeping./ Illustration by Charles Keeping from his *Alfie Finds "The Other Side Of The World"*. Copyright © 1968 by Charles Keeping. Reprinted by permission of Franklin Watts, Inc./ Illustration by Charles Keeping from *Cockney Ding Dong*, edited by Charles Keeping. Kestrel Books/EMI Music Publishing, 1975. Selection, introduction and illustrations copyright © 1975 by Charles Keeping. Reprinted by permission of the Estate of Charles Keeping./ Illustration by Charles Keeping from his *Joseph's Yard*. Copyright © 1969 by Charles Keeping. Reprinted by permission of Franklin Watts, Inc./Illustration by Charles Keeping from his *Tinker Tailor: Folk Song Tales*. Copyright © 1968 by Charles Keeping. Reprinted by permission of HarperCollins Publishers Inc./ Illustration by Maryann Kovalski from her *Pizza for Breakfast*. Copyright © 1990 by Maryann Kovalski. Reprinted by permission of Morrow Junior Books, a division of William Morrow & Company, Inc. / Illustration by Maryann Kovalski from her *The Wheels on the Bus*. Copyright © 1987 by Maryann Kovalski. Reprinted by permission of Little, Brown and Company./ Illustration by Carol Lerner from her *A Desert Year*. Copyright © 1991 by Carol Lerner. Reprinted by permission of Morrow Junior Books, a division of William Morrow & Company, Inc./Illustration by Carol Lerner from her *Pitcher Plants: The Elegant Insect Traps*. William Morrow and Company, 1983.Copyright © 1983 by Carol Lerner. Reprinted by permission of William Morrow and Company, Inc./ Illustration by Carol Lerner from her *Seasons of the Tallgrass Prairie*. William Morrow and Company, 1980. Copyright © 1980 by Carol Lerner. Reprinted by permission of William Morrow & Company, Inc./ Illustration by Carol Lerner from *A Biblical Garden*, translations from the Hebrew Bible by Ralph Lerner. William Morrow and Company, 1982. Copyright © 1982 by Carol Lerner. Reprinted by permission of William Morrow & Company, Inc./ Illustration by Carol Lerner from her *On the Forest Edge*. William Morrow and Company, 1978. Copyright © 1978 by Carol Lerner. Reprinted by permission of William Morrow & Company, Inc./ Illustration by Carol Lerner from her *A Forest Year*. Copyright © 1987 by Carol Lerner. Reprinted by permission of William Morrow & Company, Inc./ Photograph by John Shearer from his *Little Man in the Family*. Copyright © 1972 by John Shearer. Reprinted by permission of Dell Books, a division of Bantam Doubleday Dell Publishing Group, Inc.

**PERMISSION TO REPRODUCE PHOTOGRAPHS APPEARING IN *CLR*, VOLUME 34, WAS RECEIVED FROM THE FOLLOWING SOURCES:**

Oxford University Press: **pp. 42, 108**; Photograph by Helen Craig: **p. 46**; Photograph by Edward R. Noble, courtesy of Charles Ferry: **p. 49**; Courtesy of Charles Ferry: **pp. 53, 57**; Worth and Sue Gruelle: **p. 60**; AP/Wide World Photos: **p. 70**; Photograph by Steven Jack: **p. 113**; Courtesy of John Marsden: **pp. 140, 142, 145, 148**; Bob Wilcox Studio: **p. 152**; Courtesy of Jean Ure: **p. 169**.

# Children's
# Literature
# Review

# Eleanor Farjeon

## 1881-1965

(Also writes as Tomfool) English author of fiction, nonfiction, poetry, plays, and retellings, and editor of collections of fiction and poetry.

Major works include *Martin Pippin in the Apple Orchard* (1921), *Kings and Queens* (with Herbert Farjeon, 1932), *The Children's Bells: A Selection of Poems* (1934), *The Glass Slipper* (1955), *The Little Bookroom* (1955).

Major works about the author include *A Nursery in the Nineties* by Eleanor Farjeon (1935; U.S. edition as *Portrait of a Family*), *Edward Thomas, The Last Four Years: The Memoirs of Eleanor Farjeon, Book One* by Eleanor Farjeon (1958), *Eleanor Farjeon* by Eileen Colwell (1961), *Eleanor: Portrait of a Farjeon* by Denys Blakelock (1966), *Morning Has Broken: A Biography of Eleanor Farjeon* by Annabel Farjeon (1986).

The following entry presents general criticism of Farjeon's oeuvre.

## INTRODUCTION

Considered among the greatest English authors of juvenile literature in the twentieth century, Farjeon is celebrated as an especially original and imaginative writer whose works reflect her literary craftsmanship, robust world view, and understanding of children and childhood. Praised as a master storyteller and poet as well as for the prolificacy, range, and variety of her works, which address nearly every genre of children's literature, Farjeon is best known for her short stories and verse, both of which have been widely anthologized; she is perhaps most recognized currently as the author of "A Morning Song (For the First Day of Spring)," a poem from her collection *The Children's Bells* that was recorded by pop singer Cat Stevens as "Morning Has Broken." Farjeon wrote her prose and poetry to express her belief in both the beauty of the world and the essential goodness of humanity. Although she depicts death, aging, and sadness, she invests her works with an intensely personal quality that underscores her joyful attitude toward life. She is often lauded for the sensitivity, wisdom, and truth of her literature as well as for her love of language and sense of humor. Frances Clarke Sayers has written that "the miraculous quality of Farjeon's writings [resemble] nothing so much as the never-ending variety of melody and theme of Mozart's music," while Ellin Greene adds that Farjeon's "literary impulse was to waken the reader to a sense of wonder. The underlying theme in her work is 'the wise child within'." Considered among Farjeon's most special gifts is her ability to seamlessly blend fantasy and reality. Strongly influenced by traditional folktales and legends as well as by the folklore of the English countryside, she is credited with enchanting young readers by conjuring worlds of magic and wonder that are convincing, alive, and fully realized.

Critics generally agree that Farjeon's quintessential work is "Elsie Piddock Skips in Her Sleep," acclaimed by many as the perfect short story for children. In this tale, which was Farjeon's own favorite among her stories, seven-year-old Elsie is taught to skip in the fairy way by Andy Spandy, the fairies' skipping master, who gives her a magic skipping rope. When she is over a hundred years old, Elsie returns to her town to ingeniously save its playground from a greedy developer; confronting his claim that he will not break ground until the last rope-skipper has stopped, Elsie skips endlessly on the playground with her magic jump rope. "'Elsie Piddock'," says Eleanor Graham, "stands out . . . perhaps above any one story by any present day writer for the young." The tale addresses two characteristic themes in Farjeon's works, the prevailing of justice against greed and the relationship between generations. The latter is the focus of one of Farjeon's most popular stories, "And I Dance Mine Own Child," which describes the loving bond between ten-year-old Griselda Curfew and her grandmother, who is one hundred and ten. This tale comes from Farjeon's most well-received collection of short stories, *The Little Bookroom*, her personal selection from her own works. Including soaring fantasies and celebrations of love, friendship, and devotion, *The Little Bookroom* is described by Marcus Crouch as "a work of unquestionable genius," and he adds that it "shows some of the brightest facets of Miss Farjeon's art: style, a deceptively simple, clean, unadorned prose; humor, a gaiety which is never forced and never factious; a seriousness, a dignity of theme and sobriety of thought which respects the child's capacity for appreciation; understanding, the poet's detailed memory and power of penetration." As a poet, Farjeon is commended for her variety of meter, pattern, and subject as well as for her insight. Reflecting her love of nature and childhood, her poems range from the nonsensical to the numinous. Anne Harvey claims that Farjeon and Walter de la Mare "stand together as the most important children's poets of the twentieth century"; other reviewers note that Farjeon's poetry, while perhaps not as deep as de la Mare's, exceeds his in accessibility and appeal to children.

Born into a family that cherished literature and the arts, Farjeon grew up surrounded by books and music. She was privately educated at home, which enabled her to devote her energies to writing, an activity encouraged by her father Benjamin, a popular novelist. From her mother Maggie, the daughter of the American actor Joseph Jefferson, Farjeon inherited an interest in the theater. Her literary talents, particularly her taste for fantasy, were enhanced by her relationships with her three gifted brothers, Harry, Herbert, and Joseph. Her eldest brother Harry engaged Farjeon in a highly sophisticated game of make-believe and fantasy in which each portrayed personages from history, literature, and contemporary society; extremely influential in Farjeon's ability to combine fantasy and fact, the game, called TAR, was played by the siblings well into their adult lives. Farjeon began writing at the age of five, the same age at which she began to play TAR; at ten, one of her poems was published in the children's magazine *Little Wideawake*. She later composed an opera with Harry which was successfully staged in London. With the death of her father in 1903, Farjeon began to focus even more intently on developing her writing skills in order to help support her family. She published articles and verse for nearly two decades before completing her first novel, *Martin Pippin in the Apple Orchard*. A romantic love story with elements of magic and folklore, the novel describes a maiden whose mysterious captivity is ended by the power of love, incarnated in the charming Martin Pippin, a wandering minstrel. *Martin Pippin in the Apple Orchard* blends prose and poetry within the framework of the tale within a tale, a device often used by Farjeon in her later works. In a glowing review of *Martin Pippin* that helped to establish the author's early reputation, Rebecca West praised Farjeon's "richly beautiful style, which loads the pages with colour that is always relevant to form." Although intended for adults, *Martin Pippin* was adopted by young readers, gradually becoming accepted as a book for girls in the middle grades and early teens; it was reissued as a children's book in 1952. A sequel, *Martin Pippin in the Daisy Field* (1937), was published as a juvenile novel. During the 1930s, Farjeon also wrote such works as *Kings and Queens*, a light-hearted and irreverent poetic romp through the history of British monarchy on which she collaborated with her brother Herbert, and *Ten Saints* (1936), a moving retelling in verse of the lives of the

saints; she also published prose retellings of *The Canterbury Tales,* the writings of Herodotus, and hero tales from various cultures. Farjeon also began to write plays during this period, most notably *The Glass Slipper*, a retelling of the Cinderella story on which she again collaborated with Herbert, and *The Silver Curlew: A Fairy Tale* (1949), which she wrote alone; she later adapted both plays into full-length books. Although most of her works are directed to children, Farjeon wrote several novels, short stories, plays, biographies, and collections of poetry for adults; she is also the author of two notable autobiographies, the first detailing her early life and the second her friendship with poet Edward Thomas.

Farjeon's popularity suffered somewhat in the period following World War II as critics tended to deem her works as quaint and archaic and the attitude she expressed in her books as removed from the concerns of people adapting to a rapidly changing world. In addition, occasional reviewers began to see Farjeon's output as uneven due both to its volume and the deceptive facility of her literary style and verbal virtuosity. In the 1950s, however, Farjeon's popularity enjoyed a renaissance prompted by the publication of *The Little Bookroom*. Recent reviewers acknowledge the timeless quality and universality of many of her works and place her in the vanguard of authors for children. Marcus Crouch calls Farjeon "the last representative of that Golden Age which began . . . with Edward Lear" and adds that "so long as children love music and the sparkle of words, romance and the wonder of a tale supremely well told, so long will Eleanor Farjeon's books endure." Ellin Greene comments that "Farjeon's stories and poems have secured her a permanent place in the literature of childhood and in the hearts of children everywhere," while Eileen Colwell predicts: "It is certain that when the history of children's literature in our day is written, Eleanor Farjeon will be one of its most important figures." *The Little Bookroom* was awarded the Carnegie Medal in 1955, the Hans Christian Andersen Award in 1956, and the Lewis Carroll Shelf Award in 1958. In addition, Farjeon received the first Regina Medal in 1959 for her body of work. In 1965, the Eleanor Farjeon Award was established by the Children's Book Circle in London as a tribute to the author; the award is presented "to a professional of extraordinary achievement involved in any aspect of children's books."

(See also *Contemporary Authors*, Vols. 11-12; *Contemporary Authors Permanent Series*, Vol. 1; *Major Authors and Illustrators for Children and Young Adults*; and *Something about the Author*, Vol. 2.)

---

## AUTHOR'S COMMENTARY

*[The following essay is directed by Farjeon to the editor of* The Junior Bookshelf.]

And I thought I had escaped you, Mr. Woodfield! When you sent me that request for a little article on *How I Do It,* I thought, by sitting very still in my Sussex hole, and forgetting the date on your letter till it was too late, I might be given up as one of your hopeless cases. And then—

I must needs go unexpectedly to London, and find myself grabbed by a stranger on a staircase. Some scurvy villain had pointed me out to you—I was waylaid before I could take steps, up or down—and after one desperate glance over a banister that was unjumpable, I lost my head and found myself promising you I-don't-quite-know-what by I'm-not-quite-sure-when. Here it is.

But it won't say *How I Do It.* That's impossible. I can only tell you that my tables, and chairs, and beds—such as are not already strewn with Pickle the old Tabby, Nonny the young White-and-Orange, Tortoiseshell Bunny and her latest family, and Golden Coney her fairest daughter of them all—are strewn with manuscripts Almost-Done, Half-Done, Just-Begun; and that nest upon nest of drawers is stuffed with jottings and ideas, for use This Year, Next Year, Sometime, Never. Some are still clear as crystal to me, others have grown as vague as clouds which have blown out of shape since they first swam into my horizon. *This* story will never be written now; *that* poem might have been written once. What *did* I mean by this list of characters for a play? Was it a Comedy? Was it a Tragedy? Don't ask *me.* Five, or ten, or twenty years ago I could have told you. The curtain will not ring up.

It doesn't matter. My Half-Dones and Just-Beguns will last my lifetime, and new ideas come faster than I can deal with them. Where they spring from it is hard to say. A suggestion from something seen on a walk, heard in a crowd, read in a newspaper, a wakeful night, when the imagination works fiercely for its own hand; an orchestral concert, when I listen with my eyes shut. A number flows through my senses, the audience applauds, I open my eyes and am asked for my opinion; I keep rather mum about So-and-so's new Symphonic Poem; I have no opinion, I have hardly heard it. But, thanks to it, I have another story, or poem, or play clamouring for attention. I catch while I can the mood in which it was born, dashing down—sometimes a few words, sometimes a page, or several pages. If I do this at once, I generally find, when I run through my drawers a year or two later, that something has remained of the mood in which the jottings were made. In the meantime, those chance-planted seeds have ripened without my knowing it; and when the year's chief jobs have been completed, the delicious moment is at hand in which I choose my next chains. In my moment of freedom I dally with some half-dozen impatient waiters in the queue. This? —that? —t'other? At last one claims me, and the exciting day is come when I can tackle it in good earnest, and presently be rid of it for ever. There are three exciting periods in any work: the beginning, before the agony of doubt sets in—the ending, when doubt is settled for better or worse—and, in between, *sometimes,* that state of creation which one of our loveliest living poets calls "self-hypnosis." Then the work moves of itself, and writing is bliss. Woe to the morning when this magical ease is checked, for even an instant. You never pick up the flight that has dropped to earth. This ease of movement is a gift to the writer, and can't be commanded. That is why I know less about *How It Is Done* than *How It Isn't.*

The day promises to be a good one for work; and if I were a man I would lock myself into my fastness, and leave my household to get about its business as it pleases, asking only to be left uninterrupted. But just as I rise from breakfast, agog to be up in my witch-hole under the roof, and forgetting everything but my sheet of foolscap, set foot on the staircase—

"Miss! just a moment! Before you go, what about the meals?"

I say what about the meals. I re-set foot on the staircase.

"Miss! the trees have come from the Nursery, and the gardener says where do you want the weeping ash planted?"

I see the gardener, and say where. Ha, ha! the staircase!

"The telephone, miss! . . . The carrier's brought something from the station and there's ninepence to pay. . . . Mrs. Blank's in the sitting-room about the District Nurse . . . the telephone, miss! . . . Miss! Bunny's having her kittens, and the gardener says what vegetables for lunch? . . . Miss, miss! the roof has fallen on to the greenhouse, and the new pump's not working, it was put in upside-down, the grocer's brought back the tortoise, and where does the ton of oak-logs from the Estate Agent go, and you really did ought to look out of the window, there's an elephant in the orchard, and a three-headed giant coming down the lane and a flock of green dragons flying in the sky, and the laundry's sent the wrong pair of sheets . . . the telephone, miss!"

That's how it *isn't* done, dear Mr. Woodfield. Someone is *always* stopping me on the staircase.

> *Eleanor Farjeon, "How It Isn't Done," in* The Junior Bookshelf, *Vol. 2, No. 2, January, 1938, pp. 59-61.*

[*The following is Farjeon's author's note to* The Little Bookroom.]

In the home of my childhood there was a room we called 'The Little Bookroom'. True, every room in the house could have been called a bookroom. Our nurseries upstairs were full of books. Downstairs my father's study was full of them. They lined the dining-room walls, and overflowed into my mother's sitting-room, and up into the bedrooms. It would have been more natural to live without clothes than without books. As unnatural not to read as not to eat.

Of all the rooms in the house, the Little Bookroom was yielded up to books as an untended garden is left to its flowers and weeds. There was no selection or sense of order here. In dining-room, study, and nursery there was choice and arrangement; but the Little Bookroom gathered to itself a motley crew of strays and vagabonds, outcasts from the ordered shelves below, the overflow of parcels bought wholesale by my father in the sales-rooms. Much trash, and more treasure. Riff-raff and gentlefolk and noblemen. A lottery, a lucky dip for a child who had never been forbidden to handle anything between covers. That dusty bookroom, whose windows were never opened, through whose panes the summer sun struck a dingy shaft where gold specks danced and shimmered,

*Illustration by Edward Ardizzone depicting the young Farjeon from the Author's Note of* The Little Bookroom.

opened magic casements for me through which I looked out on other worlds and times than those I lived in: worlds filled with poetry and prose and fact and fantasy. There were old plays and histories, and old romances; superstitions, legends, and what are called the Curiosities of Literature. There was a book called *Florentine Nights* that fascinated me; and another called *The Tales of Hoffmann* that frightened me; and one called *The Amber Witch* that was not in the least like the witches I was used to in the fairy-tales I loved.

Crammed with all sorts of reading, the narrow shelves rose halfway up the walls; their tops piled with untidy layers that almost touched the ceiling. The heaps on the floor had to be climbed over, columns of books flanked the window, toppling at a touch. You tugged at a promising binding, and left a new surge of literature underfoot; and you dropped the book that had attracted you for something that came to the surface in the upheaval. Here, in the Little Bookroom, I learned, like Charles Lamb, to read anything that can be called a book. The dust got up my nose and made my eyes smart, as I crouched on the floor or stood propped against a bookcase, physically uncomfortable, and mentally lost. I was only conscious of my awkward posture and the stifling atmosphere when I had ceased to wander in realms where fancy seemed to me more true than facts, and set sail on voyages of discovery to regions in which fact was often far more curious than fancy. If some of my frequent sore throats were due to the dust in the Little Bookroom, I cannot regret them.

No servant ever came with duster and broom to polish the dim panes through which the sunlight danced, or sweep from the floor the dust of long-ago. The room would not have been the same without its dust: star-dust, gold-dust, fern-dust, the dust that returns to dust under the earth, and comes up from her lap in the shape of a hyacinth. 'This quiet dust,' says Emily Dickinson, an American poet—

> This quiet dust was Gentlemen and Ladies,
>   And Lads and Girls:
> Was laughter and ability and sighing,
>   And frocks and curls.

And an English poet, Viola Meynell, clearing her ledges of the dust that 'came secretly by day' to dull her shining things, pauses to reflect—

> But O this dust that I shall drive away
>   Is flowers and kings,
> Is Solomon's temple, poets, Nineveh . . .

When I crept out of the Little Bookroom with smarting eyes, no wonder that its mottled gold-dust still danced in my brain, its silver cobwebs still clung to the corners of my mind. No wonder that many years later, when I came to write books myself, they were a muddle of fiction and fact and fantasy and truth. I have never quite succeeded in distinguishing one from the other, as the tales in this book that were born of that dust will show. Seven maids with seven brooms, sweeping for half-a-hundred years, have never managed to clear my mind of its dust of vanished temples and flowers and kings, the curls of ladies, the sighing of poets, the laughter of lads and girls: those golden ones who, like chimney-sweepers, must all come to dust in some little bookroom or other—and sometimes, by luck, come again for a moment to light.

> *Eleanor Farjeon, "Author's Note," in her* The Little Bookroom, *Oxford University Press, London, 1956, pp. vii-x.*

---

### J. D. Beresford

I have been asked to introduce Miss Farjeon to the American public, and although I believe that introductions of this kind often do more harm than good, I have consented in this case because the instance is rare enough to justify an exception. If Miss Farjeon had been a promising young novelist either of the realistic or the romantic school, I should not have dared to express an opinion on her work, even if I had believed that she had greater gifts than the ninety-nine other promising young novelists who appear in the course of each decade. But she has a far rarer gift than any of those that go to the making of a successful novelist. She is one of the few who can conceive and tell a fairy-tale; the only one to my knowledge—with the just possible exceptions of James Stephens and Walter de la Mare—in my own generation. She has, in fact, the true gift of fancy. It has already been displayed in her verse—a form in which it is far commoner than in prose—but *Martin Pippin* is her first book in this kind.

I am afraid to say too much about it for fear of prejudicing both the reviewers and the general public. My taste may not be theirs and in this matter there is no opportunity for argument. Let me, therefore, do no more than tell the story of how the manuscript affected me. I was a little overworked. I had been reading a great number of manuscripts in the preceding weeks, and the mere sight of typescript was a burden to me. But before I had read five pages of *Martin Pippin,* I had forgotten that it was a manuscript submitted for my judgment. I had forgotten who I was and where I lived. I was transported into a world of sunlight, of gay inconsequence, of emotional surprise, a world of poetry, delight, and humor. And I lived and took my joy in that rare world, until all too soon my reading was done.

My most earnest wish is that there may be many minds and imaginations among the American people who will be able to share that pleasure with me. For every one who finds delight in this book I can claim as a kindred spirit.

*J. D. Beresford, in an introduction to* Martin Pippin in the Apple Orchard *by Eleanor Farjeon, Frederick A. Stokes Company Publishers, 1922, p. vii.*

## Eleanor Graham

For almost as long as I have looked with critical—albeit loving—eyes at children's books, I have been aware of a question mark in my mind against the name of Eleanor Farjeon. The query was mainly, had I failed to grasp her intention, or was she mis-classed among writers for children?

The first book I knew of hers was **Martin Pippin in the Apple Orchard,** which was enthusiastically presented to me as a book for the young. I read it with a curiosity which later turned to astonishment, and I could only presume that the people who had pressed it on me as a book of "fairy tales" had not really read it. I felt its charm—and its sophistication. I enjoyed her lovely gift for tender scenes, magic moments, the innocence of childhood and the commonplace miracles of nature. It left in my mind pictures which held for ever the transitory beauty of spring in green country. I saw also, however, the sentimentality and the false quantities in the romantic make-believe. I have always felt quite certain that its place was not alongside even Andersen's strangely romantic tales, but on a shelf apart with the elaborately mannered love stories of a past generation. In any case, it is a difficult book to place successfully. There are adults who cherish it, and a certain type of schoolgirl still dreams over it, but I have never felt it was a wise choice for an adolescent, the sentiment is misleading and cloaks the disembodied romance with unreality—too much is said, and too little. It stimulates without either satisfying or directing the flow of enthusiasm. But in actual fact, I don't believe its schoolgirl public has ever been large, though I know teachers who have, for years, bought it regularly among their prizes and for their school libraries.

Alas, even to my ears, this criticism seems ungracious and it does less—much less—than justice to the book, but a wrong label at its introduction must be blamed for starting me off with a handicap, obliging me to follow up the negative side before I felt free to go on to the positive; to clear the ground of misapprehension before I could appreciate the author's achievement in its proper field—and, make no mistake, her achievement of airy fun, spontaneous gaiety, bright imagery and delicate background of Sussex landscape, is considerable.

A few days ago, I decided to re-read the book from beginning to end, in order to get a fresh reaction to it, but the result was only to confirm me in all that I had previously felt on both sides of my argument.

Since first reading **Martin Pippin,** I have more than once met Miss Farjeon, and, to my great delight, I recognized in her just those qualities which made the book what it was. In herself is the irresponsible gaiety, the unselfconscious inventiveness, the fun, the twinkle of real naughtiness, the knife-edge pivoting of mood which swings so easily from laughter to gravity, from romance to cold reality. I found her in the flesh warm-hearted yet detached, holding each passing moment lightly in a sensitive grip, as though to extract from it every last grain of lively experience. I found it was grand entertainment just to listen to her tale of crossing the street; the more so, since she was not concerned to use it for self-advertisement. The inner motive of her story-telling seemed to be less *See how clever I am!* than *Share with me how nice is mankind!*

So I wrote to her, and asked her how she herself regarded this strange child of hers, this first book of **Martin Pippin,** and since it turned out as it did, I may as well quote her reply, which was that that this book, "somehow or other listed for children, has never been, for me, a children's book at all!"

It would be a pity to leave **Martin Pippin** the first without turning to **Martin Pippin** the second, that is **Martin Pippin in the Daisy Field**—and *there is a book of fairy tales,* though between them are interludes as archly sophisticated as anything in the first book, and not in the least likely, in themselves, to hold or attract children. But, in the stories, I think Miss Farjeon reaches her high water mark. She herself admits to satisfaction with one, **"Elsie Piddock Skips in Her Sleep,"** and I, too, feel that it comes very near perfection. All her brilliant, delicate qualities of mind, perception and imagination have contributed to it. It possesses the magic of moonlight, yet retains a close contact with the affairs of everyday life. Any child who has spent lonely mornings with a skipping rope, turning it and persuading it to her will, leaping and dancing in time to its circling, will see herself in *Elsie Piddock's* shoes, for *Elsie* was a born skipper, and could out-skip anyone by the time she was five! She skipped in her sleep with the fairies, and learnt not only the Long Skip and the Strong Skip, but the skip against Trouble, and many another besides. She skipped also on the green with the other children to the old Skipping Rhymes—and, of them all, is there any so calculated to carry even an old lady back to her childhood, as,

> Andy spandy
> Sugardy candy,
> French almond rock!
> Bread and butter for your supper's all your
>   Mother's
> GOT!

When she was a little old woman, *Elsie* became a real heroine, and skipped her village out of trouble, with the rope the fairies had given her long ago.

In this story human insight supports inspiration, and the language holds both together as lightly and exquisitely as the soap film holds its bubble of air. For me at least, **"Elsie Piddock"** stands out, not only above all else Miss Farjeon has written for children, but perhaps above any one story by any present day writer for the young.

Other stories in that volume are good too, stories any child will enjoy, e. g., **"The Tantony Pig"** and **"The Long Man of Wilmington."** Both show that spontaneity which is one of Miss Farjeon's greatest gifts, and each makes that quick contact with the child's own experience which is one of the secrets of success in all writing for children.

The fact that the author has linked these stories together in so artificial a matrix only demonstrates, I think, more of her personal make-up. She has not, you may be sure, ever planned to direct her work towards a certain public, or to fulfil certain demands. She has, I imagine, written first, last and all the time, for her own pleasure, to capture for ever the gaily bubbling phantasies of imagination, the bright visions of her spirit.

Against these, it is good to survey for a moment, the quiet dignity of her hero stories, *Mighty Men.* Not, you might say at first sight, imaginative, or particularly spontaneous . . . no? Yet I doubt if that smoothness of conception and description, that clear simplicity and dignity of style could have been conveyed so successfully to the reader, had Miss Farjeon carried in her own mind someone else's picture instead of her own, full-size and living, set up against the figured background of her own understanding of men, and human nature, and life. There is never any fumbling in her telling, no uncertainty, no awkward moments such as happen when ill-understood moments have to be glossed over. Short as they are, the pictures they present are vivid and their human values, as far as they go, are true. They are dignified and sincere.

I cheerfully suspect few will agree with my next remarks, which concern *Perkin the Pedlar,* and I wish it were otherwise, for I believe this is a favourite of the author's, but I am literal-minded over some things, and, knowing the bare rugged hill which is Yeavering Bell, I found myself revolted when asked in this book to pretend that its name came from a strange bell which came quavering and yeavering through a magic forest. I should have liked a story which took into account the actuality of scene, and on that same score, many of the tales in this book disappointed me, neither convincing nor amusing me. Yet the idea of a wandering pedlar who picked up stories of places as he passed through them was a fertile one, and the place-names are a likely collection. I felt, however, that contact was lost, thrown away, by the inconsequent ignoring of the physical nature of the subjects chosen.

The same criticism could be made of the *London Nursery Rhymes,* for the thread connecting name and story is often strained to such fineness that it is hardly apparent, but in nursery rhymes this matters very little. Nursery rhymes should be inconsequent, are often extravagant, and need not be tied down precisely to facts, though often characterized by delightfully unexpected literalnesses. Eleanor Farjeon's nursery rhymes do have just those qualities, and in addition, the extra appeal of familiar London names, music in themselves, particularly now, to all Londoners. I always remember as one of her most successful that rhyme of the **"Sevens"**:

> Seven Sisters in patchwork cloaks
> Sat in the shadow of Seven Oaks,
>   Stringing acorns on silken strings,

> Awaiting the coming of Seven
>   Kings.

> Seven years they endured their trials
> And then they consulted their Seven
>   Dials.
> "O it's time, it's time, it's time,"
>   they said,
> "It's very high time that we were
>   wed!"

There to my mind, is something very closely akin to the authentic fall of the traditional rhyme, handed down by word of mouth from generation to generation! The association of the seven-fold figures is neat, the repetition is effectively used, and there is hardly a superfluous syllable.

In her rhymes and verse, as in her prose, I feel Eleanor Farjeon is most successful when the inspiration of the moment has been captured as soon as born, and translated instantly, fully clothed, on to paper, pretty certainly needing thereafter neither revision nor polishing. I would say these are detectable, that the light shines through them, and their very finish declares them.

Such a gift, however, of its very nature, carries with it certain drawbacks. It may lead to a habit of jotting down the flashing thoughts on scraps of paper, and if the pencil falters, the world interrupts, or for some other reason the picture is broken before it has been completely recorded, the author may be left with scrapbooks teeming with half-formed ideas, brilliant suggestions not worked out, tantalising lines and haunting rhythms, or yet a clever rhyme demanding a worthy setting. It is inevitable that their creator should use some of them later on, but it is sadly a recognized imperfection of this world that the broken dream can rarely be perfectly reconstructed.

To my mind this is probably the reason for the inequality of Miss Farjeon's work, but even at that, there is always, even in the less good, the breath of real inspiration—alas, so often missing altogether from the work of present day writers for children.

I should like to end this unconventional appreciation with lines which I have greatly liked ever since I first read them, in *Sing for Your Supper.* Though written as for Christmas, they are peculiarly apt at this time:

> God bless your house this holy night,
>   And all within it;

> God bless the candle that you light
>   To midnight's minute:

> The board at which you break your
>     bread,
>   The cup you drink of:

> And as you raise it, the unsaid
>   Name that you think of:

> The warming fire, the bed of rest,
>   The ringing laughter:

> These things, and all things else be
>     blest
>   From floor to rafter

> This holy night, from dark to light,

Even more than other;

And, if you have no house to-night,
God bless you, brother.

*Eleanor Graham, "Eleanor Farjeon—A Study
and an Appreciation," in* The Junior Bookshelf, *Vol. 5, No. 3, July, 1941, pp. 81-6.*

### Dorothy Neal White

Eleanor Farjeon is one of the most prolific writers for children; indeed she has written so much it is inevitable that
the quality should be uneven. This unevenness is apparent
in her collection **Sing for Your Supper,** where poems
which can take their place with anything Blake and de la
Mare have written stand alongside second-rate verses one
might expect to find in the cheaper annuals or the children's page of a farmer's weekly. She can be guilty of weak
rhythms and jangling rhymes, but at her best she is fresh,
inventive, sensitive, and humorous. She knows her English
countryside, knows not only garden flowers, but wild
flowers and all herbs—cassia, tarragon, and balsam—
knows their physical nature and the legends of them. She
knows too, the traditional poetry of the countryside, the
counting-songs, the rhymes and singing-games many of
which are incorporated in the two **Martin Pippin** books.
She sees the countryside with a child's eye—all the more
astonishing because she was urban in her own upbringing,
a London child with a London child's pleasures.

Eleanor Farjeon always heard the sound of English as
clearly as she saw the pictures the language brought her.
One of her poems **'Cat'** describes an encounter between a
dog and a cat. The poem is the encounter, it spits out its
meaning and one hears paw and claw. Another one which
ends

> And that's why Hannibal, Hannibal, Hannibal
> Hannibal crossed the Alps

is like a chant of childhood, sometimes derisive, sometimes repeated for its satisfying rhythm rather than any
satisfying sense. Yet this same verse also catches the sense
of inevitability, of conqueror pushing forward. There is a
robustness about much that Eleanor Farjeon has written
but there is also a gentleness and a sympathy as in this portrait of **'Weston'** (a perfect gardener, deaf and dumb).

> Weston cannot speak or hear,
> Yet he has a tongue and ear
> In his fingers and each thumb.
> Weston's hands aren't deaf and dumb . . .
>
> When we meet him on the round
> He smiles and makes a muffled sound,
> But his flower beds, all and each,
> Are his music and his speech.

She has a gift too of writing of children as if she were one
of them and making rhymes as Dorothy Baruch does
about their everyday experiences, as in **'Peter in his bath'**:

> And I will get out when the water goes glug
> And I won't be sucked down the bathroom plug.

*Dorothy Neal White, "Poetry: 'Sing for your
Supper'," in her* About Books for Children,

*1946. Reprint by Oxford University Press,
1949, pp. 172-73.*

### Ruth Hill Viguers

When Eleanor and Herbert Farjeon put their imaginations
and sense of rhythm and humor to work they could make
even English history gay. Though **Kings and Queens** and
**Heroes and Heroines** are probably not read for their history, there is no doubt but that with the reading of them bits
of history may suddenly have meaning and will certainly
cleave to the memory. Best of all, they are fun. . . .

Eleanor Farjeon's poetry is full of games; she seems never
to be still. Her children are always dancing, playing, finding things, rushing off to school; in short, being children.
It is never as though she were deliberately observing children, but as though she were speaking only what she has
always known. Her understanding of children is as natural
as breathing.

Eleanor Farjeon's childhood was extraordinary and full of
variety and color. Her father was an English novelist, her
mother the daughter of Joseph Jefferson, the American
actor. She never had any formal schooling but grew up in
an atmosphere "rich with imaginative suggestion." From
the time she was a small child she and her brothers were
taken frequently to the theatre and opera, she read omniv-
orously from her father's large library and was writing her

*Farjeon at the age of eleven.*

own things by the time she was seven. All four children were very creative, their nursery life was filled with imaginative activity, their father made Christmas and other holidays the most glorious of festivals. It is no wonder that *Come Christmas,* one of her earliest collections of poetry, should contain both some of the gayest and some of the loveliest Christmas poetry in children's literature. There have been numerous collections of her poetry published: *Joan's Door* contains verses of the country and of the city, and some delightful fairy poems; *Over the Garden Wall* has more poems out of childhood, and *Sing For Your Supper* has great variety—songs about children in other countries, poem portraits of very different children, dog verses, school time verses, songs of the seasons and Christmas. There is in all her poetry a wide variety of verse patterns, delightful use of words, love of nature as a child loves it, gaiety and deep joy.

> *Ruth Hill Viguers, "Poetry," in* A Critical History of Children's Literature *by Cornelia Meigs and others, edited by Cornelia Meigs, Macmillan Publishing Company, 1953, pp. 591-604.*

## M. E. Morgan

It was on the train that I opened Eleanor Farjeon's latest book, *The Silver Curlew,* and began to read. I had not thought that it is just the book to read on a train. Its melodic prose sets to the rushing of the wheels; the fugue-like rhythm of sounds made by the train consorts wonderfully with the interweavings of the story—the repetitions, the disposal of the characters, "So much for Doll" "So much for Poll," its spanglings of rhyme, the tunes from the whistle of Charley Noon, the Man from the Moon, the cry of the Silver Curlew, herself the Lady of the Moon, the upsets between Poll and the King, the placidity of Doll, the terror of the Witching Wood, the fear of Tom-Tit-Tot—all of different patterns, but all knitting so musically into a beautiful whole. This book, so typical of its author, invites the question—What is it about Eleanor Farjeon's writing that so weaves a spell about her readers, young and old? . . .

On examining her work one fact emerges very clearly—that above all things Eleanor Farjeon is a lyrist—even her prose is poetical, and in all her writings she can scarce contain herself, but bursts into song readily and easily. In fact her first literary success was in rhyme, the two series of *Nursery Rhymes of London Town,* and among her other books entirely devoted to this muse we find *Cherrystones*—singing verse under the titles of the 'fortune' rhymes with fruit stones; *Mulberry Bush,* imaginative verse based on the games that children play; *The Starry Floor,* which consists of poems on all the constellations. From the first lines under the title **"The Earth"** we enter a rich musical world: —

> Did you know, did you know
> That the earth is a star?

There is a challenge to one's knowledge there, and there is direct appeal to each child in these lines

> Didn't you know
> You are born on a star?

Well, you are.

Her dialect, her language, varies with the story or poem as the case may be. Savour the quaintness of these lines from **"The Old Shepherds, Star of Bethlehem"**:

> Nay friend, nay friend
> Leave cudgellin' go tend
> Thy yowes and closet
> The yearlings in new straw.

If it were for her books of poems alone, Miss Farjeon would merit a high place in the field of modern children's literature, but she has essayed in many lanes. Here is a sampling of her expeditions. In mythology, *Paladins in Spain*—a story of Charlemagne and his knights and their exploits in Spain against the infidels; in biography, *Mighty Men*—thirteen tales from ancient history or legend each accompanied by a short original poem and vividly retold for young readers; or in *Ten Saints*—lives beautifully told in legendary form. We meet St. Christopher whose "eyes were the eyes of a dog" and who went "in search of God and did not know it." Perhaps the criticism might be made that there is too much fantasy and too little fact in these stories, but there will be time enough for hard facts later; for the present let us revel in these legends with their poems so suitably attached. We remember of St. Francis that

> The night and the morning,
> The water, the wind,
> The star and the daisy
> Were each of his world.

With her brother Herbert, Miss Farjeon ventures into the land of pantomime with *The Glass Slipper,* a play for older children which, while good reading, might not make for easy production. Not so her *Grannie Gray,*—children's plays and games with music and without, which are simple and entertaining as in *Absolutely Nothing,* in which the third son of the King always said nothing, absolutely nothing, but gained all that he wanted simply by lifting his finger. It is most delightful. By the end we are all chanting

> Nothing, absolutely nothing.

We see Eleanor Farjeon in a new guise, and concentrating more on the needs of the older children, when she becomes the paraphraser of Chaucer. At the outset she states that it is not an attempt to render *The Canterbury Tales* into literal phrases; she tried not merely to re-tell but generally to follow Chaucer's phrase in doing so; and what an excellent job she does. Listen to the opening of her work and compare it with the original,

> When April with sweet showers has ended the drought of March, and bathed every root in the sap of which the flower is born; when Zephyr with sweet breath has started the tender crops in holt and heath, and the young sun has run half his month, and little birds, stirred by Spring, sing half the night—the people long to go on a pilgrimage.

and the reader also longs to go on this pilgrimage with the people of the story.

In *The New Book of Days* she experimented in still new ways. In it there is something for every day of the year. As the author says, "every instance springs out of some fact, in history or legend, some truth in the real or imaginary world (for truth resides in both of them)." This last parenthesised phrase contains the quintessence of Eleanor Farjeon's ideas, and her book opens up for the children new vistas for future reading.

In all these fields she has distinguished herself and given much to the children of today, but it is as the creator of Martin Pippin that she might best be remembered. Of *Martin Pippin in the Apple Orchard* it has been said that it is still one of the best things of its kind ever produced for the romantic-fantasy period which most girls go through at some stage in their development. Its successor, *Martin Pippin in the Daisy Field,* contains Sussex legends told to a group of little girls (or imaginary little girls) by Martin.

There is joy and humour and tenderness and, above all, music in Miss Farjeon's work. She has the magic wand, and all she touches bursts into song. Like Gillian, Martin's wife, we too can sing,

> Moon for your cradle
> Dark for your cover
> Stars for your night light
> Me for your lover . . .

> M. E. Morgan, "Eleanor Farjeon: An Evaluation," in The Junior Bookshelf, Vol. 18, No. 4, October, 1954, pp. 175-79.

**M. S. Crouch**

> FANCIES AND CREAM
> The Kitten's in the Dairy!
> Where's our Mary?
> She isn't in the Kitchen,
> She isn't at her Stitching,
> She isn't at the Weeding,
> The Brewing, or the Kneading!
> Mary's in the Garden, walking in a Dream,
> Mary's got her Fancies, and the Kitten's got the
>     Cream.

Eleanor Farjeon, more fortunate, has had both Fancies and Cream. Her imagination has wandered, free as air, beyond the bounds of time and space, but she has never lost her touch with reality. Therein lies the difference between her writing and that of Walter de la Mare, with whom she is often compared. Mr. de la Mare, for all his love of earthly beauty, is always bidding it farewell and journeying to realms beyond; Miss Farjeon is content to see, to love and to interpret the things of earth.

And now Miss Farjeon has crowned a life of delighting children by winning the Carnegie Medal. Every lover of children and children's books will rejoice that the Library Association has done itself this honour. *The Little Bookroom* is no more an original book of 1955 than de la Mare's *Collected Stories* was of 1947. It is, far more important, a work of unquestionable genius, a collection of stories in which the fun, wit and wisdom of a lifetime are stored up "on purpose to a life beyond life." As one who has in the past cursed the obtuseness of those responsible

for failing to recognise the shining quality of her art, I am delighted that the Medal has been awarded for a book which so completely sums up Miss Farjeon's work. Here, indeed, are Fancies and Cream, not neatly separated but enchantingly blended in stories which treat of homely things and pierce through to the poetical and philosophical truths which underline them. This is mellow writing, free from contemporary malaise, but not complacent. It shows the child the nature of the rock upon which the happy life is founded. The stories are in the fullest sense "moral"; it is, however, in the nature of Miss Farjeon's genius that their first and last impression is one of delight. This has nothing to do with sugaring the pill. For Miss Farjeon, the beauty of holiness is no cant phrase, but a precise description; goodness and gaiety and loveliness are blended in her thought and her work.

"In my youth," she says in *Silver-sand and Snow,* "I dreamed of being a 'real' poet." All her work has to be read as that of a poet; although she is never guilty of "poetic prose" her prose writing is enlightened by the poetical imagination. In her verse she is primarily lyrical. She has sometimes been compared with Walter de la Mare because of her conspicuous success in both prose and verse; the comparison could hardly be to her advantage. Perhaps a fairer one would be with A. A. Milne. She is rarely as memorable as Milne—*Mrs. Malone,* almost alone of all her works, has become a part of the child's equipment as *The King's Breakfast* and *Bold Sir Brian Botany* have— she is infinitely more melodious than he and never, as he sometimes does, leaves the reader standing aghast on the brink of the pit of sentimentality. Her rhymes give the effect of spontaneity. They are technically of the highest excellence; they have point and wit, and the inevitability of nursery rhymes. Many of her books are in a sense "occasional" verse; individual poems suffer by being removed from their context, from the juxtaposition of other verses or of an illustration. They are not the worse for that; Miss Farjeon is no less an artist for being the senior partner in an undertaking in which artist and typographer have important parts to play.

Occasionally she sounds a deeper note. Her aged Bethlehem Shepherds: —

> "Why was it? . . . Hey? . . . Why was it? . . .
>     Why, becos it—
> Becos it—dang my wamblin' wits! why was
>     it? . . .
>     Nay friend, nay friend,
>     Leave cudgellin', go tend
>     Thy yowes, an' closet
> The yeanlings in new straw . . . Bless us,
>     why was it
> Yon Star came so
> A mort o' years ago? . . . ."

speaks out of the experiences of the centuries. But this is exceptional. She is content usually to delight with gay tunes, with swift turns of mood, with charming pictures of the changing seasons, and leaves implicit and unstated the firm philosophy from which these light fancies spring.

Although Miss Farjeon lives now in a village in London, and has celebrated the city's charms in living verse, it is

Sussex that has been the kindest muse to her writing. Those who look on Sussex now from "Amberley's green rim" or from the skipping ground in Caburn, may sometimes feel that a fate more grievous than the new Lord's malice has befallen the pleasant land; but, if Subtopia rules now, the real Sussex is preserved more truly, more securely, in the Martin Pippin stories than in the louder rhymes of Kipling and Belloc. Posterity will have its own opinion of Miss Farjeon—for if one thing is certain, it is that these books will live—but it seems likely that Martin Pippin will live as long as anything. These two books, one which captures the delicate and elusive fancy of adolescence and young love, the other so exquisitely in tune with the dreams of childhood, are of the essence of her art. She has always been a superb story-teller, and some of the stories strung on the thread of the Martin Pippin theme are among the best of the century; she loves to relate her stories to a central theme, and this the wayward wandering singer provides; her prose is always bursting into verse, and her songs here are tuneful and apposite; like all poets she is in love with words, and particularly with names; and she plays most delightfully with the grotesque and lovely place names of Downland Sussex.

As in her verse, she has captured and can recreate some of the subtle logic and music of nursery rhymes, so in her stories, she can spin out of her memory and the memory of the ages, the most convincing folk-tales. She is, I suspect, no academic folk-lorist; but she has a sure instinct which keeps her from the false tones and ideas of most inventors of fairy-tales. So, although she does not deny to her stories all the decoration and refinement of which she is capable, the tales remain fundamentally simple, elemental, as if, for all their art, they sprang from a primitive stock.

Miss Farjeon is primarily a miniaturist. She writes best within the framework of the short tale—even *A Nursery in the Nineties* is read best as a series of episodes. Her two long works for children—*The Silver Curlew* and *The Glass Slipper*—are simply charming translations into another form of stage pieces. They are a great delight, but they are not really novels. It is in the short story, with its economy, its nice balance of parts, its jewel-like symmetry, that her work can best be seen and enjoyed, as one enjoys those lyrics which have the same qualities of form and tone.

It is fortunate that Miss Farjeon has had publishers who have been aware of the nature and quality of her work, and that such fine artists have adorned her books. The Morton Sales have been particularly successful in matching, and developing, the fantastic and homely aspects of her verse, and, in *Martin Pippin in the Daisy Field,* have interpreted the charm and poignancy of the tales in a way which is almost painful in its loveliness. Helen Sewell's dignity and monumental quality, Philip Gough's elegance, Ernest Shepard's humour, all have something to add to the books they adorn. And in *Martin Pippin in the Apple Orchard,* Richard Kennedy rose to heights and penetrated to depths which even he could hardly have suspected. Edward Ardizzone brings to *The Little Bookroom* a realistic, a satiric

and a poetic touch. He, too, is equally at home with Fancies and with Cream.

Miss Farjeon's interests and sympathies range wide. She likes wild flowers, gardens, singing games, nonsense rhymes, puns, babies, all sorts of good things. Like Mrs. Malone's, her heart is so big it has room for all. That, finally, is the secret of her greatness as a writer. Children respond, above all, to warmth. They recognise the kindness of a big heart, the goodness which is made of fun and tenderness and understanding. Miss Farjeon's Carnegie Medal is a belated official tribute to a great achievement, to one who as a poet, story-teller and person, is the last representative of that golden age which began a century ago with Edward Lear.

*M. S. Crouch, "Eleanor Farjeon," in* The Junior Bookshelf, *Vol. 20, No. 3, July, 1956, pp. 110-14.*

**Frances Clarke Sayers**

Even before she had learned to hold a pencil or recognize one letter from another, Eleanor Farjeon had begun to create stories which were told to her father, and transcribed by him. All through her childhood she wrote as she read, from a necessity as immediate and persuasive as the urge to draw breath. At eighteen, an operetta for which she had written the lyrics to accompany her brother Harry's music was performed in St. George's Hall in London, and the two shy young people took their bows before an enthusiastic public who had come to hear the first opera, publicly presented by the Academy, which was the work of one of their own students. At nineteen, she received her first three guineas for a fairy tale, **"The Cardboard Angel,"** printed in Hutchinson's magazine. Now, in the middle seventies, she has chosen from the bounty of her own writing a book of stories of ageless appeal, addressed to children, which she calls *The Little Bookroom.* The publishers have given the book a format that suggests its concentrate of magic, with light and space on every page, and the incisive line of Edward Ardizzone's black and white illustrations echoing the harmony of type on the page, and confirming the characteristic reality of Eleanor Farjeon's tales of imagination.

An author is known by the worlds he creates. The measure of his greatness is the degree of clarity and the consistency with which he builds his spirit's habitation, the depth and height it offers the reader who enters it. Eleanor Farjeon's world is construed of fantasy, romance and an abounding, yea-saying joy in the experience of life. It is the stuff that dreams are made of, and as dangerous as dynamite except for those who have genius in their blood, a compassionate heart, a sense of wonder at the multitudinous miracles to be met with in one day's living in this world, and the blessed proportion of wit, humor and nonsense. All these she has. Look out upon the view that the windows of *The Little Bookroom* afford, in the English mist and sunshine, and see the origins of this, her particular enchantment.

One window looks out upon her heritage, a heritage that stretches back to generations of English actors—the Jeffersons—Tom Jefferson playing with Garrick, in a heyday of the English stage, the gifts culminating in Tom's grandson, Joseph Jefferson, the American, who was to give the definitive performance of old Rip Van Winkle, in the coming of age of the American theater. . . .

Her father was an Englishman; a storyteller, novelist and journalist, bearing in his blood the passionate response to life typical of the Jewish race, with stormy moods balancing the periods of joyous exuberance and lavish generosity of spirit. He gave his daughter the love of storytelling, an insatiable sympathy for everything that lives, and her name: Eleanor Farjeon.

That name is like a melody in a nursery rhyme, the refrain of a ballad, or the recurring lilt in a singing game. It has set a pace of melody for her, since the beginning. "I can hardly remember the time when it did not seem *easier* to me to write in running rhyme than in plodding prose," she says of herself. "If you can't be glad of your name it isn't the right one," says Nollekens, the King in **The Silver Curlew.** She must be glad of hers, "for a man can no more escape from his name than from his nature," said Robin Rue, in **Martin Pippin in the Apple Orchard,** and none knew better than he who lost his love, Gillian, to the merrier name of Martin Pippin himself.

She has a gift for names, perhaps because her own evokes such music. What names in the two novels involving Martin Pippin: Jennifer, Jessica, Jane, Joan, Joyce, Joscelyn, and Gillian; Michael, Tom, Oliver, Henry, Sally, Selina, Sylvia, and Sue! And the names she conjures for the spirits of darkness: Trimingham, Knapton, and Trunch, with Rackny, the Spider Mother in the Witching Wood.

The window of the bookroom that looks out on her childhood affords a view of the nursery in which she was brought up, saturated with music, the mystery of words, the self-invented games she shared with her three brothers, the legendary appeal of her mother's American childhood, with the most colorful men and women of the stage and London's literary life walking in and out of the household; a succession of "uncles and aunts," accomplished, beautiful—all dedicated to something beyond the common day, the diverse arts of expression—all this encompassed by fierce family loyalty and love.

There were no schools in that childhood, but teachers and governesses, and all the books overflowing shelves and tables. "We all had bookshelves, mine were crowded with fairy tales and 'The Greeks.' " In further confession of the wellsprings of her spirit she says [in **Portrait of a Family**], "Up to my twentieth year, the three outstanding 'revelations' in the worlds of poetry, music and pictures came instantaneously from *A Midsummer Night's Dream, Hansel and Gretel,* and Turner," The fairies, the folktale, and the "luminous view"! From these vistas out of the bookroom windows, one sees the stuff of which her world is made. Small wonder, being born of felicity, that the essence of it is romance, a vision of the world as it is, if you look at it just so.

Eleanor Farjeon is master at presenting the world as romance. Yet there is bite in it. Her worlds of imagination are no simpering constructions, all syrup and sugar, with fairies uprooted from their antique and awesome lineage. It is shadowed with weeping now and then, and the bittersweet of lost dreams, but the strongest note is affirmation, an exuberance of joy. Early in her writing, in that love song to London, **Gypsy and Ginger,** the theme of affirmation is stated.

> "It's all very well," said Gypsy, " . . . for us to be light-hearted in our own lives, and even in the comparatively grave matter of earning our living; but as well as that we must remember that the world is full crying of evils. . . . "
>
> "What do the evils cry for?" asked Ginger.
>
> "Reform," said Gypsy.
>
> "Then let's reform them," said Ginger. "But we needn't cry along with them, need we? . . ."
>
> "No," he said, . . . "It's no use crying over spilt evils. It's better to mop them up laughing."

Her world is not so haunted as the world of Walter de la Mare, nor so wracked with the sorrow of search and longing unfulfilled. It is not so fey and whimsical as the world of Elizabeth Goudge. There is little whimsey in it, but great magic and stout humor, wit and free-running nonsense. The miraculous quality is the freshness and originality; the themes, the incidents, the "glad invention" which well up endlessly, tale after tale, story after story, resembling nothing so much as the never-ending variety of melody and theme of Mozart's music. A comfortable practicality, a touch of common earth and ordinary bread and butter give the sanity of salt to her finest fancy. Over and over again, the common touch thrusts home the whole airy concept and leaves the reader holding the fantasy so hard by the hand there's no denying the truth of it. There is Ooney, for example, in the tale of Tom Cobble who had himself stolen by the fairies. Ooney was the daughter of the Enchanter.

"She was about as old as sixteen, Tom thought, and she was very beautiful. Like the other fairies, she had a sort of moonshine frock on, but over it she wore a big check apron with pockets, and in her hand she had a feather duster, with which she was dusting the table [**Martin Pippin in the Daisy-Field**]."

This juxtaposition of two worlds, this fusion of dusters with fairy moonlight, is always deft and successful. She has also the matchless ability of Andersen of naming exactly the object that symbolizes the real world or the world of magic. It is an eerie gift, resembling true pitch for the musician, or the infallible ear of the poet for rhyme and beat.

She has also Andersen's skill of suddenly relating a world which seems to be inhabited by men and women to the immediacy of childhood. The soldier of "The Tinderbox," you will remember, spent his wealth, it is true, in theaters and carriage rides through the Royal Deer Park. But when the extent of that wealth is being told, it is described in terms of all the rocking horses and sugar pigs it could buy. In Eleanor Farjeon's **The Glass Slipper,** when the ugly sisters were preparing for their bath, there is the same sly touch that brings the fairy tale straight to the child's own world.

*The End Cottage, Mucky Lane, Houghton, where Farjeon lived for the two years that she considered the most important of her life (1919-20). Biographer Annabel Farjeon writes in her* Morning Has Broken, *"When neighboring children gathered in Mucky Lane to skip beneath her window and sing old rhymes handed down for generations, she went out and asked them to explain the intricacies of their game and recite the words. Elsie Puttick was the deftist of all the skippers and years later became the heroine of one of Eleanor's best fairy tales,* "Elsie Piddock Skips in Her Sleep."

"The Sisters gathered themselves up, piled Ella's arms with towels and soaps and sponges and perfume *and rubber ducks,* and pushed past her to the bathroom, where she had to scrub their backs for them. They were much too lazy to do it for themselves."

And again, in **The Silver Curlew,** when King Nollekens is trying to bribe the Imp to depart forever, he says, "Look here! Here's my crown! Here's my scepter! Here's my penknife with three blades!"

The bone and sinew of her fancy and of her writing gifts derive from the sturdy art of the folktale and the folk storyteller. The direct action, the quick defining of character and conflict, the sudden flashes of dialogue—oh, what mastery of the way people talk—the uncanny choice of detail, the rich improvisation on old themes, these are close kin to the folklore of the world. The storyteller will find tales ready for the tongue in her books, the wonders rooted to a background of English earth, or Italian or French landscape, for in addition to all else Eleanor Farjeon has an avid eye for the minutiae of shifting beauty of meadows, gardens, flowers, skies, and the night.

"I was fascinated by things that came and went," she writes in **Portrait of a Family,** "things I couldn't quite touch, or really find out; the silver road on the sea to the sun on the horizon, the moon and her star, the rainbow and its reflection, the shafts of light drawn almost down to earth from a bright-edged cloud, the spot of light at the end of a green arcade of trees."

One of the windows of the bookroom looks across the peaks of solid scholarship. There are translations from the French and Italian in the writing of this author, plays for adults, short stories and romances. The English edition of O'Brien's *Best Short Stories* contained, in 1925, an exquisite ghost story, **"Faithful Jenny Dove,"** with the characteristic turn of events, unexpected, haunting, as beautiful a love story as **"The Mill of Dreams,"** the story of the weight of dreams on reality in one of the greatest of fantasies, **Martin Pippin in the Apple Orchard.**

Scholarship casts its shadow of authenticity over her retelling of the Canterbury Tales, with its forthright foreword of explanation:

"The one excuse for presenting Chaucer in any words but his own is that he may be read, and a taste for him be got by people, especially young people, who would never try to read the foreign language of his English, and so would miss forever something of the fun, the beauty, the wisdom, the humanity and romance in which he stands among our poets second only to Shakespeare."

No tale is omitted, though some are shortened, and the changing of certain names and words she explains by saying, "I have followed an instinct."

There is an inevitable rightness about that instinct. It fashions her style in the image of her subject matter. There is reverence in the sturdy prose with which she tells the lives of the saints she writes of in the book *Ten Saints.* And there is sweet grace in the poems included with the biographies of the holy men and women who lived between the third and the thirteenth centuries. In *Kings and Queens,* she becomes the gay historian telling English history in ballads and verse that take the sting out of the dates of succession.

George I

George the First, when he was young,
Couldn't speak the English tongue;
In Hanover, where he was born,
He spoke in German night and morn.

. . . .

George, George, in England they
Want you for their king to-day.
Say you will, with heart and soul!—
George, delighted, said *Jawohl!*

George the First, till he was dead,
Still his prayers in German said,
Wasn't that a funny thing
For one who was an English king?

Rhymes, verse, poetry and song have tumbled from her pen in a rush of melody. Much of it mirrors the inwardness of childhood with a sureness that betrays her understanding of incident and object which belong to their world and her remembrance of the emotions of childhood. Much of it echoes the wild, fresh poetry of ballads and singing games, and all of it is lyrical.

"I hope I shall never quite shake off my best bel-shangles. After the nursery rhymes, I found them among the Elizabethans; who, in my world of books followed the Greeks." So she writes in a little book *Magic Casements,* written for the world association of writers P.E.N., in 1941. I could wish this book in the hands and minds of every teacher in the world. In the words of Eleanor Farjeon, "The book is a plea for a return to imaginative reading, . . . not too much organized and systematized; reading for every age at any age, not running in grooves cut for the child of six, or ten, or fourteen. I would let children loose among books, as now, at an early age, they are let loose with brown paper and brush among color; where, without knowing it, they may find and give expression to the ageless spirit."

**"The Little Bookroom"** made its first appearance in this small book, when war raged in England and every beauty was threatened. It is a well of refreshment, and a candle that lights up the spirit and imagination of a rare person, giving and spending the exuberance of her richly stored imagination, her wide affection for the world and all in it. Her worlds are Elizabethan, as warm, as intoxicated with words and song, as freshly viewing the world and the men and women in it. Not even the twentieth century can diminish the exaltation this author has had from life. Best of all, she has decanted the elixir for the young.

In the introduction to her collection of selected verse, the English edition of which bears the title *Silver-Sand and Snow,* she speaks of her writing, particularly her poetry, as being inconsequential stuff, made only of "silver-sand that trickles through the fingers, and snow that melts in the sun."

She does herself something less than justice in this choice of metaphor. Looking upon the stature of her work, the range and variety of her imagination, the multitudinous invention of her fancy, and the music of her prose and verse, I bid her doff her bonnet to herself, in unaccustomed self-praise. It is a contribution of some magnitude, and for authority I cite that astute novelist and critic, E. M. Forster, whose own *Room with a View* remains a prime delight in English fiction.

Mr. Forster, in his *Aspects of the Novel,* discusses the character of fantasy. Reading his analysis, steeped as I was in the writing of Eleanor Farjeon, I caught a glimpse of what she has done.

> The stuff of daily life will be tugged and strained in various directions, the earth will be given little tilts mischievous or pensive, spot lights will fall on objects that have no reason to anticipate or welcome them, and tragedy herself, though not excluded, will have a fortuitous air as if a word would disarm her.

> The power of fantasy penetrates into every corner of the universe, but not into the forces that govern it—the stars that are the brain of heaven, the army of unalterable law, remain untouched—and novels of this type have an improvised air, which is the secret of their force and charm. They may contain solid character drawing, penetrating and bitter criticism of conduct and civilization; yet our simile of the beam of light must remain, and if one god must be invoked specially, let us call upon Hermes—messenger, thief, and conductor of souls to a not too terrible hereafter.

"The young youth of the world," as the young can see and feel it—this is Eleanor Farjeon's gift. No one else has seen it with such merry eyes, or matched the flavor of her telling.

*Frances Clarke Sayers, "Eleanor Farjeon's 'Room with a View'," in* The Horn Book Magazine, *Vol. XXXII, No. 5, October, 1956, pp. 334-44.*

**Claire Huchet Bishop**

Miss Eleanor Farjeon has now been chosen as the first recipient of the Regina Medal, and a better choice could not have been made. Few are blessed with the gift which makes them children's minstrels, and among living writers none is more endowed with this precious gift than Eleanor Farjeon. Now in her seventies, she has sung exuberantly, whimsically and tenderly for millions of children on both sides of the Atlantic.

Miss Farjeon has a rich background. Her American mother was the daughter of the great actor Joseph Jefferson, and her English Jewish father was a well-known storyteller and novelist. Her childhood was singularly privileged: she enjoyed music, art, literature and a home always open to people of distinction and rare achievement. Every day for her was an adventure of the spirit. "It would have been more natural to live without clothes than without books," she says in her *Portrait of a Family,* where she recounts how all the children of the family had special bookshelves and hers "were crowded with fairy tales and 'the Greeks.' "

Indeed, it seems almost miraculous that Eleanor Farjeon did not turn out to be just a delightful conversationalist or a refined dilettante. Happily, she did not. Her cultural background and her natural gift fused and flourished in the form of an extraordinary talent. Scholarly to the point of having integrated the joy of the past into her daily life, fluent in French and Italian, lover of Greek civilization, endowed with a luminous Christian faith and an awareness of its sturdy Judaic roots, she yet created more than fifty books for children: nursery rhymes, verse, plays, fairy tales, stories, folk tales, operettas.

In 1956 Miss Farjeon received the Carnegie Medal of England and the International Hans Christian Andersen award. And now in 1959 the Regina Medal, which bears a crown and a delicate heraldic M for Mary, and a quotation from her lifelong friend, the late Walter de La Mare: "Only the rarest kind of best in anything can be good enough for the young." Some fifty odd years before, Anatole France had said, "When you are writing for children do not assume a style for the occasion. Think your best and write your best." That Eleanor Farjeon has done, and it is the children's good fortune that "her best" is of such quality.

Hers is the gift of improvisation:

> Old Saturn lolls in heaven,
> The laziest of loons,
> Waited on by seven
> Nimble little moons.

Of lyrical fancy:

> The old sun, the gold sun,
> With lovely May returning
> Went among the chestnut trees
> And set their candles burning.

Of gentle humor: "The four sons of Mother Codling were good strong lads with enormous appetites, who said little and thought less."

And of whimsical folk-like wisdom: " 'Is it possible! A Bishop using no other carriage than his own two feet! Why any beggar has as good a conveyance. What a poor Master you must serve, who cannot provide his princes with better means of travel.' 'He can,' said Martin. Pointing at the Devil, he changed him on the spot into a mule."

She has a genius for combining the practical and the imaginative, to wit, among a host of other instances, the words of King Nollekens: " 'Look here! Here's my crown! Here's my scepter! Here's my penknife with three blades.' "

She has an unerring sense of dialogue, and a delightful musical ear. She extols the *Mighty Men from Beowulf to William the Conqueror,* and the *Mighty Men from Achilles to Julius Caesar, Kings and Queens* and *Heroes and Heroines.* And she sings most tenderly of Christmas.

History, drama, operetta, fairy tale, story, sea yarn, legend and poetry—each and all Eleanor Farjeon recreates or invents with gusto and fanciful joy. Everyone and everything is intensely alive under her pen. Her two feet are on the ground, her head in the clouds, and her imagination is never an escape but an integral part of the make-up of a whole human being. That is the reason why, as she says, "it's better to captivate a child's fancy than to teach his mind."

It would be hard to imagine a child who, at one time or another, would not be captivated by Eleanor Farjeon's voice. That this power of enchantment is not a privilege limited to children the Regina Award gives us the opportunity to discover anew. Young and old can delight in Eleanor Farjeon's books, and through them come to be, like the child in one of her tales, "pacified with wonder."

> *Claire Huchet Bishop, "A Children's Minstrel," in* The Commonweal, *Vol. LXX, No. 8, May 22, 1959, pp. 207-08.*

### Helen Dean Fish

[*The following excerpt is from an essay originally published in the February, 1930 issue of* The Horn Book Magazine.]

[Eleanor Farjeon] is a person whose eyes and mind and heart are always wide open, though one cannot read her poems without knowing that she has mightily won her joy. But she *has* won it, and has it to give away. Joy is, I think, the keynote of all her stories, her poems, her people, her music. . . .

When still in her teens she wrote poetry and light-opera librettos for which she was complimented highly by W. S. Gilbert, librettist of the famous Gilbert and Sullivan operas. Her early writings were chiefly verse and music for children, and her first published books were two volumes of serious verse in 1908 and 1911. Then came *Nursery Rhymes of London Town* in 1916 and 1917, more grown-up poetry in 1918 and several books of singing games and rounds. "Gypsy and Ginger," her first story, was published in 1920, and *Martin Pippin* in 1922 established her literary and artistic reputation more firmly than any of her previous work. *The Soul of Kol Nikon,* a fantasy, followed in 1923, and in 1927 *Joan's Door,* a volume of child poems, and *Italian Peepshow,* a book of delightful, original folk-tales, among which is the inimitably lovely "The King of Tripoli Brings the Pasta." *Come Christmas,* a gay little book of new Christmas poems, bursting full of all the joys of Christmas for young and old, came in 1928, and in 1929, *Kaleidoscope,* a charming story for older boys and girls and adults. It is made of the dreams of youth and tells of a penniless but happy young man about London who needs no more than his penny newspaper to send him adventuring in a world of romance.

And now we have *The Tale of Tom Tiddler,* again a treat

for younger readers. Here Miss Farjeon gives us fanciful tales of how the familiar and often amusing names of London streets and byways came to be—Shepherd's Bush and White-chapel, Lavender Hill and Petticoat Lane, Earl's Court and Jack Straw's Castle and a score more. The American edition includes, in addition to the tales, a number of the delightful **"Rhymes of London Town."** Who can resist:

> I went up to the Hay-market upon a summer's day,
> I went up to the Hay-market to sell a load of hay,
> To sell a load of hay and a little bit over,
> And I sold it all to a pretty girl for a nosegay of red clover.
> A nosegay of red clover and a hollow golden straw,
> Now wasn't that a bargain, the best you ever saw?
> I whistled on my straw in the market-place all day,
> And the London folk came flocking for to foot it in the hay.

Once you have met Eleanor Farjeon in one of her magical books and lived in her English countryside, you want to read everything she has written and you live in pleasant anticipation of her next book, for you know it will be written out of a rich life.

> *Helen Dean Fish, "The Spring-Green Lady, Eleanor Farjeon," in* A Horn Book Sampler *on Children's Books and Reading, edited by Norma R. Fryatt, The Horn Book, 1959, pp. 255-58.*

## Eileen H. Colwell

*[An English children's librarian, Colwell was also a well known storyteller whose friendship with Farjeon began in 1955 when she asked permission to retell some of Farjeon's works in the United States.]*

How much is an author influenced by environment in the development of his or her genius? Virginia Woolf has said [in *Granite and Rainbow,* 1958], 'How abnormal is the effort needed to produce a work of art, and what shelter and support the mind of the artist requires.' Does a sympathetic atmosphere and the interest of parents bring forth talent more quickly than one of disapproval? It would seem that creativity needs to be deeply rooted in encouragement and may fade in a hostile childhood climate. Environment, heredity, circumstance, are of importance, but the degree to which these factors affect the development of an individual must vary enormously with character and personality.

The early life of an author has significance, and especially is this so in the case of Eleanor Farjeon, for her family life was always of vital importance to her. Had she had a more conventional childhood and education, the discipline of authorship might have been easier, but, on the other hand, her natural exuberance and inventiveness might well have been subdued to the detriment of her work. . . .

[Eleanor Farjeon] was indeed, as her father said, 'an entirely new and original uproar', and a year [after her birth] he wrote of this 'Imperious Babe':

> May not those lungs which now such yells emit
> One day enthral a world with sense and wit?

He cannot have guessed how prophetic his jesting verse was to be.

There were four children in that nursery of the nineties of which Eleanor Farjeon was to write so enchantingly many years later—Harry, Nellie, Joe and Bertie. Their mother was gay, witty, sweet-tempered and musical; their father generous and excitingly unpredictable. . . .

Much the most strange and important of [Eleanor's] childhood activities was the mysterious game called TAR which she played with Harry from an early age. Its importance cannot be overestimated, for TAR lasted until she was twenty-five and she says it influenced her 'more radically' than anything else in her life. It began because of the strength of her imaginative life and her unusually close sympathy with Harry. Without him 'Nellie was not'. Even at the age of five and three respectively they could sing a duet which Harry composed as he went along and Nellie followed. TAR was an infinitely complex development of a child's game of make-believe. Harry evolved the plot and decided the characters. He had only to tell Nellie what characters they were and at once they were both lost in a world of imagination in which they were many people at once, with swift changes of thought and mood. It was an independent life, far more exciting than their everyday existence. The two children—both with spectacles, her hair untidy, his too long—would walk through the streets, he a little ahead, she trotting at his elbow, talking, talking endlessly, and oblivous to all that went on outside their secret world. On one occasion this state lasted for a fortnight. 'To play TAR shuts out all loneliness, all emptiness, all everything but itself, as long as it lasts.' It was only when Harry said 'We are Harry and Nellie,' that they returned reluctantly to the reality of everyday life.

The dangers of this 'game' are obvious, and it is certain that it delayed the development of Eleanor Farjeon the writer and person too long, for so deep-rooted had it become that to give up this imaginary life—as she eventually did—cost her pain and discipline. But through it, on the other hand, she acquired the power 'to put in motion, almost at will, given persons within given scenes, and see what came of it'. She had always had the ability to transform her thoughts during the many sleepless nights of her youth into something real and three-dimensional, so that she could, for instance, bring an orchestra to life in her mind and listen to it playing every note of her favourite music. Imagining was an ecstasy and the chief joy of her inward life.

In her adolescence Eleanor Farjeon was beset by doubts of her ability to become a writer. Writing was at the very centre of her life, yet she seemed to be accomplishing nothing in her chosen sphere. Her literary work was full of beginnings and endings with no substance. Harry was successful already—he had won a medal as the most brilliant student at the Royal Academy of Music and a scholarship for operatic composition. It is true that she had written the libretto for a romantic opera, *Floretta,* for him to set to music which had been performed in public, and that she had also received her first payment for a story, a fairytale,

'The Cardboard Angel'. But at eighteen her mother found her weeping over her 'wasted life'. Her mind was full of ideas, but she could not bring herself to complete or perfect anything, so strong was the hold of TAR.

At this time a phrase in *Die Meistersinger von Nürnberg* gave her fresh hope and inspiration. As she listened to Hans Sachs singing 'Nun sang er wie er musst, und wie er musst, so konnt er's' (now he sang because he must and because he must, he could sing). She realized that she too, like Walter, must be able to sing, for it was her life and it could not be denied.

When she was twenty-two her father died leaving the family in financial straits, and it became still more important that she should write seriously. She set out with renewed hope to overcome her dreaming procrastination. It was to be thirteen years, however, before the first of her books for children was published and she began to receive literary recognition. For many years her delight in writing had expressed itself 'in poetry and music, instead of through life', and she had written 'scarcely anything worth keeping'. Now she began to struggle from her state of almost self-hypnosis into a wider, fuller and more normal life of warm friendships and creative work.

In her circle of friends were Arnold and Clifford Bax, Myra Hess, the Meynells, D. H. Lawrence, Robert Frost and, above all, Edward Thomas, who was to mean so much to her all her life. Through her unrequited love for him, and her participation in his growth as a poet, she finally achieved maturity in her own writing. The influence of Edward Thomas also strengthened her strong affinity with nature and her response to it. She gained confidence in herself and her own powers, and grew less painfully shy.

Through all these years of apprenticeship she was writing articles, stories and poems. In 1911 her ***Dream-songs for the beloved*** had been published, in 1914 her essay on **'Trees'** and a fantasy, ***The Soul of Kol-Nikon. Nursery Rhymes of London Town*** were appearing anonymously in *Punch*, and in 1916 these rhymes were published in book form, the first of her books in the field of children's literature in which she was to become so prominent a figure.

It is interesting to catch a glimpse of Eleanor Farjeon, the woman at this time. She had many friends, including children. One of these, a son of James Guthrie, founder of the Pear Tree Press, meeting her on one of her long walks, with her haversack, stick and green leather cap with some hedge-leaves pushed into the band, wrote in his diary:

> Miss Farjeon is great fun. She stumps along with her knapsack on her back and her chalala in her hand, looking for all the world like a pilgrim . . . she turns the place into the very haunt of merriment. She is one of the most marvellous personalities I know. Her work is lively and serious.

It was walks like this one over the Sussex Downs which gave her the background for many of her stories and poems.

In 1917 Edward Thomas was killed in the Great War. His death left a gap which might have embittered a less fine character. But all through her life Eleanor Farjeon has had more thought for the grief of others than for her own, and has transmuted sorrow into love and joy.

In 1903, on the death of her father, she had been withdrawn and lost in the world of imagination encouraged by TAR, unable to come to terms with life or to achieve any real progress in her chosen career of writing. By 1917 she had had some success as a writer, was learning to control her ebullient imagination and her almost too facile ability to write verse. She was free at last to develop her genius as a storyteller, a poet and a dramatist. . . .

One of Eleanor Farjeon's greatest gifts is that of storytelling. Those who are fortunate enough to know her personally must have listened many times entranced to the recounting of something that has happened to her, something possibly quite ordinary but which became in her hands dramatic or entertaining or moving. It is this natural aptitude for telling a story which is disciplined in her written work into musical and smoothly flowing prose.

It is in the short story that Eleanor Farjeon excels; in fact all her stories for children are short ones, except for the two amplifications of folk-tales, ***The Glass Slipper*** and ***The Silver Curlew.*** Her stories are often linked together, however, by a theme as in ***The Tale of Tom Tiddler,*** or written round a personality as in the 'Martin Pippin' books. Sometimes the stories are links in a chain, sometimes beads on a thread. Even her adult books are often in the same pattern, as, for instance, ***The Fair at St. James.***

The short story demands economy in words. Within a few pages the plot must be worked out to a satisfying conclusion, the characters developed and the story set in the right atmosphere. That it is the short story in which Eleanor Farjeon is happiest, and for which she has made her name, says much for her skill.

Part of the secret of her success is probably her strong feeling for folk-tales, in which she has so delighted from her earliest days that their idiom and pattern come naturally to her. Many of her sources of inspiration are in the folklore of the countryside—children's games, fragments of tradition, legends, customs, nursery rhymes. This is seen admirably in her 'Martin Pippin' books. The way in which these stories developed affords an interesting glimpse into the mind of a creative artist.

In 1907, while on holiday on a farm by the sea in Brittany, her mind was full of troubadours and minstrels and she spent much time trying her hand at aubades and serenades. One day, she thought, she would write a story of a minstrel who rescued a captive princess and her ladies from one of these romantic islands. The ladies would have names like Elaine and Guinevere. . . . But when she returned to England the story was still unwritten except for a few songs and scraps of conversation.

Years later, as she watched her little niece, Joan, dancing in an apple orchard in Sussex, her long-forgotten story came into her mind again, but now the background was Sussex and the lovely ladies had become lovely girls with simple English names. Round the short stories she now wrote she wove interludes with the romantic figure of the minstrel and storyteller Martin Pippin as their centre. The framework of the book was a singing game, 'The Spring-green Lady', which, in spite of what she says in her beguiling preface, was her own creation. Martin Pippin helps a love-sick youth to regain his sweetheart, who is guarded by six milkmaids in an orchard. Each day he bribes a milkmaid with a tale to give him one of the keys to Gillian's prison.

Much of the book was already in Eleanor Farjeon's mind, she discovered, but her imagination and experience as a writer had transmuted the undeveloped idea of her youth into an altogether greater, although still romantic, book of love stories. The short stories in this book are adult in their conception and construction, but they are enjoyed by adolescent girls. They were in fact written during the First World War for a young soldier for whom the Sussex names and background would have associations.

Her second 'Martin Pippin' book, *Martin Pippin in the Daisy-field,* first published in 1937, is for a much younger reading public. The difference is indicated in the very titles of the books—'The apple orchard', symbol of high summer and maturity; 'The daisy-field', suggesting springtime and childhood. The minstrel is still the central figure,

*Farjeon at The End Cottage.*

but his companions are now children and the interludes are concerned not with love but with childish things—skipping-rhymes, sayings and verses about birds and trees, riddles, and the efforts of the little girls to postpone bedtime. The stories told by Martin Pippin this time are definitely for children. They include a 'tall tale' with a nautical flavour, **'Selsey Bill'**; the tender and amusing story of the Tantony Pig who makes a bargain with Saint Anthony so that he may eat as much as he likes in the daytime and the Saint will find his lost figure for him at night; the story of Tom Cobble, who got himself stolen by the fairies on purpose, a tale full of ingenious spells and magic. **'The Long Man of Wilmington'** is about Wilkin, who never grew taller than two-and-a-half feet high and became a chimney sweep, thereby breaking the hearts of his seven aunts, who hated dirt so much yet loved little Wilkin so dearly.

But the best story in the book, and Eleanor Farjeon's own favourite, for it really says 'what she wanted it to say', is **'Elsie Piddock Skips in her Sleep'.** It is the tale of little Elsie Piddock, who while she was asleep learnt to skip as the fairies do, and who had a fairy skipping rope with handles of Sugar Candy and Almond Rock. She could skip as never so:

> The Slow Skip,
> The Toe Skip,
> The Skip Double-Double,
> The Fast Skip,
> The Last Skip,
> And the Skip Against Trouble!

But little Elsie Piddock grew up, 'though never very much', and her skipping became a legend nobody believed. Long after her days a new lord came to the village and threatened to take the children's skipping ground, Mount Caburn, for a factory. A final skipping match was held there and the lord promised that he would not lay his first brick until the last skipper skipped the last skip. To the match came a little old lady—it was Elsie Piddock, 109 years old, shrunk to the size of a child again and with her fairy skipping rope in her hands. Once more she skipped in her sleep, to keep Caburn for the children 'and them and theirs for ever', and:

> . . . if you go to Caburn at the new moon you may catch a glimpse of a tiny bent figure, no bigger than a child, skipping all by itself in its sleep, and hear a gay little voice, like the voice of a dancing yellow leaf, singing "Andy Spandy" . . .

for Elsie Piddock is skipping still.

No wonder that this story—perhaps one of the best short stories of this generation—can hold children entranced and that it has been translated into many languages. It is brilliantly written and links the imaginary world with every day in a completely satisfying way.

The eight little stories in the Epilogue, each called forth by a proverb, seem somehow out of tune with the rest of the book. Only in the last few paragraphs do we return to the magic of Martin Pippin and the daisy-field.

It is the personality of Martin Pippin, wandering minstrel

of the dreams of youth, which pervades and holds together these two books. He is a unique creation, gay and witty, wise, tender, a dreamer and a poet, yet down-to-earth and practical when necessary, a contented man who finds joy in everything. In his light-hearted inconsequence and matchless storytelling he is very like his creator!

The background of these books is the real Sussex, with its flowers and country sights and sounds and scents. It is always spring and summer in these pages—they hold the sunny days of youth for us for ever. The 'Ultima Thule' of one of the children in the daisy-field is an apple orchard. 'One day,' says Martin Pippin, 'when you are there, you may look back and find it's a daisy-field.' A child will not know how true this is, but surely something from this lovely book will remain in his heart to be remembered many years hence.

One of the earliest of Eleanor Farjeon's collections of stories for children was **The Tale of Tom Tiddler.** This uses the place-names from the **Nursery Rhymes of London Town** in a series of episodes in which Tom Tiddler, who lives in a buttercup and daisy field, is the central figure. Jinny Jones and her friends come 'picking up gold and silver' in Tom's field, but are captured by the Giant Gogmagog. Tom sets out to rescue them, accompanied by a goat and an owl, but the Smith can't make a key for the prison until the Shepherd sends his dog back, the Shepherd won't return the dog until he has the Lass of Lavender Hill for company, and so on. In all there are seventeen links between Tom and the rescue. Cleverly as the London place-names are used as people in the chain—the Old Lady of Threadneedle Street, the Chalk Farmer, the Old Bailey—the process of unwinding is too long and complicated. The old folktale pattern of 'fire won't burn stick; stick won't beat dog' is too involved and episodic for use in a story as long as this. This is the least successful of her books, ingenious and witty as it is.

Although **Kaleidoscope** is more about children than for them, it contains several charming little stories which might well be enjoyed by the young. Indeed, some of them have been included by Eleanor Graham in her perceptive collection of Eleanor Farjeon's work, **Eleanor Farjeon's Book.** Many of these stories are based on memories of his childhood told to Eleanor Farjeon by her friend of thirty years, George Earle. In her hands these memories often become fantasy, which is, after all, only round the corner from reality, especially for an imaginative child. Anthony, the hero of these stories, could hear the trees grow:

> Anthony could hear them throbbing like the throbbing of his own heart. Tiny flat seeds, round seeds, oval seeds, little acorn lumps dropped from the oaks, little wings flown down from the ashes, little triangles split from the beech-nuts. The earth was crowded with them, all with their hearts beating as she rocked them back and forth.

Once he saw a young horse on a hillside:

> He stood with the sun behind him, and the short mane stood up on his arched neck like a golden comb; he frisked his flaxen tail, and a gold fountain waved up and down the air. Suddenly he whinnied and scampered, and his whole body was made of red-gold light.

Small wonder that Anthony thought the beautiful animal was the winged horse, Pegasus!

Many stories in this collection are memorable; **'The Man who Found Mushrooms'** and **'The Wonderful Clock',** for instance, and the lovely **'Eye of the Earth',** so beautiful a picture of the English countryside. Probably there are other tales scattered through Eleanor Farjeon's adult books, many of which are, unfortunately, no longer obtainable, which children could appreciate. Eleanor Graham has found one in **'The Lamb of Chinon'** from **Faithful Jenny Dove,** and there may be others.

In **The Old Nurse's Stocking-Basket** the stories once more are woven round one character, the wise old nurse whose age no one knows, she is so ancient. She allows no nonsense from her charges. 'Stop quarrelling, or you know what,' she says, and the children—and readers too—do know what and bear no malice. Her stories, usually of her previous nurselings, are conditioned by the size of the hole she has to mend in her charge's stockings. What strange and fascinating children the nurse has known, from her most beautiful baby, Irazade, to Bertha, who, having been bewitched by the Stocking Elf, had one golden foot and a perpetual hole in the heel of her stocking. These tales are of a length and simplicity for a child to read for himself, and their background is a firelit nursery with all this implies of security and comfort. Children enjoy their fun and their 'moral', and every child feels for Roly when the nurse tells the story of **'Lipp the Lapp',** who was so small that his mother could not find him. 'Then what happened?' asks Roly eagerly. 'Nothing,' answers the old nurse laconically.

**Perkin the Pedlar** has a story for each letter of the alphabet and each letter stands for a place-name. Perkin teaches the thirteen pairs of twins at Zeal Monachorum to remember their ABC by telling them stories suggested by the names of places. This may irritate an adult reader who perhaps knows the village or town and realizes the occasional incongruity—although sometimes this adds spice to the tale—but would a child mind? Most children will regard places with names like Blower's Green, Idle and Three Cocks as within the realms of fairyland, and will accept the tales that go with the queer names. Only in one or two cases does the connection between name and story seem a little forced, as in Wendover and Much Wenlock.

In 1934 came **Italian Peepshow,** the fruit of a holiday in beautiful Fiesole near Florence. These short stories are interspersed by enchanting and evocative interludes about the children's play, the local festivals and daily happenings in the villa. We see through the poet's appreciative eyes the glowing lemon and orange groves, the grey olive trees 'like round puffs of smoke', the colourful life of the countryside in which white oxen draw creaking carts and the sun shines warmly all the time. The stories grow naturally out of the interludes and were told for the children she played with and loved. The best of this collection is very good indeed; notably **'Rosaura's Birthday'** and **'The King of Tripoli brings the Pasta'.** In the former tale the flighty Rosaura who so passionately loves dancing and her varied suitors are changed into puppets in the traditional Harlequinade, and so dance for ever. In the second story the tender-hearted King of Tripoli comes to the rescue of the starving people of Italy, whose supply of pasta has failed. The many strange names for the different varieties of pasta are woven into the story—Holy Seeds, Bells, The Virgin's Tears—and there is a moving theme of compassion and innocence.

*Jim at the Corner* also appeared in 1934 and is written in a very different vein. Once again there is a central character, Jim the old sailor, who tells stories to a little boy, Derry. Eleanor Farjeon has great fun with her child readers, indulging her imagination in impossible fantasies and delightfully ridiculous tall tales. Seven stories are told in a fittingly racy and colloquial style and at a good pace, and each abounds in the kind of robust humour children love. In one story the great Sea Serpent is in tears because he has never had anyone to pet him, so Jim obligingly sets about the lengthy process of petting him coil by coil; in another a jilted penguin takes Jim as a wife, 'in a manner of speaking'. Only the story **'The Star that watches the Moon'** seems too whimsical to fit into this collection.

*One Foot in Fairyland* is divided into four sections: 'Inside', 'On the border', 'Outside' and 'Return to Paradise'. This last section contains one story only, the beautiful and moving tale of Pannychis, a favourite of its author. It tells of two children, Cymon and Pannychis, only five years old, who live by the sea in perfect happiness, until fear enters their paradise. From this moment Cymon is always afraid that something will happen to Pannychis, and his fear for her will not allow her to be happy either. One day Pannychis vanishes—for the last time Cymon hears her faint laughter and her call 'Look happy!':

> . . . the echoing laughter led him on and on, out of the wood, over the flowers, down to the shore of the sea, lapping the silver sand so softly, while in the pale green evening sky the stars came trembling out. All was pure loveliness; but Pannychis was nowhere to be seen.
>
> And she was never seen again.

All the stories in this collection are included in *The Little Bookroom* with the exception of 'The Real Leather Writing-case', a realistic story of a boy's present to his sister, bought more with his own pleasure in mind than hers—a motive not uncommon with adults as well as children!

There remain several short books of lesser importance. Amongst these are *Ameliaranne's Prize Packet* and *Ameliaranne's Washing-day*, two titles in a series in which all authors are bound to conform to a pattern, for the character of Ameliaranne Stiggins must remain consistent. Even in these slight tales, however, Eleanor Farjeon's sense of fun slips in when she decrees that Mrs Stiggins' legacy shall be 'twelve chickens, two goats and a fur tippet'.

Another slight work is *The Perfect Zoo.* This picture story book has a moral—put your toys away and do as you are bid or you will become little Beasts. This is exactly what happens to Peter, Betty and Pat, who are turning their nursery into a 'perfect zoo'. They become stuffed animals

and must remain in that form until they have found the Green-headed Beetle. A breathtaking series of adventures follows which brings them back home at last to find the Green-headed Beetle toasting cheese at their own fireside.

The repartee in this little book is clever and witty. My own favourite passage is Peter's speech, delivered with all solemnity at the wedding party:

> 'Er—er—Lady and Gentleman Bear and Dogs—er—I think this is a very nice house indeed, and I think the flowers on the table are very nice indeed—er—and the chocolate blanc-mange is really very nice—er—indeed. I am Oxford in the boat race. My Uncle has been to India, and he has got a real Elephant's tusk. My best friend at school came first in the jumping; his name is Edward Marshall; he is very good at string tricks. Er—I've enjoyed this party very much indeed so far, and thank you very much indeed'.

Slight as the story is, it is amusing and as inconsequential as a dream.

*The Silver Curlew* and *The Glass Slipper* are in a different category. Each was re-written from a play, which in turn was based on a folk-tale. Both these books are a re-creation rather than a retelling of the original tale, especially *The Silver Curlew*. Traditional rhymes and tales are a natural springboard for Eleanor Farjeon's imagination, and she adorns and enriches them. In *The Glass Slipper* the story retains its original outline, the only new character being the King's Zany, or Fool. Cinderella comes wholly to life, touched with the true magic of a poet's imagination. Romantic as is the theme, it is never sentimental, for even the Fairy Godmother says tartly, 'Keep your senses, Ella. You will need them.' And what other author who has retold this tale has made the beautiful Princess of Nowhere, her dream Prince beside her, worry about the dusting there is to be done in the palace?

Only the Ugly Sisters do not transplant easily from the play to the story, for they are essentially a pantomime property. Seen on the stage their clowning can be accepted as funny; in a book their abuse of each other becomes a little distasteful.

In *The Silver Curlew* there is a new sub-plot, the story of the Man and the Lady in the Moon. In the book's own words, the story is a 'tangle of dumplings and ducks-eggs, of wedding-bells and Christening-bells, of a witch in a wood and a fairy with a casket, of a spindle and a fishing-boat, of Doll crying and a baby crowing, of a curlew in a cage and the curlew flying. . . .' Of such incongruous elements are stories made.

So in 1955 came *The Little Bookroom,* Eleanor Farjeon's own final selection of twenty-seven tales, the cream of her prose writings for children, with a great variety of themes and patterns. Some of them could well be traditional—**'The Girl who kissed the Peach-Tree'**, **'The Miracle of the Poor Island'**, **'The Seventh Princess'**—any of these might have been handed down for generations instead of being composed within this century.

Here too are several stories in which Eleanor Farjeon's stimulating wit points a moral, as, for instance, **'In those Days'**, which tells of a sentry still keeping guard over the empty spot where centuries ago grew a Queen's favourite flower. The reason for this has long been forgotten, but the order has never been countermanded. Eleanor Farjeon has many parables of this kind, from the simple proverb tale of a few paragraphs such as those that appear in *The New Book of Days* to the subtle **'The King and the Corn'**, in which the reader perceives that the golden corn is more precious and enduring than the King of Egypt's gold, and that the simplest mind is often the wisest.

A third group of stories is inspired by Eleanor Farjeon's understanding of children. She has always loved children, and some of her best and most moving tales are about them. In *The Little Bookroom* there are several of this kind, notably **'The Glass Peacock'**, **'Pennyworth'** and **'And I dance mine own child'**. The first is the story of Annar-Mariar, the friend of all the children in Mellin's Court. To her comes the unexpected gift of a tiny Christmas tree hung about with sparkling glass ornaments. For one blissful night 'the little tree in all its gleaming beauty shone upon her dreams', but the next day she gives away the glittering treasures from the tree, keeping only the longed-for glass peacock for herself. When that too is broken by 'Willyum', her small brother, she has nothing left and yet so much. How affecting this simple story is in its restraint and the realness of Annar-Mariar.

As a contrast we have sturdy Johnny Moon in **'Pennyworth'**. Finding a heaven-sent penny, he sets off to realize his dream of extracting a bar of 'Chocklit' from the wonderful station machine. He puts in his penny—and the machine brings out a platform ticket! However, the ticket turns out to be the key to a day's ecstatic enjoyment around the station. It is in this story that a gem of childish speech appears:

> "I been to Lillamton", explained the little girl. "I'm goin' back to Clapham. I got some peppmince." She took out a paper bag of peppermints and offered them to Johnny. He helped himself to two. "My name's Dorinda. Well good-bye I must go now."

Moving also is the lovely story of **'And I dance mine own child'**. Griselda, ten, looks after her great-grandmother of one hundred and ten, but there is little difference in age between them. The tender relationship between the old woman and the child makes this a charming and touching story. Each night Griselda puts her Gramma to bed with a sweet and a story and a song. (The story is the same one that Joseph Jefferson told Eleanor Farjeon's mother and she in her turn told to Harry and Nellie and Joe and Bertie.) When the old woman and the child are at last reunited after their separation, Griselda once more puts her Gramma to bed with the old story and lullaby:

> "Once upon a time there was a Giant."
> "Ah!" said Great-Grandmother Curfew.
> "And he had *Three* Heads!"
> "Ah!"
> "And he lived in a BRASS CASTLE!"
> "Ah!" Great-Grandmother Curfew closed her
>     eyes.
> "Hush, hush, hush!" sang the happy Griselda,

> "And I dance mine own child! And I dance mine own child—!"

How many jewel-like stories there are in this book—the pure fantasy of **'Leaving Paradise'** and **'The Clumber Pup'**; the fun of that ridiculous detective story, **'The King's Daughter cries for the Moon'**; **'The Connemara Donkey'**, a favourite with children; the almost-satire of **'The Tims'** and **'The Flower without a Name'**, and the perfect story of **'The Little Lady's Roses'**. The latter is so deceptively simple, yet so perfectly balanced in phrase, that it would repay analysis by every storyteller and would-be writer.

Each story is told with the sensitiveness of a poet and the skill of a practised craftsman. Little wonder that this book, the fruit of her childhood in her father's little bookroom, was awarded the Library Association Carnegie Medal in England and the international Hans Christian Andersen Award.

> What is Poetry? Who knows?
> Not the rose, but the scent of the rose;
> Not the sky, but the light in the sky;
> Not the fly, but the gleam of the fly;
> Not the sea, but the sound of the sea;
> Not myself, but what makes me
> See, hear and feel something that prose
> Cannot; and what it is, who knows?

'What is Poetry? Who knows?' asks Eleanor Farjeon in her own poem, and indeed poetry cannot be defined. How can anyone but the poet know the infinitely complex processes by which he finds the pattern that alone conveys the emotion, the thought, the sudden apprehension of beauty that has inspired him? Still less do we know what happens in a child's mind when he hears a poem for the first time. Indeed, as Walter de la Mare has said [in *Come Hither*]:

'What is read on the printed page is merely so many words; they may mean much or little to the reader, but in either case it is he alone who out of them can create a POEM and therefore HIS poem. And this poem changes for him, as he himself changes with the years.'

In this century there have been only two poets of consequence writing expressly for children; Walter de la Mare and Eleanor Farjeon. Of these Eleanor Farjeon, while her poetry has not the profundity of de la Mare's, is perhaps nearer to the child and offers him simpler pleasures.

A facility for writing verse and rhymes has always been hers. 'I can hardly remember the time when it did not seem *easier* to write in running rhyme than in plodding prose,' she says in the foreword to her collection of poems, *Silver-sand and Snow*. At eleven she wrote an epic, 'Chaos', while brushing her hair with the other hand— surely a record for any poet! From these childhood beginnings has grown the adult poet who says modestly that she has no claim to be a 'real poet', yet who has written sonnets Walter de la Mare praised and poems which he described as 'beautiful things and solely your own'.

It is Eleanor Farjeon's perceptive imagination that is her glory. Inspiration comes to her not only from the tangible world around her, which gives her so much joy, but from the intangible also. She has a flashing awareness of beauty which results in a flowering of thought and emotion into poetry and gives it vitality. Her verses are distinguished by spontaneity and gaiety, rhythm and music, yet have a simplicity which is right for children. Her three main collections of poems, *Silver-sand and Snow, The Children's Bells* and *Then There Were Three,* contain her own selection of the best of her poetry for children.

A characteristic of Eleanor Farjeon's poems and stories is her tender—but not sentimental—understanding of children. She writes as though she herself were in the child's world, not as an onlooker but as part of it. Here in *The Mulberry Bush,* her collection of poems on children's games, is someone who knows the breathless excitement of playing Follow my Leader and the rather eerie feeling of Hide-and-seek. How well she knows the importance to a child of counting cherrystones, and as she counts them with him she spins the gay verses in **'Cherrystones'**. She has poems for the child who is bored, the child who doesn't want to go to bed, tender verses for the child who is frightened of the dark. In *The Children's Bells* she reminds us of some of the children we all know—Griselda who is greedy, Fred who 'likes creatures and has a lot of 'em', Ned who can't be got out of bed, Clare who is going to have 'waved gold hair' when she grows up, and Jessica dancing 'Innocently-wild'. These boys and girls are very real, and surely other children reading of them must often find themselves mirrored in the lively, amusing poems.

Her liking for children has inspired her to invent 'Alphabets' for the town child, the country child and schoolchildren. In the process she writes poetry on such unpromising themes as geography, dustmen and eggs. Gems of verse—**'Poetry'**, **'C is for Charms'**, **'Music'**, **'Dancing'**—are embedded in these ingenious alphabets.

It might be objected that the many allusions she uses in her poems, culled from wide reading, will be unknown to the modern child. This is true, but may not these strange names and subjects be touchstones to the curiosity of children? In any case, many will enjoy the poems simply for their rhythmic quality or their fun. It does seem, however, that the poems collected from her prose books, and so taken out of their context, may be less effective than in their original setting.

Eleanor Farjeon's poems sing in the ear and the heart. It is surprising that such carols as **'This Holy Night'**, **'The Children's Carol'** and **'Now every Child'** are not part of our Christmas music every year. A child likes poetry to sing.

Listen to **'A Girl calling'**:

'So through the falling
snow, the girl went calling,
calling . . . calling
from tree to tree;
My love,
my love,
my dove,
where can he be?'

and again:

One lime in Alfriston made sweet,
So sweet, the August night,
That all the air along the street

The shadowed air in the shadowed street,
Was swimming in delight.

A feature of Eleanor Farjeon's poems is their great variety of metre and pattern, for she is a practised craftsman. Listen to the lively rhythm in **'Dancing'** (from *A Schoolchild's Alphabet*):

A hop, a skip, and off you go!
Happy heart and merry toe,
Up-and-down and in-and-out,
This way, that way, round about!
Bend like grasses in the breeze,
Wave your arms like wind-blown trees,
Dart like swallows, glide like fish,
Dance like anything you wish.

Sometimes her rhythms are leisurely and solemn as in **'Cradlesong for Christmas'**:

Child, when on this night you lie
Softly, undisturbedly,
On as white a bed of down
As any child's in London Town,
By a fire that all the night
Keeps your chamber warm and light:
Dream, if dreams are yet your law,
Your bed of down a bed of straw,
Only warmed and lighted by
One star in the open sky.
Sweet you'll sleep then, for we know
Once a Child slept sweetly so.

Her subjects too are varied. She writes of children and their games, of nature and the seasons, of people and of places. Nonsense verses stand side by side with gem-like poems of flowers and stars; jingles are contrasted with an imaginative masterpiece such as **'The Earth'**, in which she thinks of our earth as a star seen by a child from some other planet. The ecstasy of this lovely poem is reminiscent of Gerard Manley Hopkins:

How wonderful it must be, how rare,
To be born on the bright, bright Earth up there!
How the streams must shine!
How the grass must glisten
When the dew is risen!

Inspiration can come for a poem from such contrasting themes as dogs, cats, magic, schoolchildren, heroes, a bag of chestnuts, or kings and queens, and the result is a medley of poems for every occasion and every mood.

'Pure nonsense is portion of our cakes and ale, and has always been one of my windows to a ringing welkin,' says Eleanor Farjeon in her P.E.N. booklet *Magic Casements.* This is seen in her delight in fun in real life and the spinning of nonsense in her books.

Reading her poems for children we chuckle as we read. *Nursery Rhymes of London Town,* those conceits on London place-names written originally for *Punch,* are full of nonsensical fancies:

In a village where I've been
They keep their Parson on a Green.
They tie him to a Juniper Tree
And bring him Currant Bread for tea.
A jollier man I've never seen
Than the one on Parson's Green.

So original is her invention that the incongruity of the verses is part of their charm. Edward Thomas said of these rhymes, 'They all surprise, yet not too much, just enough to make one wish one had invented them oneself.'

Her many jingles too, which could well be traditional in origin, have this element of nonsense:

> As I was going through No Man's Land
> I saw an old man counting sand. . . .

> Timothy went to Aragon
> Riding on a weasel,
> To ask the Dons for Tarragon,
> Tansy, thyme and teasel.

The rollicking rhymes in the picture book ***Kings and Queens*** were written by Eleanor Farjeon and her brother Herbert in 1932, and are an irreverent and laughter-provoking version of English history. All our Kings and Queens are here, from William the Conqueror to Elizabeth the Second (in the edition of 1953). Their character is epitomized in a few lines:

> Bluff King Hal was full of beans;
> He married half a dozen Queens.

Mary the First, who was reputed to have 'Calais' engraved on her heart:

> A truly touching thought—but who

*Farjeon's brothers, Harry, Joe, and Bertie (Herbert). She collaborated with Harry on* A First and Second Chap Book of Rounds *(1919) as well as on an opera, an operetta, and a masque. With Herbert, she collaborated on* Kings and Queens *(1932) and* Heroes and Heroines *(1933) as well as on two operettas and the libretto for a lyric drama.*

> Could say for sure if it was true,
> Since no one in those Tudor days
> Had yet discovered the X-rays?

***Heroes and Heroines*** is in [a] similar vein.

The reader may remember also the gay madness of the poems **'Consequence'** and **'Here we go looby, looby, looby'** in **The Mulberry Bush,** but there are 'catches and snatches' of nonsense in all her books, both verse and prose.

For animals and birds, and indeed all country sights, Eleanor Farjeon has an observant and affectionate eye. She loves flowers too and in the Martin Pippin books there are many charming poems about them, their old country names a springboard for her imagination. The passing of the seasons inspire some of her loveliest poems. Her sensitive ear for the *music* of words gives vivid pictures in sound, as well as visually, of birds and animals:

> Mrs. Peck-Pigeon
> Is picking for bread,
> Bob-bob-bob
> Goes her little round head.

and a fight between a dog and cat:

> Pfitts! Pfitts!
> How she spits!
> Spitch! Spatch!
> Can't she scratch!

Occasionally her poems are unequal in quality, marred by poor rhymes and pedestrian lines, but this is true only of a small number among the many she has written. Many of Eleanor Farjeon's poems will lift a child out of the everyday world and show him a new country of joy and beauty. This is the true purpose and meaning of poetry.

As well as a poet, Eleanor Farjeon is also a dramatist of ability. It is natural that she should have a feeling for the theatre, for she is the descendant on her mother's side of a line of famous American actors, the Jeffersons. From the age of four, when she went to her first play, she was able to watch the most famous actors and actresses of her day. She knew personally Ellen Terry, Henry Irving, Ada Rehan and many others. Drama was part of her life and always moved her greatly. As children she and her brother Joe were once so affected by a play that they almost wept themselves insensible, until Ellen Terry herself came to comfort them. As an adult she and Herbert produced successful musical plays together. She could always hear the lyrics in her head and knew just how the words would fit into the music she had chosen. The period during which they worked together on a play was a 'lovely, happy time', she says.

For children there are two plays, ***The Glass Slipper,*** written in collaboration with Herbert Farjeon, and ***The Silver Curlew,*** written after his death. Both are based on traditional stories. Each is a full-length play in three acts with a colourful Harlequinade and music and songs as an integral part. The tuneful music, composed by Clifton Parker, effectively suggests character and atmosphere.

In a way these two plays are pantomimes, particularly ***The Glass Slipper,*** which contains the traditional transformation scene; but while they bubble over with fun and wit, they do not use the slapstick and sometimes vulgar farce of the usual Christmas 'Panto'. The humour shades from the broad comedy of Mother Codling and her four yokel sons in their mouth-watering song, 'Dumplings is glorious! Dumplings is good!' in *The Silver Curlew,* to the ironical poking of fun at the pompous Herald with his wordy circumlocutions in *The Glass Slipper.*

*The Glass Slipper,* presented by Robert Donat at the St. James's Theatre in 1944, is the familiar story of Cinderella. With such a fairytale theme the Ugly Sisters, the romantic Prince, the ineffectual Father, need not be much more than types. The Fairy Godmother in the Farjeons' hands becomes refreshingly astringent, but it is in the recreation of Cinderella that the magic of the play lies. She is the child who escapes from the hardship of her daily life to a world of dreams and her gaiety, kindness and child-like innocence endear her to us.

The atmosphere of *The Glass Slipper* is delicate and magical in its setting of snow. As the entranced lovers hide together at the Ball they seem to be in a world of their own, enclosed in a magic circle of snow-covered gardens and echoing voices:

> Is it only you?
> Only you!
> Only . . .
> You!

What a lovely play to see, with its humour, its pathos, its beauty and its magic.

*The Silver Curlew* was produced at the Playhouse, Liverpool, in 1948, and at the Arts Theatre, London. It is robust, exciting, comic and dramatic. Here is the old story of Tom-Tit-Tot. A lazy, greedy girl eats twelve pies at a time but her mother, ashamed, tells the King she has spun twelve skeins, so he marries her. When he orders his wife to carry out this impossible feat again an ugly Spindle Imp comes to her aid on condition her child will be his within a year unless she can guess his name. In the original story she is saved by chance; in Eleanor Farjeon's version Polly, the Queen's sister, finds out the Imp's name through her courage and love. Woven into this traditional story is a second story of the Man in the Moon (Charlee Loon), and his Lady in the Moon who is the Silver Curlew. These two help Polly to outwit Tom-Tit-Tot.

Although only a fairytale, the characters are drawn with a sure hand. The four brothers are bucolic comedy figures, the King is a child like those in the audience, and Nan, his tiny old nurse, is the autocrat of nursery days. Doll develops from a selfish pretty girl into a loving young mother, whose despairing hopelessness is skilfully set against the comedy scene of the preparation for the Christening. Polly, who at first is just a child with an insatiable urge to ask questions, becomes a courageous girl who pits her strength against the terrifying powers of evil. She is merry, resourceful, unselfish, a child character not to be forgotten in children's literature.

It is said that 'Business' rather than lines makes the ideal children's play. If this is so, these plays should fascinate children. Throughout there are dances, songs, bangs,

flashes, magical tricks. The stage is never dull, the dialogue never too long without action; there is always something happening, either funny or beautiful.

These two plays are intended for children to watch rather than to act themselves. Perhaps this is true also of the beautiful little Masque for Christmas called *A Room at the Inn,* written with Herbert Farjeon and with music by Harry Farjeon. It is set in the stable on the first Christmas Eve. Here are the rustic Ox and Ass, the travellers who ask for room at the Inn, and amongst them the humble Mary and Joseph who find shelter with the beasts in the stall. The Ox and Ass, their floor only mud, their bed only straw, welcome Mary as she sings:

> The straw whereon I lie
> Was the sheathing of the grain
> That plenishes the mountain
> And furnishes the plain;
> The temples shall be filled
> And the nations shall be fed
> By the treasure of the corn
> That was sheathed in your bed.

This is a moving little play, sincere and reverent, which has been lost to sight undeservedly, for it was printed privately and only last year (1960) reappeared in the Puffin *Eleanor Farjeon's Book.*

Of plays for children to act themselves the best are in *Grannie Gray,* which contains four little plays, amongst which is a riotous farce in which a brother and sister cook dinner with disastrous results, and a successful version of the story of Snow White. The latter is in the perfect form for young children, for the actors have little to say, as the Narrator reads the story, and there is plenty of action. The Dwarfs are very different from Disney's grotesque creations, and they are given a charming song:

> She was so kind, our snow-white maid,
> For her the timid hare would stand,
> And every wild-bird in the glade
> Would take the berry from her hand.

'Were you ever in Quebec?' another play in this collection, has only four speaking characters but two pageants for any number of children. The dialogue is amusing and childlike:

> Freddy: "I say! Was you ever in Quebec, Mr.
>         Salt?"
> Freda:   "*Were* you, Freddy?"
> Freddy: "Was I what?"
> Freda:   "*Were* you ever in Quebec?"
> Freddy: "No, I weren't. Was *you*, Mr. Salt?"

As we have seen in discussing Eleanor Farjeon's plays, a good children's play needs competent construction, drama, humour and suspense, convincing characters and lively dialogue and action; but something more is necessary. To move and excite the child, to transport him to another world, a play must also have the spark of dramatic fire that brings it to life and inspires the actors. This Eleanor Farjeon has in abundance. What is more, we feel she is enjoying the play as much as the audience. She is *in* it, not only as its creator but as a spectator also.

Besides being a dramatist and a poet, Eleanor Farjeon also

has a gift for composing pleasing tunes. It is said that before she could speak she could sing in tune, and she always had a 'pretty singing voice'. She lived in a musical atmosphere, for her beloved Harry was a talented musician and with him she heard concerts, recitals and operas. When Harry went to the Royal Academy of Music as a student, she took a keen interest in all his studies. Strangely enough, she herself has never had any formal instruction in music. Yet, in spite of a lack of technical knowledge of harmony and counterpoint, she has composed many tunes—better tunes, Arnold Bax once said, than those of many of her musical friends. Melodies have always come easily to her, and she set the verses in *Nursery Rhymes of London Town* to music by humming them over to her baby niece, Joan, as she sang her to sleep. They are an excellent example of her ability to fit tempo and key to her subject. It was her nursery rhymes that she sang when she and her friend Walter de la Mare visited schools and libraries together, he to read his poems, she to sing her rhymes. What unforgettable concerts those must have been! She has also set to music her verses in *Kings and Queens*, giving unconventional musical directions such as 'Boisterous', 'Alternately merry and fervent'.

It is in her *Singing Games*, however, that Eleanor Farjeon combines to perfection her musical ability, her poetic gifts and her feeling for drama. These are original songs which children act, usually in costume. Each song has several verses and gives ample scope for many children to take part. Marjorie Gullan and Gordon Bottomley used these singing games many times at the Morecambe Festivals. They are light-hearted, fun to act and a boon to teachers as they offer plenty of opportunity for singing, dancing and dressing up, and the minimum of learning for each child. The tunes are sometimes quite difficult, but always melodic and expressive of the verses they interpret. *Grannie Gray* includes four such simple singing games. More elaborate ones were published separately in 1927-30.

It can be seen then that poetry, drama and music have each played their part in the development of Eleanor Farjeon the artist. Her response to their influence has added strength to her work as a whole.

There is room from time to time for new versions of legends and myths, for, although they may be familiar to adults, they are always new to each generation of children. It is also inevitable and right that the manner of retelling these old stories should change with changing times, even while the basic plot will remain the same.

The purpose of re-telling a story for a child is to fit it more nearly to his comprehension, thereby enhancing his enjoyment. If this means that the story must be so simplified that it ceases to have meaning or value, then we may conclude it is unsuitable for adaptation and should be left for the child to read in the original when he is capable of appreciating it. Provided that the tales are wisely chosen, however, and treated with skill and imagination, the result may be a valuable introduction to a book which the child might not otherwise have known. It may even happen that the original work is enriched in the retelling by the mind and imagination behind it. This is what often happens in Eleanor Farjeon's telling of old tales.

Her first book of this kind was *Mighty Men,* in which she gives the child glimpses of history through the adventures of famous men of all nations from Achilles to Harold, last of the Saxon kings. One story leads to the next— Alexander reads of Achilles and finds the statue of the once mighty Xerxes lying in the dust; Caesar, fired by Alexander's exploits, essays to conquer the world; the departure of the Romans brings the almost legendary King Arthur to Britain's aid. So the reader sees that nothing happens in isolation, and that all events are part of the continuity of history and mankind.

Many of the stories in this book are mythical, for, as Eleanor Farjeon characteristically says in her foreword, 'If the legends are not the very tree of history, they are the birds that sing in the tree.' Indeed, folk-tales are part of the heritage of every child, and he would be the poorer if he never heard stories such as that of the brave Patroclus over whose death even his horses wept, of Beowulf's courage in his fight against the monster Grendel or of Arthur and the enchanted sword Excalibur. It is legends which awaken the child's imagination, for they contain something imperishable of man's courage and his fight against evil. In *Mighty Men* Eleanor Farjeon recounts these old tales so stirringly, yet with such ease and simplicity, that they become a pleasant introduction to history for the child. The verses, which flow as naturally as the prose, add point and meaning to each incident.

*Paladins in Spain* was written in 1937. It is the story of the battles of Charlemagne and his Paladins against the Sultan of Babylon and his Paynims. The stories are freely adapted from the metrical *Romance of the Sowdone of Babylon* and from *Ferumbras* in Caxton's life of Charlemagne.

These heroic tales are an entertaining mixture of wonders and marvels, heroism and warfare. There is not much to choose between the Christians and the infidels. Battles are on a grand scale, with thousands killed by a handful of men; conversion is by force. Forests are full of 'lions and bears and griffins and tigers', the wicked infidels enjoy snakes fried in oil and sleep under pineapple trees. The whole background is pleasingly exotic.

Roland and Oliver have a prominent part, although the famous battle of Roncesvalles does not come into the story. Emotions and behaviour are extravagant, and one feels for the Sultan when he shouts in despair and rage, 'Down with everything!' The narrative races on with such gusto that it is all tremendous fun for the reader—and the author.

In *A Nursery in the Nineties* Eleanor Farjeon tells of her liking for reading 'the Greeks'. It is natural, therefore, that she has chosen for re-telling some of the stories of Herodotus, the Greek historian. In *The Wonders of Herodotus* a party of settlers—workers, thinkers, craftsmen, orators and children—are sailing from Athens to found a new colony. With them is Herodotus, inveterate traveller and collector of strange legends and even odder facts. Damon and Chloe, two children in the party, make friends with him and listen eagerly to his stories. So they hear of the struggle between Greece and Persia, told through the adventures of Croesus, Cyrus, Cambyses, Darius and Xerxes.

This is a bloodthirsty period of history and some horrific incidents are inevitable; but as long as an author does not dwell on such incidents children are not disturbed by them. It is usually the adult who is unduly sensitive on these points, and there is nothing here to upset anyone. Although the method of introducing the stories is an artificial one, Damon and Chloe live as real children. Eleanor Farjeon does not make the mistake of writing down, but leaves children to find out for themselves—if they wish—the meaning of such odd words as 'oligarchy' and 'satrap'. The narrative is told in lucid prose, and a book like this serves as a useful introduction to this little-known period of ancient history for children who are not familiar with 'the Greeks'.

*Ten Saints* was first published in 1936 in the United States with the distinguished illustrations of Helen Sewell. Here we are introduced to ten saints, who range from the homely Saint Christopher to Simeon Stylites, the strange ascetic who so desired to be alone with God that he lived on a lofty pillar in the desert. The poems which follow the stories differ in metre and form, as if to fit each saint more perfectly.

Legends always gather about famous men and women, particularly when, like these, they are lost in the mists of history. Of necessity, therefore, many of these stories are largely mythical. Especially is this so of Patrick, who adopted Ireland as his field of conflict with the Devil, and Nicholas, who brought back to life the boys murdered by the Innkeeper. 'The Innkeeper was pardoned his sins, and was the better for it,' says Eleanor Farjeon, and adds with a twinkle, 'He never pickled his customers again.'

The opening paragraph of the story of Saint Christopher is an excellent example of the author's skill in arousing the reader's interest. Here is perfect storytelling, conveying the character of the Saint even in the very form of the telling. The short, simple sentences are exactly right:

> Two hundred years after the birth of Christ there was a man in Samos who had not heard of him. This man had the stature of a giant. If the mightiest tree in the forest had come to life it would have resembled him. No weight was too heavy for his arms to lift or his back to bear, nothing that needed strength was too hard for him to do. His ways were rude, his mind was ignorant. His eyes were the eyes of a dog. They glowed under his shaggy hair with the look of one that longs to serve a beloved master. This giant was stronger than any man he knew, and in his simplicity had no other test. Whom then could he serve and adore? His child's heart urged him to go in search of the strongest king in the world. Taking his staff, he went alone to find him.

How beautifully these stories are written and in what limpid prose, almost Biblical at times! The pace varies with the subject, from the hurrying chase of the deer by Hubert, who afterwards became a hunter of men's souls, to the tranquillity of the serene and aged Saint Giles, who lived alone in the forest fed by a beautiful doe. Note the musical balance of phrase in these sentences:

> The season passed, grass grew long and leaves grew broad, bright summer flowers replaced the flowers of spring, nestlings began to fly and cubs to gambol. Giles sat in a green world, and dreamed of heaven: and heaven seemed all about him.

The last story in the book, that of Eleanor Farjeon's favourite saint, Saint Francis, is told with economy of phrase and the simplicity the humble saint loved. So of his passing Eleanor Farjeon says only:

> The larks flew and sang like a little choir from heaven. When night fell they went with the light, and their brother Francis went with them.

Surely any child would be the better for reading such finely told tales as these, and might well marvel at the different material from which saints are made, from the fustian of Saint Christopher to the fine cloth of Saint Francis.

In 1930 Eleanor Farjeon published her *Tales from Chaucer,* using the illustrations the famous artist, W. Russell Flint, had drawn for Chaucer's stories and had not used. The present edition, illustrated by Marjorie Walters, lacks some of the dignity of this earlier one.

In her introduction Eleanor Farjeon declares her purpose in retelling these tales. 'The one excuse for presenting Chaucer in any words but his own is that he may be read.' She has kept Chaucer's turn of phrase, however, as far as possible, for the Chaucerian idiom is so distinctive that it is an integral part of the *Tales.* So the book begins:

> When April with sweet showers has ended the drought of March and bathed every root in the sap of which the flower is born: when Zephyr with sweet breath has started the tender crops in holt and heath, and the young sun has run half his month, and little birds, stirred by spring, sing half the night—then people long to go on pilgrimages.

It is usual to give children a selection only of Chaucer's stories to serve as an introduction. Eleanor Farjeon felt that it was necessary to include all the Tales in some form or other. Inevitably this meant shortening each one or even re-writing it, as, for example, 'The Merchant's Tale'. In some cases—'The Parson's story' and 'Melibeus'—an abstract only of the original lengthy passages could be included.

Eleanor Farjeon is an inspired storyteller, and these versions of *The Canterbury Tales* are, as one would expect, absorbing and skilfully told. The whole book is full of the robust life and colour of the Middle Ages. If children must be introduced to *all* Chaucer's Tales then they could have no more delightful and lively re-telling than this. The adult reader, however, on looking again at the original, is led to question the necessity. So much must be altered or omitted if the book is to be read in its entirety by the young, it would seem perhaps that this is one of the adult classics that might well be left for young people to grow into.

In *The New Book of Days* Eleanor Farjeon has made a rich collection of 'other men's flowers' from her wide reading. Many of the stories are re-told, but the verses and proverb tales are her own. In the preface she says that 'Every instance in this book springs out of some fact, in history or legend, some truth in the real or the imaginary world (for truth resides in both of them).' There are three hundred and sixty-six 'moments of interest', a treasure house of odd facts and sayings and anecdotes, any one of which might start a curious child on a voyage of discovery in books.

Here we meet some unusual people—Bunyan playing tunes on the leg of his prison stool, a man who chose not to speak for fifty years, Mrs Ann Hicks who in 1851 so nearly succeeded in annexing part of Hyde Park for her own, and Morocco the dancing horse, which Shakespeare saw and mentioned in *Love's Labour's Lost*. There are odd items of information too—that only the rich made jam and jelly until 1780 because the poor did not cultivate fruit and sugar was a luxury; that houses only began to be numbered in 1764; the recipe for a truly awesome Yorkshire Christmas pie. Here are the origins of words, little biographies of great men, a thirteenth-century will, and suddenly a tune, for 'I think you'd better have the tune for that one!'

Derby Day sets her imagination off to a very different kind of horse, Pegasus:

> And only the poet
> With wings in his brain
> Can mount him and ride him
> Without any rein.

Even St Swithin's Day calls forth a delightful little poem, and there are many others dotted about the book; among

*Farjeon at midlife.*

them '**Loganberry Spooks**', inspired by the scarecrows in Walter de la Mare's garden. There is a riddle made in 1511 and a vivid description of the Feast of the Full Moon in Burma, something she can never have seen except in her reading and her imagination.

What a pity there is no index to help the reader to find again that curious fact or beckoning allusion that he read last month and has never had time to follow up. It would be helpful also to have a bibliography of the many books mentioned—or so it seems to a librarian! But these are trivial criticisms of so valuable a book for the enquiring young mind. Here is a book to look at any day when there is time to explore the many avenues nearly every entry can open up for the reader—a book to own.

In each of the books mentioned in this chapter Eleanor Farjeon's gift as a storyteller is evident, from the plain unvarnished tales in *Mighty Men* to the dignified prose of *Ten Saints.* She has drawn on her wide reading in 'the little bookroom' to recapture stories old and new that she enjoyed herself as a child. For many boys and girls these 'Tales re-told' should be a pleasant and stimulating introduction to new fields of interest for many years to come.

How do Eleanor Farjeon's stories and poems come into being? In an article called '**How it isn't done**' she has revealed, in spite of the title, something of her way of writing. Ideas, she says, come faster than she can write them down, inspired by all kinds of chance stimuli—something seen on a walk, heard in a crowd, read somewhere. The mood of the incident must be noted at once or it may lose its significance. Once jotted down at speed—a few lines, a page, several pages—the ideas can lie dormant with their hundreds of companions on her overflowing desk. They are forgotten apparently, but however long after she may pick them up—a month, a year—she usually finds that the chance seeds thus sown have ripened without her knowledge and can be worked into a story or poem.

Writing gets done in 'queer irregular ways at queer irregular times', and falls into three stages:

> The beginning, before the agony of doubt sets in—the ending when doubt is settled for better or worse—and, in between, *sometimes,* that state of creation which one of our loveliest living poets calls "self-hypnosis". Then the work moves of itself, and writing is bliss.

Once she has really begun she becomes immersed in the world she is creating and is no longer inventing consciously—she is *there.* This is the secret of her best work surely: it is immediate, it is happening now, it is intensely personal. In it is her gaiety, her love for children, her robustness and warm affection for the world around her. Her creative power wells up like a fountain, and, in Walter de la Mare's words in a letter to her about poetry, 'It's all fresh, crystal and happy.'

That she enjoys writing is evident. She has described it as her vice, her self-indulgence, and to be deprived of it is a real hardship. Recently, when she was prevented from writing for months by an eye-operation, she found it painfully frustrating to be unable to set down the ideas that were in her mind, and her first action when she was allowed to work again was to write and write until she had brought to life all that was struggling for expression.

With such a wealth of ideas it is not surprising that she is sometimes too prolific and not always sufficiently critical of her own work. This causes an unevenness which is almost disconcerting, the more so because the mediocre is set amongst such excellence. The variety of her work is not only in subject but in mood and form. In her verses there are always new patterns to delight the eye and ear; in her stories the reader's interest is constantly aroused by an unexpected twist in the plot, or a new and intriguing facet of character. To read so great a number of Eleanor Farjeon's books as I have done while writing this study, is an absorbing and enriching experience.

In recent years there has been a swing from the overlushness of emotion in Victorian children's books to the sterilized and 'wholesome' atmosphere of the modern book for children. It seems almost as though authors are afraid of showing emotion or allowing sorrow or joy to creep into stories for children. This is not so in Eleanor Farjeon's books—she could not write without feeling, and indeed there is always a basis of love and warmth in everything she writes. Because her stories are a true picture of life, both real and imaginary, there is sadness and pathos in them, but there is a transcending joy also, a joy that sings and exults in the beauty of life and the world. Her belief in the essential goodness of people is a safeguard for the child against too-early disillusionment.

Fun and gaiety are part of her genius. Her stories are full of whole-hearted laughter at the idiosyncracies of life and people. But although she may poke gentle fun, her humour is never malicious. It is infectious and it releases tension.

One of her gifts is her shrewd feeling for character. All her life she has been interested in people and has studied them—not as copy for her books, but as human beings. This very understanding has given her the ability to draw these imaginary characters with a sure but kindly hand. They are as real and living as anyone we know in what is called the 'real world'. Annar-Mariar, the Old Nurse, Griselda, Rosaura, Danny O'Toole, Elsie Piddock and a host of others, come instantly to mind as people one knows and likes. Even her most disagreeable characters turn into nicer ones under her genial influence, and if she cannot find any extenuating features about them she disposes of them as she did the bad landlord in **'Elsie Piddock'.** He was never seen again! . . .

Of all her illustrators, Eleanor Farjeon says, it is Edward Ardizzone who has approached most nearly to perfection in his interpretation of her work. It seems almost as though he adds details in his pictures that, although she has not mentioned them in her text, she knows to be there. 'All I feel about childhood is in them,' she says. The line drawings of this gifted artist in *The Little Bookroom, Jim at the Corner, Italian Peepshow* and *Eleanor Farjeon's Book,* are the ideal complement to the stories. There is a rare partnership between author and artist; they understand each other, they have the same sense of fun, and to

listen to the swift and witty exchange of ideas between them in conversation is sheer delight.

It is certain that when the history of children's literature in our day is written Eleanor Farjeon will be one of its most important figures. In the almost fifty years that have passed since the publication of her first book for children her name has come to be connected with that of Walter de la Mare, her dear friend of many years. Both have captured for children that other world which is so near to them. While Eleanor Farjeon has not the profundity, the eeriness of Walter de la Mare, while her muse is not so consistently inspired as his, yet her best prose and poetry are such as de la Mare loved to read and he told her that he found peace and delight in her poems. She has a more lighthearted touch than his, but her perception of beauty and closeness to the mind of children is very like his own.

Because she does not use a formula in writing for children and makes few concessions to a child's immaturity, Eleanor Farjeon's work has not the popular appeal of that of many less talented authors writing expressly for the children's book market. But her poems appear in many anthologies, her two fairytales, *The Glass Slipper* and *The Silver Curlew,* are loved by younger children and her collections of short stories are particularly appreciated by imaginative children. Most of her books are in every public library.

The secret of her appeal to the imaginative child is not far to seek. She speaks from her own understanding of a child's world, a world in which she is still at home in spite of her years. She has the child's sense of wonder and expectancy, his readiness to accept what he cannot understand. Little wonder then that fantasy, in which a child believes so easily, is the perfect medium for Eleanor Farjeon's genius. She keeps her preference still for 'things she cannot quite touch or find out'. All through her life her imagination has been 'the cloudy beam' in which she beheld 'a world refined of its material envelope'. Only from such a creative mind as hers and from such deep experience could fantasy flower in such perfection.

How great a privilege that our children should share with that rare spirit, Eleanor Farjeon, the enchantment of poems and stories that she has created out of a rich life.

> *Eileen H. Colwell, in her* Eleanor Farjeon, *The Bodley Head, 1961, 94 p.*

**Marcus Crouch**

Eleanor Farjeon, a lifelong friend of Walter de la Mare, whose work so closely follows and complements his, completed her long self-imposed apprenticeship and published her first book for children in 1916. This was *Nursery Rhymes of London Town,* followed in the next year by *More Nursery Rhymes.* These verses, which provided delightfully improbable explanations of London placenames, were distinguished by a fresh song-like quality which was to be the mark of all this author's work. Unquestionably Eleanor Farjeon "lisped in numbers for the numbers came". She has always written verse with ease, the lines and rhymes tumbling spontaneously from her mind; perhaps for this reason, although she is incapable of a bad poem, only rarely has she touched the deeper note which De la Mare sounded so often. . . .

One book of the 'twenties defeats classification. In writing *Martin Pippin in the Apple Orchard* Eleanor Farjeon was thinking not of children but of an English soldier sick for the Sussex downs. When the book first appeared it had none of the physical appearance of a book for children and it was not till 1925 that C. E. Brock's illustrations were added. It is in fact a book, not for children, but for particular people, and those who respond to its gentle melodies may be of any age. It comes near to capturing the mood of adolescent girlhood and it is in this 'age group,' if one must pin down so delicate a butterfly, that it belongs. In its subtle blending of realism and fantasy, of prose and poetry, it is most characteristic of the author whose first major work it was. . . .

The 'thirties saw Eleanor Farjeon at her best in verse and prose. She always worked best for an occasion, in sets of related verses like those in *Over the Garden Wall* and *Sing for Your Supper* or in sets of verse and prose like *Martin Pippin in the Daisy Field.* Her facile but seldom trivial rhymes, the melodies and rhythms which played continuously in her head, the mellow wisdom and kindliness of her thought, gave to her writing at this time a very personal character and distinction. . . .

There was never any doubt about Eleanor Farjeon's inspiration; she wrote because she must. One of the greatest delights of the 'fifties was the success of this veteran writer, who had first delighted children during the First World War and who in her seventies gained the homage of a new generation of readers. For this much credit was due to the Oxford University Press who reissued some of her earlier books and published new ones in most beautiful form. In 1955 *The Little Bookroom* gathered together some of the stories which she had written during a long life; for them Ardizzone provided miraculously fitting illustrations. *The Little Bookroom* won the Carnegie Medal and also the first Hans Christian Andersen Medal. The latter award was particularly appropriate, for Eleanor Farjeon belonged to the Andersen tradition. The exquisite and lively writing, the pervading humour, the wisdom, the casually fine narrative, all these were characteristics common to both writers.

> *Marcus Crouch, in his* Treasure Seekers and Borrowers: Children's Books in Britain, 1900-1960, *The Library Association, 1962, 162 p.*

## Grace Hogarth

[*Hogarth, the children's books editor at Oxford University Press, developed a long friendship with Farjeon.*]

Eleanor Farjeon once said in a letter to me: "Our friendship is one of the true things in our lives, yours and mine, complete in trust and perfect in love . . ." I could not have asked for more, and now, looking back, I long to write of her genius for loving and giving which never failed up to the very end of her life. But others will write of this because her love was, in its literal sense, boundless. I was fortunate in that, in more than thirty years of friendship, I watched her at work. I was sometimes her editor but more often I stood on the sidelines to admire, to share, and

to criticise. It has often been said that Eleanor Farjeon's writing is "miscellaneous" and "very uneven." I sometimes told her so, and though she didn't like it, she was honest enough to see this herself. It was due partly to the fact that, for many years, she wrote to live and scarcely had time to reread or reconsider what she wrote. But, beyond this, while she could be an excellent critic of other writers, she could not always judge or select her own. She hated to discard anything that some editor might want or that could possibly turn out in the end to be as good as she wanted it to be. I once read a novel that she wrote during her most productive years and made the mistake of saying that I thought it would be better if cut by a third. But she would not touch a word of it; and back it went into the cupboard where it would wait, she said, for a more sympathetic editor! We laughed, because it didn't matter. What mattered was that the good in what she wrote was so good. She and I both knew that Time would deal with the chaff.

In 1944 when I asked Eleanor for a story for a picture book, she wrote: "I enclose an awfully mixed grill! But I always have so little idea of what folk may like that you'd better see for yourself whether there's anything here." This is very characteristic, endearing, and also revealing. It was some years later that Eleanor found in John Bell the editor she needed. He held her to her best and she trusted his judgement implicitly. She began to write more slowly and to consider and reconsider what she wrote. Many of her best books came back into print, and from her overflowing cupboard he helped her to find *The Little Bookroom.* Before it was published she wrote to me:

> My big thrill was the Ardizzone drawings for my autumn book of tales. John Bell told me they were the best things he'd ever done, and he thought so, too; and when they were dropped in on me, last weekend, I turned them over, one after the other, with a lump in my throat. All I feel about childhood is in them, and I shall have two joys to look forward to this year; *The Slipper*—the book of her play *The Glass Slipper*—is adorable, but the autumn book goes deeper, and may remain for me the happiest book of my life . . .

Time will judge Eleanor Farjeon's work: perhaps the volumes of autobiography, *Mrs. Malone,* the beautiful love sonnets, and *Martin Pippin in the Apple Orchard.* Above all, what Eleanor says of Edward Ardizzone's pictures for *The Little Bookroom* can be said of her own stories in this book. All she felt about childhood is in them. For children she has been able *to be* the happy child she once was. This was her greatest gift.

> *Grace Hogarth, "From Grace Hogarth," in* The Junior Bookshelf, *Vol. 29, No. 4, August, 1965, pp. 201-02.*

## Ruth Hill Viguers

"A moment of interest may create a lifetime of curiosity," said Eleanor Farjeon in *The New Book of Days.* "My choice has fallen where it pleased me most. If it tempts any of you to look further into . . . one of a hundred other books which will bring you to a thousand others: then you will find that my speck of gold has discovered to you a gold-mine."

Such must have been the pattern of Eleanor Farjeon's education, of which she claimed she had none except what her father's library provided. Her zest for life, "her genius for friendship, her gaiety, her fun and her quicksilver intelligence" were part of a rich inheritance; her childhood fostered them, gave them so deep a rooting that, even through age and ill health, they were not lost to her.

In a poem written after he had spent "one whole beautiful day with Eleanor Farjeon," Harry Behn expressed his "impression of the timelessness that glows about her." Not long ago, I too saw her in her cottage in Hampstead. After the visit, as I walked down the cobblestone lane toward the underground, I wondered what it was about the woman I had just seen that caused my extraordinary glow of happiness. It was, of course, the timelessness and endlessness—the extending outward of her thinking, imagining, and love for people that gave her the radiance to make anyone in her company enjoy life on her terms. The sun within her warmed and illumined those about her. Its warmth and light fill her stories, her poems, her essays—none of them comes to an end. The songs keep sounding in the listener's ear, the meanings lead to new meanings in the reader's mind, and the stories go on and on in the imagination. In her "flashing awareness of beauty," others see beauty; in her love of life, others know life's value.

*Ruth Hill Viguers, "A Continuing Radiance,"*
*in* The Horn Book Magazine, *Vol. XLI, No.*
*4, August, 1965, p 341.*

### Margery Fisher

What is a "writer for children"? Is the temperament different, the approach, the vision, the occasion? Eleanor Farjeon died in June 1965; she was 84, and had been writing since she was a child. Early works of hers, published from 1911 onwards, were not specifically for children, however well suited they might be to young readers. The **Nursery Rhymes of London Town,** to take one example, were first contributed, anonymously, to *Punch*. **Martin Pippin in the Apple Orchard** (now offered, most often, to girls in their early teens) was sent in instalments to a friend at the Front, in the first world war, to remind him of his home county, Sussex; when the instalments were published in book form, in 1921, they fell into the popular category of fantasy fiction—for adults. In the second world war most of us knew Eleanor Farjeon primarily as the author, with her brother Bertie, of a delightful musical comedy, **The Two Bouquets,** poised lightly between Oscar Wilde and Noel Coward, and of sketches written for the *Little Reviews* which lightened those years with their grace and wit. Nowadays **The Two Bouquets** is a period piece, and Eleanor Farjeon is known as the author of **The Little Bookroom.** Perhaps it was not really until 1956, when she was awarded the Carnegie Medal by the Library Association in England, and the international Hans Christian Andersen Medal, that her work settled into focus and she was seen as a major figure in that branch of our literature intended "for children".

The Hans Christian Andersen Medal is given to "a living

author who is judged to have made a lasting contribution to good juvenile literature by the outstanding value of his or her works". By virtue of this citation, then, she is a children's writer. Then again, the dominant form of her work is fantasy—the form that best suited her imagination. For her, saints and fairies, angels, people and ghosts could always walk and talk together. New-style nursery rhymes, musical comedy, hagiography, love story, semantics, pantomime—fantasy is in all of them.

Does this necessarily restrict her to children as readers? Let us first look at the facts of her life, to see how her family background contributed to that versatile, active imagination. Her father, Benjamin Leopold Farjeon, was an Englishman of Jewish extraction, whose family was said to be of Eastern origin. Photographs of him suggest the rich personality which his daughter described in *A Nursery in the 'Nineties.* Always reaching towards adventure, through books as much as through real life, Ben Farjeon at sixteen went to the Australian goldfields, where he was soon running a newspaper; later, in New Zealand, he founded the *Otago Daily Times.* On the slender encouragement of a letter from Dickens, acknowledging stories he had sent for comment, he returned to London, to make himself a name as a popular novelist. In London he met and married Margaret Jefferson, daughter of the American actor Joe Jefferson whom he had met previously in New Zealand. From such parents, a passion for literature, drama, music, seems inevitable. It was a passion Eleanor was to share with her three brothers—Harry, her senior, and the younger boys, Joe and Bertie.

From her father, in particular, Eleanor received both encouragement and opportunity. There was the Sunday-Books Game, which began when she was about ten:

> We all had book-shelves, mine were crammed with fairy-tales and "The Greeks". Now Papa started giving to each of us a new book every Sunday after dinner. My first one was called *In Memoriam,* and it was bound in Real Morocco, with gold edges and a red silk ribbon marker. When the books had been given, Papa sometimes read bits out of mine with me. He told me about Lord Tennyson, and his great friend Arthur Hallam, and picked out some of his favourite verses; then I went away to read the rest for myself, and of course it was beautiful.

There had to be an outlet for the reading which, with Shakespeare, Dumas, Keats, "The Greeks" as perhaps first favourites, encompassed a very wide field. So there was the "Awake-at-night Game", when "The power to change, almost at will, flat thought into three-dimensional fancy, turned my sleepless nights into hours of glory"; and when Apollo and Diana might find themselves taking human shape as son and daughter to Warwick the King-maker, without any feeling of incongruity. At about the same time began the game called by the secret name TAR, devised by Harry, played continuously by Harry and Eleanor, with the other two children joining in from time to time. TAR, Eleanor wrote, was "the usual child's game of pretending to be somebody else; but I think in our case it was extended to a degree of intensity, complexity and accomplishment never equalled. This game began when I was about five years old, and for more than twenty years it continued to be the chief experience of my inward and outward life." This intense projection of herself and subjection to her brother's authority may well have delayed the development of Eleanor Farjeon's true talent; certainly she only worked out to a more single, independent state of mind with some pain and effort.

At the same time, the game is one of the foundations on which her storytelling rests. The storyteller must not only make his reader *want to know* what happened next, but also *believe* what happened next. It is because she lived in her stories that Eleanor Farjeon was always able to take her readers into them as well. In those nursery years, reading and imagining were a family matter. Among the Nursery Rules of the Farjeon children was the following:

> On October the Eleventh, at Three o'clock, each member of the Family shall take special note of what he or she is doing, and, if they are separated, shall tell each other.

The strength of that family feeling, with its gifts of affection and of interchanged talents, was one of the vital elements in Eleanor Farjeon's writing, as in her life.

*A Nursery in the 'Nineties* was written after her mother's death in 1933 and describes family life up to 1903 (when Ben Farjeon died). This memoir is essential reading for anyone who wants to understand Eleanor Farjeon. But they will find little *direct* description of her in it; the writer looks out, as it were, from behind her parents, her brothers, the innumerable friends who came and went through her childhood. The book is all the more revealing about her because, characteristically, it turns out to be about other people. Essential reading also is another memoir— *Edward Thomas. The Last Four Years,* published in 1958 and covering, as the author says, "the years of my friendship with Edward Thomas, from the end of 1912 to the spring of 1917".

Again, other people press into the foreground. First the poet Edward Thomas; she found maturity in her unrequited love for him, and his intense vision of the countryside released in her a flood of new impressions to be used later in her writing. Then, a multitude of men and women, young and old, intensely preoccupied with the arts and especially with words and music—Meynells and Garnetts, Arthur Ransome, James Guthrie the printer, Arnold Bax, Gordon Bottomley—the list could be infinitely prolonged. Behind them all stands Eleanor Farjeon as she was then, walking tirelessly on the Sussex Downs, talking and listening, writing stories, poems, jingles, fantasies, trying out different techniques. If the nursery years nourished her power to imagine people and identify herself with them, these years before and during the first world war must above all have stored her mind with impressions of the *places* which became background to so many of her stories—the Sussex of the Martin Pippin books, the villages of *Perkin the Pedlar,* the England of Elsie Piddock and Mrs. Malone and the Codlings. It is hardly a realistic picture that she draws, of this countryside. Fantasy colours it for the most part, and that pastoral feeling which was as essential to the times (the years of Georgian poetry in England) as were the experimental writings of Joyce and Eliot and Lawrence. All the same, it is pastoral very much in the English vein, from Greece perhaps, but by way of Elizabethan play and lyric and the poems of Keats and the evasive, evocative nursery rhyme and country tale.

The period of Eleanor Farjeon's life, 1912-1917, described in the memoir of Edward Thomas (and lovingly recalled, little more than a year ago, in her preface to a volume of Robert Frost's poems, *You Come Too*) was the second deeply formative period of her life, and much of her best work belongs to the years immediately following. She planned two further memoirs, one centred on her brother Bertie and describing her work in publishing and the theatre; another, more personal, covering 1920-1949. How much is written of these two projected books is not yet known, but meanwhile we can see how she developed as a craftsman by reading what she wrote. We can see how the lush almost enervating summer landscape of *Martin Pippin in the Apple Orchard,* crammed with blossom and adjectives, changed to more subtly suggested country scenes in stories like **"Elsie Piddock Skips in Her Sleep"** or **"San Fairy Ann."** We can see how the meandering superfluities of some of the early tales give place to a new kind of shape, seemingly casual and spontaneous, in fact carefully directed and disciplined, in stories like **"Pennyworth"** or **"The Glass Peacock."** And we may perhaps decide that the more Eleanor Farjeon changed, the more she stayed the same, for in this voluminous, endlessly inventive writer there is a very real consistency.

"Words first enter our ears as sounds without sense". She wrote this in one of her very last pieces of prose, the introduction to *The Hamish Hamilton Book of Queens,* published in 1965, a selection she made in collaboration with William Mayne. Ideas, she says, begin as sound without sense or meaning, and the ideas "born of a seed of sound grow within us as we grow, and change as we change". Words are not only the tools Eleanor Farjeon used; they could be, for her, playthings, symbols, music, windows. At its simplest, her love of words is shown in puns, double meaning or literalisms. The London rhymes are based on these (The Old Lady threads a needle in Threadneedle Street, the King is cross at King's Cross), and some of the tiny stories in *Perkin the Pedlar* which ingeniously explain the names of English villages (at Chipping Norton an old man chips stones for the road, at Kingswear the monarch is supplied with garments, at Idle nobody works). Words are handled in a free and easy way; there is no phrase or name or proverb which may not suggest a fancy that starts with word play and ends with the ghost of an idea. She tells us that her governess used to give the young Farjeons proverbs or quotations for their copybooks. One day the copy was "How far that little candle throws its beams". Accidentally the little girl blotted one of the e's and made it "blind", and her wonderings about the candle ("What were its beams like, and how far *did* it throw them, and where to?") led her to fill in all the e's—for "The Little Candle couldn't possibly throw its beams very far, if the e's were black, like the dark shutters at the photographer's".

From such simple manipulations of words to semantics. What do words mean, and what is their history? Among the diverse fragments in *The New Book of Days*—poems, stories, snatches of history—are a few Everyday Word-Meanings (neighbour, garden, cow and beef, lady, mantlepiece). These are patently simple demonstrations of the way words acquire and develop meanings. *The Silver Curlew* shows how much she could get out of one single word. The word *spinster*, with its overtones of legend and social history and old rhyme, is one of the three sides of the triangle of that beautifully worked out story. The basic tale is, of course, *Tom Tit Tot,* the East Anglian version of Rumplestiltskin, and because *The Silver Curlew* was a stage play first, a story later, it is the fairy tale that seems most prominent. It was for dramatic reasons that Eleanor Farjeon gave her country girl four brothers (who speak in a pantomime sequence) and that she turned the king, who in a fairy tale needs no character at all, into a comedy figure, a bucolic monarch with the heart of a small boy ruled by his nurse. The third side of the triangle is the nursery rhyme "The Man in the Moon came down too soon, And asked his way to Norwich". Interpreted in Eleanor Farjeon's own fanciful way, the rhyme lends a haunting poetry to the story, through those visiting spirits Charlee Loon and the Curlew, the Moon Lady disguised; it is also a useful structural addition, for it is through the sub-plot that the imp Tom Tit Tot is plausibly introduced into the main story. But sweet, brainless Doll (who never spun twelve skeins of flax but ate twelve Norfolk dumplings in one go) must not become a figure of derision, so here is the word *spinster* carefully used of her, with all its traditional meaning; she is not a silly girl but a country girl, one who spins, and the associations of the word, the implied joke (Doll can't spin but the impet can) and the overtones of ancient dignity—these, I am sure, make an important thread in one of Eleanor Farjeon's most skilful and subtle tales.

Yes, words were important to her, and music too, and the two can hardly be separated in her poetry—nor, indeed, in her prose. Music and movement are implied in the kind of arrangements she uses for her stories—for more often than not these were first published in groups, often broken up or rearranged in later years. *Martin Pippin in the Apple-Orchard* is built on a singing game, *The Spring-Green Lady,* for which she herself wrote words and music (though letting us take them as traditional). The movement of the game, where six players "fetch away" the seventh, is expanded into the story of lovesick Gillian, locked in the well-house by her father (as it seems at first) and guarded by six maidens, each with a key. Along comes the interloper, the rescuer, —Martin Pippin, a wandering jongleur who tempts each girl in turn with a story and claims her key, so that at last (and there is a typical Farjeon twist at the end) the captive emerges to new love and new beginning. The whole book is an extended game. The idea came to Eleanor Farjeon first as early as 1907, when during a visit to Brittany her mind was filled with minstrels and aubades, but it was not for some years that a Sussex orchard supplied a scene and centre for this collection of romantic, medievalised love stories.

I have already said that this was not intended as a book for children. Though it is often now given to girls in their teens, the intense cloying tone of the love stories, their fantastic, hyperbolic dialogue and other worldly back-grounds, will only appeal to a certain temperament at a certain stage of emotional development. Probably few young readers would realize or want to realize how skilfully the game is used as a framework. *Martin Pippin in the Daisy-Field* also consists of a series of tales with a linking device, but this time the tales are for children, and appropriate to them, even if, again, the framework is likely to be appreciated mainly by adults. It is high summer, and Martin, now a family man, must tempt six little girls to bed, the daughters of those maidens of the apple-orchard whom he talked out of their keys. A game develops. Martin is to tell a story for each child, and at the end he will try to guess which of the six couples she belongs to; at the same time he must discover which child belongs to him and to Gillian (the final twist in this case is a whimsical one in an adult mode of thought). Light and playful in tone, the device carries the stories, which are among the best Eleanor Farjeon ever wrote; though the little girls are attractively distinguished from one another, I suspect young readers, or listeners, will suspend attention between one story and the next, for the prattle has a slightly doting, aunty sound in it. Yet the storytelling mood, the bedtime atmosphere, is beautifully set by these affectionate preambles, with their gamesome, part-song sound. This method of *collecting* stories together is something special to Eleanor Farjeon, and it is one she excels in. This may be the moment to mention *The Old Nurse's Stocking-Basket,* for the neat, convenient scheme of this book goes to the very root of storytelling. An old nurse tells stories to her charges at bedtime, and each story is to fit the hole she is mending. So, the hole in Doris' long brown stocking reminds the nurse of Bertha Goldfoot, whom she looked after centuries ago, and of the strange enchantment that held that child; a great hole in the knee of another stocking reminds her of the time when Neptune showed her a hole that even she couldn't mend; Mary Matilda had only a speck of a hole in her tiny sock but it recalled the Princess of China, whose feet were tiny but whose silk socks took very fine darning—and so they go on, the stories, from Germany to Spain, from Persia to Norfolk, and the old Nurse claims her ancestry (as though Eleanor Farjeon were almost claiming her own):

> Let me think, now . . . Was it a hundred years ago, or two? I know it was long before I nursed the Brothers Grimm, because they were always teasing me to tell them the tale, when they were little boys, but for some reason I never told them that one. I expect they'd been too naughty or something, so it never got put down in their book later on. They were nice boys but I had to spank 'em sometimes.

The serial story, or the chain of stories, is irresistible to children; the light-hearted handling of time they will take for granted. Just as Eleanor Farjeon varies her tone from grave to gay, from witty to nonsensical, so she swings in and out of the past, not too serious about period but communicating the way *she* sees history. It may be in purely jocular mood, as in the poems about Kings and Heroes which she and her brother Bertie wrote together. It may be with a haunting pathos, as in a ghost story (for adults, initially), **"And a Perle in the Myddes—",** in which she swings unforgettably into the fifteenth century. Echoes of

# THE LITTLE BOOKROOM

*ELEANOR FARJEON'S*

*SHORT STORIES FOR CHILDREN*

*CHOSEN BY HERSELF*

*Illustrated by*

*Edward Ardizzone*

1956

OXFORD UNIVERSITY PRESS

*New York and London*

*Title page of* The Little Bookroom, *one of Farjeon's most popular collections of children's stories.*

old London, old England (and of course, often, what we have come to call Merrie England) are everywhere in her poems. Now and then she writes with a deeper, fuller tone—for instance, in **"The King and the Corn,"** one of the stories she chose to put in the collection *The Little Bookroom:*

> I seemed to see King Ra again, standing above me, saying, "The King of Egypt is more golden than the corn! The King of Egypt will outlast the corn!" And I ran out quickly to my garden, and cut down my ten ears, and thrust the golden blades among the corn the sleeping man had gathered for the King. When he awoke, he took up the sheaf and went on his way to the city. And when King Ra was buried in his glory, they buried my corn with him.

This very individual feel of the past in Eleanor Farjeon's work seems to owe much to her affinity with nursery rhyme. In her writings she has that way of dropping hints of antiquity, of offering sense and nonsense at the same time, which marks nursery rhyme as something far beyond just childhood days. This point may be best illustrated from *Nursery Rhymes of London Town:*

> Whom first shall we lay in Saint Paul's Church-
> yard?
> Whom first shall we lay in Saint Paul's Church-
> yard?
> The Smith and his Hound
> We will lay in the ground,
> May their bodies sleep sound in Saint Paul's
> Churchyard.

This echo of the past is heard distantly, again, in the story of the Long Man of Wilmington (in *Martin Pippin in the Daisy-Field*) and more nearly in the introduction of Wayland Smith into **"Proud Rosalind and the Hart-Royal"** (in the *Apple-Orchard*). The past is there, but touched with Eleanor Farjeon's preference for the gaily-coloured incident and the odd trifle; nothing is quite ordinary to her, for "romance gathers round an old story like lichen on an old branch".

There is quite another nursery-rhyme characteristic to be found in her work—the word play, the humour and the nonsense, the inconsequence that nags with hidden meaning. Some of her poems could stand very well as traditional rhymes of this kind; **"Threadneedle Street,"** for example, among the London rhymes, or the rhyme for **"Black-friars:"**

> Seven Black Friars sitting back to back
> Fished from the bridge for a pike or a jack.
> The first caught a tiddler, the second caught a
> crab,
> The third caught a winkle, the fourth caught a
> dab,
> The fifth caught a tadpole, the sixth caught an
> eel,
> And the seventh one caught an old cart-wheel.

In their convincing robustness, such poems ally themselves with the tall stories Eleanor Farjeon loved to tell—tales like **"The Tale of Selsey Bill,"** with that wonderful opening describing the good ship *Cuckoo* bound from Worthing City for Lima, with a cargo of soda-water-syphons—"They were wanted bad in Lima, where the Lime-juice was plentiful, and the water not fit to drink with it". There are the stories told by the old sailor to the small boy, in *Jim at the Corner,* always with a touch of tenderness behind their sheer nonsense, or a more traditional, toy-box rough-and-tumble in the adventures of *Tom Tiddler's Ground.*

Is all this "writing for children"? In so far as the subjects suit, certainly. The world where a king may be sent into the corner by his nurse, the world where pigs talk and mushrooms are gathered in the sky and an old woman skips into eternity—this is a world where children can feel at ease. But it is not a world they need leave when they grow up, unless it is by their own will—which may mean, by the faltering of their imagination. The themes of Eleanor Farjeon's stories are the universal themes of fairy tale—the testing of courage and love, the triumph of innocence and kindness, the discovery of what is valuable. No matter how indirect, how fanciful the medium, the themes are, like fairy tales themselves, for all comers and all capacities. How many ways—to take an example—can **"The Tantony Pig"** be read; here is a story in which comedy has its own meaning. The little pig, too thin to be accepted for market, is decorated with the bell that marks him out as Saint Anthony's pig, licensed to beg wherever he goes. His life is changed. Proud of his bell, and of the flock of sparrows following him for his crumbs, which seem like "his little train of attendants", he takes offerings until he fattens towards the shadow of market-day; but, talking on equal terms with his patron saint in the quiet church, he makes a bargain which will allow him to eat all he wants and regain his figure overnight. In this amusing, tender little tale, the narrator is one with her small listeners, enjoying the fun, but keeping a deeper point for her own. In other tales she takes a quizzical view of subjects and listeners alike, as it were protecting vulnerable childhood by the way she writes; this I feel in stories like **"Pennyworth"** or **"San Fairy Ann"** or **"The Glass Peacock,"** stories with an undertone of piercing truth about children as they are and as we know them to be. So you might say Eleanor Farjeon told tales for adults about childhood; or for children about a world shaped from the fancies of childhood; and you would be right both times, for these are both duties of the true storyteller. When Mrs. O'Toole complains to her husband (in **"The Connemara Donkey"**) "What a lot of nonsense you tell the child . . . You stuff him as full of tales as you stuff your pipe with baccy", his reply comes quick and clear—"What else would ye stuff a pipe with, or a child?" Eleanor Farjeon has left a supply of tales generous enough to satisfy children and their parents for many a long day.

*Margery Fisher, "Eleanor Farjeon: In Memoriam," in* Bookbird, *Vol. No. 4, December 15, 1965, pp. 3-10.*

**Naomi Lewis**

The quest for Eleanor Farjeon lies, very fittingly, cross-country, and curious country too. Even time plays tricks. For instance she is, we would all agree, one of the true enduring names in the field of children's writing. Yet at what point did she cross into that terrain? The works which have been appearing, in the most inviting editions, through the 1950s and '60s—*The Little Bookroom, Kaleidoscope* and the rest—are quite often re-issues or new selections of tales first published in the 1920s and '30s. Yet in that period their author was much better known for her witty theatrical productions, written, with her brother Herbert Farjeon, for adults.

Again, if we try to pin down the single essential Farjeon book for the young, what will it be? Probably, ***Martin Pippin in the Apple Orchard.*** Yet that unique, puzzling, magical book, first published in 1921 but set down earlier than that, was not intended for children at all. It was "written and posted, tale by tale, to a Sussex-loving friend in the trenches". That it came to be regarded as a children's story never ceased to surprise its author. To be sure, ***Martin Pippin in the Daisy Field,*** which followed many years later, in 1937, *is* for, as well as about, little girls, but this was consciously done, and something of the spark of the first has gone.

Time and the mood of the day must affect the course of every writer's muse. Eleanor Farjeon was born in 1881, but the dreaming, bookish, bespectacled little girl that she became, the only sister among three admired but dissimi-

lar brothers, was more than usually late in leaving the childhood world, late too in finding herself as a writer. So it happened that the time when her gifts came to flower was at a time that favoured the strongest aspect of her imagination; the golden fantasy, the cheerful fairy-tale view of human life. She had no need to swim against the tide, and this was a situation both happy and touched with danger. Yet it is fascinating to see how many works of fantasy, as well as those from the child's view (such as A. A. Milne's *When We Were Very Young*), were written for adult readers in the first twenty or thirty years of this century. Many of them are current still: *The Crock of Gold, The Man Who Was Thursday, Lolly Willowes, Orlando, Lady into Fox,* the stories of de la Mare—all of them crossing the supernatural frontier. It is with these, perhaps, that *Martin Pippin* originally belonged.

But something more must be noted about the days when Eleanor Farjeon first appeared as a writer. As we look back over half a century's distance to the last bright years—deceptively bright—before the First World War, we see perhaps the final surgings in England of an ancient pastoral dream—old enough even in Shakespeare's day to be charmingly mocked in the woodland glades of *As You Like It.* Yet it was to stay alive and green for many a day after that. For the countryside—an idealized harmony of man and creature and changing season—has been, from English poetry's first beginnings, its most persistent subject. Until quite lately indeed, when something of a revolution has taken place in the reading and writing of poetry in schools, children—often against all evidence—have gone on writing of a countryside of daisied fields where shepherds pipe all day, till dusk, when nightingales take over the tuneful lay: so pervasive is the power of this literary vision. And around 1912 and 1913—a time most vividly brought to life in Eleanor Farjeon's second autobiographical volume, we find a group of writers and artists attempting to link the pastoral fact with the pastoral idea. This was a period of the rural week-end cottage, the long tramps over country lanes, the clay pipes and blackthorn walking sticks, the cider, the newly discovered folksongs—and the reflection of these things in various "Georgian" poems.

True poetry did come out of the orchard cottage and the woodland walk—and none of it better than Edward Thomas's. For Thomas, whom Eleanor knew in the four important years that held all this poetry-writing, and then his death in war—Thomas not only lived in the country but saw it plain: the back-breaking clay, the raw new house, the rain, the way in which the recurring seasons preserve and present old griefs. He caught these things in poems of rare and poignant beauty. But to Eleanor Farjeon, trudging over the same clay fields, disenchantment never came. Summer pervades her books: milkmaids, pedlars, elves and shepherd boys people her countryside. Moreover, the pages are lit by a kind of ecstasy, a mood first known in her childish fairy-tale reading and daydream journeys, later in heightened yet dream-like moments of life itself; it remains the essential element in her work. Of this she was to write:

> Ecstasy cannot be constant, or it would kill. The
> glow comes and fades, comes and fades. . . .

> Writing gets done in queer irregular ways at
> queer irregular times. I still want everything so
> much, I don't know where to choose. If I had
> had a regular disciplined education, should I
> have learnt how and what to choose? . . .
> Would it have stopped the glow from coming so
> often, and dimmed it when it did come? I don't
> know. I have no rule to go by. It seems to me
> that there are no rules, only instances. . . .

Rule or not, she has left a number of clues to the roots,
at least, of the Farjeon gift; and for these we must turn for
a start to what many may think the greatest of all her
books, *A Nursery in the Nineties.* Here, in most striking
re-animation, she traces the life of a boy who would be in
time her father, now—in 1854—in the gold-fields of Australia, now an editor and novelist and friend of Dickens;
she traces too the story of her mother, the daughter of the
American actor Joseph Jefferson; she writes of the warm,
devoted turbulent London home, always filled with lively
literary and theatrical figures, and in which the four young
Farjeons led their own intense and close-knit lives.

Eleanor, short-sighted and shy, had no formal schooling;
on the other hand she did have an encouraging writer father (the severer disciplines came from the brothers' side)
and the free range of an enormous jumble of books. "I
never learnt how to learn," she later reflected.

> No wonder that when I came to write books my-
> self, they were a muddle of fiction and fact, fan-
> tasy and truth. I have never quite succeeded in
> distinguishing one from the other. . . . Seven
> maids with seven brooms, sweeping for half a
> hundred years, have never managed to clear my
> mind of its dust of vanished temples and flowers
> and kings, the curls of ladies, the sighing of
> poets, the laughter of lads and girls: those golden
> ones, who, like chimney sweepers, must all come
> to dust in some little bookroom or other—and
> sometimes, by luck, come again for a moment to
> light.

But the strongest influence on her mind, she reveals, was
a game called TAR—initial abbreviations of the names
Tessie and Ralph, two daydream characters with whom
she and her brother Harry, with all the force of their
strong imaginations, identified themselves.

> TAR was the usual child's game of pretending
> to be someone else; but I think in our case it was
> extended to a degree of intensity, complexity and
> accomplishment never equalled. The game
> began when I was about five years old, and for
> more than twenty years it continued to be the
> chief experience of my inward and outward
> life. . . . At an age, and long past it, when life's
> horizons should have been widening, they kept
> their narrow circle, while those of TAR widened
> increasingly. I had no desire for new adventures,
> friends, experience outside this powerful game.

"In our case . . . never equalled." At the time when Eleanor Farjeon wrote this important passage (that is, in the
early 1930s) the research on the Brontë children had not
yet reached the stage of publication. Would a harder
scene, a harder literary climate, such as the Brontës knew,
have given her work more astringency? The Brontës were

not brought up on fairy tales; their alchemy made wild romance from the seeming sawdust of political newspapers,
and even (how else did those maps arise?) geographical
textbooks.

One can never answer such questions. Eleanor had not, for
one thing, the desperate Brontë temperament. . . . There
were no imagined nymphs on the Bronte moors, nor was
summer their climate. But the practice of TAR did give
her, as it gave that family of genius, "the power to put in
motion given persons within given scenes, and see what
came of it, and . . . the flow of ease that makes writing
a delight".

This writing then—not always directed at children though
often about them—how does it seem today? Re-reading
(for remembered impression is not enough) I, for one, am
struck by the inspired craftsmanship of her stories. I
would place these above her plays—though she enjoyed
writing dialogue, had abundant humour and wit, and understood well the workings of the theatre. I would place
them also above her verse, for though she wrote many enchanting poems that will always please sensitive children,
her facility was not always her friend. Perhaps, too, she
idealized the young too much in her rhymes; this tends to
make readers uncomfortable. The best of her poetry possibly lay in her prose which—though she claimed to know
no rules—had something of the inner tensions, the design
and swift moves of poetry.

Her favourite medium (most notably seen in the Martin
Pippin books) was a framework in which a number of
shorter tales could be told. Chaucer used this of course;
so did Boccaccio. It serves Eleanor admirably; at the same
time, the separate short tales stand perfectly well on their
own. *The Little Bookroom* was her own admirable selection of such stories.

How skilfully they are told! How dazzlingly each one reveals its point, yet with a seeming casual lightness. How
many achieve, in their kind, an entire perfection of form
and content. (I would name among these **"The Kings and
the Corn," "The Barrel Organ," "The Times," "Old
Surly and the Boy," "Young Kate," "Westwoods," "The
Clumber Pup."**) And though they do not deal with adult
themes from an adult view, they are informed by the
shrewd and ageless wisdom of the folk-tale view. Even her
occasional allegory has no indigestible sediment of ear-
nestness. Perhaps she *was* too much on the side of the pret-
tiest goosegirl, the one with the longest, yellowest hair:
one can have no other complaint.

But read above all that outstanding book *A Nursery in the
Nineties.* It may be the title that has kept it from being
more widely known, for it deals with a longer time, and
with older people than either "nineties" or "nursery"
would suggest. Adults generally come to it by chance, find
themselves engrossed in its pages, report their discovery
on all sides, but part from the volume grudgingly if at all.
*Edward Thomas: The Last Four Years* continues Eleanor's story; the third volume—alas, left uncompleted—
was to centre on her brother Herbert. Perhaps we shall see
some chapters in print.

It is typical of Eleanor Farjeon that the author never was

the main figure of her autobiography. She never did see herself as the centre of the picture; indeed, it is hard to think of a writer so completely, so disconcertingly lacking in vanity. "Unlike most of us, she was not ashamed of showing her feelings", as Miss Rumer Godden writes in her memorable essay ["Tea with Eleanor Farjeon"]. With most of us, memory touches up the picture a little. Eleanor's faithfully ruthless memory was matched by her readiness to communicate all that she recalled.

Readers in search of more of Eleanor's works still have fragments to find—not least the remarkable narrative essays she wrote introducing a selection of Frost's poems published last year (1964) and a selection of Edward Thomas's, her own choice, that has recently followed it.

Eleanor Farjeon lived to be eighty-four, but her gifts did not decline, nor did her vision change. For her, in youth, the summer was brighter, the winters more delicately beautiful than they seemed to duller imaginations; and so through her life they remained. The writing of her latest days—the autobiographical essays, an occasional story such as the last one of all called **"Mr. Garden,"** show a touch as sure as in any work that she wrote when she was young. Why should this not be so? Her writing at all times was absolutely an extension of herself in words, on the page. Do not think that this is true of everybody! And because of this shining immediacy, each one of us who reads is her friend and her guest, taking tea in the room at the top of those stairs (described . . . by Miss Rumer Godden) in the house that was once a stable—a house that was, like herself, a marvel—a part of Oberon's rural England in the twentieth century London of our day.

> *Naomi Lewis, in an introduction to* A Book for Eleanor Farjeon: A Tribute to Her Life and Work, 1881-1965, *Henry Z. Walck, Incorporated, 1966, pp. 1-10.*

## Rumer Godden

Eleanor had a way of making you generous . . ., often bigger than you really were, and more understanding. I once sent her a gift of flowers and, on the same day, she gave them away. I might have felt rebuffed, hurt but, when Eleanor explained, I felt expanded and twice as warmed; she wrote, "A friend came, in great need, and your red roses especially moved him so I gave them to him. He said, 'Oh no!' but I said I had had them, fully, the moment they were sent, and he took them. So you see, love shared is love doubled."

"Love shared." Of all the poems Eleanor wrote, perhaps the best loved is the long poem—it makes a book—of **"Mrs. Malone,"** the old woman who, although so poor and neglected, always had room for one more:

> For each she had something
> if little to give,
> "Lord knows, the poor critters
> Must all of 'em live."
> She gave them her sacking,
> Her hood and her shawl,
> Her loaf and her teapot—
> She gave them her all.
> "What with one thing and t'other

> the fambily's grown,
> And there's room fer another,"
> said Mrs. Malone.

"Room for another": for a fledgling reporter, a fellow writer, an American publisher, a sad man who loved red roses, a hundred and twenty-seven kittens; but it was not only tea, or saucers of milk, or stories or memories, or petting that Eleanor Farjeon gave; it was something more, something transcendent that came out of her love so richly shared.

In *Martin Pippin in the Apple Orchard* Eleanor wrote of a river—a strange river in Sussex, Martin Pippin's country and, for years, Eleanor's, but one guesses there is such a river in every country—an exceedingly strange river, at once "the biggest and yet the littlest known, fullest of dangers and hardest to find." Only a few grown people have ever found it, yet it can be found with a child's help, which is perhaps how through her work Eleanor so clearly found it herself. Children play in it. "None but children," says Martin Pippin. "Above all the child which boys and girls are always rediscovering in one another's hearts—even when they have turned grey in other folks' sight." The source of it is a mystery, so beautiful that "after years of gladness and a life kept always young" when anyone discovers it they will never come back again.

Eleanor Farjeon will never come back again; [her] blue door is shut now, but she is not gone; she will never go as long as there are children—of all ages—to read her books and poems. As for us who had the luck to know her—if we live as Martin Pippin says, "Years of gladness, a life kept always young," perhaps one day we shall join Eleanor again in some celestial tea party, such as only she could conjure, in heaven.

> *Rumer Godden, "Tea with Eleanor Farjeon," in* A Book for Eleanor Farjeon: A Tribute to Her Life and Work, 1881-1965, *Henry Z. Walck, Incorporated, 1966, pp. 171-84.*

## Denys Blakelock

*[An English author and actor who met Farjeon when he performed the role of King Nollekens in* The Silver Curlew, *Blakelock describes his close friendship with Farjeon in* Eleanor, Portrait of a Farjeon *(1966), from which the following excerpt is taken, and* In Search of Elsie Piddock *(1967).]*

[Eleanor] told me she considered [her poem '**Mrs. Malone'**] to be one of her best—of that kind of poem at any rate. She was pleased with it technically, of its deftness, its subtle alliterations and the easy way it ran. She told me that Viola Meynell had said that the ingenious management of the extra word in the last two lines 'made' the poem. '**Mrs. Malone'** was a great favourite with audiences, to judge by its reception when Margaret Rutherford included it in a poetry programme, and on another occasion when I heard it done beautifully by Catherine Lacey.

The character of the old woman was plainly a projection of Eleanor herself. She adored animals of every kind, not only cats, and I am quite sure she would have starved herself as Mrs. Malone did, rather than see any dumb creature go hungry. . . .

Is it going over the edge of sentiment, I wonder, to picture Eleanor arriving in the next world and, like Mrs. Malone, hearing the faint echoes of those two lines which Viola Meynell admired and Father Mangan spoke at her baptism?

> 'There's room for another
> One, Mrs. Malone.'

Apart from its technical perfection this poem has an innocence and simplicity which belongs to the childlike element that was so strong in Eleanor. And yet her versatility was remarkable. 'Her Infinite Variety' was the caption that appeared above a review of one of her books by Sylvia Lynd. This was no easy compliment from one woman writer to another. It was the plain truth. Eleanor could write a story of adult love such as *Love Affair;* a satire, using a classical legend, in *Ariadne and the Bull,* which Naomi Royde-Smith described as 'brilliant'; sonnets, tender and moving, in *First and Second Love;* and the sophisticated verse of *Kings and Queens* (in collaboration with Herbert Farjeon), or *Thoughts of the Lady in the Background,* alive with *double entendre,* which she contributed to *The Saturday Book* of 1963.

All these and countless others belong to the grown-up Eleanor Farjeon; the wise, compassionate woman, whom many dozens of worried people climbed the hill to Hampstead to consult, to ask for her guidance and consolation in their perplexities.

But I should like to enlarge a little on what I have referred to more than once as 'the childlike element' in Eleanor; that psychological aspect which, I feel, provides the explanation of her power and magic, especially in her children's work.

From close and constant observation over many years I came to the conclusion that Eleanor Farjeon was in some degree a split personality. Not in the Jekyll and Hyde meaning of the term, because in her case both persons were good; but in the Dr. Dodgson and Mr. Carroll sense. So that, just as if the author of *Alice in Wonderland* in his early days had been exposed to the analyst's microscope we should never have known the delight of that Looking-Glass World, so we should have been robbed of *Martin Pippin in the Apple Orchard* and the stories that went to make up *The Little Bookroom,* if the young Nellie Farjeon had been dissected and pulled to pieces by the psychiatrists.

There was nothing Nellie disliked more than being pulled to pieces. She was always insistent that there was a special compartment of her interior self that was private ground, and was not to be trespassed upon by even her closest friends. This came out very early, as she testifies in *A Nursery in the Nineties,* where, as a small child, she objected violently to having her bumps told; and again as an old woman, when she explained the exceptional reserve of a fellow-writer: "I understand her. She doesn't want to be *fingered.*"

Neither did Eleanor Farjeon want to be fingered. This ap-

plies especially to her creative work. There were many occasions when she would be discussing some aspect of it in connection with a book she was writing, and she would break off abruptly with, "But I don't want to talk about it." She knew that the spells she wove were conjured up by a secret alchemy of her own which by analysis could only too easily be dispelled.

That alchemy belonged to Nellie, not to Eleanor. It had its roots in the far-off days of the 'Nineties, when little Nellie played a mysterious game in the nursery with her brother, Harry. She described this in great detail in the *Nursery* book: the never-ending fantasy life that went on even into their adult years. They called it 'playing TAR'. . . .

Eleanor often said that it went on too long, preventing her from maturing as early as she should have done. But I believe that it was to those long years of playing TAR, those hours of being 'rapt away from earth . . . walking round and round the table,' (like those other creative spirits, the Brontë sisters) 'absorbed in her multitudinous Other Selves'—I believe that it was to the constant and prolonged practice of this strange ritual of identification that we owe the wealth of prose and poetry that poured out from Eleanor when she once began to write. And I believe that it was the other half of the split personality that was writing; that the secret of Eleanor Farjeon was that when she wrote *it was little Nellie writing; writing as a small excited girl would write if she had the power to do so.*

Eleanor was always most insistent that she never wrote a book *for* children. Many times she said, "I didn't write *Martin Pippin in the Apple Orchard* as a children's book". This is no doubt why that book, her first best-seller, and all her writings were as much enjoyed by grown-ups as by the children for whom they appeared to be intended.

> *Denys Blakelock, in his* Eleanor: Portrait of a Farjeon, *Victor Gollancz Ltd, 1966, 160 p.*

**Eleanor Cameron**

Once upon a time in the 1890's there was a child named Eleanor, always called Nellie by her family and friends, of whom, when she was no more than a year old, her father wrote,

> May not those lungs which now such yells emit
> One day enthrall a world with sense and
>      wit? . . .

More than half of her was drawn from [her father] Ben's lavish source, she admits, but though she does not say so, we see in the adult Eleanor's work, in the quality and mood and texture of her writing, the delicacy and fastidiousness of [her mother] Maggie. As well as irrepressible humor and swift wit, we feel a fineness of judgment, as well as inspired nonsense, the considered sense, and always the implication of something deeper than what is displayed on the surface.

But Ben could know nothing of all this when he wrote those two lines about his little daughter. He was more likely expressing a general hope, the fulfillment of which he would not live to see, for Nellie was only eighteen when he died. Yet so ingrained was her sense of purpose, the sense of a certain responsibility she had to a gift which had first made itself known to her at the age of five, that after her alter ego, her beloved brother Harry, left home for the Conservatory of Music and she found herself utterly unable to work, she wept and told her mother, "I have wasted my life." "Oh, *Nellie!*" came the reply, and when Nellie looked through her fingers, there was Maggie smiling at her in tender, incredulous amusement.

What sort of child was it who, before she was twenty, was convinced she had wasted her life? For one whose tales, in the years to come, would prove the source of so much happiness and laughter and sheer delight for children and grown-ups alike, she must have been the shyest, quietest (as far as the outside world was concerned), strangest little being one could ever read of except for the Brontë children. . . .

Nellie says she cannot remember a single night of restful sleep as a child, nor can she remember being without headaches. She had glasses before she was eight, but perhaps they were not the right ones. She read constantly in the Little Bookroom and out of it, and the Little Bookroom was thick with dust so that she had one sore throat after another and nobody seemed to have thought about the cause. In order to pass the night she had an Awake-at-Night game, in which, by means of her almost frighteningly vivid imagination, she could make thought fill out from the flatness of a single dimension to rounded, progressing, three-dimensional life as real as actuality, and she would

*Farjeon and longtime companion George Earle at their home, Hammonds.*

lie in ecstasy under the spell. (I did this in some degree when I was a child, and I can testify that there is all the difference in the world between simply imagining something and making it fill out into what seems to the imaginer to be self-initiated movement, full of surprises and unexpected turns so that a play seems to be going on before one's inner eye; there is no comparison between ordinary making-up and this, and on some nights, for reasons I could never comprehend, my imaginings would not "come" but remained flat and mechanical.) All of Nellie's reading, poetry and prose, went into her Awake-at-Night game. Among "her Greeks," Apollo and Diana took the leading roles, and while other characters from both life and reading flowed in and away again, Apollo and Diana remained. Even now, she wrote as an adult, if it were dark and quiet or if she were walking rapidly along a noisy street, she could bring her shining god Phoebus Apollo to life again. . . .

At almost the same time Nellie's Awake-at-Night game started, when Nellie was five and Harry eight, TAR was begun, a phenomenon even more incredible than the continued existence of those created lives set down year after year by the Brontës in minute handwriting in the little books they made. For them these lives were anything but make-believe; they were prodigious, they commanded the landscape. And Nellie says of TAR that it was not a game, but an existence; it did not replace life, it was life; outside of it she had no desire for new adventures or friends or experiences, for the world of TAR was so much more actual, so much more fascinating, more marvelous than anything to be found outside its powerful circumference. What is more, age did not bring either disillusion or indifference to it, for as the years passed, the children's fertility and richness of invention grew so that the game of childhood had no opportunity to drop away. In Nellie's case it could be a question whether TAR was more enveloping than their imagined lives were for the Brontës, whether TAR exerted a more tyrannical power over her spirit than did their imagined worlds over theirs. Certainly Nellie did not escape into productive creativity until she was in her twenties, and perceived only later how the game had extended a lasting influence over her work, at first inhibiting it but, as time went on, proving to have been of the most enormous value. Of TAR Nellie has written that in the instance of herself and Harry, it developed "to a degree of intensity, complexity, and accomplishment, never equaled," and that she doubted "whether, among children, there have been many capable of following their leader as I followed Harry to the last time he said 'We are D'Artagnan and Porthos' from the first time he said 'We are Tessie and Ralph.' "

As the Brontës' youthful intense creations were well known when she wrote her words of confession, she must have weighed the Brontës' experiences with her own and still found hers "never equaled." But the relationship between herself and Harry, which made the game of TAR possible, was utterly different from anything known to the Brontës in the creation of their individual worlds. Theirs did not depend upon complete spiritual and imaginative unity with any one of the other members of the family. But in that unity, precisely, lay the central power of TAR: the almost unbelievable sense of identity, as if they were a single being, that existed between Harry and Nellie. . . .

It was a game that must never be told; it was *"an inviolable secret."* And though younger brothers Joe and Bertie were taken in at times, entirely unaware of the true extent and power of TAR, they were let in only a little and "never acted *à quatre* the magic we achieved *à deux.*" Soon they slipped out and away and left Harry and Nellie to go on with their own enchanted existence "in a setting as remote as that seen in a crystal globe." Harry was the creator, he was the god who called up spirits which came at his bidding.

> Like a medium I flowed into, or was possessed by, other streams of being, imagination released from all check was set vibrating and took astonishing action. . . . I had *become* for days on end creatures in Wonderland; I had lost and won duels and battles, committed crimes and heroisms, achieved nobility, endured accident, died many times in many ways, plotted against my king, rescued my king, had mistresses and been them, triumphed and been defeated on cricketfield and tennis-court, followed the Grail, felt danger and delight, starved and been rich, loved and been loved, hated and been hated, been beautiful and ugly, strong and weak—lived through a phantasmagoria of experience that life could not have offered me at that age, if ever.

With the creative imagination of Papa's side of the family and the talent for impersonation that came from Mama's were mingled that "fluid element" of the children's dual beings which made Nellie's perceptions instantly alive to Harry's even unspoken illusion, so that together they could be fifty persons "by changes of thought and mood so swift that the machinery of the drama never creaked." Nellie could not "be" anyone until Harry had ordained it, but guided by his often silent yet, to her, extrasensory direction, she flowed from character to character at his bidding—and the drama unfolded from day to day, from week to week; and within it they were utterly enclosed. Harry said "We are Tessie-and-Ralph," and they were; he said "We are Harry-and-Nellie," and they were; but so that people would never guess what was actually going on, Tessie-and-Ralph became, to any prying questions, simply TAR. "What are you doing, children, whispering away to yourselves?" "We are playing TAR."

When she should have been maturing emotionally, Eleanor writes of herself, TAR was a harmful inhibition, for it shut out natural knowledge; when the horizons of outer life should have been expanding, they kept their narrow confines while those of TAR ever widened. Because of TAR she did not become aware of herself as a woman until she was nearly thirty, and she was almost forty before emotional maturity caught up with intellectual ripeness. Such were the crippling, hindering effects of this childhood game.

And yet, she says, and yet—it gave her "the power to put in motion almost at will, given persons within given scenes," and to TAR, more than to any other experience of her life, she owed in the years to come "the flow of ease which makes writing a delight."

For Nellie everything of importance to her seems to have begun at the age of five, for it was at this age too that she commenced to write, or rather to dictate. It was her father who put down at her bidding a novel in five brief chapters entitled "My Travels and What I Saw," but she later wrote her own novel in Early Pencil Script, "The Adventures of Reggie," which she found necessary to begin all over again each time she sat down to continue it. . . .

At this age Nellie did not care for dolls, and we are reminded of Rumer Godden's saying in *Mooltiki,* "It is only people who dream and wonder who blow bubbles, children and poets—Shelley blew them," when we find that blowing soap bubbles was Nellie's favorite outdoor game—Nellie, the dreamer and wonderer. What delighted her most in childhood symbolized in a way a certain quality that would haunt all the creations to come: snow scenes in glass globes, kaleidoscopes (*kalos-eidos-scopeo*—beautiful image I see, Anthony's father tells him in *Kaleidoscope*) that shift from pattern to pattern in combinations seemingly without end, music boxes that give forth faery tunes apparently from afar, cuckoo clocks whose small figures appear and disappear. "I was fascinated by things that came and went, things I couldn't quite touch, or really find out; the silver road on the sea to the sun on the horizon, the moon and her star, the rainbow and its reflection, the shafts of light drawn almost down to earth from a bright-edged cloud, the spot of light at the end of a green arcade of trees."

And the beauty and magic that waited in Papa's study went into Eleanor's stories too: the richest treat of all, she said, was Papa's Colored Paper, a huge packet of it, large square sheets that came in a dozen different shades, and a number of which were given periodically to Nellie and Harry to carry back to the nursery while myriad possible ingenuities danced in their heads. Or else they would stay and be shown the various-hued Indian boxes, glazed and smooth, box within box until you came to the last one of all, a box too minute even to be opened; or the set of carved ivory tubes, joined to one another by brilliant silken strands which allowed a single tube to be drawn the length of the harp-like strands so that they dwindled to two, after which another tube was drawn along the two and they spread themselves miraculously into ten, where-upon *another* tube was pulled out and there were suddenly sixteen strands, then four tubes and twelve strands! Vanish—appear—disappear—multiply—diminish—reappear! What could have been more entrancing to a child's bewildered eyes? This: for the most magical thing of all was the box with the glass top that never came off, a box lined with shiny silver paper in which lay heaps of tiny, loose-limbed men, larger purple beetles and yellow butterflies, a miniature crane, and a yellow and a green and a purple ball. Now Papa takes up a rubber tube with which he rubs the top of the box and—lo and behold! —one midget man moves an arm, another a leg, the crane rises and flies, the beetle and butterfly skim and hover and swoop, the balls roll hither and yonder, the little men begin climbing over one another, faster and faster, until all is mad, dancing, unbelievable movement. Then everything begins to sink, to tremble, to fall back, and the whole scene is still until once more the Magician passes his hand over the surface of the glass.

Such were the wonders of childhood. And it is all there, all transformed into radiant life again, but differently, in the stories and plays and poems of Nellie grown into Eleanor, poured out as though now she were the Magician who reveals endless surprises, colors, witcheries and conjurings. She makes them dance from the point of her pencil as though she had only to touch the tip of it to the paper (she confessed to having always dozens more ideas than she could ever hope to make use of ), and these composed into sentences whose imagery and grace and precision continue to delight both ear and mind no matter how many times one goes back to them. But no tale is ever simply a bit of beguiling magic. No tale is only what it appears at first glance, for waiting under the iridescent surface is tenderness, wisdom, sadness sometimes, but more often humor and wit. And whether or not a child can ever speak of these things or put his finger upon them, they are there to be felt, as much the material of the story as the theme and its characters, its mood and movement.

What tales of Eleanor's I would have loved best years ago when I was Nellie's age I cannot imagine, but I know without the slightest doubt that I value now most highly of all **"And I Dance Mine Own Child."** It is for me one of the most perfect stories of its kind I have ever read, though it is **"Elsie Piddock Skips in Her Sleep"** that was Eleanor's favorite and that has been translated into any number of languages, so that I am puzzled as to why it has not been included in *The Little Bookroom.* (I can hear, as I reread "Elsie Piddock" for the third or fourth time, my English mother singing to me when I was a child, "Cups and sau-cers, plates and dishes, here comes a ma-an in calico britches . . . Bread and butter for your sup-per, that is all—the nurse has *got!*" This was part of a whole chain of verses, the end of Elsie Piddock's skipping rhyme, only Elsie's words were all closed up tight, quick, together, because she was skipping the Fast Skip, and *she* said, ". . . that is all your *mother's* got"; but then, my mother was in a hospital when she learned it and not outside skipping—indeed, after the hospital she never skipped again.) Oh, **"Elsie Piddock"** is a wonder-tale, all right, one of the lasting wonder-tales of childhood, but for me there is a special poignancy, a special tenderness, a subtlety of handling that makes **"Child,"** the story of how Griselda insisted upon bringing her old Granny home from the Almshouse and keeping her home, my favorite. It is a handling which, had it been allowed to slip a shaving this way or that, might have landed the story in sentimentality, but which, under the artist's sensitive, firm direction, keeps the dignity and strength of the tale throughout.

As Colette commemorated her adored mother in *My Mother's House* and *Sido,* so it seems to me is Maggie commemorated in a very subtle fashion in one story after another. Fully aware of Eleanor's memories of her mother as a young woman, I feel it may be quite possible we are seeing Maggie as Cinderella in *The Glass Slipper* or the princess in **"The Clumber Pup"** or the exquisite little figure in **"The Roman Puppets"** with whom Anthony fell in love in *Kaleidoscope,* or Selina, the little chambermaid who married the young king in **"Westwoods"**—Selina, dainty, clever, reserved, but secretly loving—exactly like Maggie! —and all of them gowned for the ball and lovely as Maggie, with her tiny hands and feet, her leaf-smooth cheeks and gray-green eyes, ready to go to her own ball in silver and white. "She looks as though she ought to be put on top of the Christmas-tree." At least we know with certainty that Eleanor is hearing her mother tell the children their special story when she makes Griselda tell Granny the old woman's favorite to soothe her to sleep: "Once upon a time there was a Giant! And he had *Three* Heads!! And he lived in a BRASS CASTLE!!!"

**"The Lamb of Chinon"** I put only a little below **"Child,"** and along with **"Lamb," "The Glass Peacock."** Nellie said of her brother Joe, "He will go to Heaven when he dies. Whatever happens to the rest of us, Joe will quite certainly go to Heaven . . . I am sorry, Joe; I am trying to tell the truth, and you had the least selfish nature of any child I have ever known." So it is with Annar-Mariar. Her unselfishness is never spoken of, it is shown, and it is never painful, nor does it seem in any degree conscious or unnatural. Above all—*above all*—Annar-Mariar's actions do not point a moral, for her giving is as much a part of her as her breathing. When, after Christmas, a little trimmed tree is bestowed upon her in a neighborhood where the children experience almost nothing of the lavishness of Christmas, and Annar-Mariar and her brother least of all, it simply follows that she will call the children to come and strip the tree—except for the glass peacock at the very top. But that night, because Willyum, her small brother, had broken his Farver Crismuss, "Annar-Mariar gave Willyum her peacock." He dropped it, of course, after he had fallen asleep, and Annar-Mariar "heard it 'go' " as she lay there awake beside the little dried tree, shorn of its ornaments.

As I go over my other favorites, I am struck by the number of "simples" Eleanor Farjeon has raised to a special place, who perform a wonder or who speak an unexpected wisdom. In **"The Lamb of Chinon,"** it is André Doucelin, beautiful with his tawny hair, his pale, colorless, tawny skin, eyes dark and with immense depths. Gentle and quite harmless, his grandmother said he was, but touched, and every night of his life he saw the Maid of Orléans, who had saved him when he was seven years old. Another is Simple Willie in **"The King and the Corn,"** who got the better of King Ra in ancient Egypt, the proof of his triumph evident in his father's field in our own day. He, too, is described as tawny-haired, fair-skinned, so that we cannot help asking, Was there a tawny, wise, and simple man somewhere in Eleanor's life? We find, as well, the old reprobate Jem Stokes, in liquor for six months of the year but sober for the other six when he would lie listening in the woods, for he was **"The Man Who Heard the Trees Grow."** There is Silly Billy, **"The Man Who Found Mushrooms,"** at times and in places no one else could find them. There is Joe, the unassuming young woodman in **"The Clumber Pup,"** who through modesty and direct intuition found his way to the princess, whom he married (a variation on the Youngest Son cycle in folklore). And there is Eli Dawe in **"The Man Who Pretended to Eat,"** the old carpenter who, when he was young, had had so little money and so many children that every day he only pretended to eat his cheese at lunch, and who told Anthony that the great thing was to get his surface true to begin with, for if his surface wasn't true, all the rest would be wonky. "And as 'tis with carpentering, so 'tis with life."

Of her own writing, Eleanor has said,

> Ecstasy cannot be constant, or it would kill. The glow comes and fades, comes and fades as it has always done since I was a little girl. Writing gets done in queer irregular ways at queer irregular times. I still want everything so much, I don't know where to choose. If I had had a regular, disciplined education, should I have learned how and what to choose? Should I have made more of the glow when it came, or would it have stopped the glow from coming so often, and dimmed it when it did come? I don't know. I have no rule to go by. It seems to me there are no rules, only instances; but perhaps that is because I learned no rules, and am only an instance myself.

Yes! One is one and all alone and evermore shall be so—green grow the rushes O.

> *Eleanor Cameron, "A Fine Old Gentleman,"
> in her* The Green and Burning Tree: On the
> Writing and Enjoyment of Children's Books,
> *Atlantic-Little, Brown, 1969, pp. 317-34.*

### Frank Eyre

[*The following excerpt is from the revised edition of* British Children's Books in the Twentieth Century *published in 1971.*]

In a long life associated with writing and publishing one meets a number of authors who are better known and admired for what they were than for what they wrote and Eleanor Farjeon would come high on any such list. She was an outgoing, warm-hearted, impulsive, completely genuine human being and no one who knew and loved her would ever want to write slightingly of her work. But it must be acknowledged that her substantial and, at the time, well-deserved reputation was established largely because she began writing at a time when, apart from Walter de la Mare, there was little else that was worth notice being written for children. At a time when there was little quality to be found she cared for quality, and as a writer of graceful verse and a born story-teller with a light sense of humour, she achieved many successes in a long and prolific career. The best of her genuine talent is found in her short stories, such as *Jim at the Corner* and the two *Martin Pippin* books, and this was acknowledged by the award to her, towards the end of her writing career, of the Carnegie Medal in 1955 and the first International Hans Christian Andersen Award in 1956, both for another collection of stories, *The Little Bookroom.* But though she was a much-loved writer she wrote little at full length, and despite a remarkable second flowering of her work after its re-discovery by Oxford University Press, it seems unlikely that it will endure, because it belongs essentially to an age and an era of writing for children that is now past.

> *Frank Eyre, "Fiction for Children," in his*

British Children's Books in the Twentieth Century, *revised edition, Longman Books, 1979, pp. 76-156.*

### Margery Fisher

Martin Pippin, a wandering singer, comes to the village of Adversane in Sussex one April morning and meets a young man broadcasting seeds and weeping bitterly, for his lovely Gillian is locked with six keys into her father's well-house, with 'six young milkmaids, sworn virgins and man-haters all, to keep the keys'. Using stories and songs, riddles and games, Martin Pippin beguiles the maidens one by one and persuades each to give up her key. But in the end, strangely, it is Martin who wins the silent prisoner and not Robin Rue, lamenting outside the enclave.

Martin Pippin owed his inception to a holiday in Brittany in 1907 which filled Eleanor Farjeon with thoughts of troubadours and *aubades.* She moved the troubadour, a colourful, enigmatic and riddling fellow, into rural Sussex, for she planned *Martin Pippin in the Apple Orchard* partly for the consolation of an English soldier in France, and gave each story a setting which the exile would recognize.

As framework to the stories, which all reflect the *amour courtois* of the thirteenth century, she gives Martin long, provocative sallies with each of the six girls. The particular chaste boldness which belonged to the medieval Courts of Love seems to have spilled over into the Interludes, with their songs and dalliance, and there is a faintly enervating atmosphere in the book which recalls *Restharrow* and Mary Webb and Quilter's Merrie England tunes. Perhaps to those who met Martin when he first appeared he did seem debonair, witty and attractive: most young readers nowadays would probably think him prolix and facetious (at least in the apple-orchard, if not also in the daisy-field) and would dislike his attitude to women, whom he treats as queens and children in the same jaunty breath.

*Martin Pippin in the Apple Orchard* was probably not planned as a book for children, though its febrile emotionalism has given many adolescents the kind of pleasure they can derive also from the romantic novels of Georgette Heyer. *Martin Pippin in the Daisy Field,* a sequel written specifically for children, contains stories which are among the best of Eleanor Farjeon's offerings to the young. In this book Martin Pippin is, apparently, the father of a baby; he teases and plays with six small girls (Stella; Sally, Sophie, Selina, Sylvia and Sue) who enjoy the delightful illusion that it is they who are deceiving him and putting off their bedtime.

The teasing is light and free from the disagreeable overtones of the first book and Martin Pippin enjoys his adult jokes in an easy, acceptable way, but a surprise ending, in which we realize that he has in fact been dreaming on the day of his wedding to Gillian, abruptly turns him back into the troubadour. By introducing reality, of even such a relative kind, Eleanor Farjeon disturbs one with the feeling that she has packed into this ambiguous figure elements which do not truly harmonize.

> *Margery Fisher, "Who's Who in Children's
> Books: Martin Pippin," in her* Who's Who in
> Children's Books: A Treasury of the Familiar

Characters of Childhood, *Holt, Rinehart and Winston, 1975, pp. 207-09.*

**Sheryl B. Andrews**

In his poem "Pan With Us," Robert Frost has the piper toss his reeds " . . . far out of reach" for "[t]hey were pipes of pagan mirth,/ And the world had found new terms of worth."

Eleanor Farjeon, too, was a piper of magic and gentle mirth whose song celebrated the quiet dignity of the commonplace and the childlike joy of the innocent heart.

Quiet dignity. Childlike joy. Not phrases to herald a brave new world of totally honest, brutally frank books for children. Today we seem to be in a publishing phase that is mainly comfortable with the realistic and the literal. This is not to suggest that writers such as John Rowe Townsend or Isabelle Holland, in *The Man Without a Face,* cannot deal with mature subject matter. They can and do. Rather it is to suggest that there must also be a place on publishing lists for fantasy and romance, with the proviso that they, too, touch some human need or dilemma—and do it with sensitivity.

*The Glass Slipper,* Eleanor Farjeon's retelling of the classic Cinderella story, is such a fantasy. Her vision was not on the grand scale of Tolkien's nor did she deal with the fundamental issues of good and evil as did C. S. Lewis or, in a modern vein, Madeleine L'Engle. Instead, she saw the ordinary and made it lustrous. The Things in Ella's kitchenmaid-slavey world—Grandfather, the clock; the broom; the fire—are friends who stand as brothers against her Stepmother when she attempts to prevent Ella from trying on that glass slipper.

The girl-in-the-ashes fairy tale is taken out of the splendid realm of Perrault and Lang, and we find ourselves in a world where a Prince's Zany helps a meek little man in a thin overcoat steal bonbons for his daughter at home, while the Princess of Nowhere looks on and whispers to the Prince that the Father is not guilty, but "very innocent." In Eleanor Farjeon's world, man is very human, but he doesn't sin so much as he stumbles; even the two Stepsisters—"stupid and greedy and fat and flouncy" Arethusa and "peevish and sly and thin and scratchy" Araminta—are charitably dismissed when their past behavior is put down to "thoughtlessness" by Ella, the Nobody from Nowhere, a land "where wishes come true" and loving kindness matters.

Yet while the author's vision was definitely rose-colored, her books do not drip with honeyed phrases nor sticky-sweet sentiment. Pomposity and arrogance always receive their just comeuppance in the sharp if humorous slash of the writer's pen: "The fat man with the gold hammer was the Toastmaster. . . .and his heart was as soft as the Herald's was stiff. But then he had not come of a Good Family, like the Herald."

*The Glass Slipper* is a magical book about ordinary things. There is a kindness and a wisdom in it that are hard-to-find commodities in today's literary market; yet it is one of the financial casualties of a sophisticated publishing world. . . .

For twenty years, *The Glass Slipper* has sparkled for young people. It will continue to do so; all they need is a chance to read it.

> *Sheryl B. Andrews, "A Second Look: The Glass Slipper," in* The Horn Book Magazine, *Vol. LIII, No. 2, April, 1977, pp. 193-94.*

**Edward Ardizzone**

[*Biographer Annabel Farjeon calls Ardizzone "the finest and most understanding of all the artists who ornamented [Eleanor's] work." He became a personal friend and accepted the Carnegie Medal for* The Little Bookroom *on her behalf.*]

As a child before the 1914 War I lived with my family in a Suffolk village. Telephones and cars were few; the cinema was hardly known and the radio not at all. It was still the world of the horse, with the pony trap, governess cart and wagonette much in evidence.

It was also for us a small world bounded by the village and its surrounding fields, and one in which we made most of our own amusements. There were the plays which we wrote and in which we acted and the family magazine, highly illustrated by me, to which every member of the family, young and old, contributed. We read much and knew and loved the works of Hans Andersen, Grimm, Charlotte Yonge, Mrs Ewing, and other nursery classics. We played long and elaborate games of make believe, and then, too, there were the rural tasks such as helping with hay and harvest. We were very young and it is only fair to admit that our mother was behind much of our more ambitious activities.

You will see that though our world was small it was a busy one, but what I think was special about it, was that in the realms of the imagination it was a very wide and spacious world indeed.

Now the point I wish to make is that on reading Miss Farjeon's stories I was immediately transported back into this old imaginary world of ours. It was as if some responsive chord had been struck. To put it vulgarly, the stories clicked. They were stories that were somehow both new and fresh, yet to me familiar.

I also found something else in these stories which was important to me as an illustrator. It was the poetic quality.

Miss Farjeon is a poetess and her prose is a poet's prose. It is sparing in description. One might say that she hardly describes at all, and yet, owing to that magic which belongs to poetry, each sentence or paragraph is evocative of a very precise visual image. It is a prose which never leaves one in doubt as to its meaning.

I would like to quote a passage from *The Little Bookroom* to make my meaning clear, but alas, can find none short enough for the space at my disposal!

However, take the opening of the story called '**Young Kate**'. Miss Daw lived in a narrow house on the edge of the town and young Kate was her little servant. Now it was a tall house because one is told it had an attic and it was a cliff-like house because houses on the edge of a town have a cliff-like quality. Besides it was inhabited by Miss

*Farjeon at her desk.*

Daw and Daws are cliff-dwelling birds. From the attic Kate could see all the meadows that lay outside the town, and that must have been a wide vista indeed.

But doesn't this conjure up an exact picture clear and sharp in the mind? I can hardly see how it can fail to do so.

Now what more can an illustrator ask of his author's work than this evocative quality plus an imagery in key with his own? Given this, stories almost illustrate themselves, invention is no labour, only drawing remains to be done and that is the least of our difficulties, and work becomes a joy.

MISS FARJEON HAS IT ALL.

> *Edward Ardizzone, "On Illustrating Miss Farjeon's Work," in* Chosen for Children: An Account of the Books Which Have Been Awarded the Library Association Carnegie Medal, 1936-1975, *edited by Marcus Crouch and Alec Ellis, third edition, The Library Association, 1977, pp. 78-82.*

**Diana Waggoner**

[*The Glass Slipper* is a] retelling of "Cinderella," based on a play which Farjeon wrote with her brother Herbert. Ella's enemies are her hypocritical stepmother and her petulant, clumsy stepsisters; her friends are her henpecked father, the Grandfather Clock, and the Prince's zany, who never speaks. The descriptions of the Prince's other possible mates and of the grand feast at the ball are just sumptuous enough to be funny; the scene in which the father and the zany steal sugar-plums to give to Ella is just funny enough not to be heartbreaking. A beautiful balance between melancholy and merriment.

> *Diana Waggoner, "Farjeon, Eleanor, 1882-1965," in her* The Hills of Faraway: A Guide to Fantasy, *Atheneum, 1978, p. 183.*

**Anne Harvey**

Eleanor Farjeon never forgot the child she once was, and never stopped enjoying the act of writing. Her final piece of work, an introduction to a selection of Edward Thomas's poems for young readers was completed the day before her eighty-fourth birthday, four months before she died. The advice she offered to would-be children's writers in the 1930s she certainly followed herself:

> Don't "write down" to children; don't try to be on their level; don't think there is a special way of addressing children, a special tone they will respond to. Don't write on the still waters where the great ships have arrived; launch the best ships you can on running water. . . . Don't be afraid of words and things that you think the children can't yet grasp.

In this year of the centenary of her birth two of her collections are back in print, representing some of her most original writing. *The Little Bookroom* is her own choice from tales told over many years, and takes its title from that real bookroom of her own late Victorian childhood, "that dusty bookroom whose windows were never opened, through whose panes the summer sun struck a dingy shaft where gold specks danced and shimmered, opened magic casements for me, through which I looked out on other worlds and times than those I lived in . . .". With no formal education Eleanor and her three brothers made free of the eight thousand books in their father's library. This wealth of literature, combined with a feast of imaginative play was to provide Eleanor with "that flow of ease that makes writing a delight". She passed through the early stages of journalism (indulgent essays where trees became "Temples of Pan") to becoming one of our finest storytellers. She wanted her readers to believe as she did that "Each book is a magic box/Which, with a touch, a child unlocks". *The Little Bookroom* expresses all that she feels about story-telling. The range is wide and drawn from her rich store of knowledge. One turns from the romantic tale of the kitchen maid who marries the prince in **"Westwoods"** to the down-to-earth **"Connemara Donkey"** which tells of Danny O'Toole whose Dad came from Connemara where there *were* donkeys whatever tough old Albert Briggs said. My own favourite is **"And I Dance Mine Own Child",** the sad-sweet story of ten-year-old Griselda, and her Great Grandmother Curfew, a hundred years older, who is the great-great-great-great granddaughter of Thomas Dekker. A book with his writing in it is where Bella the doll sits ("it props her up beautiful") and it turns out to be worth a lot of money; so that Gramma need not go to the Almshouse and Griselda can go on singing Dekker's old song written for that other long-ago Patient Grissel, "Hush, hush, hush . . . /And I dance mine own child. . . ." This ageless book, to be appreciated on many levels won the Carnegie, Hans Andersen and Lewis Carroll awards in the 1950s.

Another reprint from 1931 makes delightful reading aloud, and children over seven will enjoy for themselves the individual pieces that make up *The Old Nurse's Stocking Basket.* As with many of her collections Eleanor Farjeon liked a handle to hang the items on—one recalls earlier Alphabets of London, Sussex and Magic; Perkin the Pedlar; and Martin Pippin, that inveterate tale-teller of Daisy Field and Apple Orchard. Here, she used the device simply but skilfully: Old Nurse tells bedtime stories to Doris, Ronald, Roland and Mary Matilda while she darns. Old Nurse has been around a bit and nursed such charges as King Neptune, the Spanish Infanta "who had to be best at everything", and tiny Lipp the Lapp who was so small that his Mother couldn't find him. A strong down-to-earth humour pervades this book.

Edward Ardizzone was the illustrator who served her perfectly in both these books and with whom she is often associated. He pronounced her stories "to put it vulgarly, 'money for jam'. They almost illustrated themselves. One's pen or brush danced to her tune so easily". . . .

Eleanor Farjeon's critics would be right in suggesting that at times she allowed less than her best to appear. She was not always aware of her tendency to pour out words too lightly, too sweetly, and she resisted editing. But her best is far better than one at first realizes, and when she combined her light-hearted wit with her brother Herbert's more caustic touch the result was piquant. It would please many devotees of their *Kings and Queens* to see this treasured book back on the shelves; here you can brush up on important facts like "Edward the Second/Is commonly reckoned/One of the feeblest of all our Kings".

When the fuss of the centenary dies down it will be asked "Given the vast range of modern children's books, is she going to last?" I think, yes, if only for the originality of her ideas, the real sturdy quality of her characters, and because her huge personality is one with the writing. Comparing her to the Old Nurse, Edward Ardizzone said she was "the perfect Nanny and the perfect Poetess. Could anything be better?"

> *Anne Harvey, "The Perfect Storyteller," in*
> The Times Literary Supplement, *No. 4069,*
> *March 27, 1981, p. 344.*

### Eileen Colwell

One sunny day in September twenty-five years ago, I walked down a cobbled lane in Hampstead to visit someone I had never met but felt I knew well through her poems and stories—particularly the story called **"Elsie Piddock Skips in Her Sleep,"** which I had told so frequently. I knocked at the blue door with its brass knocker, and it was opened by an old lady. Her gray hair was tied, almost literally, into a knot; her shape resembled a cottage loaf (her own description); and her sparkling eyes were hidden behind thick spectacles. Her first words showed her to be no ordinary person, for stranger though I was,

she seized my hands and said, "Let me look at you. Yes, you are just as I thought, just right for Elsie Piddock!" From that moment we were friends, and our friendship was to continue until her death. . . .

Eleanor's childhood was unconventional. She had little formal education and never went to school, but she was let loose in a room full of books and allowed to read at will. From her earliest days she was taken to see plays and to hear music; and many famous people—Ellen Terry and Henry Irving, among others—were frequent visitors in her home. From the beginning she wrote compulsively, for writing was "her life and her vice." She relates that when she was a girl, she once wrote a long poem with her right hand while combing her hair with her left! Everything she wrote she submitted to her father, and her proudest day came when he said, "I have hopes of you, Nellie!" The four children were inseparable in that nursery she described so touchingly in *Portrait of a Family.*

The bond between Harry and Nellie was particularly strong, for it was with him that she played the imaginative game they called TAR (the first letters of the names of Tessy and Ralph, two characters they had seen in a play). They imagined themselves to be characters from books and plays and history, and at once they *were* those people. Local inhabitants became accustomed to seeing Harry with Nellie trotting at his elbow, both bespectacled and rather untidy, walking along the Finchley road and talking, talking, talking—oblivious of everything that went on around them. Until Harry said, "We are Harry and Nellie," they were lost in their imaginary world, a world more real to Eleanor than the one in which she lived. It was not until she was twenty-five that she broke away from TAR. Undoubtedly, it was through these early essays in imagination that she developed the power to "put into action almost at will, given persons within given scenes and see what came of it." Her inspired imagination gave her a brilliant awareness of beauty, emotion, or truth, and it never failed her. At the age of eighty she showed me boxes and drawers full of slips of paper on which she had noted ideas she would never now have time to use. "I have always been kept busy with more varied ideas than I could ever finish and have had fun of all sorts with them," she said.

Her output was diverse and prolific: poetry, plays, singing games, lyrics which she set to music herself, stories for children, novels for adults, scholarly translations and retellings of legends and history, a volume of autobiography. Yet when I told her that I was to give an hour's talk about her, she said in obvious surprise, "How can you possibly talk about me for so long!"

She was thirty-five when her first book appeared in 1916, *Nursery Rhymes of London Town.* Later she set these verses to music. Her only attempts at journalism were her weekly contributions to the *Daily Herald* for thirteen years and later to *Time and Tide.* Apart from these, she lived precariously on her books; she was never a rich woman. At one time she collaborated with her brother Herbert in his revues. She would "splosh down" verses, and he would edit their exuberance. These lyrics she set to old tunes or composed others for them. She had no formal knowledge of music or of harmony, but her musical friends—Arnold Bax was one of them—corrected her mistakes. This was "a lovely, happy time," she said.

Her novels for adults were mostly delicate fantasies, whimsical stories with gay, elusive characters. They are nearly all out of print today, but her short stories for adults sometimes appear in anthologies, notably her moving ghost story **"Faithful Jenny Dove."** Her novels could perhaps be called period pieces; they are possibly too gossamer for modern tastes.

Eleanor Farjeon was always interested in drama and was a keen critic of the wide variety of plays she took pains to see. Her taste was catholic, for she was open to new ideas. It was natural that she should write plays herself. The best known are her two fairy tale plays *The Glass Slipper* and *The Silver Curlew,* both based on folk tales familiar to everyone. *The Glass Slipper* was written with her brother Herbert in 1944 and is sometimes produced for children at Christmastime. It is enchanting; the entranced lovers move in a magical world of snow-covered gardens haunted by echoing voices. Both plays were later rewritten as highly successful novels for children.

It is for her stories and poems for children that Eleanor Farjeon will be remembered. The short story, one of the most difficult of literary forms, was always her most successful medium. Such stories need directness, economy of words—but exactly the *right* word—and a feeling for drama and characterization developed within a small compass. To be bound by these rules was a necessary discipline for her exuberance. She spoke of her stories as "a muddle of fact and fiction, fantasy and truth," but it was an inspired muddle. This can be seen in the two books in which Martin Pippin, a wandering minstrel, is the central figure. Round him are woven delightfully imagined short stories. *Martin Pippin in the Apple Orchard,* never intended for children, is appreciated by adolescents (especially in Japan); *Martin Pippin in the Daisy-Field* was written for children. It contains the most famous of all her stories, **"Elsie Piddock Skips in Her Sleep."** The story was her own favorite, and Eleanor Farjeon told me that it said more than any other what she wanted to say. Happily, it is loved and told by storytellers everywhere. . . .

It is in the short stories that we see her love for and understanding of children. "I have had no children of my own," she said, "and yet so many! There is a part of me that loves the things children love, so I just write as myself. Always we must write as ourselves, for only then shall we put into our work that something special that we alone can give." Wise advice for any writer.

There can be few anthologies of poetry which do not include some poems by Eleanor Farjeon. She found it easy to write verse, *too* easy sometimes, so that her very facility produced work of uneven quality. But the best of her poems sing in the heart and the memory. **"What is Poetry?"** she asks and continues:

> . . . .Who knows?
> Not a rose, but the scent of the rose;
> Not the sky, but the light in the sky;
> Not the fly, but the gleam of the fly;
> Not the sea, but the sound of the sea;

> Not myself, but what makes me
> See, hear, and feel something that prose
> Cannot: and what it is, who knows?

There is an ecstacy reminiscent of Gerard Manley Hopkins in her poem **"The Earth":**

> How wonderful it must be, how rare,
> To be born on the bright, bright Earth up
>     there!
> How the streams must shine!
> How the grass must glisten
> When the dew is risen!

Her poems have spontaneity and gaiety, rhythm and music that make them memorable: Listen to **"A girl calling":**

> So through the falling
> snow, the girl went calling,
> calling . . . calling
> from tree to tree;
> My love,
> my love,
> my dove,
> where can he be?

And children enjoy the fun of such evocative poems as **"Cats."**

Eleanor Farjeon's poetry does not have the profundity of that of her dear friend Walter de la Mare; it is more lighthearted and childlike, but de la Mare himself praised her sonnets and found delight in her poems. At one time the two toured schools in the East End of London—she to sing in her "sweet singing voice" and he to read his poems. Do any of those long-ago children remember the experience, one wonders?

Eleanor Farjeon will live for the warmth and vitality of her writing and for her joy in all things lovely. Her stories are full of laughter, too, and are expressed in a limpid prose which, though deceptively simple, is the work of a craftsman. She found such pleasure in writing that she smiled as she wrote. Always her preference was for fantasy, for things she "cannot quite touch or find out." . . .

Eleanor Farjeon had a genius for friendship. Her friends seldom met each other, however, for she preferred to give each one her undivided attention. Her judgment was shrewd but never malicious, her sympathy warm but giving no encouragement to self-pity. She was warmly generous; once I asked for a rose, and immediately, to my dismay, she cut off the whole top of a magnificent rose tree and gave it to me with her love. Part of everything she earned was given away as a matter of course, not out of charity but with loving compassion—and usually anonymously. Her curving smile showed the beauty of a spirit eternally young and exhilarated by the wonder and beauty of the world and of life. "I'm so glad to be alive. It's so interesting and such fun!" she said to me when she was eighty.

On what was to be my last visit to her, she said in parting, "Be happy, my dear! That is what matters." For in spite of much sorrow and the loss of loved ones, she was essentially a happy person, with an inward happiness. For her countless friends the rare person who was Eleanor Farjeon is implicit in the words of her own poem **"Mrs. Malone"**:

> Whose havings were few
> And whose holding was small
> And whose heart was so big
> It had room for us all.

> *Eileen Colwell, "Eleanor Farjeon: A Centenary View," in* The Horn Book Magazine, *Vol. LVII, No. 3, June, 1981, pp. 280-87.*

### Margery Fisher

Can a classic really date? If not, Eleanor Farjeon's works are hardly classics, for there are certain strains of whimsicality and lushness which have not lasted well. Yet she created a unique world, partly Arcadian and partly toy-cum-fairy-kingdom where stories that start like 'Cinderella' or 'Tom Tit Tot' end with surprising twists. She had something of Hans Andersen's gift for making a homely object memorable (a puppy, a glass ornament, a chocolate bar, a rose) and a deep tenderness for childhood, perhaps seen at its best in the haunting **'And I dance mine own child'**. The stories she chose herself for the collection named, from her childhood, *The Little Bookroom,* deserve to live still to please readers who have the sensuous imagination to absorb the colours and textures of her world and the literary sense to appreciate the grace and rhythm of her prose and her skilful variations on old themes.

> *Margery Fisher, in a review of "The Little Bookroom," in her* Margery Fisher Recommends Classics for Children & Young People, *Thimble Press, 1986, p. 11.*

### Zena Sutherland and May Hill Arbuthnot

When Eleanor Farjeon began to write, she always took her manuscripts to her father's study, pushed them under the door, and then ran away. "I had a stomach-ache till he came and told me if he liked it," she wrote. "He never kept me waiting. Even if he was writing his own stories, he stopped at once to look at my last poem, and came straight to the Nursery to talk it over with me."

Her first book was the amusing *Nursery Rhymes of London Town,* for which she wrote her own music. This was followed by the lively historical nonsense, *Kings and Queens,* and from then on she wrote prolifically, both prose and poetry.

*Kings and Queens,* written with her brother Herbert, was republished in 1953 and will delight children wrestling with the solemnity of English history. For instance, **"Henry VIII"** opens with:

> Bluff King Hal was full of beans;
> He married half a dozen queens;
> For three called Kate they cried the banns,
> And one called Jane, and a couple of Annes.

And it continues with blithe irreverence to account for the six ladies and their much-marrying spouse.

At their best, Eleanor Farjeon's poems for children, whether nonsense or serious lyrics, are skillfully written. Her rhythms are often as lively as a dance; her meters and rhyme schemes are varied and interesting; and her subject matter has exceptional range.

Unfortunately, the quality of her poems is uneven. She is not, for instance, so adroit at describing the modern child's everyday activities as A. A. Milne, but the moment she turns imaginative, something wonderful happens:

### The Night Will Never Stay

> The night will never stay,
> The night will still go by,
> Though with a million stars
> You pin it to the sky.
>
> Though you bind it with the blowing wind
> And buckle it with the moon,
> The night will slip away
> Like sorrow or a tune.

This curious and lovely poem might well give children their first sense of time, rushing irresistibly along in a pattern of starry nights that will not stand still. In *The Children's Bells,* her **"What Is Time?"** supplements this poem in a lighter mood. Children like the sound of her companion poems, **"Boys' Names"** and **"Girls' Names,"** and the surprise endings amuse them.

> *Zena Sutherland and May Hill Arbuthnot, "Poetry: Eleanor Farjeon," in their* Children and Books, *seventh edition, Scott, Foresman and Company, 1986, p. 305.*

### Annabel Farjeon

[*Farjeon is an author and critic who is the daughter of Eleanor Farjeon's brother Herbert.*]

From a very early age [Eleanor] had been a voracious reader, with an insatiable appetite for words. Her progress must have been accelerated by the desire to keep up with Harry, for she was competitive. "I want a different same," she would say, when not quite able to enjoy equality. But literary guidance was given by Farjeon to all the children with a wisdom which would have been exceptional had he enjoyed the best formal education. If he was fortunate in having children whose tastes were compatible with his own, so were they in being allowed to enjoy the eight thousand books spread everywhere about their home.

'Of all the rooms in the house, the Little Bookroom was yielded up to books as an untended garden is left to its flowers and weeds. There was no selection here. In dining-room, study and nursery there was choice and arrangement; but the Little Bookroom gathered to itself a motley crew of strays and vagabonds, outcasts from the ordered shelves below, the overflow of parcels bought wholesale by my father in the sale-rooms. Much trash and more treasure. Riff-raff and gentlefolk and noblemen. A lottery, a lucky dip for a child who had never been forbidden to handle anything between covers.'

This was written in the preface of one of Eleanor's most successful collections of children's stories, *The Little Bookroom,* where she would forever be seen in the Ardizzone illustration: a small girl hunched short-sightedly over some fable, with musty volumes piled and tumbling about her.

Like all true readers, as she grew older she did not relinquish those earlier much-loved books, but went on absorbing more and more, apparently at random. She read greedily with an undisciplined mind that never learnt how to know all of one thing while it gleaned smatterings of a thousand others. . . .

Promiscuous reading complemented her writing and left her with a literary education of extraordinary richness and variety. Her wide knowledge was relied upon all her life by great numbers of people far more diligently taught.

'That dusty bookroom whose windows were never opened, through whose panes the summer sun struck a dingy shaft where gold specks danced and shimmered, opened magic casements for me, through which I looked out on other worlds and times than those I lived in.' . . .

In January 1917 Captain Victor Haslam, serving in the Royal Garrison Artillery and Royal Flying Corps Balloon Company, had written a fan letter to Eleanor Farjeon praising one of 'the most delightful books' he had read: *Nursery Rhymes of London Town,* published by Duckworth. It consisted of verses that played upon the names of districts or monuments in London. The two became acquainted by letter and then, as Eleanor commenced a new book, she posted the chapters one by one to the soldier in the trenches; and very fresh, remote and whimsical they must have seemed by contrast to his grim surroundings.

*Farjeon in her studio.*

When Haslam returned to England they met, and for a short while it seemed as though a romance might develop, but three years later Eleanor explained to [her longtime companion] George Earle: 'For more than a year our friendship and affection seemed leading up to the gift of all I had to give, and when I found he wanted so little of it, it fell back on me heavily for a while. (It had blown away like thistledown before April two years ago.)' . . .

The joyful *Martin Pippin in the Apple Orchard,* whose success set the pattern of a prosperous career, was the book whose chapters were sent to Haslam at the front. Its prologue begins: 'One morning in April Martin Pippin walked in the meadows near Adversane, and there he saw a young fellow sowing a field with oats broadcast. So pleasant a sight was enough to arrest Martin for an hour, though less important things, such as making his living, could not occupy him for a minute. So he leaned upon the gate, and presently noticed that for every handful he scattered the young man shed as many tears as seed, and now and then he stopped his sowing altogether, and putting his face between his hands sobbed bitterly. When this had happened three or four times, Martin hailed the youth, who was then fairly close to the gate.

"Young master," said he, "the baker of this crop will want no salt to his baking, and that's flat."

The young man dropped his hands and turned his brown and tear-stained countenance upon the minstrel. He was so young that he wanted his beard.

"They who taste my sorrow," he replied, "will have no stomach for bread.' "

The young man goes on to explain that he loves Gillian who is locked up in Old Gilman's well-house, where she weeps beside the well. Six milkmaids, all sworn virgins and man-haters, keep the six keys of the gate, and live in the orchard outside. So Martin the minstrel finds the orchard, tells the girls six love stories and, overcoming their hatred of men and their prudishness, wheedles and tricks the keys from them. Finally the freed Gillian goes off, not with the tearful sower of oats, but with Martin Pippin himself.

This fanciful tale was written in a mood of delight: a caprice set in the Sussex countryside, where the flowers and woods, the downs and valleys, had become personal to Eleanor, with place names like Hawking Sopers, Open Winkins and Pillygreen Lodges full of wayward meaning. Adversane was one that seemed to her to have been taken from Malory, and evoked the world of troubadours which had so intrigued her on holiday in Brittany before the war.

*Martin Pippin in the Apple Orchard* was not written as a children's story, although it is now known as such, being a neatly patterned, whimsical pastoral, the main theme dovetailed with songs and stories improvised by the minstrel hero, in a way which Eleanor herself would have improvised for anybody in her company. The affected, antique mannerisms of language are not what [her friends, poet Edward] Thomas or [novelist D.H.] Lawrence would have approved, but they would have suited brother Harry in a game of TAR. The book is vivid and coherent, its artlessness full of craft, while the picture of this English Arcadia is curiously individual. Descriptions of munching apples in apple trees, of the spring grass which grew 'high and full of spotted orchis, and tall wild parsley spread its nets of lace almost abreast of the lowest boughs of blossom' are pictures full of Eleanor's light poetic vision.

Martin's lilting roundelays are wrapped about the names of wild flowers; there is wit and wrangling in the coy conversations, where a girl will jib at the word 'kiss'. But the converted milkmaids at last climb up and down the double apple-picking ladder over the hawthorn hedge and away with some last minute lovers, while Martin takes Gillian to his cottage hidden in a lush Sussex valley where 'all flowering reeds and plants that love water grow' and the 'pussywillows bloom with grey and golden bees'. . . .

[It was before the completion of this book that] Eleanor found a place of her own: The End Cottage, Mucky Lane, Houghton.

A rutted way, scarcely a cart track, led to this primitive dwelling, two-up, two-down, thatched, with a seven-sister rose bush beside the porch and a well in the garden.

Here Eleanor lived alone for nearly two years. She wrote that these may have been the most important years of her life. . . . [Here] she wrote and went to bed leaving doors and windows open. It seemed to her an almost perfect way of living, filled with natural and necessary things, like collecting wood and fir cones, picking flowers and mushrooms from the fields, watching the seasons change, learning to grow vegetables, and above all learning to lose fear. . . .

When neighbouring children gathered in Mucky Lane to skip beneath her window and sing old rhymes handed down for generations, she went out and asked them to explain the intricacies of their game and recite the words. Elsie Puttick was the deftist of all the skippers and years later became the heroine of one of Eleanor's best fairy tales, **"Elsie Piddock Skips in her Sleep."** . . .

Doubtless during the two years in End Cottage she suffered a great deal, mourning the loss of [her close friend Edward Thomas, who was killed in the war], but the loneliness was soothing, while the writing of prose and verse for children filled her mind with visions. . . .

When in 1921 *Martin Pippin in the Apple Orchard* charmed the public, a professional career was established, and by 1928 twenty-two books of verse and stories, mostly for children, had been published. This average of over two publications a year would be satisfactory for any author. It seemed as though the store of ideas which had piled up in Eleanor's imagination for forty years now flooded out.

One of the important results of living alone in Sussex had been that in losing fear Eleanor emerged resilient to the buffets of the world. As with her father, a natural optimism kindled continual hope, and although her judgement sometimes went astray, she could now accept failure and learn from it rationally, without disenchantment. When selling her work she became almost immune to disappointment, each manuscript going off to a publisher as

on a journey, from which, if rebuffed, it would be welcomed home with her faith in its worth unshaken.

In the early 1920s Eleanor was asked to write some hymns and readily produced three for which the fee was nine guineas. After her death the hymn called **"Morning Has Broken"** was taken by the pop star Cat Stevens and sung on records and at concerts. The three guinea hymn soon became 'Top of the Pops' both in Britain and the United States with a blast of notoriety and royalties that would have amused and delighted its author.

When writing verse Eleanor liked to discipline herself within some definite form. In the sonnet she achieved a mastery which was in danger of becoming facile, as Lawrence discerned; with light-hearted rhymes the alphabet became a favourite framework. The Town and Country Child, the School, Sussex, Magic, the Seaside, Twins and the BBC each had its own ABC. A pipe-smoker's ABC was planned which might have been dedicated to Thomas, Earle or [her brother] Bertie with equal warrant. Most of the ABCs have charm and wit, but in the hurry of composition and the effort to earn money, poor quality work could pass uncensored.

But **"E for Express Messenger"** shows how effectively and simply the chosen form was generally mastered. . . .

**"W is for Waves"** can be appreciated by a four-year-old as well as an adult, and in some of Eleanor's short poems there glows a clarity that approaches Blake's vision of innocence. Her stories for children are lucid and to the point, while the best have an underlying complexity, with the moral not forced but gently and firmly stated. . . .

[In 1929 Eleanor and Bertie collaborated] on a series of verses about the kings and queens of England. . . . [They worked together], with the maxim of 'collaborator's honour' which, Bertie told his sister, meant that neither ever revealed who wrote what. . . .

This popular, unceremonious history book was admired by the royal family, even though fun was poked at their antecedents. Bertie had written to his sister: 'Let's have no nonsense about it. The Bad Kings are Bad, and the Good Kings are Good, just as they were when we were children.' Diana Cooper remarked, "I learned all my history of England from Bertie and Eleanor Farjeon's *Kings and Queens*." . . .

In 1937 a sequel to *Martin Pippin in the Apple Orchard* was published: *Martin Pippin in the Daisy-Field.* This was in the old style, with more fanciful convolutions of conversation. It is significant that although seventeen years had passed since the first Martin Pippin, although Eleanor had now experienced a varied life knocking up against the world and earning her living, the youthful concern with playing mothers and fathers, with games and rules, fair and unfair, revived as fresh as ever; and with it the child's astute single-mindedness. . . .

There is a sprung rhythm to this dialogue, to the whole of the Martin Pippin fantasy. The minstrel's flirtation with the girls remains curiously sexless despite innuendo, much like that which Harry adopted in real life, a philosophic banter that showed off his ability for word-spinning.

*Martin Pippin in the Daisy-Field* was yet another success. . . .

In 1943 Bertie received a letter with a new suggestion from the film star and actor-manager, Robert Donat. 'I wondered if I dare approach you and your sister with the idea of writing the First Real Children's Pantomime.

'I have always felt that a lovely job could be done in the theatre for children and children only, with no distortion of the story, no inclusion of snappy modern songs, no jokes about beer and mothers-in-law; just a simple and honest concentration on the story and its faithful telling with all the great traditions and glamour of the theatre to help it . . .'

Donat wanted to put on the show for his young sons.

Eleanor and Bertie were delighted with the idea—there was no more talk of never again writing for the theatre from Bertie—and they at once began work on *Cinderella,* with a Christmas production in prospect. Clifton Parker was their chosen composer. . . .

By autumn Donat had acquired the beautiful St James Theatre (so wantonly torn down in 1957) for [the now renamed] *The Glass Slipper.* Hugh Stevenson designed exquisite décor, the actors were perfectly matched to their parts.

The plot follows the traditional story, that strange balance between the fairy world of ideal princes, princesses and magic, and the grim reality of jealous sisters, not enough to eat and dirty-washing up. The play was linked by songs which enhanced both the unearthly and the domestic. There was a flow to this collaboration, which seems to have been one which Bertie enjoyed as well as his sister. . . .

At Christmas the show was a triumph. Beverly Baxter's review in the *Evening Standard* stood out as fulsome as any author or composer greedy for praise could wish. . . .

The final paragraph runs: 'If we have left the authors to the last it is only because they deserve a final award. They have contrived to combine wit, phantasy and charm with unerring taste. *The Glass Slipper* is something no one who loves the creative theatre should miss. After many vicissitudes the lordly St James's has found a piece worthy of its past.' . . .

The urge to write remained constant when the three powerful characters in Eleanor's life, Harry, Bertie and Earle, were gone. She finished a children's play, *The Silver Curlew,* which was produced in Liverpool's Playhouse for Christmas 1948. The story was based on the Norfolk version of *Rumpelstiltskin,* with music by Clifton Parker.

There were fey additions: a man-in-the-moon bewitched into a loony fisherman, and a lady-in-the-moon bewitched into a silver curlew. The heroine turned out a greedy, lazy, dreamy cabbage-rose of a girl, who gobbled dumplings, leaving none for her hungry brothers. The dumpling song was very much better than the good food song for the 'Poor of London' in the Soyer operetta.

King Nollekens of Norfolk, who marries the lazy girl, on the understanding that she will spin a roomful of flax once a year, turned out to be a man with a double nature, wilful, affectionate and weak. There is much foolery and fun in this play, which alternates between the coy and charming. It was back to a Martin Pippin style of badinage, whimsicalities which would never have passed through the net of Bertie's criticism. The moral is cleverly overlaid by happy fantasies. The dialogue whisks along and there are good homely songs. . . .

At the christening four gifts are presented to the baby: a kind heart, happiness, magic and beauty. Eleanor herself had been given the first three, which is more than can be expected for most of us. . . .

During the 1950s new editions of old works for the young were republished by Michael Joseph and Oxford University Press. *Silver Sand and Snow* and *The Little Bookroom* are still her finest collections of poetry and prose, lively, imaginative and varied, works which are more complex than they appear and support her maxim that children grasp more than they can understand. . . .

*The Little Bookroom* was illustrated by Edward Ardizzone, the finest and most understanding of all the artists who ornamented her work. His drawings express more nearly than any others Eleanor's especial sense of the cosiness, dreaminess, and strangeness of childhood. In a letter to Grace Hogarth she wrote: 'My big thrill was the Ardizzone drawings for my autumn book of tales. [O.U.P. editor] John Bell told me they were the best things he'd ever done, and he thought so too; and when they were dropped in on me, last week-end, I turned them over, one after the other, with a lump in my throat. All I feel about childhood is in them, and I shall have two joys to look forward to this year; the *Slipper* is adorable, but the autumn book goes deeper, and may remain for me the happiest book of my life, so far as collaboration is concerned.' . . .

[Eleanor] never gave up wanting life to be a glorious feast of love and enjoyment, and never gave up the struggle to make it so, with remarkable success.

*Annabel Farjeon, in her* Morning Has Broken: A Biography of Eleanor Farjeon, *Julia MacRae, 1986, 315 p.*

# Charles Ferry

## 1927-

American author of fiction.

Major works include *Up in Sister Bay* (1975), *O Zebron Falls!* (1977), *Raspberry One* (1983), *One More Time!* (1985), *Binge* (1992).

## INTRODUCTION

Ferry is the author of several historical novels for young adults that are praised for their vivid characterizations and evocative sense of place as well as for their faithful recreations of the atmosphere surrounding the American youth subculture of the 1940s. In addition, he is recognized for creating a young adult novel that provides a graphic and controversial account of contemporary teenage alcoholism. His works commonly address such themes as the maturation process, racial prejudice, and the quality of life in small towns during the wartime years. Often setting his books in the Midwest while attempting to capture the flavor of the Big Band, Wartime era, Ferry profiles male and female adolescent protagonists whose experiences and relationships help them to cope with the vagaries of life. While some critics have found that his early novels involve complicated and improbable subplots, most have praised the careful balance that he achieves through his incorporation of fast-paced narratives and vivid description with insightful reflections on the emotional lives of his characters. Although he includes death, dismemberment, and other unflinching details in his books, Ferry also addresses such themes as the importance of friendship, falling in love, and other of, as he calls them, "life's sweet moments."

Born in Chicago, Ferry spent many of his summers in northern Wisconsin, the setting for his first novel, *Up in Sister Bay*. He served in the Navy from 1944 to 1949 before beginning a long career in journalism and radio. Although he received awards for his work in these fields, Ferry's efforts were progressively undermined by his continuing battle with alcoholism, an experience that later inspired *Binge*. As a young man, his dependency on alcohol led him into car theft, burglary, forgery, and other criminal activities; caught in Michigan at the age of twenty-six, he was incarcerated for several years. After his parole in 1970, Ferry began a successful recovery program and became a full-time writer of fiction. His first novel for young people, *Up in Sister Bay*, weaves stories based upon his childhood vacations into a narrative that examines the tribulations and challenges faced by four ambitious Wisconsin teenagers in 1939. In the highly acclaimed novel *Raspberry One*, which he calls "my little prayer that [war] will never happen again," he embellishes his own recollections of his experiences in the Navy with thoroughly researched accounts by other participants to create the story of two young crew members aboard a torpedo bomber, forced to confront their fears of death and eventually to

face injuries sustained at Okinawa before returning home. Paul Heins has noted that "rather than intellectualizing the wartime situation" the novel provides "a restrained but effective account of the varied experiences, not all of them unhappy, of two young Americans of the era." With *Binge*, Ferry departs from historical subjects to explore the problem of teenage alcoholism. Writing that *Binge* "is my personal redemption—and I have a lot to redeem," Ferry details the semi-autobiographical experience of an eighteen-year-old alcoholic and petty thief who wakes up to discover that his drunk driving accident has resulted in the loss of his foot and the death of the people struck by his car. The unabashed candor with which Ferry describes the results of his character's addiction and the absence of a happy ending have fostered controversy about the work, which was rejected by twelve major publishers of young adult literature. Forced to publish *Binge* independently, Ferry has been championed by several reviewers and other children's literature professionals. Considered a nonjudgmental and revealing story which is accessible despite its painfulness, *Binge* was described by Mary K. Chelton as an "incredibly powerful, mesmerizing, tragic, read-in-one-sitting little book with an authenticity and understanding rare in adolescent literature." Ferry notes: "If the book spares one young person the ravages of alcohol, I will consider it the greatest achievement of my life." *Raspberry One* was named the best book of 1983 by the Friends of American Writers as well as a Best Book for Young Adults by the American Library Association and a Best Book of the Year by *School Library Journal* in the same year. *Binge* was named an ALA Best Book for Young Adults in 1993, the first self-published book in the history of the organization to receive this award.

(See also *Contemporary Authors New Revision Series*, Vol. 16 and *Something about the Author*, Vol. 43.)

---

# AUTHOR'S COMMENTARY

*[The following excerpt is from an interview by K. Fawn Knight.]*

Charles Ferry's third novel for young people, *Raspberry One,* was published at a time of particular interest in war and its effects on children and children's books. A 1983 conference at the Cooperative Children's Book Center in Madison, Wisconsin, for example, examined "War as Metaphor" in children's literature. *Raspberry One* is set during World War II and deals with the effects of combat on two young Navy crewmen. It was listed as one of the best books of 1983 by both the Young Adult Services Division of the American Library Association and the *School Library Journal.* The Chicago-based Friends of American Writers recently presented Ferry with an award for *Raspberry One* as the best juvenile book of 1983. Not long ago, I had a chance to visit Mr. Ferry in his home and to talk with him about his work.

The Ferry home is a modest, ranch-style house in a subdivision of Rochester, Michigan. The house is well-loved and well-lived-in—"laid back," as Mr. Ferry cheerfully announced. Most of his writing is done in a corner of the living room with equipment no more pretentious than a portable typewriter posed on an end table and an A&P bag for a wastebasket. As we talked, we sat at the kitchen table in a dining room pleasantly awash with mementos of family, vacations, old friends, and past political campaigns.

Mr. Ferry has published two previous novels for teenagers, *Up in Sister Bay* and *O, Zebron Falls!* Writing fiction for young adults is a fairly recent development in his life, but communications is not. His professional career stretches back over thirty years in journalism, radio, and television, primarily in Texas and Michigan. Was his background in journalism a help when he began his first novel? He's not sure: "I knew how to compose a literate sentence, which fiction requires, after all." But the need for strict accuracy, so much a part of his journalism training, occasionally hampered him when he first began to write fiction. Readers of his first two novels know that they are set in actual places—*Up in Sister Bay* in the upstate Wisconsin of Charles Ferry's youth, *O, Zebron Falls!* in the Rochester of forty years ago. His new freedom to make changes in the actual geography to better fit the story was unsettling at first.

Still, it was his journalistic instincts, in part, that prompt-

ed him to write *Raspberry One.* Mr. Ferry has a passionate distaste for what he believes is historical "revisionism" in the treatment of World War II in many current novels for young people. It seemed to him that the authors of the books he read had a total disregard for either the facts or the feel of the period. He was determined to make his book an accurate account of the attitudes and experiences common to people in this country in the 1940s.

Ferry's book takes place in 1944 and recounts the experiences of two young Navy crewmen assigned to the dive bomber *Raspberry One,* stationed on the fictional carrier the U.S.S. *Shiloh.* Mr. Ferry wanted Nick and Hildy's story to be representative of the experiences of young men who fought in World War II. To that end, the actual writing of *Raspberry One* was preceded by more than a year of research. He read histories of every major naval engagement in the Pacific, studied every carrier, read eyewitness accounts of combat in the area, and interviewed two men who had survived the devastating Kamikaze attack on the U.S.S. *Franklin* (the prototype of the *Shiloh*). The result is a meticulously researched historical novel, permeated by a strong sense of patriotism and personal conviction. If some of the values expressed make readers today uneasy, Mr. Ferry is unapologetic. "None of my characters shed a tear when the [atomic] bombs are dropped," he says flatly. "People didn't—not in this country, not then." They were relieved that the United States had not been invaded and that the war was over.

It is, he believes, enormously important not to "write down" to young people. World War II, he emphasizes, was a war "fought by young people." He himself was only 16 when he "sneaked" into the Navy and was sent to flight school. The main characters in *Raspberry One* are all in their late teens. Young people should know their own history, presented accurately: "I didn't try to tell a moral. Pointing out how bad war is was not in my mind. I just tried to be faithful to the material."

The book was almost a "pure conception" to him. He knew immediately what the focal point of the novel would be: a newsreel seen in a theater forty years ago, but never forgotten, of the *Franklin*'s heroic entry into New York Harbor. The *Shiloh* was modeled after "Big Ben." Curiously, his intention to make the harbor scene the climactic one in the book altered as he wrote. When he had finished his talent show scene, in which the few grievously wounded survivors of the *Shiloh* put on a cheerful show for their rescuers, he decided that this was the emotion he really wanted to capture. Consequently, the harbor scene was never written.

Other changes, major and minor, were made in the earliest versions of the book as well. Originally written in the first person, the novel was rewritten in the third person, broadening the conception beyond the experience of only one flyer. Hildy changed, too, as the novel developed. "He surprised me!" Mr. Ferry admits. Originally intended to be an emotional casualty of the war, Hildy just wouldn't stay down. "He just kept saying, 'I'm not giving up.'"

He usually works from legal pads on which he has jotted ideas, "prompts," as he calls them. From these snatches and pieces, he types successive drafts, writing and rewriting extensively, moving from chapter to chapter and back again. Although he wrote his first two books back-to-front, as it were, beginning with the final chapter, *Raspberry One* was written roughly in chronological sequence. Part I (and Chapter 1) were written first, and then Part III, the closing chapters of the novel. He avoided the combat scenes because he was worried that they were the only part of the novel where he would not be drawing on his personal experience (the war ended at about the time he finished flight school), but he actually wrote them rather rapidly and with comparative ease once he came to them.

Does he think of himself as a writer for young people? "I don't write for *young* people. I write for people of any age. I know that what I write is most applicable to young people, but that's all that is in my mind."

In a sense, he writes for himself. He quotes Emily Dickinson: "How can I know what I think until I see what I have written?" Franny's and Nick's fathers, both warm and sympathetic men in *Raspberry One,* are products of a new understanding of his own father.

Robbie Van Epp, the main character in *Up in Sister Bay,* rarely sees his father. Lukie Bishop, the 16-year-old protagonist of *O, Zebron Falls!*, struggles painfully to communicate with her father. "Sometimes she thought she loved [her beloved Uncle Farnie] more than she loved her father—and felt guilty about thinking that way." Only in researching *Raspberry One,* Mr. Ferry says, did he begin to understand what his own father, a gunner in World War I, must have endured. "All my characters are 'me,' " he muses, "composites of people I've known. Next time I'll do a father *in spades.*"

Occasionally a character is suggested by a particular person in his life. Sister Joan Therese, Charles Ferry's own eighth-grade teacher at St. Joseph School, was transformed into Robbie's dear friend, and her pet phrase, "stick-to-it-iveness," appears in *Sister Bay,* as well.

There is a sense of audience, however, in the seriousness with which he views his own writing. He is, he says, "spinning yarns," but not only that. He is also trying to write "honestly," a term he borrows from Hemingway. Any conversation with Charles Ferry, one quickly discovers, is full of allusions to his favorite authors: Hemingway, Dickinson, Salinger. From Chekhov he quotes the idea of the "concrete universal," the one evocative detail that will stand emotionally for all the other details that might have been included. He tries to include just enough detail to trigger the reader's own imagination. When he deals with sexuality, as he does in all three of his novels, he tries to suggest intimacy, rather than detailing it, both from respect for the young reader's privacy, he says, and from a belief in the power of the imagination. He uses profanity sparingly, even when writing about life in the Navy, from the same conviction: gratuitous detail kills a book.

One also can't talk long with Mr. Ferry without realizing that he is a man with vigorous opinions on a wide range of subjects. A slightly built man in his mid-fifties, he is graying and so thin he appears almost frail, an impression that fades as he talks energetically about his hobbies and particular concerns. Politics, natural foods, the mass media, and values are all areas of strong conviction. Although he graduated from high school and "dabbled" a bit in college, he is fond of saying that he is the product of a "good eighth-grade education" and laments that schoolchildren today don't seem to him to have the same exposure to fine writing and music as earlier generations.

A distinct vision of life in the rural Midwest, as an earlier generation experienced it, permeates both *Up in Sister Bay* and *O, Zebron Falls! Up in Sister Bay* is set in the last year or so before the outbreak of World War II. It is 1939. Robbie and his friends Libby, Jim, and Charlie plan to homestead Loon Lodge, but their plans are threatened by hidden small-town scandals, by racial prejudice, and by the coming war. Critics have applauded Mr. Ferry's ability to evoke a particular place and time in his novels. *Up in Sister Bay* is, in part, an evocative celebration of the seasons and tempo of life in rural Wisconsin.

*O, Zebron Falls!* celebrates small-town life. Lukie Bishop lives in a rural Michigan town of Tuesday night Musicales, community fish fries, hometown football games, and seemingly unshakeable stability. Lukie imagines that she and her classmates will always live in the Zebron Falls she knows: "That was how it had always been . . . and that was how it would be with them. It was the one great certainty of her life." The intrusion of World War II into her placid world, and the death of her Uncle Farnie, force Lukie to wonder for the first time if Zebron Falls *will* always be the same and finally bring her to the painful realization that the town she knows is not the same town for others—notably, her best friend Billy, the only black student in her high school. But, in both novels, the security and goodness of small-town life and values are ultimately confirmed.

It is tempting to suspect some nostalgia here, and at least one critic has suggested that Mr. Ferry's books attribute a rather rosy-colored hue to the lives of people forty years ago. Are his books nostalgic? No, he says, they don't represent a hankering to go back to an earlier period of his life. They are, he believes, authentic—showing what a particular period of our history was like. His books try to say, believe it or not, "this is the way it was."

Certainly the battle scenes in *Raspberry One* are powerful and present a horrifying picture of war. They are a serious treatment of combat for young readers. The scenes aboard the floundering *Shiloh* are, I think, the best that he's written to date.

*K. Fawn Knight, "Interview with Charles Ferry," in* Children's literature in education, *Vol. 16, No. 1, Spring, 1985, pp. 15-20.*

## TITLE COMMENTARY

### *Up in Sister Bay* (1975)

The best of all possible worlds . . . Sister Bay, Wisconsin just before the outbreak of World War II, where Robbie and his buddies—Libby who had polio, the Chippewa orphan Jim and "spastic" Charlie—dream of an even better life they'll build on a communal homestead they plan to call Loon Lodge. But first Charlie (he's the only one old enough to apply for homestead land) must be cleared of charges that he burned down the tannery, and that means finding the will left by the town's recently suicided great (and often drunk) lady to expose the scheming, disinherited Herr Doktor. The plot unfolds in snatches of dialogue, homey colloquies from the bachelor Swede who takes an interest in their future, and much glorying in the season of youth, the rightness of small town life and the rhythms of nature in general. Often this goes too far, as with Libby rhapsodizing over her own efflorescence and glorying in the day when she finally "blooms" (though she decides at the last minute not to share all this with Robbie until after marriage). But the misty lakeside setting, the characters' isolation from news of the impending war, and Robbie's own innocence of the dark, small town secrets that threaten his dream all dovetail with the Ecclesiastes-like philosophy. And Ferry's narration—not innovative surely, but somewhat more sophisticated than the single viewpoint, 1-2-3 chronology juvenile authors so often rely on—makes a pleasant change of pace. You want to believe in Loon Lodge and in these north country gothic characters, and you can if you want to believe long enough to see Robbie through a mystery that threatens to shatter his faith.

> *A review of "Up in Sister Bay," in* Kirkus Reviews, *Vol. XLIII, No. 16, August 15, 1975, p. 924.*

When Ferry, remembering, writes of the fresh smell of rain blowing in from the northwest, of the flight of a majestic blue heron, of the terrifying sensation of swimming through a set of dangerous rapids in the dark, I am with him doing my own remembering.

As long as he is describing these wonders and Robbie's dreams for holding onto them by homesteading on Big Chetac with his three best friends, Ferry is successful. Unfortunately, he has chosen to involve Robbie in a trite gothic plot featuring the mysterious death of an heiress, a missing will, a secret tunnel and a menacing Prussian "Herr Doktor." The book is also marred by too many all-knowing adults who keep giving the kind of advice about life which my teen-age sons would characterize sarcastically as "heavy. . . . very heavy." ("Nothin' comes free, Robbie. Sooner or later we all have to pay the piper.")

It pains me to write this way about Ferry's novel because I believe he is capable of better work. When he can describe with such poignancy the land and the vulnerability of being 17, he doesn't need to let his characters indulge in ponderous philosophizing. Nor does he need to manufacture melodramatic events better suited to Transylvania than to Wisconsin.

> *Susan Terris, in a review of "Up in Sister Bay," in* The New York Times Book Review, *November 2, 1975, p. 10.*

In the story the dialogue is sometimes strained and stilted, and some awkwardness and contrivance exist in the plot. But the author has achieved in his first book something not always within the grasp of more seasoned writers—a sense of place. Impressions of small-town Wisconsin—the

prejudices and communality, the beauty of the land—filter through the prose, giving the book its feeling of stability and timelessness.

> *Anita Silvey, in a review of "Up in Sister Bay," in* The Horn Book Magazine, *Vol. LI, No. 6, December, 1975, p. 601.*

So many events and attempts at characterization are jammed into the first few chapters that readers are overwhelmed. Sorting out who died, who's in jail accused of arson, why Livvie lives only for the time when she'll marry Robbie, how insensitive Robbie is to unfair treatment of his Chippewa friend Jim, and a variety of other small-town incidents and personalities is tiresome and pointless. One thing is clear—teenagers Robbie, Livvie, and Jim, and their older friend Charlie dream of an idyllic, self-sufficient homestead on the Up Holly (outside their town of Sister Bay, Wisconsin). But problems abound—only Charlie is old enough to sign the homestead papers, Robbie's family moves to Chicago, Jim is sent to the Indian reservation, and the three teenagers feel they need to solve the mystery of Alvia Ivors' death and the subsequent fire in town. None of these is particularly well developed, and neither are any of the characters: Jim and Robbie behave much younger than 17 and the adults, when they aren't shadowy, are weak or bickering or they die young.

> *Susan Sprague, in a review of "Up in Sister Bay," in* School Library Journal, *Vol. 22, No. 4, December, 1975, p. 59.*

---

### O Zebron Falls! (1977)

In retrospect the 1940's, war and all, appear to be nearly a golden age of domestic tranquility. Zebron Falls, Michigan, is a cozy small town in which young and old are friends, young people are hardworking and respectful, and the future seems certain and secure. Lukie Bishop, sixteen years old at the beginning of the novel, is an amiable girl, a loving daughter, and a serious student. Essentially, the novel is the story of her last years in high school from 1942 to 1944—when she is elected Class Sweetheart—a happy, exciting time of football triumphs, parties, and dances. Her dearest friend is Billy Butts, football hero, valedictorian, president of the student council, and the son of the only black family in town. Some tragedies inevitably happen—a young man is killed in the war, Lukie's uncle dies in an explosion in a munitions factory, and her beloved dog Lady dies of old age. The only real flaw in the golden society is the fact that the long relationship between Lukie and Billy—a true love—can never, under any circumstances, come to maturity. Somewhat reminiscent of Maureen Daly's *Seventeenth Summer*, the fine, realistic novel contains the sweetness of a simpler time but emphasizes that every era has its unsolvable problems.

> *Ann A. Flowers, in a review of "O Zebron Falls!," in* The Horn Book Magazine, *Vol. LIII, No. 5, October, 1977, p. 539.*

The characters' malt shop dialogue with its "gollies" and "darns" is believable and, despite the remote setting and

*Ferry with wife Ruth and, he writes, "beloved Belgian sheepdog, 'Darling Girl'."*

much-too-saccharine ending, young readers will easily identify with Lukie's heartbreaks and concerns.

*Jack Forman, in a review of "O Zebron Falls!," in* School Library Journal, *Vol. 24, No. 2, October, 1977, p. 123.*

Lukie is a teenage girl of a generation ago. Yet today's young reader may readily identify with her problems and fears: growing up, falling in love, maturing sexually, relating to one's parents, and deciding one's future.

The book shows the secure closeness of small-town America but it also contains the prejudices and stereotypes that existed pre-feminism and pre-Civil Rights. For example, adults advise Lukie to get an education because "girls should have something to fall back on—like teaching or nursing." Also, Lukie's very popular black friend, Bill Butts, is always aware of the unspoken racial barriers in Zebron Falls—the limits which he must never transgress.

Lukie's anxieties stem from her unsure relationships with the men in her life: her father and his twin brother, Farnie; Billy Butts and Harvey Toles. Once she understands her feelings and places them in proper perspective, she begins to mature. She can now deal with, and accept, changes in her life.

Lukie's graduation day is a symbolic and literal climax,

described in detail, and brimming with emotions familiar at graduations: wistfulness, happiness, sadness, melancholy, anticipation, excitement. Yet, even as Lukie makes the wish to hold onto this day, she will never truly lose it. For Lukie, this is not only a graduation, but a commencement: the beginning of adulthood coupled with optimism about the future.

Charles Ferry has capably made his point about the young person of 1944 and his 1977 counterpart: in the fundamentals, nothing has changed.

*Marianne M. Rafalko, in a review of "O Zebron Falls!," in* Best Sellers, *Vol. 37, No. 9, December, 1977, p. 293.*

In those good old days when Charles Ferry and I and one or two others were young, life was a lot simpler. People were 95 percent kindly, the sun shone, the war seemed far away. Really? Of course not. Mr. Ferry has sprinkled his story with a variety of problems: strained family relationships, a young boy's incipient blindness, a smattering of racism, the battlefront death of a classmate.

But nostalgia for a vanished Never Never Land of innocence shimmers over every part of this story like a mist, obscuring certain realities and making of it finally only a fiction. I was there, in the Middle West, along with those one or two others, and what I remember—vividly—is that the war was our total environment. Mr. Ferry all but ignores the Victory gardens, the scrap drives, the testing of those terrible air-raid sirens in the schools, the ominous blackout curtains, standing endlessly in line for everything from shoes to meat to sugar. It was a grim, glorious, anxiety-ridden time. Surely Lukie Bishop would have been touched more deeply.

Further, it seems to me improbable that Lukie would have been permitted an almost-sweetheart relationship with a black boy; that he would have been the only black boy in town, and football captain, president of the Student Council and candidate for valedictorian to boot. Not impossible. Improbable. The nation was innocent in those days, but innocence cuts two ways: We didn't always know when we were being cruel. Finally, I can't believe in this young black, Billy. I can't believe that Lukie could be homecoming chairman and still have no date for the prom, or that, the following year, she could be elected Class Sweetheart. Those things always went to the most-popular girls.

And I can't believe in an entire senior class so stirred by the chance of breaking a school scholastic record that it studies extra hard for final exams. Mr. Panella, a teacher, says, "It seems abnormal." I agree.

*O Zebron Falls!* is a gentle book, full of love, and there's no use denying that it squeezes the heart. But only that corner of the heart where we over-40 types store our most sentimental memories. I don't think the current young will be impressed.

> *Natalie Babbitt, in a review of "O Zebron Falls!," in* The New York Times Book Review, *March 5, 1978, p. 26.*

---

### Raspberry One (1983)

A story of wartime friendships, loves, and tragedies views World War II in the Pacific (1944) through the close-up perspectives of two young air crewmen. In the first section of his novel, Ferry introduces Hildy and Nick, his 19-year-old protagonists, and the college girls they meet at a reception for servicemen—Franny, the Jewish girl whom Catholic Nick decides to marry when he returns from the war, and Diane, the dedicated artist who designs an insignia for the **Raspberry One,** the plane that the airmen will fly. Exciting flight sequences pepper the latter part of the novel, which follows the fliers to Iwo Jima then on to Okinawa as they struggle with feelings of cowardice, cope with the death of comrades and the grisly reality of war, and experience emotional and physical injuries that forever change them. Slow to start but battle scenes are vivid and the 1940s stateside atmosphere is effectively and carefully rendered.

> *Stephanie Zvirin, in a review of "Raspberry One," in* Booklist, *Vol. 79, No. 18, May 15, 1983, p. 1196.*

The military aspect of the novel is presented objectively and makes extensive use of the vocabulary of tactical communications; but the horror of the situation breaks through as Nick becomes aware of "limbs flying through the air," mutilated bodies, and the ever-present sharks ready to attack unfortunate men in the water. Rather than intellectualizing the wartime situation, the three sections of the narrative—"Good Times," "The Pacific," and "The Hospital"—give a restrained but effective account of the varied experiences, not all of them unhappy, of two young Americans of the era. With a glossary of World War II expressions and idioms.

> *Paul Heins, in a review of "Raspberry One," in* The Horn Book Magazine, *Vol. LIX, No. 3, June, 1983, p. 310.*

Long on action and strong in characterization and description, this is the well-written story of Nick and Hildy, who serve as Navy torpedo bomber crewmen aboard the *U.S.S. Shiloh* in the South Pacific during the latter part of World War II. Ferry skillfully sees to it that by the time they receive their "baptism by fire" at Iwo Jima, we know these two young men and their girlfriends and have empathy for them, their backgrounds and the times in which they live. Nick, we learn, lives in constant fear of cowardice; however, when their pilot is wounded and Nick loses his hand during a *Kamikaze* attack on the Inland Sea, he draws upon his inner resources to deal with these situations and their aftermath. A moving narrative that rises above a plot and events common to many war novels.

> *David A. Lindsey, in a review of "Raspberry One," in* School Library Journal, *Vol. 30, No. 1, September, 1983, pp. 132-33.*

Characters are well realized and are a slight cut above stereotype. Hildy is the All-American midwestern boy-hero who falls apart when wounded; Nick is the more contemplative, from an upper crust Philadelphia background, fearful of battle, but who develops a strong quiet inner strength.

The story is told primarily through dialogue, there is a cinematic sense reminiscent of the war movies of the late 1940s. There is plenty of action and a hint of romance. This certainly captures the sense of history of the time period, without any glorification of war and will provide a feeling for what the generation of young people in the 1940s experienced in their teen years. A glossary of terms is included.

> *Micki S. Nevett, in a review of "Raspberry One," in* Voice of Youth Advocates, *Vol. 7, No. 1, April, 1984, p. 30.*

---

### One More Time! (1985)

Ferry's new novel immerses teenagers in the era of the big bands at the onset of World War II. The Gene Markham Orchestra tops the charts, and lead clarinet Skeets Sinclair tells the story of events during the company's last national tour before its breakup. Excitement, apprehension and a tinge of melancholy affect the musicians in different ways. Skeets loves Polly Breen, the 18-year-old singer, but doesn't think he has a chance with her; he's short, near-sighted and 4-F. Harry Swanson, Skeets's buddy, drinks some; he's a whiz at the piano, but he's depressed by his fiancée's sneering at his profession. Road manager Gus Oshinsky worries about his soldier son when he's not laying down the law to Harry and the other young musicians. Reserved, "by the book" Gene is regarded as cold until his people find out about their leader's reaction to the manager of a Detroit ballroom who calls the cops to evict black customers. The author compels deep interest in all the characters and, above all, in the splendid music of a bygone day, described so that it's almost audible.

*A review of "One More Time!," in* Publishers Weekly, *Vol. 227, No. 13, March 29, 1985, p. 73.*

There's no real hero in Ferry's latest novel. Short, "four-eyes" Skeets Sinclair, who narrates the story, somehow doesn't quite qualify for the traditional title. Nor, in fact, is there much in the way of sustained plot excitement to propel the book along. Yet Ferry has done an extraordinary job of evoking the flavor of big-band music at its peak and capturing the nostalgia and the trepidation of the American people as they look back on an era of peace and ahead toward the unknown. Characters, while not three-dimensional, grow distinct as the story evolves; the backdrop is exceptionally vivid; and Ferry demonstrates an easy familiarity with musical conventions. But its riches notwithstanding, the novel will be most appreciated by the special reader in touch with swing or in search of a glimpse of how World War II affected some of those at home.

*Stephanie Zvirin, in a review of "One More Time!," in* Booklist, *Vol. 81, No. 18, May 15, 1985, p. 1325.*

Putting to work his skillful powers of characterization and description (previously demonstrated in **Raspberry One,**) Ferry has constructed yet another well-crafted narrative which artfully gives readers a detailed knowledge of and an empathy for his characters and the milieu in which they live. . . . Strong on setting and characterization but lacking the fast action and tension found in most stories set during World War II, this story of the Big Band era and those who were a part of it may have limited appeal to junior high students.

*David A. Lindsey, in a review of "One More Time!," in* School Library Journal, *Vol. 31, No. 10, August, 1985, p. 74.*

A genuine stroll down memory lane, **One More Time!** is an engaging first-person account of the tribulations and triumphs of the Gene Markham Orchestra during its last cross-country tour in 1941 and 1942. Narrated by nineteen-year-old Skeets Sinclair, tenor saxophonist and lead clarinetist, the story recreates the period through references to timely topics, such as the draft, the bombing of Pearl Harbor, and America's entry into the war, and through the more homely details of transportation, salaries, and family backgrounds. There is a bittersweet quality in the telling. . . . The pace is energetic; the descriptions of life on the road during the big band era are realistic; the earthier aspects of the relationship between Skeets and Polly are handled almost as discreetly as a 1940s flick featuring Van Johnson and June Allyson. A well-crafted, lovingly nostalgic look at times past, the book has all the

right ingredients for a musical as intoxicating as the band's theme song "Moonlight Cocktail."

*Mary M. Burns, in a review of "One More Time!," in* The Horn Book Magazine, *Vol. LXI, No. 5, September-October, 1985, p. 563.*

---

*Binge* **(1992)**

# AUTHOR'S COMMENTARY

**Binge** is my personal redemption—and I have a lot to redeem. The very last page of the book tells of my 25-year battle with alcohol and of some of the horrors it caused in my life. It says, "Ferry openly admits that he drank his way into seventeen different jails, three of them twice." That is quite a record, but it is not the entire story. It should say, "Ferry drank his way into seventeen different jails, three of them twice, and one of them the largest walled jail in the world: the State Prison of Southern Michigan."

For over three years, my address was 4000 Cooper Street, Jackson, Michigan. My number was 89750 (you'll find that number in the book). And my zip code, so to speak, was "5-2-13"—Five Block, tier two, cell thirteen. For over three years, I lived with screams in the night and the rumbling of heavy steel doors. One week, in the Hole (solitary confinement), I lived in a darkened cell and lost track of time.

Why was I sent to prison? Forgery and uttering and publishing—three-and-a-half to fourteen years. The sentence was handed down in Ann Arbor by the late Judge James M. Breakey. His sentence may seem rather harsh, but it wasn't. You see, Ann Arbor was merely the tip of the iceberg. Ann Arbor was the culmination of a six-month, nine-state binge, during which I was a mini-crime wave. Two stolen cars, one abandoned, one totaled. Five break-ins, most of them senseless. Bad checks, whenever I got my hands on a blank one. Larceny, whenever there was an opportunity. Anything to keep alcohol flowing through my bloodstream.

In addition to Michigan, the states were Illinois, Wisconsin, Texas, Vermont, Massachusetts, New York, Pennsylvania, and New Jersey. It was in New Jersey that I left a young man, drunk and passed out, in a motel room, with nothing but his underwear, and made off with all of his possessions—his car, his clothes, his money and personal records. In **Binge,** the central character, Weldon Yeager, does the same thing and then assumes his victim's identity. Weldon becomes Richard C. Wessell; I became F. William Ross. And after totaling Mr. Ross's car, I came to Ann Arbor with his money and academic credentials and registered at the University of Michigan, an impostor.

I could continue recounting my masquerade in Ann Arbor. I could tell you about the apartment on William Street, above a bicycle shop, which I shared with two other students and where my chief activity was organizing parties. Or I could tell you about how I was a familiar figure at the Pretzel Bell, freely spending stolen money. But it is enough that you know that I soon ran out of money and decided to commit another crime.

Now, when an alcoholic commits a crime, he looks for familiar surroundings or circumstances, which will give him a sense of security. I chose St. Andrew's Episcopal Church. I am an Episcopalian. Before my disintegration, I was active in the church in Texas, where I worked in radio. Professionally, I had a solid reputation for talent and ability. In newspapers, I had done award-winning work. In radio, one of my documentaries had been carried by the CBS radio network. One of my scripts had been narrated by a prominent Hollywood actor of that time, Dana Andrews. And now the talented journalist was going to knock off a church.

One Sunday evening, while activities were in progress downstairs, I slipped unnoticed into the parish library. No one was there. I sat down in an easy chair, with an open book in my lap, and pretended that I had fallen asleep. Soon the lights went out and everyone left. I was alone in the church.

Groping in the dark, I made my way up to the church office, searching for money. I found none, but in the desk of the rector—the rector at that time, 1955, was the Reverend Henry Lewis—and in Father Lewis's desk I found a large business-type checkbook on the church's seminarian fund. The next day, at two different branches of the old Ann Arbor Bank, I cashed two checks—each for $150, each made out to Charles Ferry (there was no Charles Ferry in town; I figured I was safe), and each signed by Henry Lewis.

I had no difficulty in cashing the checks; I never had difficulty in cashing bad checks. Why? Because of my appearance. I was a clean-cut young man. I was personable and had a nice smile. And I was a con artist. All alcoholics are con artists; they have to be to get away with their drinking. And so I would engage bank tellers in a pleasant conversation, distracting their attention. At the Ann Arbor bank, they never bothered to check my ID. Weldon Yeager does this in *Binge,* with a stolen credit card.

There was a kind of pattern to my binge. I kept returning to places where life had been good, where I had been good, as if those places would make life good again. Instead, I simply replaced good memories with bad ones. I dirtied up my past.

And whenever I got my hands on some money, I would resolve, quite seriously, that this would be the end of the binge. I would use the money to pull myself together. I would get a job and start rebuilding my life. I would do that tomorrow. But tomorrow never came. For an alcoholic, one drink is too many; a thousand aren't enough.

And so the binge went on. I continued my high living. I even opened a checking account in my assumed name, which was a reckless thing to do. Give an alcoholic a checking account and he will cash bad checks; it's as certain as death and taxes. Soon, I had forged checks out in the name of Charles Ferry and bounced checks in the name of F. William Ross. I was leaving a trail forty miles wide.

And then one Monday morning, I was alone in the apartment above the bicycle shop, sleeping off a Sunday drunk. The door was unlocked. Two detectives came in and shook me awake.

"Mr. Ross?" one of them asked me. "Have you ever used the name Charles Ferry?"

The binge was over. The disgrace was about to commence. First, in the press—the *Michigan Daily,* the *Ann Arbor News,* the Detroit newspapers, the wire services, radio, television, the works. The University of Michigan impostor was quite a story. And then being led through the streets of downtown Ann Arbor, with other prisoners, from the county jail to the old courthouse on Huron Street. Friends I had made at the university stopped their car and stared in disbelief at the clean-cut impostor, in chains.

One day at the county jail, I was taken down to the room where lawyers conferred with prisoners. The court had appointed a public defender for me. But today, it wasn't my lawyer; it was the Reverend Henry Lewis, the man from whom I had stolen, the man whose church I had violated.

We had a long talk, and Father Lewis saw in me something worth saving. He was in the courtroom when I was sentenced. Without him, I'm sure I would have gone to pieces. For hearing a judge sentencing you to prison, at age twenty-six, has to be the most emotionally devastating experience there is. But Father Lewis was there; someone cared.

He said he would come visit me, and he did. Not just once, but several times. He was my only visitor in prison; my family knew nothing of my whereabouts.

In fair weather or foul, Father Lewis would drive from Ann Arbor to Jackson. Then a long walk from the parking lot to the administration building, followed by a long wait in the visitors' lobby. When his number was called, there was the indignity of being frisked by a guard. Then through an enormous steel door, twelve inches thick, which was locked behind him. Then through a second thick door, which was also locked behind him, while I came out through a third thick door and met him in the visitors' room, this distinguished, silver-haired Episcopal priest, in a blue suit and a Roman collar, a truly remarkable man, whose friends included the great American historian Samuel Elliot Morison, whose father had founded the University of Pennsylvania Law School and served as its first dean. He did all of this for a fifteen-minute visit with me, number 89750, three or four times a year. He did it because he had seen in me something worth saving.

But Father Lewis did much more than just visit; he became an important influence in our prison life. He arranged for the rector of the Episcopal church in the city of Jackson to hold monthly communion services for the Episcopalian inmates (there were only three of us). And when he learned that one of the inmates had never been confirmed in the church, Father Lewis arranged for Bishop Richard Emerich to come to the prison and confirm him.

Our services were held in the Protestant chaplain's private

*Ferry with Brian Wildsmith (left) and Robert Cormier, 1984.*

office. Our altar was a large window sill. The window looked out on the entrance to Fifteen Block, thirty feet away. Fifteen Block was the infamous "Hole," where I had once lost track of time. And that was the backdrop for a priest and a bishop administering the sacraments of the church to our tiny congregation. It tells you a lot about the Episcopal Church; it tells you a lot about Henry Lewis.

When I came up for parole, Father Lewis arranged a job for me, in Detroit, and referred me to a young adult fellowship group that met Sunday evenings at St. Paul's Cathedral. Three months after I was paroled, I attended a meeting of that group. I was immediately struck by a very attractive and vivacious woman who gave a report on a forthcoming St. Patrick's Day party at her duplex in Royal Oak. Six months later that woman became my wife. But before Ruth and I were married, I took her to Ann Arbor to meet Father Lewis. He was overjoyed by the news of our plans to marry. I think he felt that his work was done, that I was now in good hands. And I was, but I still had a twelve-year battle against alcohol.

It was the last time I ever saw Father Lewis. I learned just recently that he passed away two years ago at his retire-ment home in Brunswick, Maine. He was ninety-seven years of age. The Reverend Henry Lewis was a true man of God. He was my salvation. As you will learn, I couldn't have made it without my loving wife. Without Henry Lewis, I never would have met her. My life, my books, everything—I owe it all to Henry Lewis.

Ruth was unaware of the bumpy road that lay ahead. She was unaware of how severe my alcohol addiction was— but she soon learned. A year after we were married, I joined Alcoholics Anonymous, but it was on and off, up and down, good years, bad years. I was dysfunctional for most of that time; I couldn't hold a job for very long, and I had a few good ones. Ruth, who was executive travel co-ordinator at the J. L. Hudson Company (the big down-town store), held everything together, but it wasn't easy. For example, in 1969, on Halloween actually, I had collected some money owed me for some work I had done. The money was to be applied to household bills. Instead, I stormed out of the house in a drunken rage, took our only car, and ended up five days later in the state of Wyoming. Ruth, meantime, was left stranded. A friend had to drive out from Royal Oak each day, drive her to work, and then drive her home at night.

But blessedly, her ordeal was nearly over. In 1970, I bottomed out. For me, hitting bottom was a matter of totally running out of gas, so to speak. I was completely drained of energy. I didn't have the energy to pour a drink or put a gun to my head, which is what I felt like doing, I didn't have the energy to think. I was in a black pit of despair.

But once you hit bottom, I learned, once you decide that you're tired of the pain and anguish, tired of kicking yourself in the head, tired of the vomit and urine of drunk tanks, tired of seventeen different jails, three of them twice and one of them the largest walled jail in the world; once you decide you're tired of all that—there's no way to go but up.

Somehow, I found the strength to start clawing my way out of the pit. I wasn't at all hopeful; I had tried to lick alcohol so many times before and had always failed. But inch by inch, with the help of my loving wife, the principles of AA, and William Shakespeare—I made it. I am now in my twenty-third year of recovery.

You're probably wondering how William Shakespeare figures into this story? Very importantly. From him, I learned a rule of life that I recommend to everyone, especially alcoholics:

Hamlet, Act I, Scene 3. Polonius, the father of Ophelia, is speaking:

> This above all, to thine own self be true,
> And it must follow, as the night the day,
> Thou canst not then be false to any man.

I have revised those words and added an important proviso: "This above all, be true to the best that is in you/And help other people." We all need help. Everyone reading this needs help; the only difference is in the intensity of the need.

This above all, be true to the best that is in you, and help other people. When we help other people, our own troubles fall away. Of course, all of this is in the *Bible*, which is an appropriate point to conclude, specifically with St. John.

St. John tells us that the truth shall make us free. And it will. And it has. First, before Rotary International, in the town where I once disgraced myself, and now here, I am free at last.

> Charles Ferry, "How 'Binge' Came to Be Written," in Voice of Youth Advocates, *Vol. 16, No. 4, October, 1993, pp. 206-08.*

---

Think about this: There's a little soft-cover book you should read between now and prom night, or the next wet event. That's "should" as in you'll be glad you did so. You won't be bored. Guaranteed.

The book is titled, **Binge.** It's a short novel, written by Charles Ferry of Rochester Hills. He's a nonpracticing alcoholic who was once a kid and remembers how it was to be young, invincible, immortal and frequently thirsty.

**Binge** is about how alcohol can seduce and destroy young lives. No, it does not preach. . . . This tale illuminates,

as in turning on lights in a dark place. It neither judges nor condemns. It only reveals, chillingly.

You'll recognize the main character. He's someone you know and like, because he's a great guy. Maybe he's you. You'll recognize other characters, too. They're a lot like people, all ages, that we all know.

Ferry wrote his book to share his knowledge and understanding with the age 12-and-up crowd, but he couldn't find a publisher. Sometimes that happens.

Maybe publishers thought **Binge** was too realistic, candid, unsugared for a young audience. Who can figure publishers? Ferry finally published the book himself, with help from an anonymous benefactor.

That's the kiss-of-death to most reviewers. Ditto booksellers. Ferry's work was outside the commercial publisher-reviewer-book-seller chain of distribution.

The American Library Association (ALA) took a look, however. The ALA awards committee read **Binge.** Members were delighted with the work.

"It reads like a bullet," said Dr. Helen F. Flowers, a member of the committee. "Once I began it, I couldn't put it down; nor could other members of our committee."

In late January, **Binge** beat out 309 other nominations for the ALA's Best Book award in the young adult category.

**Binge** is a good story by an author who doesn't talk down to his young audience, or pretend kids are as innocent as parents wish they were and kids try to pretend they are, especially on prom night.

> Nickie McWhirter, "Illuminating Book about Kids Drinking Turns on Lights in Some Dark Places," in The Detroit News, *April 4, 1993, p. 7C.*

Eighteen-year-old Weldon Yaeger wakes up in a hospital, unable to remember how he got there. In the next several hours, he learns that he not only has killed two people and gravely injured two others in a drunk driving accident for which he is under police guard, but also that he has lost his right foot in the same accident. Under the sympathetic, watchful eye of Nurse Weatherby, he is methodically interrogated by a police lieutenant, for whom he has to reconstruct how he managed to get to where he is right now. As he answers Lieutenant Becker's questions and remembers events leading up to the accident, we learn that he is first and foremost a drunk who can't hold a job, maintain his grades, get his father's respect, or get it up for a girl—even a willing one—and that he has been an unacknowledged alcoholic since he was offered a whiskey sour at a neighborhood wedding as a young adolescent. By the time he has the accident, he has also become a car and credit card thief, and a murderer. His last thought as the book ends with the television news announcing that the fourth person in the accident has died, is "He needed a drink. God, how he needed a drink."

This is an incredibly powerful, mesmerizing, tragic, read-in-one-sitting little book with an authenticity and understanding rare in adolescent literature outside Chris Crutcher's work and *Crosses* by Shelley Stoehr. It pulls no punches, offers no pat endings, just describes a kid mired in his own alcoholic denial. A particularly disgusting and deliberately provocative scene describes Weldon's attack of dry heaves, coupled with bowel and bladder loss in a motel where he stayed after a binge on a stolen credit card. While painful to read, the author makes the point relentlessly that alcohol kills in many ways, including destroying the person who drinks. There are no little feel-good sermons here about the dangers of drinking. Ferry lets the facts of Weldon's impotence, bowel and bladder dysfunctions, and his drunk driver murders speak for themselves. This is not for squeamish adults, but I can only agree that it will probably give a few kids second thoughts. It is an absolutely superb book, highly readable, and relentlessly constructed to make its point, without being a tract. It is a considerable compliment to the members of the 1992 YALSA Best Books for Young Adults Committee that they selected it, and an indictment of main-stream publishing that the author had to find a small press willing to subsidize its publication. We've needed a book like this for a very long time. *Princess Daisy,* good as it is, doesn't even come close.

> *Mary K. Chelton, in a review of "Binge," in* Voice of Youth Advocates, *Vol. 16, No. 2, June, 1993, pp. 88-9.*

This is a brutal book with a strong moral impact. It walks a thin line between being a tract on the evils of alcohol and a novelette and, thanks to the skill of Mr. Ferry, it succeeds.

We come upon our antihero, Weldon Yeager, 18, as he wakes up in a hospital room, where an understanding nurse becomes the human figure in the tale. We soon learn that there has been a car accident and that his right foot has been amputated. Apparently he ran over four teenagers; two are dead; the remaining two are clinging to life.

All that is horrible enough, but there is more. Weldon is addicted to alcohol and has been for a couple of years. He has become alienated from his parents and has failed to graduate from high school.

He gives his testimony to a police officer; through a series of flashbacks, we get the details. *Binge* spares the reader nothing; the vomiting and diarrhea as his body tries to handle the alcohol abuse; the false courage that alcohol gives him as he steals and lies his way along.

At the time of the accident, Weldon had been trying to return to the place and the girl, Livvie, of his pre-alcoholic days. We learn at the same time he does that one of the victims of his drunk driving was Livvie, and at the end of the book, we learn that she, too, has died.

But Weldon's mind cannot deal with that fact.

As I said, the book is brutal, and it is powerful, a compelling story that overrides the cautionary tale it contains. It is also very brief, and the reading level is not difficult. It just might cause some teenage students to stop and reevaluate their attitudes toward drinking.

While *Binge* is strong, perhaps too strong for some middle school students, that's where and when it can do the most good.

> *Carol Otis Hurst, in a review of "Binge," in* Voice of Youth Advocates, *August, 1994.*

# Johnny Gruelle
## 1880-1938

(Full name John Barton Gruelle) American author and illustrator of fiction.

Major works include *Raggedy Ann Stories* (1918), *Raggedy Andy Stories* (1920), *Raggedy Ann and Andy and the Camel with the Wrinkled Knees* (1924), *The Paper Dragon: A Raggedy Ann Adventure* (1926), *Raggedy Ann in the Deep Deep Woods* (1930).

Major works about the author include *The Animated Raggedy Ann & Andy: An Intimate Look at the Art of Animation* by John Canemaker (1977), *Johnny Gruelle: Creator of Raggedy Ann and Andy* by Patricia Hall (1993).

The following entry presents general criticism of Gruelle's oeuvre. It also includes a selection of reviews to supplement the general commentary.

## INTRODUCTION

Best known as the creator of the twin rag doll characters Raggedy Ann and Raggedy Andy, Gruelle was a prolific cartoonist and illustrator who crafted a number of adventure stories for primary graders that blend the familiar and the fantastic. Many of these works feature his popular, mop-haired, button-eyed heroine Raggedy Ann, whose shape, according to Margery Fisher, "has lasted almost as long in the nursery world as that of the Teddy Bear" and who is described by Selma Lanes as "a junior-size American folk heroine." Emphasizing Gruelle's belief that "books for children should contain nothing to cause fright, suggest fear, glorify mischief, excuse malice or condone cruelty," his stories shun violence while promoting ideals of courage, honesty, and virtue. Thus in a typical tale Raggedy Ann and her sibling and other stuffed nursery-mates come to life when the "real for sure people" are away, learn moral lessons through a series of mishaps and encounters with a variety of essentially harmless villains, and make a timely return to their former positions in the nursery before their secret life is discovered. Discussing *Raggedy Ann Stories*, Sam Leaton Sebesta and William Iverson have written that "each chapter has just enough gentle incident—a bit of danger followed by a return to security—to entice a child." Occasional commentators, however, have found Gruelle's stories excessively simplistic and predictable, and fault his insistence upon an often awkwardly blatant moral didacticism. Some agree with Selma Lanes that the stories are currently of interest primarily as period timepieces, "each tale transmit[ting] a continuing stream of goody-goody messages" through which "shines the seductive optimism and snug insularity of a more innocent America." Nevertheless, most critics acknowledge that the appeal of Gruelle's lively illustrations, fanciful characters, and good-hearted humor is universal. Martin Williams has also credited Gruelle with a pioneering role in the creation of a new type of children's

writing. Noting that the author's style is "whimsically child-like" in its playful vocabulary, use of alliteration, and tumbling rhythms, Williams adds: "Adopting the narrative manner and the style of children in telling his stories for children—that is Johnny Gruelle's unique contribution to their literature."

Born in Illinois, Gruelle was raised in Indianapolis, Indiana, where his father gained renown as a landscape and portrait painter. The elder Gruelle was a close friend of the so-called "Hoosier poet" James Whitcomb Riley, whose regional verse highlighted scenes of rural life and common folk characterized by humor, warmth, and sincerity. Riley's work exerted a notable influence on young Johnny Gruelle, whose Raggedy Ann was named after Riley's poem "Raggedy Man." Selma Lanes has noted that Gruelle's stories bear similar regional trademarks, maintaining that "the middle western origins of Raggedy Ann are central to the character's ingenuous, hayseed charm." A self-taught artist, Gruelle began work at age eighteen as a cartoonist for the Indianapolis *People*, later moving to two other local papers, the *Sun* and eventually the *Star*. He frequently finished his assignments early and spent the remainder of the day writing stories for his daughter Marcella, some of which his employers published. In 1910, Gruelle was awarded first prize in a *New York Herald* Sunday comic strip design contest, earning $2,000 and a job with that newspaper. He subsequently moved with his family to the artist's colony at Silvermine, Connecticut, where he prolifically crafted cartoons and illustrations for a number of periodicals while contributing illustrated children's stories to such journals as *Good Housekeeping* and *Woman's World*. As a small child, Gruelle's daughter Marcella discovered a faceless rag doll that had belonged to Gruelle's mother; when the artist painted a face on the doll, Raggedy Ann was born. In 1917, Marcella died at the age of fourteen from exposure to a contaminated vaccination needle. The following year, *Raggedy Ann Stories* was published in her memory. Dolls made for bookstore displays garnered so much interest that Gruelle approved mass production, prompting rapid, widespread renown for Raggedy Ann.

Gruelle's early stories are essentially "around-the-home" adventures depicting the playful mischief Marcella's dolls engage in when unattended. The *Raggedy Andy* collection, for example, features a suspense tale called "The Taffy Pull" in which the dolls invade the kitchen, make candy and a resultant mess, and manage to clean up and resume their former positions just before the family returns. Gruelle progressively incorporated many common fairy-tale motifs into his later works, which feature helpful dwarves, fairies, and magic objects, along with frequently appearing, enchanted sources of candies, cream-filled cakes, and other childhood delicacies in endless abundance. All of these conventions and more are encountered in *Raggedy Ann and Andy and the Camel with the Wrinkled Knees*, wherein the sibling duo and their stuffed companions pursue pirates who have kidnapped Marcella's new French doll Babette. This story takes the reader into Gruelle's "deep deep woods," which Martin Williams describes as "a very American enchanted place, by which I mean it is a singular combination of European elements and ones that he made up himself, using a very American imagination." The deep deep woods were a prominent feature of many of Gruelle's later titles, including the fantasies *The Paper Dragon* and *Raggedy Ann in the Deep Deep Woods*. In addition to his tales about Raggedy Ann and Andy, Gruelle created works featuring popular characters such as Beloved Belindy and Wooden Willie, several of which were later merchandized successfully as well as fairy stories, poems, and songs. Despite his success during his lifetime, Gruelle has not received extensive critical analysis. Reviewers most often acknowledge his understanding of children and of what appeals to them, his inventiveness, and his technique as an illustrator as his finest attributes while predicting enduring popularity for his most famous creations. Summarizing Gruelle's achievement, Martin D. Williams notes that at his best "Gruelle was an exceptional children's author," while Jack Zipes writes, "The Raggedy Ann and Andy stories are cultural landmarks: the pristine nature of the dolls and their desire to be good to everyone in a land of milk and honey, the apple-pie cheeks and kind hearts of the sexless, guileless, and blissful brother and sister, the good clean fun found in all the harmless adventures—these elements constitute the innocence of the American dream, and Gruelle used

them for his stories and illustrations at a time when the dream was losing its validity and America its innocence."

(See also *Contemporary Authors*, Vol. 115; *Dictionary of Literary Biography*, Vol. 22; and *Something about the Author*, Vols. 32, 35.)

---

### The Canadian Bookman

[**Raggedy Ann Stories** features] Raggedy Ann again, in some more of her jolly moods and happy pranks. One feature is that most of the pranks are played by others, and that Raggedy Ann is almost always on the receiving end, but she is such a jolly doll, and so patient, so kind, so lovable, that every little boy and girl who has not already made her acquaintance, will revel in her delightful adventures. A circumstance of major interest in this connection is that this is only one of six books in the series—all full of similarly engaging contents!

> *A review of "Raggedy Ann Stories," in* The Canadian Bookman, *Vol. XVI, No. 10, November, 1934, p. 154.*

### Bulletin of the Children's Book Center

Mild and rather dull story [**Raggedy Ann's Merriest Christmas**] of how Raggedy Ann, the other dolls, and Santa Claus work together to get for Marcella the puppy she wants for Christmas. Mediocre writing and illustrations. Not recommended.

> *A review of "Raggedy Ann's Merriest Christmas," in* Bulletin of the Children's Book Center, *Vol. VI, No. 4, December, 1952, p. 32.*

### Martin Williams

Raggedy Ann is found everywhere: in card shops, doll shops, dime stores, bookstores. There are some twenty books in print, from the original Raggedy Ann series. Yet, if you look in any standard reference volume, you will find no entry on her or her author, Johnny Gruelle, dead since 1938. He was not even in *Who's Who*.

Johnny Gruelle was a hack. Or, to put it more politely, he was a prolific author and illustrator. He turned out a mound of children's stories, illustrated books, comic strips, drawings. He even illustrated an ambitious edition of the Grimm Brothers, very handsome stuff considering it was done by a self-taught illustrator.

Now if a man is that prolific, if he writes so many books in a series, and other material as well, one is apt to view his work with suspicion. His writing couldn't be very good if there's that much of it. And generally speaking, much of Gruelle's writing isn't good. But the interesting thing to me is that the best of Gruelle is very good indeed, and unique, as far as I know, in children's literature.

Probably I do not need to say that some hacks write well on occasion. Robert Greene, the Elizabethan playwright, might be considered a hack, but he is still read, and some of his plays are very good. Daniel Defoe is the standard example of a hack whose best work is still read. Here in America, we have the example of another children's author, the man who wrote *The Wizard of Oz.* L. Frank Baum wrote an incredible amount of material, under various pseudonyms, some male and some female, in addition to some fourteen books about Oz. We are only beginning to acknowledge that Baum was a very good writer and that some of his books are really excellent—say, *The Patchwork Girl of Oz,* or *Tik Tok of Oz,* or even better, a non-Oz book called *Queen Zixi of Ix,* which I sometimes think is the best American children's story ever written.

The problem with people who are prolific is that one has to read all in order to find any real good works. One has to sift, examine, and look at all, and that's not necessarily easy. I don't mean to say that I've done something terribly hard in reading Gruelle, but I have read a great deal of him, including all the Raggedy Ann books, and I have come to certain conclusions about him.

Biographically, from what I can discover from talking to a few people, and from looking Gruelle up in the few places where one can look him up, this very talented, very prolific man was a born innocent. It seems that he went through most of his life, almost until the end, without a moral problem to his name. He was kind to everybody simply because it didn't occur to him to be any other way. He was never tempted to be rude or mean. And it is that kind of moral innocence which is both the virtue and the limitation of his writing.

Johnny Gruelle was born in Arcola, Illinois, in 1880, but he was raised in Indianapolis. His father, Richard B. Gruelle, was a self-taught painter, well-known in the Middlewest for his landscapes. I think the American Middlewest, its ways, and its language are very much present in the Raggedy Ann books. If you want to find out attitudes and speech patterns of people of that time, I think you'll discover a lot of them in Raggedy Ann.

Gruelle and his brother Justin and sister Prudence apparently had healthy, somewhat casual upbringings. The father seemed to have let his children come and go pretty much as they wanted to, within reason. But they were all brought up with the idea of the importance of art with a little "a," rather than of a refined, somewhat snobbish thing called Art, with a capital "A." If one drew and painted, one produced art—whether it was editorial cartoons, comic strips, portraits of the wealthy or landscapes or whatever. Quality wasn't what made it art or not art. One did his best and didn't worry about Art.

While still in his late teens, Johnny Gruelle had become the cartoonist on *The Indianapolis Star,* and then a few years later, on *The Cleveland Press.* He did every kind of drawing that a newspaper might require of a staff cartoonist. He drew weather cartoons, political cartoons, and he illustrated stories for which there weren't photographs. He got through his work so fast and so well that he had time on his hands. He used that time writing and illustrating original children's tales. It turned out that the editor liked these, so he published them in the paper too.

Then in 1910, Johnny went to visit his father, who had by then moved to Norwalk, Connecticut. While he was there, the New York paper which was then called the *Herald* held a contest to see who could come up with the best idea

for a Sunday comic feature. Johnny Gruelle entered the contest twice, under two different names, and he won the first prize and the second prize. The first prize went to the adventures of an imaginary little elf named Mr. Twee Deedle, which continued for several years in the *Tribune* and the *Herald Tribune,* and was syndicated to other papers as well.

Johnny, married by then, had moved his family up to a town in Connecticut near Norwalk, called Silvermine, an artists' colony. In Silvermine, he began turning out an incredible quantity of material for everything from *Physical Culture* magazine to joke magazines like *Judge,* and he wrote and illustrated children's stories for *Good Housekeeping,* and *Woman's World.*

Gruelle was a not uncommon combination of laziness and industry. Behind a man like that there is often a driving woman. Gruelle's wife Myrtle was apparently just that. She used to stop him if he felt like going fishing or like playing with the neighborhood children. She might drag him in to his studio and sit him down and say, "You've got some drawing to finish for *Life* magazine." And while he drew—this man-child Johnny Gruelle—she would sit and read him fairy tales.

The Gruelles had a daughter named Marcella whom they loved much. (At that point they had no other children; there were subsequently two sons, Worth and John Junior). Marcella died unexpectedly when she was fourteen years old. She had had a rag doll that had belonged to Prudence, Johnny's sister, her aunt. It was called Raggedy Ann, and in memory of Marcella, Gruelle wrote and illustrated a series of stories about the doll, and Marcella's other dolls, little short tales of imaginary about-the-house adventures. These became **Raggedy Ann Stories,** published in 1918. They were so popular that they were followed by sequels. Indeed, there was a sequel almost every year, and sometimes two a year, until 1937, the year before Gruelle died.

In the meantime, of course, the popularity of the Raggedy Ann books had meant other uses of the character. In the mid-1930's, for instance, Gruelle used to do a single newspaper panel drawing each day for a small distributing syndicate. Daily, there was a little drawing of Raggedy Ann with a verse, or a bit of advice, always very cheerful and happy and sun-shiny, as the stories usually are. Also in the '30's, partly for reasons of health and perhaps other reasons that I'm not quite sure of yet, Gruelle moved his family (the two small boys by then) to Miami. There this adult innocent met his first real temptations and, it seems, succumbed to them. Unexpectedly, he evidently gave up his former way of life. People in Silvermine tell me that when he would return north for a visit, he would be overweight, bloated, puffy-eyed, and talking away about the fact that he was busy every afternoon attending cocktail parties. Within a few years, Gruelle was dead. It was a combination of his illness plus the suddenly fast life he had begun to live in Florida, it seems. And as I have said, there was very little attention paid to his death, although his books were still selling then, as they still are now.

The first group of **Raggedy Ann Stories** is based on the

Rare copies of the original Raggedy Ann Stories (1918) and Raggedy Andy Stories (1920).

*First editions of* Raggedy Ann Stories *(1918) and* Raggedy Andy Stories *(1920).*

idea, not a new one, that dolls have a secret life. They come to life when people are asleep or when people go away on a trip. They can walk and talk and have all kinds of adventures on their own. The dolls find a puppy and adopt it and have to make arrangements for the puppy when "the real-for-sure folks," as Gruelle calls them, return. Or, Raggedy Ann falls in a bucket of paint and has to be scraped and washed and have another face painted on. There one gets a double perspective of the way the real people are thinking about all this—the way Marcella particularly is thinking about it—and the way Raggedy Ann (without ever admitting it to the real people, of course) is thinking about it herself.

These first stories were followed almost immediately by a collection of *Raggedy Andy Stories.* Raggedy Andy is of course the brother doll to Raggedy Ann. Some of these tales, I think, are charming. One of them tells how all the dolls sneak down into the kitchen one evening while the real-for-sure people are away and have a wild taffy pull. There's a last minute escape, when the dolls get everything cleaned up and everything exactly the way it was. Before the adults come through the front door, they all scatter up to the nursery and back into bed and get back in the same position as they were when they had been left.

Many of the stories in these early books are trivial. But children often like them. They like the premise of the secret life of the dolls and they don't mind the repetitious-

ness. There are other, later, collections of short Raggedy Ann tales. One is called *Marcella Stories,* and another is called *Beloved Belindy.* Now, Beloved Belindy was a black "Mammy" doll of a kind that would never be written about now. I don't think she's really patronized. I think she's just a nice matriarchal being in the midst of the other dolls, who happens to be black. I do think that some of the black servants in Gruelle's books are patronized but I don't think Belindy was. Anyway, *Beloved Belindy* was the fourth collection of short domestic tales about the dolls.

To go back a little bit, however, the third Raggedy Ann book, meanwhile, had been of a different sort. It is not a collection of short stories but a long tale called *Raggedy Ann and Andy and the Camel with the Wrinkled Knees.* (Long titles, and long phrases like that, charmed Johnny Gruelle, and he used them all the time.) In this story, Gruelle took us into his own version of fairyland, which he called the Deep Deep Woods.

It is supposedly a wooded area behind Marcella's backyard. But Gruelle's Deep Deep Woods is a very American enchanted place, by which I mean it is a singular combination of European elements and ones that he made up himself, using a very American imagination. There are witches but they aren't really very evil; they're unkind maybe, but that's the worst you could say about them. And there are wizards and magicians, some of whom are a little mean, and some of whom put spells on you but they aren't really very bad spells. And sometimes they hide people away. But that's about it.

Then there are princesses and princes: they are all very handsome or beautiful and sometimes they're disguised as other people or other things, and reveal themselves in the end. And there are kings, some of whom are grouches of course. Along with this there are little magical beings with names like Sniznoddle, Snarleyboodle, Little Weekie the Goblin, the Bollivar, the Snoopwiggy, and his friend, the Wiggysnoop, and Mr. Hokus, who of course is a magician. And there are magic spells that can be broken with riddles like "why does a snickersnaper snap snikers?" That's not very European, is it?

The Deep Deep Woods is—again like Gruelle himself—an innocent kind of world, mostly full of niceness and kindliness and some naughtiness. Raggedy Ann herself early acquires a heart that is sewn inside her, a candy heart on which is written, "I love you." Well, if you've got "I love you" written all over your heart, you don't have many moral decisions to make. They come easy.

There is one device in these stories that comes up over and over again, one which is typical of the popular children's writing of the time—it also shows up in British children's literature—and that is the almost endless feast of sweets: donuts, creampuffs, ice cream sodas, ice cream. Book after book has mud puddles which turn out to be chocolate ice cream rather than mud, or fountains in the middle of the woods, enchanted fountains, which put out sodas, or bushes on which grow cookies or cream puffs or donuts. Everyone stops and eats his head off. It's enough to make a diet-conscious adult sick to his stomach.

There's another aspect of Raggedy Ann's kindliness that I find a little disturbing. On occasion, Raggedy Ann behaves like a real busybody in the Deep Deep Woods. She finds out that owls eat mice and she doesn't like that, so she converts the owls to cream puffs. You know, she has a wonderfully uncomplicated idea of what's best for everybody else. (Sometimes it reminds me of American foreign policy.)

But then there are marvelous small touches. For instance, in the book called **Raggedy Ann in the Deep Deep Woods,** the two dolls are wandering along, looking at the sights and saying hello to the animals, and they run into two old owls who live in a tree top. Mama Owl, who's old, and Papa Owl, who's also old and tired from having worked for years in a buttonhole factory. It's typical of Gruelle's inventiveness to make up that kind of thing.

But in reading these books, one may decide that this man is just pouring out words, and pouring out plots and ideas and incidents, and one may wonder: does he have any writing *style?* Does he have any sense of how to put words together gracefully? Or is he just pushing the plot along?

I think he did have a writing style, and I think it too was distinctly American. The hint comes from those words like the Snarleyboodle, and the Snoopwiggy, and Little Weekie. That's the kind of word-making that little children indulge in, making words and names out of bits and pieces of other words and sounds they've heard adults use. And I think Johnny Gruelle succeeded in several ways in writing stories by using the methods of a child, not an adult. For another example, there are the little repetitions he uses. Hookey the Goblin is always Hookey the Goblin. He's never the Goblin and he's almost never Hookey. That's his name, the whole thing:

> "Mary Jane Adams lives down the street."
> "Oh, Mary Jane?"
> "No! Mary Jane Adams."

We've all heard children do this kind of thing, particularly small children. They're just learning to talk, perhaps, and just learning names, just learning the fact that most of us have three names, (and some of us four and five) and they like to say it all. It's a verbal game with them, and Gruelle used it in his books.

In **Raggedy Ann and Andy and the Camel with the Wrinkled Knees,** there's a character named the Tired Old Horse, but sometimes he's the Old Tired Horse, sometimes he might be the Tired Horse and sometimes he might be the Old Horse but usually he's the Tired Old Horse or the Old Tired Horse, and he is never, never just the Horse. Elves and gnomes and fairies, or fairies and gnomes and elves, or gnomes and elves and fairies, and so forth—any order in which you can put the three together will show up eventually, but hardly ever two of the three and certainly never just one of the three.

In **The Camel with the Wrinkled Knees** there are princesses and princes, and there is a Loony King and there is a witch, and there is the Old Tired Horse. But soon we meet a group of pirates who have a ship, a great big pirate ship that navigates on the land by virtue of the fact that it has four wooden legs which walk the ship along like a great

horse. These pirates run around doing pirate things to the dolls and the people. But very early, Gruelle's charming drawings begin to reveal something to us: the great big red nose on the pirate leader is a false nose, and the bandanna on the mean looking pirate covers up the curly hair of a little girl. Gruelle's drawings reveal to us that this assemblage is really a group of Marcella's friends who are playing a game, pretending they are pirates. Soon we realize that the whole story is a game being played by the children about the dolls, and that they're making it up as they go along. We have all done that as children, surely. We start making up a story and acting it out with a group of our playmates. And it rambles and rambles; it goes in this direction and that. It goes in every direction it can go in until mother calls us for lunch or supper.

Johnny Gruelle put these tales together with the same kind of easy whimsy, the same kind of casualness, which children use when improvising a story-game for themselves. And he's the only writer that I've ever read (I may be ignorant of others) who consciously uses an imitation of the way children make up stories in writing a book for children.

**Raggedy Ann and Andy and the Camel with the Wrinkled Knees** is a very good example of it, and there are several other very good ones. For instance, **Raggedy Ann and the Magic Wishing Pebble.** (Now a magic wishing pebble is a wonderful thing if you find one. Look for one: it is absolutely white and absolutely round. If you find an absolute white and absolutely round pebble, it will give you all the magic wishes that you want.) As I say, it's a good book, but the characters do spend some time in the opening pages sitting around a cookie bush, gorging on soda and donuts.

Did Gruelle write any *great* books? I think he did write one great book: the book which was originally called **The Paper Dragon: A Raggedy Ann Adventure,** and is now published as **Raggedy Ann and the Paper Dragon.** It's about a little girl named Marggy who has lost her father. Well, he's sort of misplaced actually; it isn't a very bad situation. Nobody is anguished about the old boy. He's probably all right, but, you know, somebody's sort of misplaced him somewhere so we ought to find him. There's a naughty magician involved, and there's Marggy's mother in the story. And Raggedy Ann and Raggedy Andy are typically helping them in finding Marggy's father, or Marggy's Daddy as Gruelle would put it, in the Deep Deep Woods. The dragon of the title is a very Oriental dragon until it gets a hole punched in his side and is patched with a Sunday comic section stuck on with some filling from a cream puff. That Americanizes him.

The dragon is completely hollow inside and at one point the bad guy of the story props his mouth open with a stick because he wants to use him for a chicken coop. But that doesn't work very well because if the chickens can run in easily, they can also run out easily. The dragon is also full of dry leaves; it seems that a lot of fallen leaves blew in while he was yawning. Raggedy Andy gets put inside him at one point. He wanders around for a little while, and, as I remember, he can't find anything or anybody. All he finds are these dry leaves which have the dragon coughing from time to time, and eventually have him coughing Raggedy Andy out. It's that kind of rambling, meandering narrative which Gruelle does very charmingly, and particularly in this book.

The book also has good characterizations. Of course they are brief, almost blunt. Characterizations generally are brief and blunt in children's books, and very much so in this book, particularly of Raggedy Andy. He loves to get into boxing and wrestling matches. They never really amount to much, but he likes to box and wrestle. The villains and the bad magicians are always irascible and usually rather foolish—propping the dragon's mouth open so that the chickens could get in, but also get out. At one point, the villain says something like, "If you want to find Marggy's Daddy, you must do something for me first. That's the way it always is in fairy tales." And Raggedy Ann says, "But this isn't a fairy tale." "Of course it's a fairy tale!" he answers. "How else could you two rag dolls be walking around and talking if it wasn't a fairy tale?" That's blunt, and that's probably a child's way of looking at it.

There is one other Gruelle book which I'd like to recommend especially. As I said earlier, there's a whole collection of dolls in Marcella's doll nursery, and one of them is Uncle Clem the Scotch Doll. There's a book built around him called ***Wooden Willie,*** in which the Scotch Doll and the doll called Beloved Belindy have an adventure. Incidentally, this story originally appeared as a newspaper serial in 1922, and in that version it is a Raggedy Ann and Andy adventure.

I haven't said very much about Gruelle's illustrations, but anyone who has ever seen Gruelle's drawings, in that soft line of his, knows he has seen something special. To know how good they are, simply compare them to those in the books published after Johnny's death that have illustrations done by others, chiefly by Justin Gruelle, his brother, or by Worth Gruelle, his son.

I think there's no question that Johnny Gruelle's reputation would be much higher, and that he would be in the histories of children's literature, if he hadn't written so much. But he did write some very good books. And he had his own way of depicting a child's mind and a child's outlook. So I would like to think that before my life is over, we can read about Johnny Gruelle in volumes on American writers and in volumes on American artists.

> *Martin Williams, "Some Remarks on Raggedy Ann and Johnny Gruelle," in* Children's Literature: Annual of the Modern Language Association Seminar on Children's Literature and The Children's Literature Association, *Vol. 3, 1974, pp. 140-46.*

### Sam Leaton Sebesta and William J. Iverson

A number of early childhood fanciful stories that have remained popular through the years aren't exactly critical favorites. The sixteen volumes about Raggedy Ann and Raggedy Andy, beginning with ***Raggedy Ann Stories*** by Johnny Gruelle, are cloying to most adults, but some children still like them. Each chapter has just enough gentle incident—a bit of danger followed by a return to security—to entice a child. Raggedy Ann herself is indestructible and dependably cheerful, even when she loses her stuffing.

> *Sam Leaton Sebesta and William J. Iverson, "Fanciful Fiction, Color Portfolio of Picture Books, Folk Literature, and Fanciful Fiction: 'Raggedy Ann Stories'," in their* Literature for Thursday's Child, *Science Research Associates, Inc., 1975, p. 196.*

### Kirkus Reviews

For the first time between hard covers, Raggedy Ann [in ***More Raggedy Ann and Andy Stories***] winks her shoebutton eyes and Raggedy Andy chuckles deep down inside his cotton-stuffed tummy as they scamper through ten cunning stories seeking happy hearts and wishing stones, conversing with Witchie Wiggle Waggle and the Camel with the wrinkled knees, and asserting their belief in the fairies of the Deep Dark Woods behind Marcella's backyard. Oh my goodness gracious sakes, won't grandma be delighted.

> *A review of "More Raggedy Ann and Andy Stories," in* Kirkus Reviews, *Vol. XLV, No. 5, March 1, 1977, p. 225.*

*From* Raggedy Ann Stories, *written and illustrated by Johnny Gruelle.*

**Ann L. Kalkhoff**

These ten stories [in *More Raggedy Ann and Andy Stories*] have never been published in book form before. The illustrations were done by Johnny Gruelle, his son, and his brother. All the beloved Raggedy Ann and Andy characters are here, but the stories lack any life. Recommend purchase of the earlier books instead of this mediocre-to-poor collection.

> *Ann L. Kalkhoff, in a review of "More Raggedy Ann and Andy Stories," in* Children's Book Review Service, *Vol. 5, No. 12, Spring Supplement, 1977, p. 115.*

**Selma G. Lanes**

Can a wholesome Hoosier rag doll survive that ultimate American peril—success—and still hang onto some shred of her homespun integrity?

The film, "Raggedy Ann & Andy: A Musical Adventure," currently being touted as "the first feature-length animated musical comedy produced in this country," was released nationwide at Easter by Twentieth Century Fox. With $4 million spent on the production of this lavish spectacular by I.T.T. (the Bobbs-Merrill Company's conglomerate owner), and up to $3 million more earmarked for its promotion in the family film market, it should come as no surprise that some 115 other companies have been licensed by Bobbs-Merrill (which controls all copyrights on the Raggedies) to produce everything from Raggedy Ann and Andy cameras to room dividers, toothpaste dispensers and umbrellas; and that a host of new Raggedy Ann and Andy books, in both hard and soft covers, are here to join in this spring's multi-media, coast-to-coast hoopla.

In the beginning was, of course, the book, *Raggedy Ann Stories* (1918), written and illustrated by Johnny Gruelle, a political cartoonist for the *Indianapolis Star*. Gruelle had breathed life into the floppy character to entertain his ailing young daughter, Marcella. Legend has it that, one day, Marcella discovered in the family attic a rag doll that had belonged to Gruelle's own mother. When the artist obligingly painted a new, irresistibly contagious smile on its face, a junior-size American folk heroine was born. After Marcella died in 1916, at 14, Gruelle decided to publish the tales. And, in all probability, the affecting sweetness of the best Raggedy Ann stories and Gruelle drawings owes much to the poignancy of a father's memories of this cherished only daughter.

The first Raggedy volume was published somewhat reluctantly by the P. F. Volland Company, and only then because an earlier Gruelle book, *My Very Own Fairy Stories* (1917) had been an immediate success. The gamble paid off handsomely. By 1940, the original book had gone through 15 editions; all of Gruelle's 30-odd children's books together—the bulk of them Raggedy sequels—had sold more than 5 million copies.

Following Gruelle's death in 1938, his widow, a son, Richard, and Howard Cox, formerly of Volland, organized the Johnny Gruelle Company and managed to keep the Rag-gedy books alive until 1960, when the company was sold to Bobbs-Merrill of Indianapolis.

In some crucial way, the Middle Western origins of Raggedy Ann are central to the character's ingenuous, hayseed charm. Through all the tales shines the seductive optimism and snug insularity of a more innocent America. Gruelle's noble credo was that "books for children should contain nothing to cause fright, suggest fear, glorify mischief, excuse malice or condone cruelty." Thus his heroine's cottonstuffed head is filled only with sunny thoughts. Most of the characters she encounters are "kindly"—even a Big Bad Wolf turns out to be "very fond of children." And each tale transmits a continuing stream of goody-goody messages: i.e. "The only magic required is the magic of a loving kiss"; "One little fib is just like a seed. It grows and grows until, in the end, you have a large clump of fib weeds"; "Whenever you try to injure others, you always harm yourselves." Among Raggedy Ann's claims to fame is the first successful heart implant: During one of her earliest adventures, she falls into a paint bucket, and the good lady who scrubs and re-stuffs her inserts a permanent candy heart with "I love you" lettered on it.

Like L. Frank Baum's "Wizard of Oz" tales, the Raggedy Ann books have flourished outside the cultivated garden of high children's literature. Certainly their staying power owes nothing to literary distinction. Gruelle's 96-page stories are carelessly—almost heedlessly—written. They are, in fact, stuffed with words much as Raggedy Ann dolls are stuffed with cotton rags—for bulk, not backbone. And curiously, Gruelle never improved upon or deepened his earliest inspiration. The later tales refer to, and often build on, incidents in preceding adventures, but with waning invention and spontaneity.

For all the sweetness and light he dispensed, however, Gruelle was a canny fellow, in no way averse to merchandising his product. At the end of the first Raggedy Ann book, he tacked on "a stranger friend" who borrows Raggedy Ann and takes her to a room "where girls in aprons make patterns of her—shoe button eyes, cheery smile and all," thus setting the stage himself for the multi-million dollar doll industry that may well be more responsible for Raggedy Ann's staying power than the books themselves. Early on, Gruelle also sensed that his stories would have broader appeal if Raggedy Ann had a male counterpart. Thus, in *Raggedy Andy Stories* (1920), he introduced a stout-hearted, long-lost brother. Gruelle's unerring instinct for promoting his characters turned them into celebrities by the mid-20's: Jerome Kern composed a song called "Raggedy Ann," and Raggedy Ann mother-and-daughter dresses, Raggedy Ann haircuts—and even a Raggedy Ann salad (shredded carrot topping?) —were the rage. By then, his son, Worth, and a brother, Justin, had joined Gruelle in writing and illustrating the books.

The Raggedies, actually, are a perfect vehicle for animation. Gruelle's charmed notion of a nursery world in which dolls spring to secret life as soon as any "real-for-sure people" are out of sight is tailor-made for filming. And "the Deep, Deep Woods" outside Gruelle's fictional nursery window is the author's own fairyland, a setting conducive to action-packed, magical adventures. The main character, too is endowed with a number of endearing—and cinematic qualities: When Raggedy Ann runs her rag hand through her yarn hair, she is deep in thought. And if she should think—or smile—too hard, she is likely to pop several stitches in her head.

In 1977 the Gruelle family's wildest dream was achieved: a full-length animated film.

But what of Raggedy Ann herself? Has our floppy, soppy heroine survived it all? Virtually intact. Perhaps a rag-stuffed head can't be turned.

> *Selma G. Lanes, "Raggedy Ann to Riches," in* The New York Times Book Review, *May 1, 1977, pp. 30, 39.*

### Margery Fisher

The tales of Raggedy Ann belong to the 'twenties; [*Raggedy Ann and Andy and the Camel with the Wrinkled Knees* and *Raggedy Ann's Magical Wishes*] were published first in 1924 and 1928 respectively. It was a period of middle-class readership, a time when books had more often than not a paternal or avuncular voice, friendly but authoritarian (or even, in England, the gently reproving admonitions of Nannie). If stories for the young were not necessarily more didactic than they are now, the lessons were delivered as of right, with none of the apologetic irony which is apt to colour purposive tales in our own time. I wonder, then, how children today will regard Raggedy Ann's words when the greedy Snoopwiggy and Wiggysnoop ask why she did not keep the secret of the strawberry-flavoured spring to herself:

> . . . you will find out . . . that if you share your pleasures with others, the pleasures will seem ever so much better to you; 'cause, every time you give to others and make them happy, you catch some of their happiness, and that makes you just that much happier yourself! And the more you give away, the more you have yourself. . . . When one is stingy, it is just like shutting every door and window in a house and expecting the sunshine to come in!

Perhaps one should read into this and other improving utterances of the candy-hearted little rag-doll a sly comment on American materialism. Certainly the author seems to have used his tales, as Frank Baum used the Oz books, to reflect national pride—in ingenious machinery, for example—and though he may at times strike a satirical note, presumably he means to be taken seriously when the King and Queen of the Purple Mountain, freed from the land of the Loonies by a witch turned Fairy Queen, decline to take up their throne again:

> The people here, if they wish, can have a republic, like the United States of America; but we would rather be just plain, everyday folks in a plain, everyday house with plain, everyday people for friends!

The mixture of the homely and the fantastic in the Raggedy Ann stories is in many ways similar to the atmosphere of the Oz books. Strange but somewhat commonplace creatures like Mister Gruffy Bear, Mr. Hokus the magician and the Loonies find their hostility melted and,

indeed, their characters changed by Raggedy Ann's gentle but firm influence. The delectable and tooth-destroying comestibles dear to children play a large part in the stories and, together with the descriptions of cosy cottages and the emphasis on nursery virtues, define the limits of adventure—excitement and surprise but no real danger and no great distance to stray from the security of home. The plots of the two stories discussed here have the rambling shape of the Oz books too. The first concerns the search for lost Babette the French doll, the second (which is still more episodic) plays round the point that Raggedy Ann has a magical wishing-pebble sewn inside her with which, not without moments of mischief, she changes people and circumstances alike.

Perhaps in the end the charm of these artless tales, if it endures at all, is simply the charm of a rag doll endowed with magical attributes. Children of any generation, even those sated with television marvels, might imagine for themselves just such a quaint, squashy figure as Raggedy Ann with her submissive consort Raggedy Andy, her candy heart and her magic pebble safely hidden in her stuffing and her awkward habit of splitting the stitches in her head when she thinks. It is not hard to forgive her for her sententious moments because she has, in the end, the pleasing personality of a doll—one, moreover, whose invented shape has lasted almost as long in the nursery world as that of the Teddy Bear.

> *Margery Fisher, in a review of "Raggedy Ann and Andy and the Camel with the Wrinkled Knees" and "Raggedy Ann's Magical Wishes," in* Growing Point, *Vol. 16, No. 2, 1977, pp. 3140-41.*

### John Canemaker

The search for information about the distinctly American career and life of Johnny Gruelle, the creator of the stories and illustrations of Raggedy Ann and Andy, is not an easy task. Considering that he was such a prolific and famous artist, there is amazingly little reliable information; instead, legends have sprung up and grown into the gaps in the truth.

Martin D. Williams, Director of Jazz Programs at the Smithsonian Institution and an authority on Gruelle's work, once wrote in *Book World* his opinion as to why Johnny Gruelle is so elusive: "He turned out a vast quantity of children's stories and illustrations during his lifetime. . . . Our critics and literary historians are apt to suspect anyone as prolific, and as frankly uneven, as Johnny Gruelle. At his rare best, however, I think that Johnny Gruelle was an exceptional children's author, and his work has qualities found nowhere else that I know of in writing for children."

Sixty-five-year-old Worth Gruelle, one of Johnny Gruelle's two sons and a valuable source of information about his father, agreed with the above opinion in a letter written in 1976:

> [Johnny Gruelle] would work mostly at night either on illustrations or an old typewriter—he could get more beautiful work done in the shortest time! He never had to do any art work over.

*From* The Complete Fairy Tales of the Brothers Grimm. *Written and illustrated by John B. Gruelle. Translated by Jack Zipes.*

It was always approved and accepted the first time.

Worth gives us a thumbnail description of life with his father:

> My dad and I were great buddies. Everyone loved him and he loved everybody. . . . When he was able in the '20's and '30's to have a good sized boat [there] would be firemen, police, the mayor, the governor, actors, artists, singers, truckdrivers, prizefighters all in a heap. No class problems as long as they were with my father. . . . He was 5' 8", slight but supple—played baseball and was a great pitcher. . . .
>
> The myths [and] conflicting stories of course are typical [of] famous people who didn't intend or expect to be famous—their lives could have been calm, peaceful, happy and maybe even uneventful and mediocre. However, most of this was true in our family—except for uneventful and mediocre—it was a happy family!

Johnny Gruelle was born in Arcola, Illinois, in 1880, the son of Richard B. and Alice Benton Gruelle. Johnny and his sister and brother, Prudence and Justin, were raised in Indianapolis, Indiana.

Worth says:

> He was born into a family of writers and artists. His father, Richard B. Gruelle, was one of the originators of the famous "Hoosier" group of artists. James Whitcomb Riley was among the friends that swarmed into grandfather's studio—he wrote a poem about my dad, "The Funny Picture Man," so of course he was right in the middle of all sorts of art and must have loved every minute of it. As Grandmother Gruelle said, he was never without a pencil.
>
> My grandmother (who lived with us most of the time) said my dad as a very young boy drew pictures, wrote verse, prose, etc., usually disrupting his studies.

When Johnny Gruelle was fourteen he and a friend hopped a boxcar and ran away to Cleveland. Broke and hungry, Gruelle got a job, it is said, playing piano in a saloon where he met a police officer named McGinty, a character he used in some later cartoons. Johnny drew the cop's picture with soap on the window of a back bar.

McGinty told the kid he thought he had "the makings of a good cartoonist" and offered to stake him until he could get a job on a newspaper. Gruelle appreciated the encouragement, thanked the policeman and returned home. A few years later, when he was a cartoonist on *The Cleveland Press,* Gruelle became good friends with Officer McGinty and his family.

Gruelle began working for the *Indianapolis Sun-Star* and *Sentinel* (later shortened to the *Star*) in 1903; he drew weather cartoons and political cartoons and illustrated news articles when there were no photographs available.

Some of his fellow artists on the newspaper resented Gruelle's quick ease with a pencil; William F. Heitman, a veteran *Star* staff artist, once recalled, "Johnny loved to fish. He'd even have the gall to show up at the office in old clothes and fishing boots, draw his cartoon for the day in less than an hour, then tip his fishing hat to the rest of us as he left for the day."

He married Myrtle Swann in Indianapolis in 1900, and two years later a daughter was born. They named her Marcella. Around 1909 Gruelle worked as a staff cartoonist on the *Cleveland Press.*

In 1910, while on vacation visiting his parents, who were then living in Connecticut, Gruelle learned that the *New York Herald* was conducting a contest to select a new comic page; his mother suggested he submit one. Along with five hundred other applicants, Gruelle entered the contest. The judges eliminated all but a hundred, then narrowed these down to two. It was a tie, and both winners turned out to be—Johnny Gruelle! His "Mr. Twee Deedle" won first prize, and his "Jack the Giant Killer" won second.

"Mr. Twee Deedle" ran as a Sunday comic strip for four years, then was suddenly discontinued by a new Sunday editor. The *Herald* publisher, James Gordon Bennett, noticed the omission while traveling in Europe.

"What became of Twee Deedle?" cabled Bennett.

"Discontinued by Sunday editor," was cabled back.

"Discontinue Sunday editor," was Bennett's succinct reply. "Mr. Twee Deedle" lived another four years.

According to Worth Gruelle,

> The Herald was just one of his regular jobs. At the same time he had dailies in the New York World, Woman's World, Cleveland Press. He had a studio in N.Y.C. —did daily juvenile publications—stories and illustrations. "Yapps Crossing" was in Judge around 1911, also ran as a monthly for years—then "Yahoo Center" in the old Life, then "Punkin Center" in College Humor until 1938. "Brutus" in [the] Herald ran from 1932-38 and stopped at his death in 1938.

Gruelle moved his wife and daughter East, and in either late 1910 or early 1911 he built a house in Silvermine, Connecticut, where they lived for six years. Worth was born there in 1912, and another son, Richard, was born in Norwalk, Connecticut, in 1917.

Worth Gruelle remembers his sister Marcella:

She was quite ill and rested a great deal, but at times seemed to get a bit of energy, and we played in our large back yard in Silvermine—ran around and even swam in our (then clean) little river. Naturally we were supervised, and Marcella's illness was a very sad time for my parents. Due to a vaccination—when they lived in N.Y.C.—Marcella developed an infection which affected her heart and caused her untimely death. It was a lingering, deteriorating illness and cause[d by an] unsterile needle or vaccine. . . . She died at 14 and had been a healthy girl prior to the vaccination—there was no TB.

Marcella's death [on March 21, 1916] was the reason for selling the Silvermine House and they moved to Norwalk. . . . It was closer to the R.R. Station for N.Y.C. also.

I feel Marcella was a very little (young) girl when "Raggedy" stories began. The illustrations for the book (using them as a guide) showed her as maybe 6 or 7 years of age. The folks were very, very busy throughout my younger years of age. But [they] hid their sadness [over Marcella's death] and bitterness, too, quite well, I remember.

Regarding the legend that Marcella started the whole thing by discovering her grandmother's old rag doll, Worth believes:

> It's true. I remember an old stringy rag doll— but it must have been found before my folks actually moved to Conn. Maybe on a visit to their folks.

He also thinks Johnny Gruelle made up the Raggedy Ann stories to amuse his ill daughter.

In the preface to the first Raggedy Ann book, titled *Raggedy Ann Stories* and published on September 10, 1918, by P. F. Volland, Johnny Gruelle writes: "I have before me on my desk, propped up against the telephone, an old rag doll. Dear old Raggedy Ann!

"The same Raggedy Ann with which my mother played when a child . . . what lessons of kindness and fortitude you might teach could you but talk, you with your wisdom of fifty-nine years. . . . "

*Raggedy Andy Stories* appeared in 1920 and was dedicated to "Marcella's Mama." In the preface to this book, Gruelle's mother has supposedly written a letter dated January 12, 1919, from Wilton, Connecticut: "Living next door to us, when I was about four years old, was a little girl named Bessie; I cannot recall her last name. When my mother made Raggedy Ann for me, Bessie's mother made a rag doll for her, for we two always played together. . . . Bessie's doll was made a day or so after Raggedy Ann, I think, though I am not quite certain which of the two dolls was made first. However, Bessie's doll was given the name of Raggedy Andy, and one of the two dolls was named after the other, so that their names would sound alike."

Other accounts suggest that Johnny Gruelle named his mother's doll after the James Whitcomb Riley poem "The Raggedy Man," for which his father had done the illustrations. (Harold Gray worked briefly for the *Star* before he moved to the *Chicago Tribune,* where he launched his "Little Orphan Annie" comic strip, which was based on a Riley poem.)

In the May 13, 1923, *Indianapolis Star,* Gruelle spoke of how he came to put the Raggedy stories into writing:

> It was in a room with fourteen other artists, and I only had to draw this one picture, and was generally through by noon, and when I'd start to go out the other artists would look at me, and I'd feel kind of ashamed and decide to stay around a while longer. So I got to doing things to take up the time—writing sketches and bum verses— you know the kind—and finally got to writing Raggedy Ann in verse, and making pictures for it. Raggedy Andy came later. P. F. Volland, the publisher, suggested I do it in prose, so I did, and it's been in prose ever since. Ann is in some of Andy's books but Andy doesn't get into any of her books. The stories write themselves; I've written as many as seventeen in one morning.

Worth Gruelle helped his father illustrate the Raggedy books from "around 1922," and in 1940, "when Donahue [which followed Volland as publisher] stopped printing the books and the Johnny Gruelle Company [had] formed, I illustrated all of the books except a couple that my Uncle Justin did.

"I worked with my father for years. I helped first with coloring, then inking, then layouts, etc. I had my own column with George Matthew Adams. I did the 'Raggedy' column also for Adams Syndicate . . . of course with [the] Johnny Gruelle sig[nature]."

*Publishers Weekly,* October 26, 1940, reported that the original **Raggedy Ann** sold 750,000 copies in fifteen editions, and "all the Gruelle books together have sold more than 5,000,000 copies."

Paul Volland, the original publisher of **Raggedy Ann Stories,** was not initially enthusiastic about the book, but he wanted to keep the good will of writer-illustrator Gruelle, whose earlier work, in 1917, **My Very Own Fairy Stories,** had been an immediate success.

"The book no sooner reached the retail counters than reorders began to pour in, and for the rest of the year every printer in Chicago with an idle press was printing **Raggedy Ann Stories**," recalled Richard L. Cox, publisher of the books from 1939 to 1960.

After the books came the Raggedy dolls, which became perhaps even more popular than the books. One story suggests that the demand for the doll began at Christmastime in 1920 when Marshall Field & Company in Chicago made up a special Raggedy Andy doll for a window display. Supposedly an insistent customer bought it the second day it was in the window, and the rush for the huggable dolls was on.

Gruelle then turned most of his attention to writing and illustrating children's books. Before his death, more than twenty-seven of those books had been published, eighteen of which were Raggedy Ann and Andy books, including two songbooks. Jerome Kern composed a song called "Raggedy Ann" that was showcased in a Broadway musi-

*Gruelle drawing Raggedy Ann in chalk for a group of Miami schoolchildren in 1933.*

cal of 1923, "Stepping Stones." At the peak of popularity there were Raggedy Ann mother and daughter dresses, Raggedy Ann haircuts, and Raggedy Ann salads. By the mid-twenties, Johnny Gruelle was both famous and wealthy.

The Gruelles moved to Miami Springs, Florida, and it was here that Johnny Gruelle died on January 9, 1938, of heart disease. His death was unexpected, although he had been in ill health for three years. The *Star,* where he first worked professionally as a cartoonist, described him as "a jovial companion, enthusiastic, venturesome and popular among all who knew him. . . . It is unfortunate that a man who brought so much gladness into the world should succumb at the age of fifty-seven."

In 1939 Johnny Gruelle's widow, Myrtle; his son Richard; and Howard Cox, formerly of Volland, formed the Johnny Gruelle Company. They owned all Raggedy Ann publication rights, as well as motion picture and commercial rights. According to *Publishers Weekly,* Volland had handled almost all of Gruelle's work until 1934, when they liquidated their book publishing division. Publisher M. A. Donahue acquired the Volland plates and by arrangement with Gruelle continued to publish most of the Raggedy Ann titles.

Worth Gruelle blames a temporary decline in the popularity of the dolls and books on an infringement suit we had to put into effect due to a Philly doll concern which started manufacturing Raddys [sic] by the thousands. We won this suit, of course, but it took about 5 years to do so, I believe. At the same time, Gerlach died [Gerlach-Barklow, who were publishing the books].

Donahue took several years to start publishing again, slowly but successfully. Then Mr. Donahue passed on.

My mother, brother Richard and Howard Cox started the Johnny Gruelle Co. with only one book—mine—Raggedy Ann and Andy in the Magic Book. Through the years they were able to get one book at a time from Donahue and Co. My mother became ill and [in 1960] Cox sold to Bobbs-Merrill [then owned by Howard Sams, later a subsidiary of ITT].

In 1962 the Knickerbocker Toy Company acquired exclusive rights to manufacture the Raggedy Ann and Andy stuffed rag dolls.

The licensing of more than five hundred Raggedy Ann products in the past ten years has helped Ann and Andy stage a spectacular comeback and paved the way for the feature-length film about them [*Raggedy Ann & Andy*].

What are the qualities in Raggedy Ann and Andy and their stories that have made them so popular for so long? Martin D. Williams feels that Gruelle is the only writer to make conscious use of a "great natural resource of childhood"—namely, "Let's pretend."

Williams explains, "Gruelle himself spins out his best tales in a kind of rambling but controlled literary extension of the same breathless uncomplicated what-happens-next that children use when they improvise their own story games."

The first two books contain short domestic adventures that take place in and around Marcella's house; the tales are based on the ancient notion that inanimate dolls have a secret life and can have taffy pulls, rescue a puppy, adopt kittens, enjoy a picnic or a dance as much as "real-for-sure" children do.

Beginning with the book *The Camel with the Wrinkled Knees,* Gruelle introduced his own version of fairyland, which he named "the Deep Deep Woods." It is a place full of witches, elves, and strange wonderful creatures like the Snicksnapper, the Hungry Howloon, the Snarleyboodle. In these tales Gruelle's work takes on classical dimensions. Child psychologist Bruno Bettelheim has explained that all children "fear being deserted by their parents and lost in the deep dark woods like Hansel and Gretel [or Raggedy Ann and Andy], or being swallowed by wild animals [or, as in the film, a Greedy?] like Red Riding Hood. On their own these childhood nightmares have no solutions. Fairy tales tell the child he is not alone in having such anxieties and that he has nothing to be ashamed of."

A child's identification with Raggedy Ann and Andy and their simple adventures may be one of the secrets to the dolls' durable appeal. Williams mentions that the silly character names in the Deep Deep Woods are "extensions of the kinds of names that little children make up for themselves." Such names prove, to Williams, that this "seemingly style-less man had real style."

Williams points further to Gruelle's "elaborate verbal repetitions": "The Tired Old Horse may be The Old Tired Horse or, less often, The Old Horse or The Tired Horse, but he is never simply The Horse. Children love such elegant verbal ritual, and Gruelle used that love in his writing."

"I don't think he wrote just for Marcella alone," sums up Worth Gruelle, "or for Worth and Dick either, but for children of all ages."

> *John Canemaker, "Johnny Gruelle and His Million-Dollar Dolly," in his* The Animated Raggedy Ann & Andy: An Intimate Look at the Art of Animation: Its History, Techniques, and Artists, *Bobbs-Merrill, 1977, pp. 63-75.*

**Margery Fisher**

The nursery tales of the 'twenties had a curious coy didacticism much diluted from the robust, unself-conscious moralising of Victorian children's stories. The virtues of kindliness, courage and honesty are implicit, and often directly advocated, in the Raggedy Ann tales, and present-day reprints will need to be accepted as period pieces if children are to feel comfortable with them now. Possibly they will come to terms with them through the illustrations, since rag dolls are currently enjoying a revival in the nursery world. At least there is plenty of lively action in [*Raggedy Ann Stories* and *Raggedy Ann and the Hobby Horse*]. *Raggedy Andy Stories* tell how this engaging doll, made for the author's mother to match her Raggedy Ann, makes friends with the rest of the dolls, enjoys a taffy pull with them and rides on the new wooden horse, is rescued from the snow by Grandma and is given a new smiling face by Father Christmas after being badly stained with orange juice. In the second book, a hobby horse escaped from a cruel magician is helped by the rag dolls, in a series of enchantments reminiscent of the Oz books. The humour in the books is good-hearted and helps to swing one through a good deal of what, today, seems like verbiage.

> *Margery Fisher, in a review of "Raggedy Andy Stories" and "Raggedy Ann and the Hobby Horse," in* Growing Point, *Vol. 17, No. 4, November, 1978, p. 3405.*

**Michael Patrick Hearn**

The year *Raggedy Ann Stories* appeared, Johnny Gruelle also published the now forgotten *Funny Little Book.* It is delightful nonsense: A funny little man meets a funny little woman who invites him to meet her funny little family in her funny little house, and it turns out that she is his funny little wife. They have just been playing a funny little game. Because all of the characters are wooden dolls, Gruelle adopted an uncharacteristic but no less engaging mock-cubist style for this funny little picture book.

> *Michael Patrick Hearn, "The Lost Classics of Childhood," in* Book World—The Washington Post, *November 6, 1988, pp. 17-18.*

**Patricia L. Hudson**

Johnny Gruelle's particular gift, both as an author and an illustrator, was his ability to capture the simple yet heart-felt dreams of children. "He was always a boy at heart," says [biographer Patricia] Hall. "There was a part of him that never lost touch with the deepest feelings of child-hood."

*Patricia L. Hudson, "Still Smiling at Seventy-Five," in* Americana, *Vol. 18, No. 5, November-December, 1990, pp. 52-5.*

# Charles Keeping

## 1924-1988

(Full name Charles William James Keeping) English author and illustrator of picture books.

Major works include *Charley, Charlotte and the Golden Canary* (1967), *Alfie and the Ferry Boat* (1968; U.S. edition as *Alfie Finds "The Other Side of the World"*), *The God Beneath the Sea* (by Leon Garfield and Edward Blishen, 1970), *Through the Window* (1970), *The Highwayman* (by Alfred Noyes, 1981).

### INTRODUCTION

Keeping was an award-winning illustrator of a number of highly regarded works who also created his own often controversial books for primary graders. An inventive stylist who is lauded for helping to broaden the scope of picture-book art during the 1960s, he is described by Elaine Moss as "arguably the greatest picture-book artist of our time." Lauded as brilliant, profound, and courageous, Keeping created books that are often called visual tours de force and reflect what is considered a mature and often disturbing personal vision. Keeping regarded his books, which are acknowledged for their powerful illustrations and complex themes, as an art form not unlike film, a series of impressions to be followed from beginning to end in succession; his works are noted for this quality, with a continuum of images flowing one into the next. Praised as a brilliant innovator, Keeping declared that his primary aim as an illustrator was not to reflect the action of the story but rather to interpret feelings. His texts are spare, nearly plotless, and considered almost inconsequential to his pictures, which he insisted were the key to understanding his messages. While his early work was more clearly representational, his art became increasingly atmospheric and expressionistic, filled with fine—and often sinuous—line and dramatic use of light/dark contrasts. In paintings that utilize black and white India ink, gouache, tempera, watercolor, and other mediums, Keeping created a world of impressions, sometimes troubling, with background and foreground merging, or figures dissolving into abstraction. Keeping is also lauded for his design sense. Although he did not draw landscape, he frequently utilized urban textures of wood, brick, glass, and textiles to depict certain background objects, then employed line to join the figures with the setting. In using color he rarely employed naturalistic hues, offering instead a variety of shades as a means of expressing specific emotions or to signify sounds of the city. He also manipulated color to show that it never remains the same; for example, a character's clothing may change hue as the light of day wanes or as the character walks by certain artificial sources of light.

It is often noted that color adds drama to Keeping's books, as in *Wasteground Circus* (1975), where two boys witness a circus arrive at an abandoned site, perform, and leave. The drab illustrations of the urban setting become increas-

ingly bright as the circus completes its setup; the performance is ablaze with color, and the hues fade as the group leaves. A few strips of color, however, are left behind, symbolic of one character's conviction that the site is now blessed with the possibility of wonderful opportunities. Keeping has fashioned many characters similar to the two through whom he narrates the *Wasteground Circus*. In several books his child protagonists, usually lonely boys, play in enclosed yards littered with debris, viewing the squalor and destitution of East End London through windows or fences, as did Keeping at an early age. Although seemingly unflattering, the artist's unadulterated portrayal of the human and animal inhabitants of this environment captures the appeal of their strength and simplicity in both text and illustration. While he thus offers the reader much to ponder, critics have lamented what they consider a regrettable lack of levity in his works. Because he does not recoil from the elements of life which are unsavory, frightening, and violent, he is often accused of producing books which, while technically impressive, are thought to be inappropriate for children. John Rowe Townsend has written: "[Keeping] has never made any concession to supposed childish tastes, and his work raises in acute form the question whether picture-book artists sometimes demand too much of their audiences and waste their endeavors on those who cannot yet appreciate what they are doing." Keeping, however, contended that books set in "a land of sugar puffs and cream" fail to capture the true essence of life, which children inevitably gain awareness of through the media. Jean Russell is one of several commentators who have applauded Keeping's unique style, maintaining that his "greatest asset is his conviction in what he is doing and his knowledge of exactly where he is going." Frank Eyre adds: "[Keeping] has a strangely hypnotic style which seems to be either greatly liked or strongly detested; and he is unusual among what are perhaps too loosely described as 'picture book artists' in being passionately interested in ideas."

The son of a professional boxer and a grandson of street traders, Keeping was born in the South London borough of Lambeth in 1924. Respecting his father's wish not to play in the streets, Keeping intently watched the activities in the neighboring stable yard and on the street, creating stories out of the train of people and events that passed before him. He was apprenticed in the printing trade at the age of fourteen and served in the Navy during World War II. Thereafter, he worked as a cartoonist for a newspaper and as a commercial artist. Keeping began illustrating books in 1956, working for more than a decade on scores of titles by such authors as Rosemary Sutcliff, Henry Treece, Kenneth Grahame, Emily Brontë, Mollie Hunter, and Alan Garner. Encouraged to write and illustrate his own texts, he began offering his impressions of a child's life in London. One of Keeping's first books, *Charley, Charlotte and the Golden Canary*, explores a motif common to many of his stories: that of the child isolated by his urban environs. Acclaimed for its startling color mix of bright incandescent yellow, deep violet, blue, and orange, the story relates the adventures of two small friends, Charley and Charlotte, who are separated when Charlotte moves away but reunited when Charley's canary escapes and flies to the window of her high-rise apartment. *Alfie and the Ferryboat* describes a young boy's travels across the Thames—in the child's view, an exotic trip to the other side of the world. The book's pictures are filled with a sense of enchantment; not interested in simply recording the sites Alfie observes, Keeping drew spirals of color and abstract images to try to capture the wonder with which his young protagonist would have viewed these scenes. *Through the Window* explores more serious themes. In this story, young Jacob's life is defined by what he experiences vicariously while peering through the front window of his home. When he sees an elderly woman grieve because her dog has been killed, Jacob breathes on the window and draws a picture with his finger in which the dog is alive and its owner happy. Described by *Junior Bookshelf* as "brilliant, profound, disturbing as only Keeping can be," *Through the Window* garnered a mixed reception from critics. While Margery Fisher praised Keeping for "mak[ing] us open our eyes and exercise our feelings," Kevin Crossley-Holland commented: "It is high time Mr. Keeping realised that he has a responsibility not only to his art but also to his audience. Precisely because his pictures are so fine, there is every possibility that this arrogant book . . . will profoundly disturb a large number of those children who are unfortunate enough to see it."

Keeping continued to address pensive themes with *The Railway Passage* (1974), his story of children who live and play in an abandoned railway passage, cared for by "aunts and uncles" who together play the Pools in an effort to escape their extreme poverty. The generally disappointing results of these gamblers' eventual winnings are viewed through the eyes of the children. Considered unique in its focus on adult characters, *The Railway Passage* was praised by Marcus Crouch as Keeping's "best story to date"; Crouch adds: "Here is an artist who knows urban poverty and paints it in all its unwitting beauty." *River* (1978) and *Adam and Paradise Island* (1989) examine urban growth and renewal–in the former, as contrasted with its unchanging natural surroundings. The characteristic depth of feeling in his books is also evident in the pictures he has done for other authors. For example, in his award-winning illustrations for Leon Garfield and Edward Blishen's *The God Beneath the Sea*—which Alan Garner described as "more terrible and beautiful than Goya"—and Alfred Noyes's *The Highwayman*, Keeping has been commended for the intensity of his pictures and the mastery of his images, but the violence of his depictions of the dead Bess or the tortured Prometheus have led critics to note the dilemma in assessing Keeping's opus. While questioning the effectiveness of his complicated work, reviewers nonetheless nearly unanimously rate Keeping one of the most singular and talented visionaries in contemporary children's literature. *Charley, Charlotte and the Golden Canary* was awarded the Kate Greenaway Medal in 1967, an award also won by *The Highwayman* in 1981. *Joseph's Yard* was named a Greenaway honor book in 1969, and *The God Beneath the Sea* received a Greenaway Medal commendation in 1970. *The Spider's Web* won a plaque at the Biennale of Illustrations Bratislava (BIB) in 1973, and *Railway Passage* won a golden apple at the BIB in 1975, after gaining a Greenaway Medal high commendation in 1974. *The Wildman* was given the W. H. Smith Illustration Award in 1976, a prize Keeping received for *Charles Keeping's Classic Tales of the Macabre* in 1988. In addition, Keeping was runner-up for the Kurt Maschler award in 1985 for *The Wedding Ghost* and won the Maschler award in 1987 for *Jack the Treacle Eater*.

(See also *Contemporary Authors*, Vol. 125; *Contemporary Authors New Revision Series*, Vol. 11; and *Something about the Author*, Vols. 9, 56.)

---

## ILLUSTRATOR'S COMMENTARY

*[The following excerpt is from a speech which was delivered at the Exeter Conference on Children's Literature in 1969.]*

[One] of the strange things often said about me is that I have forgotten the child. This is terribly funny because I think the child is one of the few people who does appreciate certainly some of my more recent work. I can prove it if anybody wants to put it to the test. In Islington they actually lick my books—that seems to me real proof! Books are physical things. They are not just drawings in a group of pages—they are physical things to hold in your hand. If my books are sensuous and the kids lick them, great, that suits me fine. That's what happens. Most of my students, when they leave art college after 3 to 5 years, 70 per cent of them drift into teaching because there is not much work around or because things are not that well paid. Many of them teach in primary schools, secondary modern schools, grammar schools; they are teaching from the primary school level the very children who are going to the library to see a book that I or anybody else like myself will produce. These children are *far* more in touch with what is happening and what it's about when it comes to the art side of it, because these children have been brought up on art that isn't just stuck in a certain type of nineteenth century rut. They are quite willing to accept any type of change at all in the structure and they understand it. Let's make this quite clear. They do understand it.

One of my last books you've seen was *Alfie and the Ferry Boat* which was probably the beginning of the move away which I am certainly going on to now. *Alfie and the Ferry Boat* dissolved in the centre into forms of design which a lot of people found very worrying, which prompted somebody to say 'very nice, until we got to the page of squiggles.' This was terribly important because what I was doing was trying to dissolve the whole scene in a certain type of way that could be an experience that a child could easily have itself. Far from forgetting the child I think I was remembering the child most positively and most children have understood this and accepted it. There were words like, 'Alfie moved along with the crowds' and all the people were faced with was this large page of rather movable colour. Well, quite honestly, I don't think at that point in the book Alfie would have seen crowds anyway, because he was going through a new experience. He would have been concerned only with light and colour and therefore any child I think would understand this and accept it. It is the adult whose mind has been fixed and who probably has not had an art lesson since he was about sixteen who would not accept this as being a valid visual thing to do.

The next point is the 'fact' that some of our picture books today are disturbing children. It is almost so funny, you can't even take it seriously. How the devil I can disturb anybody I really don't know. One of my books was referred to in this way, 'What world do the children think they are going to have when they are faced with this? Why was a boy outside a knacker's yard?' I have a new book here in proof stage which was a film concerned with death, so you have really got worries.

I have felt for a long while, as I have explained to you and as you have probably noticed by my earlier remarks, that we have got, at some time or the other, to move away or move in other directions from where we have been going. This doesn't mean to say that there is no place for any sort of book, I can perfectly well appreciate the work of a man like Maurice Sendak despite the fact that to me Sendak is almost a nineteenth century illustrator. His work's all nineteenth century and I can appreciate it for what it is. We are always going to have a book for the left, a book for the right and a book for the centre, but what I want to see is a greater range of pictorial expression coming into children's books. I want to see many more younger people, and I do my best to encourage the best of my students into children's work, because I believe that a time is coming when we must accept this or sink. Now when I say 'sink', I think you all know what I mean, in the sense of the competition that most of the book world is going to get and continue to get from television.

I am one of those people who accepts television because it is here to stay, and it's not only here to stay it's going to develop. It's going to get better and better and better and it's going to be in colour and it's going to cover half your wall in the end. In fact you are probably going to have a television room and children today are going to see this come about. . . . It's going to be an essential part of education. I can see a time coming when television probably would even do away with teachers, as such, in a room. I am sure many people, if they stop to think, will agree on this. This is going to be more and more important because there might be a touch of Big Brother, it might all get sudden horrible shades of Orwell. But the development will come and we can't stop it, no more than we can stop people going to the moon. We might not like it but they are going to go. They are not going to ask your permission and the more you get a development of television, the more people are going to go over to it.

The book, if it is to survive against this onslaught of television, has to do one or two things. At the moment we are making a compromise. We are making film and we are making some of the film afterwards into book form. But if the book is to survive at all it must be accepted that it is a three-dimensional, physical thing. In other words, it is not unlike a film in that it is not a sort of book as we know a book, something with pages, with drawings on it. It is, in fact, a thing in itself, like any other thing is a thing in itself. Like you yourselves are something. Many people open a page of a book and say, 'I don't like that drawing.' Now the way I see a book you cannot open a book and say, 'I like that drawing' or, 'I don't like that drawing.' What you do is you either like the book or you don't like the book. I would put something that might be quite bad by some people's attitudes in the book because it was a part of the book, because I wanted to say something bad at that point. A book should never be a singular set of drawings, but a complete thing. A picture is something which you look at, which you see sitting there, if you like, and it is an experience which you either have or do not have in that position. A piece of sculpture is something that you can't do this with. It has a time element. In other words if this glass was a piece of sculpture you would have to move around it. From where you are you can only see one side. You have to move round it to get the complete experience. Surely the same goes for a book and a film? You can't go down to the cinema here and look at a few stills outside and say, 'Blimey, that was a good film.' Nor can you go in, sit down, watch three shots and walk out or look at the end of it. You have to sit down and sit for a time and this is the same with a book. That is not interesting. What is interesting is the time pattern through this book and whether the thing, like a film, adds up in the end to an experience or non-experience. It must be one thing or the other.

I have taken this very much to heart and therefore I am beginning slowly to make films and books of this type. I don't want any more to make books like my early books.

I have been working on a group of three books or three films, whichever way you like to look at it. One is called *Joseph's Yard,* the second *Through the Window* and the other one will eventually be called *The Garden Shed.* Actually *The Garden Shed* isn't even signed up yet so we will have to wait and see about that, but the other two are finished. *Joseph's Yard* and *Through the Window* are in fact already films and are on the way to being books. *Joseph's Yard* which I actually started nearly two years ago is for me quite old. But the thing is that these three ideas don't go very far away from what we find in so many of our folk poems and our folk tales, if we look back. We used a lot of the same ideas and dealt with the same problems. All three books are based on my own experiences as a child because one of the things I have found very hard to do is to write about somebody else. I find it very difficult ever to know anybody else or anybody else's environment and situation. I wouldn't dream of doing anything about somebody in Manchester, because I have never been to or lived in Manchester. To me Manchester is just a sort of railway station and therefore I know nothing of it. I must write and work—I must create ideas that come from myself. These three ideas were the original ideas, strangely enough, that I took to the Oxford University Press some six years ago, but at that time the temperature in children's books was not right and, quite rightly I think, Mabel George felt that they were maybe a little too sophisticated. Therefore we have kept them over. I have done other books which I think you probably all know which have used things which you won't find happen in these. *Joseph's Yard* deals with such things as loneliness, love, jealousy and death. These are things which I found as a boy were all terribly important to me. Maybe I have failed in my attempt to deal with them; one never knows, I am only putting forward to you the attempts that I have made. If I were to say, 'I have done this,' this assumes that I have succeeded. I never say I succeed in anything. I find that within a month of doing them most of my works are, to me personally, failures. Not in the reviewer's sense of the word 'failure' but to me with my knowledge of what I wanted to do.

I believe that these feelings do concern young people and I think it depends how you deal with them to bring out a certain mood or feeling within them, that one child somewhere will identify with. What I want to do is to deal with children in a given situation in which they find themselves, in which they tend to suffer their own inward feelings alone, and how, if you like, they can explore this position through accident or through consciousness. In *Joseph's Yard* the boy solves it by discovering flowers; he also discovers through flowers both love and, naturally, jealousy because his love of the flowers is so great he tries to protect them at all costs from anything, only losing all his other friends in the meanwhile. *Through the Window* deals with boredom, a very common feature of the human race—nothing strange there. It also deals with indifference, that is the visual experience which is thrust upon you without you necessarily being that interested. It also deals

with the rejection of what you see because you don't like it and the solving of it in your own visual terms. There is a sudden violence again which results in *Through the Window* in death which nevertheless is never spelled out; it is shown visually, but not shown in its worst sense. It is through the visual ideas that you understand this and the final drawing is by the child who has seen it all himself and this attempts to solve these problems. The third book will be concerned with something I feel very strongly about, the problem of humiliation. In these books I use symbols to express that it is happening to the character. In other words I am not going to have a child in it who is humiliated, I use symbolism which will sum this up. Now all of these three as you can imagine are suitable for films as well as for books; with a film of course we can have added things like music so therefore we get much greater evocative feeling and this is the sort of thing I personally now want to work at.

What the next stage will be I don't know. I have never done more than a certain amount without moving onto something else if I feel it later. This may be the end of three patterns or it may be more but this is what I am moving towards. That's what I am doing but what I want to see happen is other people coming in with their ideas. I am not one of the art teachers who try and keep people out. I know so many lecturers at art college . . . one came up to me one day and said, 'Here, Charlie, did you give that girl the address of so and so publisher and so and so gallery?' I said, 'Yes.' He said, 'You will run me out of business.' This is absolutely ridiculous. What I want is everybody in, not everybody out. I don't know what he thinks he is going to preserve, whether he wants to stand alone on some pedestal. It is absolutely ludicrous. You won't save your soul by doing that, please believe me. If anyone has got more to say than you have they'll have it and you will be forgotten. You won't save yourselves. You encourage them all in because you will have a lot of friends then. I always like the old saying, 'Be nice to them on the way up because you'll meet them all coming down.' Seriously, I do always encourage all my students to come in. I have a boy at the moment who has been working in a sort of optical form of art. He has done a beautiful book for me at the college and we also printed this book and it was very lovely. I don't know one publisher that would touch it with a barge pole but it's lovely and I think that it's something that they will have to touch one day. They will have to accept it because I think unless they do we have got no interplay of ideas going on.

Take friend bunny rabbit—all these books that seem to be in a land of sugar puffs and cream—it doesn't exist, you know. Turn your television on any day and you will see that. Vietnam is happening and you can't dismiss it by living in a world of sugar puffs. Kids know it is happening, therefore violence and all these things are a part of their life. So is modern art in its shape and form as completely non-figurative, non-suggestive of anything. In other words, real art and these things are establishing themselves very strongly in children's minds. They have been taught it, they see it, they go to exhibitions. They know. They are going to want this. We can even have books that are completely three dimensional. I am not talking about the old fashioned ones, years ago, you know, about Snow White and the Seven Dwarfs that popped up. Somebody said to me the other day, 'Kids like bangs.' Well, what about a book that explodes? Has anybody thought of that, because that is the sort of book I would like to see in as well. Why not? There is not only this sort of poem stuff. I know kids like that and my kids say to me, 'Oh, poems—rubbish.' They like big bangs. What about a book that stretches or squeaks or does anything? Let's have some ideas. What about a round book? What about one that is a circular tube with lots fitting inside it? We have tried that at the college actually. It's not a great success. Really I am only trying to ask you all to see the funny side. We must at some time or other introduce this unless we are to live in a world of bunnies whose ears bend over. The funny thing is my kids have got two bunnies and I have never seen one of their ears fold over. If anybody has got a rabbit whose ears fold over, let me know. I will give them one of those sugar buns.

> *Charles Keeping, "Illustration in Children's Books," in* Children's literature in education, *No. 1, March, 1970, pp. 41-54.*

*[The following excerpt is from a speech which was originally delivered at the Tenth Annual Conference of the Children's Literature Association, held at the University of Alberta on May 13-15, 1983.]*

I was born in Lambeth. I don't suppose anyone here knows it, but there is a very famous song called "Lambeth Walk" written about it. It's by the river and it's an area of small, mainly Victorian and Georgian, houses with small gardens. The people there were the "poor but honest" sort, and my family was part of what I can only describe as comfortable working class. We certainly weren't poor—there was much poverty around us, but we weren't poor ourselves—and we had a large household, full of aunts, uncles, goodness knows who else. We were terribly spoiled, my sister and I, and we were encouraged to create, to do everything: singing, reciting, talking. You had to tell a story every time you came home; if you didn't they wondered what was wrong with you; they thought you were ill. My grandmother always delighted in saying, "Now what have you done today?" and it had to last half an hour. She would laugh at all the appropriate moments and cry at all the appropriate moments and make your story interesting. Incidentally, she also told very, very lengthy stories herself, and you had to listen to those, too.

My grandfather was a merchant seaman. He'd been to sea for forty years, he knew the Far East and Australia long before there was a Panama Canal, and he told stories of the sea. All these things were very stirring and very exciting to me as a child.

Of course, my own vision as a child was not so broad. One only saw what one experienced oneself, and when it comes to my own actual work later in life, I tend to keep within what I could see as a child. That was mainly a small garden, a fence, and a large black wall. Against that black wall many things took place. It was a yard which had cart horses, and I would see these vast shapes of horses moving across this wall. These very simple images attracted me, I know, as a very small boy. And I used to like the cats and the birds and things that came into the yard and sat on the flowers. This was an exciting, tiny world to live in.

I also enjoyed being taken into that yard next door and sat on the backs of cart horses. This was a very, very exciting thing for a child. It had an element of fear, because the animals were so large, and it had a feeling of almost sensuous comfort because the horses were furry and warm. When I got back home, I used to draw those horses and what I had seen in that stable.

The feeling was that by drawing it you had it again. You'd really got it for yourself, and no one could take it from you. It was yours; you were actually putting it down and owning it. It sounds a terribly selfish attitude, but drawing is essentially a very selfish pastime. You want to keep something; you want to hold it. If you were frightened, as a child, by a cat that came in the yard and tried to kill a bird, you could then exorcise this fear by drawing the cat. You could even tear the drawing up afterward, you know, and then you'd destroyed the cat. I quickly discovered there were many sorts of things you could do in drawing.

I really never missed a day drawing. In fact, I spent so much time drawing, I was very bad at most other things at school. Looking back on it, I would go so far as to say I was pretty appalling, because I really wasn't interested in it. When you're so passionate about something, as I certainly was about drawing, you want to do it all the time, and you cannot find the concentration to do those things which you don't like or you don't want to do. This is something that I feel very strongly, and it's something we all ought to think about when we're saying a child is not very good at something. We might be looking to see what he is, or she is, good at.

Now my world would quickly break away from the little yard. I was going to go out into the outside world and learn about other things. One of the first things was, we used to go on holiday. My father had a little open car, a Morris Cowley. When we went to the seaside, he drove along the main front of the seaside, and they used to have colored lights strung across the road. To a child, this was like a fairyland. It was years later—I'll tell you when we come to it—how I used that fairyland. I remember there was a waitress at the hotel where we were that I fell madly in love with, and I drew her—I was only twelve or something at the time—and I drew her on the menu. This was a way of preserving her and taking her back to town with me. You see, it is a question of capturing the things you like and the things you love, and I think only later are you trying to give them to somebody else in your books; at the time you're only concerned with holding on to them.

This type of thing happens to many children, I am sure, but later on when they grow up, it's destroyed. They become things like chartered accountants and what have you. I have the pleasure of telling you I've never grown up. They tried very hard in the Royal Navy, but it didn't work awfully well. I spent four years in it, but I somehow managed to escape without losing that romanticism I had as a child.

It's not easy, to get a start in illustration. First of all, I do believe that you have to go to art school. And after the war

*From* Charley Charlotte, and the Golden Canary, *written and illustrated by Charles Keeping.*

I did. But it wasn't easy in those days to study full time, and I spent quite a while as a rent collector in a dreadful area in London, a really poor, rundown area, for pennies. Looking back on it now, it was a great help to me later in my understanding of people, of poverty and of how people live. I think I saw more real poverty at that period than I had seen even as a child. Because as a child you're not really conscious; you know there are poor people around you, you see some boys coming to school in ragged clothes, but you're going back to your own little castle in your own little world, and you can forget. But you can't forget when you are older, and much of my work has been colored by those years in Paddington, when I really felt that people were underprivileged.

Now in art school, I did endless drawings. If you've got anyone in your family who wants to be an illustrator, tell them for goodness sake to learn drawing, because it's terribly important. It's one thing knowing what you want to say. It's another thing knowing what to do with it, how to control it, and that is essential.

After art school it was pretty grim. I found myself needing to earn a living. I certainly didn't want to do rent collecting again, and the only thing that was going in the world of art was a job on a daily newspaper. I took it on for three years. I suppose, if anything, it taught me design, because I did a daily cartoon, with another man who did the writing, and it was a topical drawing; to fight your way on the front or the back of a daily newspaper with crosswords, pin-ups, goodness knows what, to try to make your statement, is absolute hell, and it really taught me design. It taught me how to attract people's attention, how to make them look at my work and not just miss it over. You know,

it's far better if a book in a bookstore is in a pure white jacket with a black circle, because all the others look like fruit salads, and if you put all the fruit salads together and stick your one white book in the middle, people will pick it up. That's psychology—they do. And this I learned on the newspaper.

I quickly got away from it because it really was not my scene. But I did try advertising, and it was a disaster for me. I am not made to sell people's dog food or toilet bowls, and I found it absolutely soul destroying.

I decided to ask my agent to get me more book work, and I eventually was invited by Oxford University Press to come along to meet a very formidable editor, one of the greatest London ever had, called Miss Mabel George. The O.U.P. then was in Maidenhead Square opposite St. Paul's, and Mabel George had a little office right on the top floor. I went up there—it was a job to find it, you had to go through all kinds of little passages and places all thick with books, and it was like a broom cupboard. She gave me this large manuscript, and she said, "It's about Romans." And I thought, oh no! Not all those blokes clanging about with shields! I hadn't the slightest interest in them. But you can't just turn things down, so I took this thing home. On the way home I started reading it, and I found it wasn't so much about Romans, at least not Romans that clang about. In fact, it was a brilliantly written piece of work, by Rosemary Sutcliff, a very, very lovely lady whom I worked with on three or four books. And that was my intro into the O.U.P.

I also worked with Henry Treece, who was very into Vikings. I didn't know much about those either, so I invented my own. I was a bit shocked once to see some drawings of Vikings that looked very like the ones I'd drawn, and I thought, "Good God! I invented those. They're not Vikings at all." This was in an educational book, so it shows you that you want to stay away from education.

I invented my own Vikings because I can't believe they actually were what people say. If you look at what life must have been like in those days, it was jolly cold in the parts of the world they came from. I think they would have wrapped themselves in anything. And they must have been pretty filthy people, they must have been in a right state after sailing about on those little boats. The smell of them must have been disgraceful. So I took my Vikings from my own imagination, and I didn't take them much from anywhere else. I don't think anyone really knows much about them anyway.

But I grew a little tired of them in the end. I kept getting people asking me to illustrate books about Vikings. I'd done so many of them I was beginning to look like one, and I was jolly pleased when Mabel George said, "Look, would you like to do a picture book?" At that time I had never been involved in picture books. I didn't see myself as a picture book illustrator at all. I thought one of my old friends, Brian Wildsmith, who is a very, very good designer and colorist, was ideally suited for picture books, but I wasn't sure I could see any place for myself in this world.

But I have a way of doing things like a diary. I'm not very good at writing, I can't even spell awfully well; that's why

I don't write anything out to talk to you about, because I wouldn't be able to read it. But I make these little writings, these little poems and things, and I brought them in to Mabel George. She said, "Look, none of these are suitable to make a book of. Could you just take bits from the writings and make a sort of composite book?" It was called *Shaun and the Cart Horse,* but it really was a composite book that I just made up from these other writings. I did it in a lot of bright color, not out of conviction but because I felt at the time that was what people wanted. That was not very honest, because at that time I was very much involved with black and white illustrations, but picture books seemed to be about color and I felt I ought to do it.

Strangely enough, it was very well received. They made me runner-up for the Kate Greenaway Award for it. Mabel George was quite pleased, and she said to me, "Look, we better have another one from you. Have you got another idea?" So I said, "Oh, yes, I've got one. I've got a good one. It's about a man who catches sparrows, and he paints them to look like canaries and sells them." She said, "Good God! I've never heard anything so cruel in my life. We can't do a thing like that for little children. It's out of the question, and anyway it never happened." I said, "Well, I'm sorry, Mabel, but it did, my uncle used to do it. He also used to sell pigeons in the market, and he trained them to come back so he could sell them again." But Mabel George said, "No, I'm not having that sort of thing written for children." Well, I left there, and as I walked over London Bridge through an area which was terribly bombed in the war, I noticed that although some of the old streets were surviving, much of it had been destroyed, and they'd built a great new world of glass, great tower blocks which were, to my mind, impersonal and aloof. They make it very beautiful at night when they're lit up, but I wouldn't like to live in them. I was still involved with sparrows and annoyed about the rejection, and I noticed that the sparrows in the old streets were very happy, and so were the children playing in the streets. Then I looked up at these wretched flats, and on all these little balconies all the way up, I could see little children holding onto the railings, looking down, and I realized that these children could never come down, they could never come down on the street because they would be too far from their parents. They were perfectly safe but they were all in little cages, maybe twenty, thirty floors in the air. And it struck me that there was a great similarity between them and the canaries in their cages. Now if you look at a canary in a cage, it seems to be perfectly happy, it's certainly very comfortable, and it's certainly well fed by the people who own it; but what sort of existence has it got? And yet in the street there are the sparrows; they get squashed by vehicles going through, they get killed and die, snows in the winter kill them off, yet they have a much better life while they're around, you know, because at least they're free. I decided somebody ought to make a statement about this; we do need to make these personal statements in children's books. So I produced a book called *Charley, Charlotte, and the Golden Canary.* It went on to get the Kate Greenaway Award, and because of that, Mabel George asked me to do more.

Personally, I still had some doubts about this field. I wasn't really doing books for children as such; I was really doing things for myself. I was talking about what I had seen and I called them children's books. On the other hand, I felt I was doing something that could be interpreted to children, even if the children didn't get the point themselves; and I was asked to persevere, so I did.

I went to Southend to produce a book called *Alfie and the Ferry Boat.* Now we have a ferry that runs across the river from Woolwich, and I felt this was a good vehicle for the element of adventure. I mean, can you imagine how the big ferry boat with its lights on looks to a child? He doesn't know where he's going on it; he could be going anywhere, any place in the world, any place in his imagination. To him, the other side of the river might as well be China, might as well be anywhere, because he only knows where he lives.

At that same time, I was talking to a man in a pub—I do learn a lot from talking to people in pubs; they're great institutions. Well, I was with my brother-in-law in this pub (and I'd known my brother-in-law as a boy); we were talking to this man, and he was talking about how he could've played for a famous football club—I believe you call it soccer. Well, one thing led to another, and my brother-in-law said, "Oh, God, yes, I've often told my son I almost got chosen to play for Chelsea, and had I played for Chelsea, I think I would have played for England." Well, I didn't remember that, and I knew him when he was at school. But he had been telling his son these things, you see, and I realized that his son would grow up saying, "My dad nearly played for Chelsea, or my dad could've played for England," and I thought, it's crazy how people pass on these things that children will believe. So I invented a man who told a child about how he used to go to the other side of the world. Now would a child know this was untrue, that "the other side of the world" was only a path outside? And would a child crossing on the ferryboat, and reaching, maybe, Southend on the other side, with its beautiful colored lights, see it as a fairyland, as I had when I was a child? It wasn't when I went back; all I saw then were loads of drunks sort of lolling about with funny hats on with "Kiss Me Kate" on them. But you know, it doesn't matter to a child, you don't see that side of it, you only see the lights, and therefore I did a book that showed the actual path as a path, but also showed that there *was* another side of the world, in the imagination, and that any child could imagine that themselves.

I've often been accused of making things very violent in children's books. Mabel George was always frightened that I would suddenly bring violence into my picture books, and I thought of that when I was at Southend. It's a long pier; it's a mile long, and I was right down at the end of it looking back on Southend and watching the lights. There were some little children playing. The pier had chains. You could fall in the water if you were careless, but there were chains, and there were little children swinging over and over on the chains; you know how they do. And there was a man standing there in a uniform, and I think the uniform had given him some sort of feeling of superiority over everybody else. He was a tall man; he stood at attention with his hands behind his back, like this, you see, and this cap on, and this braid; and he suddenly turned to these children and he said, "Stop doing that; you'll fall in the water." And he turned away again and immediately stared off, you see. They all stopped, but then they went on again. Well, he was really affronted because there he was, this great big man in his uniform, and these kids took no notice of it. So he said, "If you do it again, you'll all be drowned. A dog fell in there the other day, a dog," he said. So one little girl came up to him and she said, "Did it die?" And he said, "Yes, of course it did." So she said, "What did it look like when it was dead?" Well, he'd seen me standing there and I suppose he thought, "God, my authority's all gone," so he said to this little girl, "Oh, his eyes were hanging out." I'm not joking; he said that. And another little girl, she had a big bow in her hair, she came up and said, "Can we see it?" Well, I don't believe he ever was the same man again.

I really learned a lesson that day. Children are not so easily frightened. I'm told so often that something I've done in a picture book has frightened the life out of children. But really, I don't think you can. I think they all frighten the life out of me.

Well, at this point I started on a series of books like *Joseph's Yard* and *Through the Window*. I think *Joseph's Yard* becomes self-evident in all I've said. It was the first one where I returned to my writings. I felt this book was necessary because so many children are made conspicuous by being, I don't know, crippled, by wearing glasses, by being very fat; maybe nowadays in many schools they can be sorted out and picked upon for their color. Therefore, my Joseph was a marvelously scruffy little boy, he wasn't very beautiful and he wore glasses. It's easy to make a pretty little boy a hero; most people respond to it. But it isn't always easy to make an ugly little boy a hero.

I felt that if I used the idea of trying to own something a child might learn that life is about sharing. As you may know, I showed how in his endeavor to own the flower he had planted in bleak yard, Joseph constantly killed it. He had to learn to share his flower with the birds and the insects and the cats. I hope that it was the type of book that could get a real discussion going. Basically I think that is what these books were about.

The one that followed on from that was *Through the Window*. Many people say I killed a dog in it, but actually I didn't. They just assume the dog is dead. I've always felt that when you go through life you often look at it through a window. You do that when you look at television, and you do it when you are driving along in your car. I'm sure there must be people here that come home of a night in their car, and they've looked out of the window, maybe they've stopped at the lights, and they've seen an accident, someone knocked down, two cars smashed, police there, you know. Yet they drive on; they don't stop. And they go home and they say to their wives or husbands, "I just saw a shocking accident down the road." And they say, "Did you?" "Yes," and then they just say, "I've got supper ready" and "Do you want a drink?" The thing goes; everything is a passing thing in your life, visual things come and they go and they move. In a way it's like the

stage. I use the window for this effect in the book because the house I lived in as a child looked out onto the street. My father was a great stickler for the dangers of the road, even back in the thirties, and he wouldn't allow me to go out in the street as a small boy, and therefore I looked at most of it through the window. It's surprising how many things you see and note and enjoy.

My greatest hero then was a man who drove a van, a horse van. In the book I made him into the road sweeper. I just wanted to be like him, I don't know why, I thought he was terrific. Years later I told this story to my mother and she said, "Do you know, that man had about ten children, his wife died of tuberculosis when she was in her early thirties, and he was left with all these children. At least half of them died very young, also of tuberculosis, and he himself eventually died of tuberculosis." He was the most tragic, poverty-stricken man, yet as a little boy, I somehow fixed on him for my hero. As children, we can find heroes anywhere, and therefore I decided to use the ordinary people of the street in the book. I made the man who drove the beautiful brewery horses that go past the boy's window the great hero. I made the lady with her dog the pathetic person, the sad person.

I also decided that, when anything happens outside your window, you can't see all of it. It's like a stage, or like being offstage. So I made everything pass one way, and I made it all come back the other way, and then I took it back slowly, a procession back through the window the other way. But the boy never actually saw anything important at all; he only saw all the actors in the play, if you like, moving past him toward and away from the stage. But another boy in the street did see it all, and that brings in the whole question of envy, because we all envy the chap who can see it all when we can't see it. So we have many interplaying ideas in the same story.

They made this book into a short television film. It looked very good, and I think because of that I decided to do the next one along the same lines. But I'm afraid that one was a bit of a disaster. It was called *The Garden Shed* and I apologize for it; I don't think it was very good. Incidentally, after I'm finished I think most of the things I do are pretty awful. It's the one thing that makes me do another one.

I followed up *The Garden Shed* with another one in the same group called *The Spider's Web*, which I do think was a good one, as good as they can be anyway. It was again looking at things from an enclosed world, and I was trying to get over the idea of how we are afraid of things, yet we become terribly brave when we find that someone else isn't afraid. The boy is afraid of the chicken until he finds that the chicken is afraid of the dog, and then he thinks the chicken's silly, because he immediately associates himself with the dog. In the end the bravest one is the little girl, and that's why the book got a lot of criticism in England. Fancy showing a little boy hiding behind a little girl! Well, I can assure them I hid behind my sister often.

I did a book soon after that called *The Railway Passage*. I was in a pub again—horrible, isn't it? And I was talking to a man about my car, which had broken down. I'm not very good with motor cars, and he said, "I'll mend that for you, no trouble at all." He had been telling me that he was a gritter on the road and that he earned, and this was a lot of money at this time, £100 a week, gritting the road when it snowed. Well, it doesn't snow very often in England, so I said to him, "You know, I don't want to be rude, but what do you do apart from that?" He said, "Oh nothing," he said, "we have to sit around and wait until it snows." So I thought, he's got a pretty nice job there, for £100 a week. He said he would come and fix my car, and he did. He spent all day on it, and when he had finished, he was covered from head to foot in grease, and he looked a right state. I felt very sorry about that. This man gets £100 for sitting there waiting for it to snow, and it never does, and he comes round and mends my car and he looks like he's been down the drain, and you know, I can't give him £100. So I said to him, "Look Ted," that was his name, I said, "What do I owe you?" and he said, "Don't you insult me, Charlie, don't insult me," he said, "Nothing, I won't take a penny off you." I suddenly realized that people will do many things they like for nothing, but if they don't like it, they want to be paid a lot of money. I thought he'd fit nicely into my story about seven old-age pensioners.

We have a thing called football pools. You put down what will happen at each football match on a lot of coupons, and if you get them all right, you win thousands and thousands. I had all these old people going in for the pools, and everyone was a bit worried about this book. You couldn't do a book about old-age pensioners for children. I couldn't see why not; I thought they would be quite interested in old people, so I did it.

I decided that each one would represent a different human characteristic, and if you see the book, I think you'll recognize people you know. There's the lady in it who has a fish, and I based her story on my own children. They had a guinea pig; it had a special house and it was given a name and it was really cared for. Unfortunately, they got another guinea pig, and as you know, guinea pigs don't stay two guinea pigs for very long, especially if they are of the opposite sex. In no time at all, I think we had about fifty guinea pigs, and nobody seemed to care much about them. There were guinea pigs everywhere, and you couldn't make out who they all were. I've never seen so many, and the children couldn't cope with them all. So the lady in the book had a fish called Sam, and she loved it; but when she won all the money, she bought thousands and thousands of fish, and of course she could never find Sam again. I think this is a moral point in life. We should remember, when we've got something, not to want a lot more. I also put in the man who mended bicycles, who, like my friend with the car, was content to just do the things he liked, and the money didn't mean a lot to him. I was very cruel to some of the people, and I got severely reprimanded for it in New Zealand, where a man came on the radio and said I was a disgrace to the working class. But it was about greed, and I don't think that particular characteristic belongs only to working people. At this stage we were in a bit of trouble in England. The books weren't selling enough. A lot of people found controversial books unacceptable and wanted a return to the old comfortable sort of things they knew. Because of the recession in England, many publishers decided that books had to be more popular and that you had to sell at least thirty thousand the world over. Mabel George had retired by this time, and the new men who had taken over at O.U.P. started talking in terms of wanting books that would appeal to everyone: the Japanese, the American Continent, the French, the Germans. I don't think you can do that. I don't think you can make a character in a book look like everyone. The mind boggles at what you'd have to do visually. I mean, cars with steering wheels in the middle? And the way you'd draw human beings blows my mind. And what's wrong with having books about different people? I don't want to see a book from Africa all about white people, I want it to be about Africans; I want to see how they live. We should be broad enough to be able to accept books from other countries, but people can't. I've had books turned down, in foreign sales, for that reason. They say they're too local, too much concerned with London. It's absolutely crazy. I beg you librarians to bear in mind what would happen if we pursue this. Books are already fast becoming no more than a commodity, like a bit of dog food on the shelf in the supermarket. Do we really want to see books reduced to that, books that offend nobody's ideas, offend nobody? Books *should* offend sometimes; there *are* offensive things that we should talk about in children's books. The great children's stories of the past were all about ugly things that really happened. Let's remember "Little Red Riding Hood" really wasn't about a wolf; I mean, there weren't many wolves roaming about the streets of London, but there were an awful lot of men that acted like wolves. Children today still need to be warned more about men in cars with sweets than they do about wolves. I once suggested this, and the editor went through the roof. He said, "How can you talk about a child molester or a rapist in a children's book?" But why shouldn't you? We should be talking about practically everything in children's books, and I think it's very sad that we're not.

In the late seventies, many of us found that the ideas that we had were not acceptable. At this time, I produced two books, one, called *Inter-City,* about a train journey. Basically it's okay, but I don't think it said an awful lot. It proved that when you go on a train you go through the tunnel, and you go through the city, and you go through the country, and you go through a tunnel, and then you're back in another station. In *The River,* I showed what we do with the river. I don't know if it happens here, but in London, they used to build big brick walls in front of the docks to stop pilfering, and when the docks fell into disrepair and were finished and useless, the wall was left. Rather than pull the lot down and show the landscape as it is, they paint a river on the wall! It might look nice, but why not look at the real river? It seems crazy, painting this make-believe world, and I thought I'd do a bit of a send-up of this type of thing. But *The River* also was greatly criticized; people even accused Oxford of producing books that were only suitable for the Oxford dons' children, and it didn't do very well.

That's when I decided with the editor to try a poem. Now *I* wanted to do "Gunga Din," because I think Kipling's poems could be done very well as a sort of formal picture book for children, slightly older children maybe; but they wanted me to do **"The Highwayman."** I knew the poem well at school; of course, everybody had it, and it struck me that it was the sort of thing that, if you are going to do it, you've got to really do it. You can't just do yet another little colored-up version. It doesn't need color at all; it's got plenty of color in the actual words, and one of the things I feel you must never do is let the drawings and the words say the same thing. So I decided to do it in black and white.

**"The Highwayman"** is a poem about rape, it's about murder, it's about intrigue, and it isn't really a very nice poem. Now I cannot do a thing without being conscious that it's not very nice, and once I get conscious that it's not very nice, that not-very-nice feeling comes over in the work. Well, after it won the Kate Greenaway Award, a critic in The Telegraph said, "What is it coming to, when a children's book that wins the Kate Greenaway Award is about rape?"

He might have said that years ago, when it was written by Noyes back in the beginning of the century; it was hardly me who invented it. But I couldn't do that book and run away from those facts.

In their wisdom, O.U.P. followed up **"The Highwayman"** by asking me to join with Kevin Crossley-Holland on **Beowulf**—and that's the latest one. Many people think of **Beowulf** as just pure good against pure evil. But I don't think there's anything, really, that is that evil, or anything that's that good. Even the nicest people often do things for their own ends. Even the saintly figures like Mr. Ghandi and Mother Teresa must get some sort of secret pleasure from doing those things, and if you are deriving pleasure from what you're doing, you can't be doing it only out of goodness. I also don't think there is anything totally evil, and I've always thought of Grendel in **Beowulf** as a cripple. I think that to be such an outsider and shunned by everyone else, because you are not quite one of them and because you are so ugly and misformed, is a pretty dreadful thing, and it could easily make you want to wreak vengeance on the rest of mankind. So I treated him that way. My drawings have been greatly criticized by some people, but none more than Kevin Crossley-Holland himself. He doesn't agree with a word of it; he says "Yes, there is total evil, and Grendel was." As he reads pure Anglo-Saxon, which I can't, I'm sure he knows best; but I must say that visually I can't accept that, and as a human being I can't accept that, and I had to do the drawings the way I did them.

I would like to mention a new book I'm doing with Leon Garfield. As many of you may know, we did **The God Be-**

Alfie was so excited he ran and joined the stream of people moving down an iron gangway and into the ship—and no one, not even the sailors, seemed to notice him.

*From* Alfie Finds "The Other Side of the World," *written and illustrated by Charles Keeping.*

*neath the Sea* and *The Golden Shadow* and we've joined together now to do [*The Wedding Ghost*]. What we're trying to do in it is to mix a certain reality with fantasy—not fantasy of the type Alan Garner is such an expert at, but a type of dream fantasy. How many people, married to the most comfortable looking lady or the most comfortable looking man, look at some glamorous film star, or at an ad that shows some glamorous person, and think, maybe that's the person I'd like to be with. I don't suppose they would, really, if they could, but we always dream about these things and I feel that we could make quite an interesting book out of this.

In some places we want to let the drawings tell the story visually, rather than have the words do it. We tried that a bit in *The Golden Shadow;* I sometimes showed how it would happen in my mind quite apart from what Leon Garfield was saying. For instance, Garfield wrote about two men who fought over a girl. Now this was quite a long chapter, and I decided to get away from the type of illustration you used to get in the old nineteenth century books, where it would say, "Tom punched Jim on the nose," and you had him doing it in a picture. The picture wasn't doing anything, it was only showing what it said in the text, and normally it didn't even appear on the same page; you got the drawing before you got to the bit about the hitting, and it would say, "See page so and so." I'm sure you remember those dreadful things; they stuck them in on glossy paper. Well, in *The Golden Shadow* we tried to get away from that. Instead of the fight I just show a man's head, slowly being battered by the other man until he was battered out of recognition. Pretty brutal, but it was a brutal chapter and the Greek myths were about brutal things, so I think it was a good way of showing it. In [*The Wedding Ghost*] we extend this idea into the idea of the whole book. I think it would be a good thing if more illustrators would experiment in this way. We ought to be doing far more books that are experimental, not because they're toys, but because they mix visuals and words, cut out the writing where it's not necessary and let the visuals take over, and reduce visuals where the writing can do the job. There's many things writing can do that drawing can't, and there's many things drawing can do that writing doesn't need to do.

People often ask me how much I think of children when I'm making these books. Well, not an awful lot. You can't. If you start thinking who's the book for, you would be lost to start with. I couldn't begin to produce a book that would please everyone here. No one could do it. I defy anyone, writer, illustrator, anyone, to do a book that would make all of you happy. It can't be done, and it can't be done for children either. I once said that the only book all children would like would be an exploding book; you know, it'd blow up with a great bang. They'd love it; they'd go around blowing it up all over the place. It would be wonderful for sales.

Children like books for all sorts of weird reasons. I was in Islington Library once, and a little boy came in and took out a book of mine that the librarian said children couldn't read. She said I'd put lettering all over the drawings and children couldn't read it, and I said, "But look, he's taking

it out," and she said, "He doesn't read it," so I said, "What does he do with it?" and she said, "He licks it all over." That's absolutely true—he liked the look of it; like a sweet, he liked the colors, and because it was covered in acetate, he used to lick it. I spoke to the printers about that. We thought of making peppermint-flavored ink.

We can't figure out what children will like. But we ought to be looking for books that give more to children than just amusing them, for we can't do things that would please them all, all the time.

*Charles Keeping, "My Work as a Children's Illustrator," in* Children's Literature Association Quarterly, *Vol. 8, No. 4, Winter, 1983, pp. 14-19.*

---

# GENERAL COMMENTARY

## Jean Russell

One well known children's book editor has said of Charles Keeping that his style is too sophisticated for young children and that she feels he is better suited to older children as in the Rosemary Sutcliff books. Indeed he does not appeal to all young children and those brought up on 'pretty' picture books have little stomach at first for his dramatic world. One six-year old returned tearfully home from school and refused to touch her newly cherished *Joseph's Yard* because 'only me and Miss liked it'. Perhaps Keeping's greatest asset is his conviction in what he is doing and his knowledge of exactly where he is going. No one who has read *Shaun and the Carthorse* will be surprised to hear that he had a coster grandfather and lived as a child next to a stable yard. The greatest compliment a young acquaintance of mine can pay to any house he visits is to liken it to "Knicky knackers yard".

In Charles Keeping's coming book *Through the Window* a child sees the action outside of himself—as a play. When as a child Keeping's favourite horse, the one he used to tie a ribbon on was sold for ten quid for horse meat, he felt exactly as the boy does when a dog dies. People criticise his books for not being pretty enough, but the world is a cruel place. Life floods children with visual approaches, they see Vietnam on their Television screens, they see starving children refugees of the Biafran war in the very centre of their security, in their own living rooms. So they should understand the emotions of Joseph who loves and protects the rose in his yard so much that he kills it until he learns with each successive bloom what freedom and the right order of things is about.

Keeping is an emotional illustrator who can portray moods, noise and emotions in colour, not flat as in a painting, but vital, vibrant three dimensional colour that made a small girl in an Islington library actually lick the pages. Nothing is static, a red dress will become purple under a neon light, it is never quite the same, it looks different at the front, from behind, the side. This pre-occupation, one might almost say obsession, with colour leads him to use it boldly so that each page will have one dominant colour only. This is particularly so of *The Garden Shed*—his latest book idea which he hopes to start working on in the autumn to complete the trilogy of *Joseph's Yard* and *Through the Window.* (He always works in threes, and unlike many of our best illustrators will not repeat himself but is constantly seeking new interpretations of simple ideas.) Two of these books have also been made into films for B.B.C. 2. They were in fact drawn on film and 65 feet of pictures were used to create the book. His critics say that the text is hard to read and certainly young children not familiar with such a kaleidoscope of colour, do find this a problem. The rather meaningless controversy which raged last year about *Vicki* and *Hide and Seek,* two books without words by his wife Renate Meyer, shows that parents and critics of children's books are not yet ready for this purely visual approach. But what of the children for whom after all these books are intended; are they concerned with text at this age? Does not what they actually see, the emotions they experience, the meaning of the book to them, matter most not whether they are able to read every word.

There is a need for change, a need for reality to children. As Keeping has said, "The days of the potted Red Riding Hood are over". The original Red Riding Hood, you may recall was frightened by a wolf dressed as her Grandmother. It was written when wolves were a menace in the countryside, a man would not travel in the forest at night for fear of them. Children were warned of the dangers of wolves as we may today warn them of the menace of a man in a car offering them sweets. Imagine the outcry if a children's picture book had this for its theme.

> *Jean Russell, "Charles Keeping," in* Books for Your Children, *Vol. 6, No. 1, Autumn, 1970, pp. 2-3.*

**Frank Eyre**

In the years immediately following the war the early objections to the work of such artists as Ardizzone and Kathleen Hale began slowly to disappear. Younger parents, with a new generation of children brought up in a different atmosphere—and at a time when many of the older books were temporarily unobtainable—were readier to accept unconventional-looking books. There was less prejudice in the air generally and it began to be seen that illustrations of this kind were more in keeping with the century in which we live.

It was from this atmosphere of freedom from inhibitions, combined with an intense professionalism, that the children's book artists of the last decade arose; almost, it seemed, from a kind of spontaneous combustion. One minute, it now appears looking back, we were all reasonably satisfied with the sort of illustrations to which we had been accustomed for the past twenty years—and then there was Wildsmith. Other artists, no doubt, were at work at the same time; other books of roughly the same kind were published, or about to be published, but it was the early work of Brian Wildsmith that accomplished the first breakthrough, and for a time aroused much the same sort of antagonism as had the earlier modernists. He is a prolific artist, obviously working best at full stretch, when he has a lot of work in hand, and it must have taken a courageous publisher to commission so much work in colour, in so short a time, from a then relatively unknown artist.

In the space of five years between 1961 and 1966 he illustrated an *ABC,* editions of a number of La Fontaine's fables; a collection of poems for children edited by Edward Blishen; *A Child's Garden of Verses; The Arabian Nights* and a *Mother Goose,* all in full colour—and what colour! Before the *ABC* he had illustrated a number of children's books in line, using colour only for the jackets, but his black and white work has never been so successful as his colour and it is as the leading exponent of the exuberantly colourful contemporary picture book that he is best known. . . . He is an artist to whom a whole generation of children must already be grateful and whose work is likely to live a long time.

An artist whom many critics link with Wildsmith is John Burningham. . . . His colour is almost equally brilliant, but more controlled, more immediately accessible, and there are many who consider that his books appeal to more children than do Wildsmith's. He has illustrated many books, of many kinds. Like Wildsmith, he has done an *ABC,* but he has also done a number of beautiful books of his own, including *Trubloff, Cannonball Simp, Humbert, Mr. Firkin, and the Lord Mayor of London, Seasons, Harquin* and *Mr Gumpy's Outing* all lit by a controlled delight in colour and a strong sense of fun. . . . It is difficult to think of any twentieth-century artist, with the possible exceptions of Ardizzone and Ernest Shepard, who has given children more pleasure. . . .

Charles Keeping, on the other hand, seems less obviously interested in giving pleasure. His colour is almost as brilliant as Wildsmith's; he has a strangely hypnotic style which seems to be either greatly liked or strongly detested; and he is unusual among what are perhaps too loosely described as 'picture book artists' in being passionately interested in ideas. In a contribution on 'Illustration in Children's Books' to the first number of *Children's Literature in Education,* he had a number of things to say about his work which, although convincing and of great value to anyone trying to understand what such an artist is trying to achieve, make one wonder whether the age for which picture books are still, presumably, produced, is really a suitable one for the introduction of such conceptions. His work is extremely sophisticated; to get the full benefit from it the reader should really understand what the artist is seeking to communicate; but for what age, one wonders, is it intended?

Charles Keeping originally made his name as an illustrator in black and white. Some of his work in this field was greatly admired—a set of dramatic illustrations for one of Rosemary Sutcliff's books for example—but much of it aroused strong dislike from some children and critics. His work in line is stark, compelling, theatrically effective and whether it succeeds or fails, never negligible. He is, one feels, an artist first and an illustrator second, and nothing that he draws is carried out in the way any other artist would have treated the same theme. But despite the vividness of his line drawings he first came into real prominence with a series of books in full colour which he produced as both artist and author, *Shaun and the Cart Horse, Charley, Charlotte and the Golden Canary* and *Alfie and the Ferryboat.* Some of his work in these books was immediately attractive because, despite what a few critics said, children could see immediately what was intended and *Charley, Charlotte and the Golden Canary* is a delight from beginning to end. But the beginnings of the style that many readers have criticised was already apparent in these books and his two later books, *Joseph's Yard* and *Through the Window* apparently indicate the direction in which he wishes to go. He is an exciting artist, whose work it is impossible not to admire, even if one does not always *like* it, and his future work promises to be as important as that of any artist working in children's books today. But it is difficult to see how such an approach can be carried much further without taking picture books directly into the area of social commentary and the age at which picture books are of value is still, I believe, too young for such conceptions.

> *Frank Eyre, "Books with Pictures," in his* British Children's Books in the Twentieth Century, *revised edition, Longman Books, 1979, pp. 38-58.*

## John Rowe Townsend

The British picture book, after many disappointing years, came to vigorous life in the 1960s. The leading names of the decade were those of Charles Keeping and Brian Wildsmith, but many other artists also came to prominence. Keeping remains the most powerful and the most controversial. He has never made any concession to supposed childish tastes, and his work raises in acute form the question whether picture-book artists sometimes demand too much of their audiences and waste their endeavours on those who cannot yet appreciate what they are doing.

An artist, like a writer, is always entitled to say that he does the work he has it in him to do, and what becomes of it afterwards is not his business. So perhaps the question is primarily one for publishers, librarians and parents (though . . . anyone whose work is to appear on a children's list must consciously or unconsciously have a special sense of audience; it is not really possible to operate from an ivory tower).

I do not know of any study that has been made of the graphic preferences of small children. Certainly their tastes can be very different from those of visually educated adults. Grown-ups should not, I think, deprive children of what they find for themselves and enjoy; but in actually introducing them to books I believe it wise to stick to the principle that only the best is good enough. Picture books are a child's first introduction to art and literature, no less. To give him crude, stereotyped picture books is to open the way for everything else that is crude and stereotyped. And even if children do not always appreciate the best when they see it, they will have no chance of appreciating it if they don't see it.

Judged as graphic art, I have no doubt that Charles Keeping's work is very fine. It is unfortunate, I think, that, . . . he has written texts for himself that do not match the quality of his artwork. *Charley, Charlotte and the Golden Canary* is a stunning book to look at; the colours are so wild, glowing and vibrant that it is hard to take one's eyes off them to attend to the rather ordinary little story. *Through*

*the Window,* considered as a whole, is a better book. Jacob's world consists of what he can see through the gap in the curtains. Excitement is followed by disaster when runaway horses from the brewery come galloping down the street, and the poor old woman picks up and cradles the limp body of her dog. But the conclusion, if not exactly happy, is positive, for Jacob, breathing on the window and drawing, has the old woman upright and smiling, her dog alive and alert in her arms.

In *Railway Passage,* Keeping's colour has cooled a long way from the vivid blaze of *Charley, Charlotte and the Golden Canary,* and there is more emphasis on draughtsmanship and pictorial character-creation. The six tenants who live in Railway Passage are old and rather poor; the children call them uncles and aunties. They always fill in a joint football-pool coupon, and one day it comes up and they are rich. Not a child-centred subject, admittedly; but children, like the rest of us, are intrigued by the idea of sudden wealth, and we can all consider which of the uncles and aunties spend the money wisely.

In *Cockney Ding-Dong,* Keeping, a Londoner in blood and bone, built a rowdy, energetic, eye-filling and massively nostalgic book on the foundations of the songs that were sung at the old London singsongs and in the music-halls. His presentation of the Alfred Noyes poem *The Highwayman* is stark, almost brutal, and exemplifies a sombre streak that runs through much of his work. Although *The God Beneath the Sea* and *The Golden Shadow,* by Leon Garfield and Edward Blishen, are not picture books, Keeping's illustrations are so powerful and integral as to make him a full partner in the enterprise.

> *John Rowe Townsend, "Picture Books in Bloom: British," in his* Written for Children: An Outline of English-Language Children's Literature, *third revised edition, J. B. Lippincott, 1987, pp. 317-25.*

## Elaine Moss

Charles Keeping is an artist whose work can be seen either as a barrier breaker or as having come before its time. Often, as I listen to conversations in bookshops or libraries, I have heard this major artist condemned because his exploration of the emotions is outside the comprehension of a five-year-old. His work—from straightforward *Richard,* which portrays the life of a police horse, to *Inter-City* and *The River,* textless picture books that perplex even the experienced adult—could fuel a doctoral thesis. Indeed, it probably already has.

My interest here is merely to point out that the books whose interest level lies between these two extremes have texts and pictures that thrust deep into the growing emotional consciousness of the prepubescent youngster. *Through the Window, Joseph's Yard, Wasteground Circus*—to take three of many—are personal and demanding books that use the medium of colour printing to convey messages about human weakness, violence, fear, love. *Through the Window* is the most heart-rending and terrifying, the story of little Jacob "alone in his front room . . . He moved across to the window and looked out. The street was all Jacob knew of the world, so it was the whole world to him." Death comes into his net-curtained world when the brewery horses run amok, killing the skeleton-thin dog who is life itself to an old woman. The book ends with Jacob finger-drawing the crone and her pet (smiling, content in each other's company) on the breath-steamed window pane. How else should we remember the dead? What is the meaning of resurrection? Jacob knew.

*Joseph's Yard* is a lesson in love. Joseph exchanges the rusty old iron in his yard—"A brick wall, a wooden fence, stone paving and a rusty old iron; that's all there was in this yard"—for a plant. The plant is a living thing. Joseph is responsible for it, and he smothers it with love, protects it from birds, insects, cats, and even from the sun and rain. The plant withers. And Joseph is bitterly ashamed that he has betrayed "the beautiful thing in his yard". But spring comes, and with it new life—for the rose tree, for insects, for cats, for birds, but above all for Joseph. In *Wasteground Circus* Keeping uses colour, grey or bright, to show how a circus on a piece of waste land affects two boys after it has gone. For one the wasteground is suffused with the afterglow of excitement, a place for ever bright; for the other it becomes grey again as though the circus had never been.

It is a paradox that arguably the greatest picture-book artist of our time should be exploring the world of the underprivileged child so brilliantly, yet should go unrecognized by those who search for art and literature that reflect other than the middle-class experience. Keeping's pictures need concentration, but older children look at pictures with an intensity (given the right surroundings, and a teacher with controlled enthusiasm) that literate adults cannot match.

*Elaine Moss, "Them's for the Infants, Miss,"* in Signal, *No. 27, September, 1978, pp. 144-49.*

**Brian Alderson**

England has not been immune from the movement towards a more or less self-conscious exploitation of graphic effects in picture book illustration and, without any doubt, the artist who has caused the most discussion and who has exhibited those characteristics which continental critics tend to call "expressionist" is Charles Keeping. Where it would be ludicrous to imagine Quentin Blake, say, or Helen Oxenbury figuring very prominently in the judgments of the Biennale of Illustrations Bratislava or Andersen juries (and we know with what incomprehension the work of Edward Ardizzone is met by continental connoisseurs), Charles Keeping is a different matter: he has indeed won a Golden Apple at Bratislava for *Railway Passage* and, like Wildsmith before him, figured as a runner-up in the Hans Christian Andersen stakes.

It is not difficult to see the appeal which Keeping has for eyes attuned to the displays of illustrators like Janosch or Max Velthuijs or Misha Damjan; but it should not be attributed solely to special pleading, if a case can be made for the validity of his picture books, at their best, as much intenser versions of books celebrated as "the English tradition." The reason for this is that in, for example, *Joseph's Yard* or *Through the Window* Charles Keeping is making a unified statement in which a great tension subsists between the narrative poles of word and picture. Unlike so much continental work where, . . . the text is but an excuse for the graphics, these books are a powerful fusion of the two. Subtler variations in Keeping's "expressionism" can also be seen in his beautifully muted *Christmas Story* and in his *Spider's Web,* a book bordering on a dream, but vastly more resonant than the querulous fancies peddled by Lieselotte Schwarz's dream-maker.

*Brian Alderson, "A View from the Island: European Picture Books 1967-1976," in* Illustrators of Children's Books: 1967-1976, *Lee Kingman, Grace Allen Hogarth, Harriet Quimby, eds., The Horn Book, Inc., 1978, pp. 20-43.*

**Treld Pelkey Bicknell**

Charles Keeping did only fifteen drawings for *The God Beneath the Sea,* but what drawings, what breaking of new ground, what influence this book has had upon his own work and that of others! Here are the unfolding myths of Gods and Men, treated with compassion, pathos, strength, horror, and intelligence. Charles Keeping used the harshness inherent in the stories and in the magnificent writing of Leon Garfield and Edward Blishen, as a dramatic quality in his illustrations. How better to express the eternal problems of humanity?

So powerful are these black-and-white drawings that although it is not a picture book, the Greenaway Award committee was startled into making *The God Beneath the Sea* first runner-up for that award. Had Keeping as artist been given the award itself, *The God Beneath the Sea*

And then up spoke the little cabin boy,
And a fair-haired boy was he,
"I've a father and mother in fair Portsmouth town,
And tonight they will weep for me."

*From* Tinker Tailor: Folk Song Tales, *written and illustrated by Charles Keeping.*

would have gathered a unique double award for its creators, since it had already earned the Carnegie Medal for its authors.

Unfortunately the American publisher of the book had commissioned new illustrations from another illustrator. Zevi Blum chose to exaggerate and stylize the figures to a grotesque degree. His gods are surrounded by a space-age mimicry of Greek architecture, drapery, and helmets. Blum's Prometheus—his liver tickled by a beakless turkey—is a camp, stagy charlatan, superficial and insincere: Keepings' Prometheus is the embodiment of a human spirit in extremis. Not surprisingly the English edition has become a modern classic; the American edition is out of print.

Keeping has explored areas which other picture book artists do not explore, but it is in his work for the older child that he comes into his own. His *Cockney Ding Dong,* in which he combines portraits of his family and friends at Saturday evening gatherings where songs were sung and good fellowship abounded, is a perfect example. The aunts and uncles who played and sang, the young who cuddled and the younger still who snoozed, are shown with their slack jaws, gap-teeth, wrinkles, and podgy knees—but how lovingly! The illustrations to the songs themselves are more fictional, more literary and abstract. The real and the imaginative elements balance on a tight-rope throughout Keeping's long "backward glance," making it so much more than just a wallow in nostalgia. Judging by the letters he has had, and the requests the publishers have had for proofs of this picture or that picture, adults all over the country are using the book to share this all-but-lost past with their children. If communication is what illustration is all about, this is communication at its highest level. Yet the illustrations would at any time stand alone as works of art.

> *Treld Pelkey Bicknell, "In the Beginning Was the Word: The Illustrated Book 1967-1976," in* Illustrators of Children's Books: 1967-1976, *Lee Kingman, Grace Allen Hogarth, Harriet Quimby, eds., The Horn Book, Inc., 1978, pp. 58-89.*

### Aidan Chambers

I rushed into one of my local children's libraries recently needing a Keeping picture book for some work I was doing. The librarian said, 'Oh yes, we've got it of course, and it will be on the shelf. Keeping isn't very popular.' Confident of her words, she took me to the stacks. Not one copy of any Keeping was there. 'Typical!' she said. And indeed that sort of thing does happen just when you least expect it. But I fancy she was unconsciously parading the received opinion about Keeping's subtler picture books: that they aren't children's books because their artwork is too sophisticated. This isn't a view held by Jill Hopes, a teacher of infants in a Swindon school. She wrote to me:

> When I consider the hundred or more picture books I have in my room . . . in most of them the author/artist's intentions are quite clear-cut. But Keeping leaves gaps for the imagination to fill in a very definite way and in a manner which infants do not often experience . . . Keeping

uses colour actually to set the scene for strong emotions . . . His books usually carry obscure meanings, which children have to be encouraged to find. He makes no concessions to age, and one of the strongest features of his books—and, I believe, an invaluable one—is the depth of the texts. They are usually sparsely worded but with an extension of language which is unusual in picture books. A general criticism made of Keeping seems to be that children will not understand his books. Young children understand more than we give them credit for.

I asked Jill to show me somehow the truth of that. What I got back was not another letter but a book, called *A Book All About Books,* made for me by her six-year-olds, and all about Keeping, accompanied by a cassette of the children talking about their reading of **Charley, Charlotte and the Golden Canary,** of **Joseph's Yard** and the rest. Jill says in her covering note: 'After a fortnight of almost pure Charles Keeping, I did wonder yesterday whether I had overdone it, as when talking of the recent assassination attempt in America [against President Reagan], I asked for the name of the president. It was not forthcoming, so I said, "Come on, who is one of the most powerful and important men in the world?" Lee answered immediately and with great confidence, "Charles Keeping".'

Here are just two of the children's responses to Keeping from their book about him, sentences extracted from surprisingly long accounts, considering the ages of the children:

> CHRISTOPHER: The pictures look like when I dream because they are scribbly and you can see the shape but they do not look really real.

> LEE: When Charley found Charlotte with the golden canary, I felt happy and I don't like losing my friends because Craig was my friend and he has gone to the Isle of Wight and I miss him and feel sad.

On and on through this lovely book: six-year-olds as critics, and enjoying themselves enormously. Open, intelligent, their experience of reading books some say are too difficult for them captured in their own words and drawings. Would that adult critics and reviewers could be so direct, so honest, and so ready to allow a book to shape their lives. I cherish especially one sentence heard on Jill's tape. One of the girls was talking of losing her friend Kevin; she finished by saying with sudden brightness, 'But I've still got Kevin in my head.' Surely this is a transformation, a coming to conscious understanding of experience, that has resulted from her reading of Keeping's fiction about **Charley, Charlotte and the Golden Canary.**

> *Aidan Chambers, "Axes for Frozen Seas," in* Booktalk: Occasional Writing on Literature and Children, *The Bodley Head, 1985, pp. 14-33.*

### M. S. Crouch

Charles Keeping was very much a man of his own time and place. Born a Londoner South of the Thames, he clung tenaciously to his cockney accent, and was happiest in portraying the squalor and the mystery of the streets and alleys he knew best. His preferences were clearly demonstrated when, after he had served a ten-year apprenticeship illustrating the work of other writers, Oxford published the first of his picture-books to his own text. There followed a succession of evocations of the London scene, a scene unguessed at by the tourist. Typical among these was *Alfie and the Ferry Boat,* in which Keeping found magic and glamour in the lights of the Woolwich Free Ferry and in the spill of colour from the tawdry stained-glass of a back-street pub.

These picture-books gave Keeping his deepest satisfaction. He continued with his book-illustration in an unbroken stream of titles, children's books and also, thanks to the percipience of the Folio Society, major adult books. From this vast mass of work a few books stand out. His early drawings for Rosemary Sutcliff's historical novels are notable. I cannot believe that he shared the author's Kiplingesque vision of the past, but he recognised the strength and grandeur of her writing and matched them with his own sinewy, spiky drawings. He may have been less in harmony with Henry Treece's tough, sometimes heartless stories, all of which he illustrated conscientiously, but this author's last and most enigmatic book *The Dream Time* (1967) called forth some of his most memorable designs, hauntingly tender as well as strong. He explored too, rewardingly, the Scotland of Mollie Hunter and the Wonderland of Nicolas Stuart Gray. His controversial drawings of Greek gods and heroes in two books by Leon Garfield and Edward Blishen (*The God beneath the Sea,* and *The Golden Shadow*) brought praise and condemnation in roughly equal proportions. More recently he seemed to have found a kindred spirit in Charles Causley. The anthology *The Sun, Dancing* (1982) contains some outstanding work in monochrome, and the recent collection of original poems *Jack the Treacle Eater* is even more successful, as it is more restrained, in colour. . . .

No illustrator in this century has worked harder. Even Ardizzone, in a longer life, cannot match his output. He established an individual style at the beginning of his career and stayed faithful to it. When in tune with a writer he could add another dimension to a book. What he lacked was a sense of fun. His world is one of terror and wonder, of light and darkness, not one of laughter.

> *M. S. Crouch, "Makers of Images," in* The Junior Bookshelf, *Vol. 52, No. 4, August, 1988, pp. 173-75.*

---

## TITLE COMMENTARY

### Shaun and the Cart-Horse (1966)

Mr. Keeping has served a long apprenticeship in the illustration of other men's texts, to which his highly individual talents have sometimes contributed powerfully. Here is his own picture book. The story—of a little boy who loses and recovers a horse—is adequate, if a little thin. The coloured pictures of London landscape and life are extremely vigorous and disturbing. They come bursting out of the page in great daubs of brown and blue and purple. It does children no harm to be shaken up, even perhaps terrified as

they may well be by Nicky Knacker's sudden appearance, but is there any yardstick of normality by which they can measure this strange, uneasily beautiful world? Certainly it is a book which cannot be ignored. It selects itself automatically for the Greenaway short-list. It will upset a great many adults, perhaps not so many children.

> *A review of "Shaun and the Cart-horse," in* The Junior Bookshelf, *Vol. 30, No. 5, October, 1966, p. 305.*

Shaun lives with his grandfather in London and sometimes gets a ride with old Charley Peel when he takes his fruit cart to market. But Charley falls ill, a stranger leads Queen away, and Shaun determines to save her from the knacker. The story is sure to please animal-loving children, but they may find the pictures ugly, with their staring colour and impressionistic scenes; the style hardly seems to suit the essential humanity of the story.

> *Margery Fisher, in a review of "Shaun and the Cart-Horse," in* Growing Point, *Vol. 5, No. 5, November, 1966, p. 802.*

When Shaun, a little Cockney boy, learns that his good friend Uncle Charley Peel has had to sell his cart-horse (Shaun's "very *best* friend"), he finds a way to bring the horse back to Uncle Charley. The story is simple but satisfying and does not patronize. "Shaun knew that all the costers there loved Queen and they would be sad about her, too." The word "coster" is not explained, but on the next two pages, Shaun visits the ice-cream man, the old-clothes lady, the fish-stall man, and the coffee-stall man. The pictures are distinctive and vital; dazzling in color, they appear shot with light from behind some of the figures.

> *Della Thomas, in a review of "Shaun and the Cart-Horse," in* School Library Journal, *Vol. 13, No. 6, February, 1967, p. 59.*

Shaun is a small boy who lives in London with his grandfather; he is distressed when a friend's horse is sold to Nicky Knacker, the horse dealer. Shaun goes around to other adult friends at the market, and they all agree to chip in and buy the horse back. The story line is thin, especially for American children to whom the Cockney environment is unfamiliar. The illustrations are absolutely lovely, especially in the use of color; the technique is distinctive, and the faces in particular will be recognized as uniquely Keeping by those familiar with his black and white pictures in children's books by other British writers.

> *Zena Sutherland, in a review of "Shaun and the Cart-Horse," in* Bulletin of the Center for Children's Books, *Vol. 20, No. 11, July-August, 1967, pp. 171-72.*

---

### Black Dolly: The Story of a Junk Cart Pony (1966; U.S. edition as Molly o' the Moors: The Story of a Pony)

This is the story of a junk cart pony—hardly a story so much as a series of episodes in the life of Black Dolly, born in the mountains, cherished and decked for shows, taken to the city to pull a rag-and-bone cart, falling down in the rain, restored to the fields in old age. The story is told, really, in the tenderly beautiful pictures, with their suave orange, green and petunia held in with swirling lines and shadings. Seeing and feeling are one and the same in this book.

> *Margery Fisher, in a review of "Black Dolly," in* Growing Point, *Vol. 5, No. 5, November, 1966, p. 802.*

Charles Keeping, second to none at drawing beasts of burden, takes the life history of **Black Dolly,** a Welsh mountain pony pressed into service pulling a junk cart through a 'place of rust and rags, bones and bottles,' as the subject of his visually thrilling new book. His text is astringent, elemental, just the right thing, while the pictures swirl with feeling and movement and make wonderful use of a limited palette: shocking pink, tangerine, rust and olive green. It is quite extraordinary that Mr Keeping has not yet won the Kate Greenaway Award: may this book secure it for him.

> *Kevin Crossley-Holland, "In the Picture," in* The Spectator, *Vol. 217, No. 7220, November 11, 1966, pp. 627-28.*

Here is Black Beauty's story much abbreviated in the life of a pony. The text, a short paragraph to each double-paged spread, is told with a matter-of-fact air that occasionally brushes close to poetry. "Men came and caught me with ropes./They took me down to green fields/where the grass was long and tasted good." Mr. Keeping's illustrations are suffused with color and could well be the child's first introduction to art, for though they may puzzle, they will also please.

> *Jean C. Thomson, in a review of "Molly O' the Moors: The Story of a Pony," in* School Library Journal, *Vol. 13, No. 7, March, 1967, p. 121.*

There are echoes of Black Beauty for adult readers of this book, but whether or not children know that story, they sympathize with the hard times the junk cart pony has to go through and delight in his final good luck. Older children found more to interest them in the illustrations, questioning why Keeping had used colours as he did and concluding that it was his way of setting the mood for us. I usually find that Keeping's work evokes a great deal of discussion, and this book did just that.

> *Rene Suter, in a review of "Black Dolly," in* The Signal Review of Children's Books, *2, 1984, p. 14.*

---

### Charley, Charlotte and the Golden Canary (1967)

Keeping's story of **Charley, Charlotte and the Golden Canary** [needs] a text, for the pictures are of that boldly artistic kind which is often thought to be beyond a child's comprehension. Not this time. This is a book for *feeling,* and Keeping, as always, is leading you to feel by the shock of his blurred, sprawling, rich colours and the fluid, almost filmic figures in movement, always expressing emotions— of wonder, sadness, joy. Paradise Street, with its boy and

girl separated and united again, its shining singing bird, is a place that creates itself through vivid, shocking yellows and purples, through the sheer height of sketched-in buildings.

> *Margery Fisher, in a review of "Charley, Charlotte and the Golden Canary," in* Growing Point, *Vol. 6, No. 4, October, 1967, pp. 973-74.*

Charles Keeping will offend just about as many readers as he will please. It is difficult to remain neutral in the face of all these brilliant yellows, blue-greens and oranges. Probably it will be mostly the children who will like **Charley** and their parents who will hold up their hands in pained distress. Next to Wildsmith, Keeping is the most original English artist working in the picture-book field, and even less than Wildsmith does he make concessions to his more conventional readers. In this book he accompanies his own text—a very good one—with most remarkable explorations of the colour, shape and character of the London slums. Keeping sees most vividly the beauty of everyday things and here he shares his vision generously with those whose eyes have not been dulled into an unseeing acceptance of their world.

> *A review of "Charley, Charlotte and the Golden Canary," in* The Junior Bookshelf, *Vol. 31, No. 6, December, 1967, p. 372.*

Fortune triumphs over the depredations of urban renewal in a slight story with an improbable happy ending that will probably satisfy the read-aloud audience. Separated by fate, two small friends are reunited when Charley's canary escapes and flies straight to the window of Charlotte's new apartment in a highrise building. This was published in England last year and has just won the Greenaway Medal for 1967, and well it might. The pages glow with ravishing colors: incandescent yellow, brooding violet, melting blue—and glimpsed through them, Charley's big-eyed, sad waif's face.

> *Zena Sutherland, in a review of "Charley, Charlotte and the Golden Canary," in* Saturday Review, *Vol. LI, No. 29, July 20, 1968, p. 30.*

---

### Alfie and the Ferryboat (1968; U.S. edition as *Alfie Finds "The Other Side of the World"*)

Yet another view of a child's London through the eyes of Charles Keeping. This time it is the river and the fog, and the story of Alfie and his friend Bunty, the old sailor, with his pram, gramophone and dog, Stoker. Alfie lives near the docks behind a sugar factory in Hope Street. His real world is very small, but his imagination ranges to the "other side of the world" thanks to old Bunty's yarns. One foggy day Bunty disappears—to the other side of the world perhaps? —and Alfie, lost in the fog, finds himself by a "big ship" (a Thames ferryboat). He steps aboard and is taken to the "other side of the . . . (Thames)", full of bright lights and people where miraculously he finds Bunty, who takes him home again. There are some glorious visual effects, but as a whole the book does not have the impact of the artist's medal-winning **Charley, Char-**

*lotte and the Golden Canary.* It might have been an idea to stop the narrative when Alfie steps off the ferryboat, and let the pictures speak for themselves until Bunty's dog appears suddenly out of the fog. But with all reservations, a book by Charles Keeping is not to be missed and certainly not by those children for whom he has created it.

> *G. V. Barton, in a review of "Alfie and the Ferryboat," in* Children's Book News, London, *Vol. 3, No. 4, July-August, 1968, pp. 185-86.*

*Alfie and the Ferryboat* appears, most happily, just at the right time to underline the rightness of Charles Keeping's award of the Kate Greenaway Medal. He is an artist of uncompromising high standards, a man with a strong personal idiom, technical skill of the highest, and what one might dare to call vision. He is, like John Burningham, a city man, seeing as Burningham does but with greater intensity, the beauty latent in the squalid back streets of London. In this new book Alfie goes, unwittingly, for a ride (or cruise) on the Woolwich Free Ferry. It seems like a voyage to the Promised Land or at least to "The Other Side of the World". Mr. Keeping sees it, as a small boy would, as a confused glory of blazing colours standing out from the murk of the river and the mean streets. Is it all much larger and more brightly coloured than real life? Of course, it is the larger-than-life, twopenny-coloured vision of a little boy straying for the first time from the comforting meanness of Hope Place. A fine, disturbing book, incomparably Keeping's best to date. How the uncles and aunts will hate it!

> *A review of "Alfie and the Ferryboat," in* The Junior Bookshelf, *Vol. 32, No. 4, August, 1968, p. 222.*

The striking originality of the pictorial execution is somewhat flawed by a flat, toneless text which fails to bring down to earth the book's exuberant abstract art. The virtual bombardment of light, color and energy will excite any eye that chances on *Alfie,* though the layout often makes the text difficult to read. A cockney boy from England's blighted factory district, Alfie has seen nothing of the world beyond his home. But, having heard exotic sea yarns and believing his old, disheveled ex-sailor friend Bunty has gone to the other side of the world, Alfie eagerly hops a ship in hopes of finding Bunty. From the dull browns, greens and blues of factory streets, the paintings undergo a transformation that brings forth abstract swirls and shapes of psychedelic hue and intensity as Alfie approaches an amusement park he's never seen before. When Bunty and his dog Stoker appear in front of a pub advertising itself as "The other side of the world," Alfie's journey is explained away as having been just a jaunt to the other side of the river. A storytelling letdown but for potential viewers, an inviting, visually exciting treat.

> *Joyce Baumholtz, in a review of "Alfie Finds 'The Other Side of the World'," in* School Library Journal, *Vol. 15, No. 4, December, 1968, p. 38.*

In this picture-book, which heralded an exciting experiment in illustration, Charles Keeping sets out to convey by visual means not personality but emotion. In scenes where shapes and figures are sometimes represented and sometimes suggested in the midst of a blaze of seemingly shifting colour, he conveys Alfie's reactions to a journey that takes him from dingy, fog-bound streets to the stirring, crowded night-life of the city. Keeping has been criticized for his use of symbol and abstraction in this and other books but children, less hidebound than their elders, are usually ready to let the point of the story enter them through their eyes so that they, in their turn, may enter into Alfie's imaginative experience.

> *Margery Fisher, "Who's Who in Children's Books: Alfie and the Ferry Boat," in her* Who's Who in Children's Books: A Treasury of the Familiar Characters of Childhood, *Holt, Rinehart and Winston, 1975, p. 11.*

---

### The Christmas Story (1968)

To a text that talks in monosyllables—"One winter's day, a man named Joseph and his wife, whose name was Mary, had to go to a town called Bethlehem"—Charles Keeping has appended drawings of considerable subtlety and technical refinement, some of which are quite affecting while in others the manner overwhelms the matter. The result is a book that's aesthetically titillating for adults but inconsistent as an entity and inaffectual at the read aloud level.

> *A review of "The Christmas Story," in* Kirkus Reviews, *Vol. XXXVII, No. 1, January 1, 1969, p. 1.*

[*The Christmas Story*] is a very simple, matter-of-fact retelling. The large pages in this 8 ½" x 10 ½" book are devoted mostly to the lack-luster illustrations in dark green and purple-blue on greyish-pink and putty-colored backgrounds. The tones are intentionally somber to suggest the poverty of the surroundings; however, this results in a dreary looking book. Keeping's line is both sensitive and dynamic, but is often smothered by areas of flat dead color or over-powering texture. The book is praiseworthy for its lack of sentimentality, but there are many more distinguished renditions of the story. . . .

> *Marilyn R. Singer, "Inside the Vacuum of Reverence," in* School Library Journal, *Vol. 16, No. 2, October, 1969, pp. 168-71.*

---

### Tinker Tailor: Folk Songs (1968; U.S. edition as Tinker Tailor: Folk Song Tales)

A collection of folk songs, following the traditional rhyme "Tinker, tailor. . . ." Sources of words and music are given at the beginning.

As a picture-book artist, Charles Keeping is making increasingly heavy demands on his reviewers. Considering it objectively one is filled with admiration for his latest offering. The subtle atmosphere which he introduces into the illustrations supports and expands the text of the folk songs. Within the pictures themselves there are successive layers of experience, so that one is continually being surprised into a new dimension of appreciation.

*From* Joseph's Yard, *written and illustrated by Charles Keeping.*

However, when one comes to consider the book in relation to the children for whom it is intended, the doubts crowd in. Since it is marketed as a picture book it is reasonable to assume that it will find its way into the hands of the three- to seven-year-olds, and I have grave doubts as to what they will make of it. Aside from the fact that the text is almost certainly beyond them, how can they interpret pictures that depend so much on assumed experience for their understanding? Far be it from me to advocate unimaginative photorealism in picture-book illustration, but when one knows from experience that small children have difficulty in recognizing even the most obvious portrayals, one realizes that for all but the unusually mature, *Tinker Tailor* is going to be little more than a chaotic blur of colour. This does not mean that there should not be books like this—only that there should be more "bridging" books to lead children on so that they can obtain the maximum experience from them.

> *V. C. Alderson, in a review of "Tinker Tailor,"* in Children's Book News, *London, Vol. 4, No. 1, January-February, 1969, pp. 19–21.*

Charles Keeping has chosen eight folk-songs to match the traditional counting game—Tinker Tailor—and has decorated these in his most vigorous manner. The pictures are brilliantly done and extremely disturbing. His treatment of textures is especially clever; one likes or loathes it, but

there can be no question of indifference. Some of the juxtapositions of pictures are unfortunate; one feels that not as much thought has gone into making the book as in drawing the individual pictures.

> *A review of "Tinker Tailor," in* The Junior Bookshelf, *Vol. 33, No. 1, February, 1969, p. 16.*

The eight folk poems in Charles Keeping's book, although entertaining in themselves, are simply excuses for filling each page with splendid and extraordinary illustrations. Secondary school art teachers who are concerned with printing and design will find each page to contain original combinations of techniques which are, incidentally, most accurately and evocatively in harmony with the verses they accompany.

> *David Churchill, in a review of "Tinker Tailor," in* The School Librarian and School Library Review, *Vol. 17, No. 1, March, 1969, p. 113.*

Charles Keeping has arranged the folk song tales around the old nursery rhyme, "Tinker, tailor, soldier, sailor." Unfortunately the idea fails to come off. Choosing a folk song for each of the characters in the rhyme, Mr. Keeping, for all his illustrious reputation, has produced a quite ghoulish series of pictures. They are very difficult to decipher and put together with pages of music in which the notation is so reduced that a pianist would have difficulty even seeing the notes. It seems a pity that such a good plan could fail so miserably in every respect.

> *Mary Reed Newland, in a review of "Tinker Tailor," in* The New York Times Book Review, *November 9, 1969, p. 67.*

---

### *Joseph's Yard* (1969)

Charles Keeping is an artist who tries over and over again in his beautiful books to bring his singing, spinning view of matter within reach of children, and particularly of town children shut in flats and small dark streets. *Joseph's Yard* tells of a boy who clears the junk from his yard, grubs up a stone in a corner, and plants a tiny plant: the seasons come and go, and through the plant insects and birds come to the yard; when Joseph tries to protect his plant by putting his coat over it, it withers, but each spring it puts out new green. It is interesting to compare this with last year's *The Yellow Flowers,* by Fiona Saint aged six (Dennis Dobson); Fiona's story is much the same, except that her flowers are killed deliberately, and not by kindness, but her point of view, as reflected by Ralph Steadman's drawings, is so much more practical: with Fiona to lead them on, perhaps children will respond to the higher glory of Charles Keeping's vision.

> *"For the Young, Fantasy Begins at Home," in* The Times Literary Supplement, *No. 3536, December 4, 1969, p. 1393.*

Some help may be needed for the point of *Joseph's yard* to be understood, but it must also be emphasised that this is a book whose sensuous appeal could be felt at one stage and a deeper meaning could satisfy children already reading to themselves. This is a moral tale. It exists to state a point of human behaviour and the point is clearly shown in the sequence of pictures, where a boy who has planted a rose in his backyard first loses a bloom because he cannot resist picking it and then spoils the plant in trying to hide it from insects and birds. The lesson is plain, salutary and to be accepted as essential. It is illuminated not only by the eager passion of Keeping's statements but also by the passion of a Londoner for colour in blackness. I can remember the sooty back gardens of Camberwell from my own childhood and I believe Keeping has expressed the desire for beauty in a wholly effective and simple symbol. This is a strongly personal book. Nobody else could have made it such a burstingly effective whole and nobody else could have reached from particular to general, reached out to children through the colour and shapes that embody the story.

*Margery Fisher, in a review of "Joseph's Yard," in* Growing Point, *Vol. 8, No. 8, March, 1970, pp. 1482-83.*

With a minimum of text and a maximum of beauty Charles Keeping has produced a striking and moving picture book which will keep the tongues wagging for some time. All the adolescents whom we have shown it to want copies of their own; the reaction of the threes to sixes has been as varied as the children themselves, but no child remains indifferent. The technique displayed in these pages seems to have taken a leap forward in depth; the child gets inside the picture this time. Although all the earlier work can be seen to contribute to this production, the range and intensity and subtle interplay of colour and texture combined with feeling tone are breathtaking. The story is of Joseph, tousled and bespectacled, in whose yard is only junk, until he trades some of it for a plant—a rose—which he tends with covetous devotion, killing it twice, until he learns the way of living things. I propose that this book be read and shown to all children who share Joseph's dilemma. Myopia was never more brilliantly analysed. A new stage in picture books where the standard is already very high.

*Margaret Meek, in a review of "Joseph's Yard," in* The School Librarian, *Vol. 18, No. 1, March, 1970, p. 126.*

Charles Keeping seems not to fret at his narrow cell. **Joseph's Yard** represents yet another step towards full mastery of his difficult medium. Mr. Keeping has most of the equipment of the picture-book artist. His sense of design is unerring. He draws with great power and penetration. His colour is superb. . . . He uses words well too, with feeling and economy. If only he had a trace of John Burningham's humour. One longs for his solitary little boy—he is good at loneliness—to discover that life is not only sad and beautiful, it is also fun.

*A review of "Joseph's Yard," in* The Junior Bookshelf, *Vol. 34, No. 2, April, 1970, pp. 78-9.*

Keeping's illustrations are always a delight in their high sense of design and dramatic use of color. Here the first pages are not particularly effective as an accompaniment to the story, although artistically interesting, but the succeeding pages are intrinsically complementary to the story as well as handsome. A small boy who has planted a seedling learns, by hard experience, that one cannot expect growth if a plant (or child?) is deprived of a natural environment. When he cuts the first rose, there are no more blossoms; the next year Joseph learns that he cannot cover the plant to protect it from birds and insects, because it needs the sun. Seasons pass, the plant grows bigger. The last pages show a luxuriant plant, birds and cats, and a happy boy. The message, possibly intended, seems to be freedom, love, and sharing. Not a strong plot, but a strong theme.

*Zena Sutherland, in a review of "Joseph's Yard," in* Bulletin of the Center for Children's Books, *Vol. 23, No. 11, July-August, 1970, p. 181.*

[There are] some excellent author-illustrators who do not flinch from the harshness of urban life. One of the best is Charles Keeping. At the Exeter Conference on Children's Literature in 1969, Keeping told his audience that he consciously uses the techniques of television, treating his story as a visual medium that requires few words to make it comprehensible. **Joseph's Yard** deals with loneliness, love, jealousy and death. It is impossible to understand the plot or capture the mood without the help of the pictures. A brick wall, a wooden fence, stone paving and rusty old iron denote not only the sterility of Joseph's yard but also of Joseph's life. Drab greys and browns represent Joseph in his yard, when the story begins. The greenness of rain, the hot yellow and orange of sun, the blueness of threatening cats, the hot pinks of exploding anger, the yellowish green of jealousy, and the triumphant reds of the flowering plant that finally fills Jacob's yard vividly symbolize the development of Joseph's character. Because it shows the destructiveness of anger and jealousy, the regenerative power of love and the consolation of nature, **Joseph's Yard** is just as much a moral tale as those that appeared in earlier times. Yet Keeping had to delay publication for six years because, in the view of his publisher, the book was too sophisticated—'the temperature in children's books was not right'.

*Muriel Whitaker, "Louder Than Words: The Didactic Use of Illustration in Books for Children," in* Children's literature in education, *No. 16, Spring, 1975, pp. 10-20.*

[Children's picture books have shown] a development which is symptomatic of the reinterpretation of the role of English teaching in schools, which has over the last forty years moved from seeing literature as a "storehouse of recorded values" to seeing it as a powerful stimulus for creative and imaginative work by and among children. This drift has meant that the meaning of the word "moral" has changed: instead of being obvious and signifying "instructional to feelings and intellect", it has become a wider term signifying the drawing out and stimulating of creative response in children. As such, of course, it is still based firmly on moral principles like good-and-bad and fair-and-unfair, but it is now more part of a process that invites and draws out the recognition of these things rather than lays them down like the Ten Commandments. Charles Keeping's *Joseph's Yard* demonstrates what happens. A little boy has a yard where nothing grows and into which no insects or birds or animals come. He decides to grow a flower, and from that starts nature's return to the garden. This is not "moral" in the sense that growing gardens is something all good children ought to do (as might be advised in *Sandford and Merton*); nor is it moral in the sense that gardens are part of God's creation and growing gardens is a good way of acknowledging the fact (as would be implied throughout Kingsley's *Glaucus* and *Madame How and Lady Why*). *Joseph's Yard* is moral in the sense that it evokes a feeling of rightness and of something worthwhile achieved, of personal achievement and of leaving something better than you found it. It demands that the child respond, decide, actively react, not just passively accept. And the vivid pictures make the response pictorial as well as verbal.

> *Stuart Hannabuss, "The Moral of It All (Part 1)," in* The Junior Bookshelf, *Vol. 40, No. 3, June, 1976, pp. 131-35.*

---

### Through the Window (1970)

*Through the window*—through a gap in net curtains—a little boy confined to the house looks at the street that is 'the whole world to him'. He looks at the church opposite and the roofscape behind. He sees the road-sweeper and nasty Georgie who spits and Old Soap with her skinny dog and the proud dray horses from the neighbouring brewery. All these characters, familiar to him, he sees as static figures; their movements are halted as in a film close-up, for him to look at. Then movement comes, terrible and bewildering. Why is everyone running—the men from the brewery, the sweeper? Why are the horses galloping and why is Old Soap bent over so strangely? Something has happened down in the street but Jacob can't see. He can only see Old Soap; and the climax of the story as he wants it is drawn with his finger on the pane of glass—a strong upright woman and in her arms an alert, alive dog. This is one of those books that hits you with a bang. The pages explode with colour and yet the colour is carefully organised and disciplined. They explode with movement like a film, and then slow down to close-up. They explode with feeling, never stated, always forced out of what we see and what Jacob sees. With every new work Charles Keeping is extending the range of the picture-book, to make us open our eyes and exercise our feelings.

> *Margery Fisher, in a review of "Through the Window," in* Growing Point, *Vol. 9, No. 3, September, 1970, p. 1578.*

*Through the Window* is brilliant, profound, disturbing as only Keeping knows how to be. It is the story—if you can call it a story—of Jacob who watches the world from his window and sees everyday things and a tragedy. It is all half-comprehended, by him and by the reader. The pictures are immensely powerful and haunting; one does not readily throw off their impression. This artist becomes more and more fascinated with textures and with prob-

lems of depth, but he resists the pressure to make technique an end in itself. The subtle, complex designs advance his theme and point his social comments. This will be a minority book but an influential one.

> *A review of "Through the Window," in* The Junior Bookshelf, *Vol. 34, No. 5, October, 1970, p. 278.*

Charles Keeping is a prime thicket man, and his latest book, *Through the Window,* takes us farther in than ever. A Hitchcock eye stares through the crack in a grimy lace curtain—it is dusk; lengthening shadows creep through the mean streets and plant a cross, from the top of the church opposite, on to the watcher's forehead. The face at the window belongs to a boy, Jacob; the pictures show what he sees as he gazes from his eyrie at the crepuscular scene below. What he sees is tragedy—an old woman's dog is crushed by galloping dray horses—but Jacob's reaction is to pretend it did not happen: he breathes on the window and draws the woman smiling, holding the dog, alive, in her arms. Anybody drawn to this sombre little saga (and the dustjacket picture is really closer to Hammer films than to Hitchcock) is likely to take the pictures as seriously as they deserve; the child's facile (and indeed incredible) reaction makes nonsense of what has gone before.

> *"Pictures with a Purpose: Prisons and Palaces," in* The Times Literary Supplement, *No. 35, October 30, 1970, p. 1260.*

Let me take as my text this autumn a statement drawn from the blurb to Charles Keeping's *Through the Window.* 'This picture-story captures exactly the small child's awareness of life, and his intuitive acceptance of it.' Leaving aside the gesturing largeness of the formulation, one is still entitled to a couple of questions. How, short of staying so childish that words like 'intuitive' would hardly be part of one's vocabulary, can anyone confidently talk of the experience of a kid experiencing events? And why, anyway, should it be assumed that a child would welcome such an extraordinary feat of empathy? He probably wouldn't even recognise it. Mr Keeping's minimally worded book concerns a mangy dog run over by a pair of drayhorses, the outline of the happening being witnessed by little Jacob peering between lace curtains in the East End. The colours and contours of the framing curtains shift bewilderingly; the people have a Henry Moore, or posed and stony, look; Jacob makes a cheery, uncomprehending breath-and-finger drawing on the window. It seems to me a thoroughly sophisticated enterprise, aimed at a certain kind of grownup who is less interested in children than in his reactions towards them. Striking it may be, but my home panel of two thumbed through it without relish.

> *John Coleman, "Pick of the Pix," in* New Statesman, *Vol. 80, No. 2068, November 6, 1970, pp. 612-13.*

*Through the Window* is at once the most singular and most exceptional picture or picture-story book of the season. Its conception seems to me to be a mistake on the part of Charles Keeping and its publication irresponsible on the part of the Oxford University Press. This might not matter so much if Mr Keeping were not one of the finest illustrators working in this field in England today, and if the Oxford University Press were not associated with children's books of the very highest quality. As it is, the book is certain of very wide exposure and therefore, influence. . . .

Heaven knows, I am not opposed to the judicious presentation of reality to young children—and this book is for very young children; the publisher indicates an age-range of three to six. But this grim and unrelieved little saga, which presents but does not comment, in effect asks a child how much he or she can take. The events described may be true to life, but they are only part of life; they are presented within no context, and they are therefore seen out of perspective. By sealing off the end, moreover, with the drawing on the pane—the child's conscious or unconscious attempt to mend the broken link, to reassert normality—Charles Keeping absolutely precludes any escape into healing fantasy. Jacob's reaction is certainly an interesting and, I think, true comment on how children behave; but that is a matter for adults, not material for a children's book. It is high time Mr Keeping realised that he has a responsibility not only to his art but also to his audience. Precisely because his pictures are so fine, there is every possibility that this arrogant book—in which the shadow of the cross on the church opposite recurs again and again as a symbol of death—will profoundly disturb a large number of those children who are unfortunate enough to see it.

K. Crossley-Holland, "Artistic Licence," in The Spectator, *Vol. 225, No. 7432, December 5, 1970, pp. xii-xiii.*

---

*The God Beneath the Sea* **(1970)**

[The God Beneath the Sea *is written by Leon Garfield and Edward Blishen.*]

## ILLUSTRATOR'S COMMENTARY

When I first met Leon Garfield he asked me would I like to join with him and Edward Blishen to do the Greek myths. And I thought 'My God, what a horrible idea.' Mainly because I did not like the Greek myths in any shape or form, but because I liked Leon I said 'Oh yes, Leon, I will.' So I came home and said to my wife 'How do I phone Leon now to tell him that I am not the slightest bit interested in the Greek myths?' It was a terrible problem.

I would like to tell you why I didn't like the Greek myths. First of all the myths were presented to us at school in the most boring fashion. I can remember them being read on Children's Hour on the radio in those days. There was one or two of them I liked but I have a terrible blind spot for names, particularly when it comes to Greek names. I find it difficult enough to remember names like Fred and Mary. When it became Greek names I couldn't sort out one from t'other. So I tended to mix up every possible myth there was. I knew there was some woman who turned men to stone and some other fellow went out and tried to cut her head off. Later in life when I was an art student the other

side of the myths came out through studying the great periods of Greek art, although I must confess it was not the most attractive art form to me. It seems cold and dispassionate, particularly at that time. Graphically however I got to like the fine ideas presented on many of the vases in the British Museum. And one of the things I've noticed is that everybody who ever illustrated anything to do with the Greek myths seemed to end up with these same drawings off these vases. There was always stylized figures— the guy in the same sort of chariot, the same sort of fellow pulling the bow, they always had the same brass gaiters on their legs, and the women always had the same sort of thing high up here and dangling down. I thought this was an utter bore. I couldn't see anything in it for me. I hasten to add that as a Londoner I found my heroes and my heroines and my monsters more among the local people on the street or in the family or somewhere else. I certainly didn't take them from what somebody had written down years ago. Also if I was to get involved with these myths, they did present me with this terrible problem: what the devil could I do with it? Then Leon phoned me up and said 'Well look, I'm taking my source from Robert Graves.' You must remember that at this time I'd never seen a word Leon had written. To be honest I'd never read one of his books. But I liked him as a person and had heard a lot about his work. So a very good friend gave me two Penguin editions of the Graves' myths which I started to read. Even at that stage I was still pretty worried because I think one of the worst things you can do when you're reading Graves' Greek myths is to read them from the beginning because every one seems to be almost identical. They seem to be the same old thing over and over again. They seem to follow a strange sort of pattern. And you must remember that I'm at a disadvantage since both Edward and Leon are doing the writing. I have got to do fifteen drawings.

Now visual art is a totally different thing from written art. How do I cover all the ground they've covered with fifteen drawings? First of all let's consider: a drawing is an image. If we have any given shape of paper on that paper we are going to create an image and that image has got to convey something. Now it doesn't matter how that image is done. It can be realistic, it can be abstract, it can be anything but it's got to convey something to somebody looking at it. You must remember that drawn images came long before writing. They're the new boys in the field. They have these miles of pages on which they can indulge themselves in wonderful flights of fancy and literature but all I've got is fifteen blank shapes. And in those fifteen blanks I've got to do something visual which gets this over.

Now when I started reading it let's be honest, these things are really quite disgusting! I found no love in them and I'm very fond of love. I think love is one of the great qualities that the human race has but these things are completely devoid of any love. This is all lust, rape, revenge and violence of every possible kind. It goes on and on and on. I wondered first whether this was just the *Oh Calcutta!* of its time or whether it really had something a little deeper than that, a significance, and whether it had some philosophy to tell us. I found that it did have some philosophy. I also found that many of the stories linked tremendously with the Bible and other stories that one knows from other cultures and other religions. It seemed to me that there were some basic human passions there which we could use. Since I had only fifteen shapes to make I had to take a group of shapes that would project what this meant to me.

You've got this dreadful problem of costume if you're doing a thing like this. I've always hated costume for this reason. I dislike it intensely for many reasons. First of all if I use a Greek costume I'm back to the familiar illustration. People don't walk around like that today so the children who see this book may get the same reaction I used to get. What does it mean? What does it do? Am I just delving back in the past? If I use modern dress which would be more to my taste, this would be old fashioned within another fifteen years, I mean the mini skirt's out of date, so my drawing's going to look ridiculous. So I always come to the conclusion in the end that the best thing is not to bother overmuch with definite costume at all. I used a few people and animals and outside that I wanted to get away from this whole idea of having any form of recognizable costume but on the other hand you have to be terribly careful that you don't use anything that is appertaining to our particular moment in time. These are visual problems

which many of you probably don't fully appreciate. You may have ideas too which take you outside of the realms of people's understanding. Therefore as it's concerned with people I think the only thing one could do is to use a figurative art. There's nothing else in it as far as I'm concerned except people, their emotions and their reactions to emotions. Therefore I produced a set of drawings much to my disgust not all awfully good. I think there are one or two—or three or four—which might be good. I don't know yet. I need a passage of time to tell. But I know these things were violent, I know they were cruel and I know the people concerned in them were cruel and violent. My form of projecting cruelty and violence becomes very difficult because I've got to project it visually. Therefore I took a symbolic line, so if you look at them you will find there's a symbolic overtone in them. Whether I succeeded or not I don't know but I can tell you I'm looking forward to the next one we do together because I'm hoping to redeem some of the mistakes of the first one. If illustration wasn't about progressing from one stage to the next then it wouldn't be worth doing. If I started again to illustrate the same myths tomorrow the results would be quite different and that's how it should be. My own fresh experiences together with new discoveries in the legends would trigger off quite another set of images and so on and so on.

*From* Through the Window, *written and illustrated by Charles Keeping.*

*Charles Keeping, "Greek Myths and the Twentieth Century Reader," in* Children's literature in education, *No. 3, November, 1970, pp. 52-4.*

The pity of it. Like Sisyphus, whose story occupies no less than three chapters of this book, the authors sweat purple words as they roll their new version of the Greek myths by inches up the ascent, and what happens? The stone gets heavier the further they push it, only to roll back to the bottom, taking Messrs. Blishen and Garfield with it. It is difficult not to be influenced by the cloudy rhetoric of this book. Put plainly then, Edward Blishen and Leon Garfield conceived the idea of retelling a selection of Greek myths "not as a collection of separate tales but as a continuous narrative", written in "the literary voice of our time" (quoted from the Afterword). With them on the journey went the artist Charles Keeping. His contribution is magnificent. Pain stares naked from the tortured figure of Prometheus; the horses of the sun stream across the page; Pandora looks slyly past our shoulders, her mouth and eyes drowsy and sensual; Demeter's grief for the lost Persephone is audible to the ears of the imagination, so powerfully has Charles Keeping delineated her anguish. From this book, it is Keeping's interpretation of the "enormous violent energy" of the Greek myths that will be remembered. . . .

In contrast to the spare yet flowing line of the drawings, the text is lush, meandering and self-indulgent. It is larded with those lazy adjectives, "mighty", "terrible", "lovely", and weighed down under laborious similes. Simile was the stock-in-trade of the great classical poets, from Virgil himself to Milton and Pope. Similes suit a leisured book, but they have their dangers. Metaphor is cleaner, swifter, harder-hitting. The opening sentences of the book set the pace. Nearly fifty words containing two extended similes are used to describe a pinpoint of light moving across the sky. A further fifty lines of print follow to tell us that the infant Hephaestus, hurled out of Olympus, has arrived in the ocean grotto of Thetis and Eurynome. This opening is used—undoubtedly an excellent device in itself—to allow the book to start dramatically. What has gone before is then related to Hephaestus by his guardian goddesses. He learns of Chaos, of the rise and fall of the Titans, of mad Cronus and the rule of Zeus.

An attempt to "humanize" these primitive myths only ends in weakening their impact. The story of Demeter and Persephone, for instance, is reduced in power by anthropomorphism.

In the story of Cronus and later of Prometheus, something of the grandeur of these myths does come through, even if only fitfully, and this increases one's bitter disappointment in the work as a whole. It could have been so splendid. At first, Keeping's awe-inspiring picture of Cronus swallowing his child dominates a slack text, but suddenly, when Cronus is forced to disgorge his children, the literary rope tautens. In a terse paragraph, the authors describe how the mad king "spewed out the fiery inhabitation of his belly" and "stared in dread at what he'd brought forth. They rose before him like columns of fire: the children he had consumed". This is true Garfield horror, as the death

of the first man is told with the tenderness of the author who created "the poor thing" in *Black Jack*. We are genuinely moved as our first mortal ancestor is carried over the Styx, sadly questioning his escort, Hermes, "Why? Why?" But the authors cannot sustain the pace or the tension. The over-writing has become chronic, and it is only just to lay some of the blame upon an editor who did not see how urgently the book needed honing down, who did not notice upon page after page the plethora of empty superlatives. "Zeus", we read, "was overcome by the largeness of his gestures." The words are ominous for the reader. If this is "the literary voice of our time", God help us.

*"Stones Not Bread," in* The Times Literary Supplement, *No. 3583, October 30, 1970, p. 1254.*

We live in strange times. A character in a story, with his mother's help, cuts off his father's genitals, has children by his own sister and eats them at birth. This seems to be OK for children to read. In a different story, 'bastard' and 'arse' occur, and a teacher sends a letter to chide the publisher for printing filth. The crucial difference between the stories is that the first is a myth and the second is a modern novel.

There is an apparent belief among some established teachers, librarians and child manipulators that myth (with its subdivisions of folk lore, fairy tale and fantasy) is safe for children to read because it's not 'true'. The younger, hardheaded generation, who prefer 'realism', criticise myth on the same grounds. Yet myth is no escapist entertainment. It is distilled and violent truth. Anyone who reads it is handling spiritual gelignite. Should children be let loose among the stuff, or are they at risk? The question may seem idiotic to the adult who has forgotten childhood. My own answer is clear. Children should indeed know myth, but it must be presented with the greatest skill.

There are three basic ways of handling the material. The writer may re-absorb and transmute (often subconsciously) the elements of the myth; or he may translate existing texts; or he may re-tell. Re-telling is the form most practised, since any competent literate can crib from a translation, although a few writers do have genuine ability in this narrow field, and can read both text and translation and retrieve what the scholar has lost. Translation is normally an accurate text from which the essence has gone. It is workable slag, which some steal and one or two build on.

Hardest of all is the absorption of myth, not the shape but the spirit, and making it relevant to the present moment. This absorption, if it works, is the most positive form for the myth to take, because the life of the myth is handed forward. It doesn't matter if the story changes, since what we take to be the original story is no more than the earliest form that we have. When it works, the writer is a transmitter, not an archivist. . . .

Can, or should, Classical myth survive? And if so, how? My inclination would be to send a Modern Greek linguist into the mountains and not let him out for five years. The gods can't be killed: they'll be lurking somewhere while we and our children yawn at their bleached replicas.

An effort should be made to restore Classical myth to its original vigour, and an effort has been made. Leon Garfield and Edward Blishen have set out to write a continuous story from a part of the complex theology of ancient Greece, and somehow a collection of line drawings by Charles Keeping has come to be bound between the same covers.

With so many books published annually, and so little space available to a critic, it seems extravagant to pay attention to rubbish, but in this case there may be a lesson to be won from the experience. *The God Beneath the Sea* is very bad. It is almost impossible to read, let alone assess. . . .

Leon Garfield and Edward Blishen have fallen into the trap they tried to avoid. The prose is overblown Victoriana, 'fine' writing at its worst, cliché-ridden to the point of satire, falsely poetic, groaning with imagery and, among such a grandiloquent mess, intrusively colloquial at times. . . .

The text of *The God Beneath the Sea* demonstrates what is dead in our feeling for Classical myth. But if that were all, there would be no justification for wasting energy on the book, except to warn readers from being conned into buying it on the strength of the authors' prestigious names. The trouble is Charles Keeping and his illustrations. It's unbelievable that these clear statements are his reaction to, or have anything in common with, the fudge that surrounds them. They are a singular vision of what Classical myth must have been. They are what happens when great gifts are put at the service of the subject. Two drawings especially—Cronos and Prometheus—are more terrible and beautiful than Goya.

Charles Keeping, thank God, is one of those men who won't be categorised, and book readers are lucky that a part of him expresses itself in this form. If you want to see the survival of Greek mythology justified, buy *The God Beneath the Sea*, discard the text, take Charles Keeping's drawings, and frame them.

> *Alan Garner, "The Death of Myth," in* New Statesman, *Vol. 80, No. 2068, November 6, 1970, pp. 606-07.*

*The God Beneath the Sea* by Leon Garfield and Edward Blishen is a collaborative attempt by two distinguished writers to establish a new version of the Greek myths. They have bulldozed through the stories, so long landlocked for the young in school-book cosiness, to reveal an ocean of frightening violence and seminal poetry. Once embarked upon these seas monstrous imaginings loom upon us.

The Titans spawned of Chaos beget the Gods who fashion Man. The artist-god Hephaestus is cast from Olympus, clambers back—linking us to our present Christian ethic—only to fall again because of pride and the tyranny of Zeus. Names such as Zeus, Prometheus, Sisyphus, Persephone resound again, this time with the clangour of immediacy; warning bell-buoys of the rocks within ourselves.

There are so many couplings you feel they could only be properly contained within an Ark, but the narrative-voyage is handled with dramatic, and comic, awareness of the epic voyage into our creative origins. It is a remarkable book for any reader and should evoke a response from anyone clogged within the classics, wanting to see the poetry afresh.

The illustrations by Charles Keeping are totems of potency, so alien and yet so recognisable as ourselves, that they—as indeed does the book—make us grateful for the landfall of an eventual humanity.

> *Tom Hutchinson, "Not for Infants," in* The Spectator, *Vol. 225, No. 7432, December 5, 1970, p. vii.*

---

## The Garden Shed  (1971)

This haunting book about a world of dreams and possibilities is imbued with feeling for the past but at the same time alive to the advantages of change and new experience. Through the peephole in the front of his private place, the garden shed, Daniel can see his house and the world he knows; through the splintered glass of the window at the back he looks out on to a derelict railway yard dating from a time when steam trains and horses were the main means of transport. Although he is fascinated by the yard and by the statue of a lady that stands in it, Daniel recognizes sadly that they are dead remnants of a vanished time, and he is filled with excitement and anticipation when the yard is demolished to make room for something new. Charles Keeping's sombre, mysterious paintings show a real appreciation of the child's mind and vision.

> *A review of "The Garden Shed," in* The Times Literary Supplement, *No. 3640, December 3, 1971, p. 1515.*

Through the broken glass of the garden shed Daniel looks out at a rather dreary clutter of abandoned railway buildings, enlivened only by a stone lady. Daniel is a typical Keeping boy, solitary, melancholy, rather repulsive. One day the derelict buildings catch fire, and Keeping has a wordless sequence in which the intrinsically ugly takes on gorgeous and colourful beauty. The resulting desert of smouldering ashes offers Daniel, rather surprisingly, a promise for the future. A very strange book, even by this artist's standards. The design is marvellous, the draughtsmanship masterly, but the book scarcely communicates. Symbolically, the brief text is dropped into the midst of dark pages in such a way that it is barely legible. Here is a great artist at work, but what is he trying to say?

> *M. Crouch, in a review of "The Garden Shed," in* The Junior Bookshelf, *Vol. 36, No. 1, February, 1972, pp. 22-3.*

It is even more evident in this book than in the two previous ones that Keeping is concerned with an idea, a moment of revelation, rather than a story. Whether or not this new book reflects his own childhood or not, it has an absolute unity of emotion and setting, illustrating a moment of illumination and growth in a child's life. Framed in a peephole in a shed door Daniel sees a derelict railway yard where (grandfather tells him) cattle and sheep used to be mustered for transit. In this untidy, fascinating no-man's-land the object that really catches Daniel's attention is a statue; the remote marble figure of a woman seems to him to borrow warmth from the flowers he puts in the window. Then one day the old dead world of the yard is coloured indeed, by the dangerous red of fire; and though the statue is visible throughout the destruction, the boy realises that new objects and uses will now come to the yard. This most abstract of Keeping's picture-books is built from immensely sensuous colour and a symbolic use of contrast—for instance, of the boy's eye glaring through the knot hole and the statue's flat, empty eyes. Once more the artist has extended the range of the picture book as a vehicle for feeling and imagination.

> *Margery Fisher, in a review of "The Garden Shed," in* Growing Point, *Vol. 10, No. 8, March, 1972, pp. 1900-01.*

---

### The Spider's Web  (1972)

[Illustrations] appeal more immediately to the senses than to the understanding. The brilliant colours of modern printing shout to a child from the pages before him. He *has* to look, and if the picture is strange and unexpected, he tends to look longer and longer. His curiosity is aroused and he may suffer the artist to lead him on to wider and different experience in a way he would not permit a writer to do. But it is extremely important such an artist should know where he is seeking to lead and why.

Charles Keeping, who may be described almost as king of the modern experimentalists, *does* know—and is not too highminded to make his aims and intentions perfectly clear. *The Spider's Web* is the latest of a series of strikingly original, colourful and moving books in which he tries to show a child's view of the drab, puzzling, concrete modern world—books, one feels, that although they contain not a written word about himself can aptly be described as biographical, with pathos, wonder and hope strangely blended. And because they are so personal, so vivid, so intimate, he has to supply his own text, kept to the absolute minimum length and maximum simplicity. A lonely child stands in an empty yard bounded by a fence. A spider spinning a web seems at first to be the only other living creature. But, looking at the spider's web, the child becomes aware of the yard beyond his own, and of other signs of life—a butterfly, a goldfish, a cat, a hen, a dog, a horse, a man, and at last another child. The book is a beautiful work of art, but its appeal may be greater for adults than for the children to whom it reaches out so nostalgically.

> *Alice Andrews, "Experimenting," in* Books and Bookmen, *Vol. 18, No. 2, November, 1972, pp. xi-xv.*

This is the most beautiful of Charles Keeping's picture books to date. Once again he has shown us a vision of the world through the eyes of a young child, a boy peering between the slats of a garden fence and commenting on what he sees: a spider making its web, goldfish, a butterfly, a cat, a chicken, a dog, a man, a little girl and a horse. There is no attempt at a narrative structure, the text reads like a film scenario with stage directions interposed between the boy's comments.

Without a defined narrative thread there might have been a lack of dramatic tension but the force and flow of the visual images interacting with the boy's apprehensive comments on what he sees, create their own inner tensions which are marvellously resolved in the concluding pages.

Visually the book is a *tour de force*—each object is seen framed between vertical or horizontal planks, the dark grain of the wood creating a decorative counterpoint to the enclosed images, many of which are seen through the delicate network of the spider's web. The colours are muted with restrained browns, greys and steely blues enriched by blushing pinks and sudden, glowing reds and yellows.

This is not the book for a pre-school story hour but older children should be given the opportunity to absorb it in solitude or pore over it with their friends.

> *Eleanor von Schweinitz, in a review of "The Spider's Web," in* Children's Book Review, *Vol. II, No. 6, December, 1972, p. 180.*

Mr. Keeping's problem is increasingly one of communication. He has never drawn better than in *The Spider's Web,* but what will children make of this little boy's interior monologue and of the strange, disturbing vision of a commonplace world which he sees through the threads of the web. It is supremely well done, but who is it for?

> *M. Crouch, in a review of "The Spider's Web," in* The Junior Bookshelf, *Vol. 36, No. 6, December, 1972, p. 368.*

A small boy peers through a spider's web spun between two fence posts and reflects on what he sees on the other side. Much of what he sees frightens him, and it is hard to believe that it will not frighten the child who reads this book as well. Mr Keeping is a courageous maker of books, and it may well be that most picture books err on the side of cosiness and reassurance, but the pictorial images presented in these often over-worked pages seem unnecessarily disturbing.

> *A review of "The Spider's Web," in* The Times Literary Supplement, *No. 3692, December 8, 1972, p. 1495.*

---

### The Nanny Goat and the Fierce Dog  (1973)

This is one of Charles Keeping's nightmarish, claustrophobic studies of vulnerability and fear. The little nanny goat finally triumphs over the enemy who lives on the other side of the fence from her, but so much fear and solitude go into the text and so many strange, frightening images appear in the pictures, that the story is only to be recommended for the very stout-hearted.

> *A review of "The Nanny Goat and the Fierce Dog," in* The Times Literary Supplement, *No. 3734, September 28, 1973, p. 1126.*

As so often in the picture books of Charles Keeping it is not so much the story that matters here as its implications.

The nanny goat who lives in the 'weedy patch' at the city's edge and fears, but finally confronts, the fierce watchdog in the junkyard next door, is both hero (heroine?) and emblem. Her marvellously delineated poses: terror and loneliness, calm and triumph are not merely 'pictures in a story about animals' but symbols of those qualities themselves.

This, it would seem, is the answer to those critics who have objected to Mr. Keeping turning his back on the realism of his own story. The mutability of the nanny-goat's colouring, the insistence on *rusty* cars a sombre shade of blue, are really matters of no account. They may attract attention because of the simple and unpretentious tones of the text, but, as we should know by now, Mr. Keeping's texts are the muted back-drop to quite other dramas. They make it easier for us to take the impact not of surface colourations but of feeling. *The Nanny Goat and the Fierce Dog* is a book of eyes: the shattered headlamps of the cars, the cold pupils of the goat, the electric glare of the dog, the dotty group of hens. Read the pictures, read the eyes. It's all there.

> *Brian W. Alderson, in a review of "The Nanny Goat and the Fierce Dog," in* Children's Book Review, *Vol. III, No. 6, December, 1973, p. 171.*

A minimal story about a little nanny goat who lives in a junkyard with some chickens and fears the fierce watch-dog behind the fence, but who after a year of swiftly passing seasons butts the dog away and never fears him or anything again. It's all in the pictures and the pictures—bold blue and green prints—are all design, taking on a scary luminosity to suit the abandoned junkyard setting and the confrontation with the dog but generally too sophisticated for the story and without the involving personal appeal necessary at this level.

> *A review of "The Nanny Goat and the Fierce Dog," in* Kirkus Reviews, *Vol. XLII, No. 14, July 15, 1974, p. 736.*

---

## Richard (1973)

This is Charles Keeping's second picture story book about a horse, but a very different one from Queen the carthorse who appeared in *Shaun and the Carthorse* in 1966. It is appropriate to compare the two for *Richard* illustrates the development of Keeping's techniques only hinted at in the earlier book. For a while at least the constricting sombreness of the *Garden* and the *Window* are left behind. The story of the daily life of a police horse is related in Keeping's evocative style—the housing, grooming and exercising, the daily round of duty in the city streets and controlling the crowds in London. Richard and his fellow police horses will be popular with boys of five to eight particularly those living in London who will have seen many Richards. Children in general will perhaps find the latest Keeping more readily acceptable than the more impressionistic atmosphere of *Joseph's Yard* and the titles which followed, yet it is perhaps because of this that there is a sense of disappointment. Keeping is nothing if not an innovator. His recent work, whilst controversial and not easily ac-

cepted by some, has depicted a continuing search for fulfillment in the use of his rare gifts and techniques. One feels, and hopes, that with *Richard* Charles Keeping has paused only for a while before presenting some new idea brilliantly interpreted in colour and line. He is one of the most exciting illustrators of the day; one who, in the space of less than a decade, has changed and extended the world of picture-story-book illustration.

> *Edward Hudson, in a review of "Richard," in* Children's Book Review, *Vol. III, No. 5, October, 1973, p. 139.*

A short, simple text describes the training and work of a London mounted policeman and his horse. As though to challenge critics, Keeping has transferred many of his decorative devices to a sequence of pictures of great beauty which are basically and directly descriptive rather than symbolic; with total accuracy he shows the dapple-grey and its rider in stable and street, and the soberly beautiful pages speak eloquently of the loving eye he casts on the city and its inhabitants. Alternations of light and shade, line and colour, can be enjoyed singly as well as in the filmic sequence so characteristic of this artist.

> *Margery Fisher, in a review of "Richard," in* Growing Point, *Vol. 12, No. 5, November, 1973, p. 2270.*

---

## Railway Passage (1974)

Charles Keeping has his best story to date. The children play in Railway Passage, from which the railway has long departed, watched by the "aunts and uncles" who live in the squalid houses. The aunts and uncles have only one thing in common; they do the Pools together. When they come into the big money, it affects them in various ways, bringing happiness to only a few. Keeping shows the drabness of their lives, shot through with threads of brilliant colour. Here is an artist who knows urban poverty and paints it in all its unwitting beauty.

> *M. Crouch, in a review of "Railway Passage," in* The Junior Bookshelf, *Vol. 38, No. 6, December, 1974, p. 336.*

Sympathy and satire in rare association in a chronicle, formal in structure, describing the inhabitants of a row of six houses—tidy Aunt Adelaide, Red-oriented Uncle William, Aunt Ada who loves cooking and Aunt Emma who loves her goldfish Sam, Uncle Harry, an ex-sailor, Uncle and Auntie Meanie, one miserly, the other fashion-mad, and finally Uncle Ernest, who once rode in the Tour de France and now rebuilds old bikes from scrap, to the admiration of his nephew Pete. £250,000 and three pence, won in the pools, changes their lives; some react surprisingly, others predictably, and only Uncle Ernest is content to live as before. The illustrations are in a style similar to that of *Richard*—a combination of intricate line and sharp, acid colour, disciplined by careful composing of figures against an emphatic background, and with the personalities of the "Aunts" and "Uncles" shown through the boy's eyes as well as through the shrewd, humane gaze of Keeping himself.

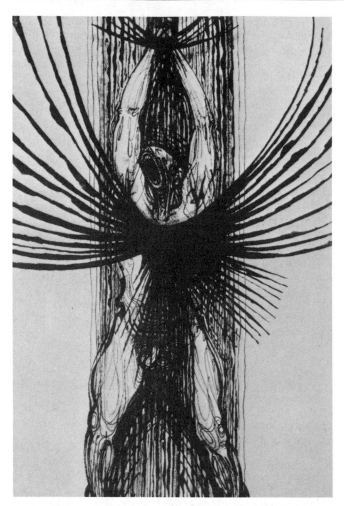

*Prometheus. From* The God Beneath the Sea, *written by Leon Garfield and Edward Blishen. Illustrated by Charles Keeping.*

*Margery Fisher, in a review of "Railway Passage," in* Growing Point, *Vol. 13, No. 8, March, 1975, p. 2582.*

In this book Charles Keeping's attention has swung from the loner back to the community, but a community composed of real individuals also familiar as types, and ranging from the pathetic through the tragi-comic to the ebullient. Railway Passage consists of a terrace of six cottages rented out to eight elderly tenants, who have all been dubbed 'Uncles' and 'Aunts' by the local children, regardless of their avuncularity.

The story is really about the effect of sudden wealth on these eight individuals, as witnessed by the children (with whom the reader comes to identify). The story is entirely plausible because of Charles Keeping's secure purchase on his knobbly characters. Children should find it amusing, absorbing in its detail, and illuminating in its portrayal of a spectrum of attitudes towards wealth. The text is largely functional and therefore not conspicuous, it is pointed up by the action and detail manifested in the drawing.

The pictures are as exciting as ever, Keeping's observation is just as keen, and his talent for pattern making undimin-

ished and under control. His depiction of characters ranges from a closely observed almost documentary approach, as in the drawings of Uncle Harry before the great event, or of Aunt Adelaide after it, across the narrow dividing line into caricature, as in his handling of the new, improved Auntie Meanie. Colour is used subtly; a pervading sepiatone is shot through with passages of pure bright colour, and one gradually becomes aware that each character is also associated with a particular colour. And look at the first picture of Uncle William for an example of the effective and characteristic use of contrast in brush (and pen?) strokes, and of the modulation of an apparently free organic line.

The tenants of Railway Passage bear no relation to the plastic persons who people *Janet and John*'s world, but if it were not for Charles Keeping's affectionate and amused portrayal, and, of course, for the transforming event of the story, one might be left saddened by the plight of some of the inhabitants of Railway Passage.

*Clive Phillpot, in a review of "Railway Passage," in* Children's Book Review, *Vol. V, No. 1, Spring, 1975, pp. 12-13.*

Charles Keeping's child's eye views of life are relentlessly real, yet touched with magic because their focus is so intense and isolating. Bereavement and loneliness have been the separate yet linked themes of earlier sombre picture books; in **Railway Passage** he explores, with a new-found joy in his heart, what happens to the elderly inhabitants of six run-down railway cottages in a cul-de-sac "play area" when these pensioners jointly win a large sum of money on the pools. What does happen? Well, they all begin to indulge in what had been their small pleasures in a large way. Aunt Adelaide makes a lovely garden for the street children to play in; Uncle Meaney sits counting lots of money; Aunt Ada cooks—and eats—far too much food; Uncle Ernest goes on making bicycles, and can now give them to the children; Aunt Emma buys so many goldfish and such a huge tank that she can no longer spot her beloved Sam; and Uncle Harry, the retired sailor, buys a Mini and starts exploring the world all over again. A perceptive, mature, earthy and outstandingly beautiful book.

*Elaine Moss, "Picture Books: 'The Railway Passage'," in her* Children's Books of the Year: 1974, *Hamish Hamilton, 1975, pp. 19-20.*

### Cockney Ding-Dong (1975)

This is a very personal book by the illustrator, Charles Keeping, who offers us an attractively produced record of his mother's family songlore. "Ding Dong" is Cockney rhyming slang for "Sing Song" and these songs are those which were sung round the piano on Saturday nights up to quite recently, never stopping even during the Second World War. The family custom was to sing the songs in character; Mr Keeping's Dorset-born grandmother sang mostly ballads, his grandfather, a sailor from Portsea, sang nautical songs, while Uncle Bob and Aunt Em were 100 per cent Cockney in their tastes. His father favoured Irish songs.

In one of the illustrations you can see his father, a one-time professional boxer who appeared under the name of Charlie Clark, shown on a poster sparring up outside a boxing hall, with other posters showing Fred Newman and Bob Wise. The song they illustrate is "That's where my Love lies Bleeding", collected (as are many others in this book) by Charles Keeping himself from the Cockney oral tradition:

> He only fought a round or two and he felt queer.
> All his teeth were missing, and half an ear,
> Lying in the gutter, blind to the world;
> That's where my love lies bleeding.

They could laugh at themselves and enjoy it. The situations, the humour, the singers, the songs and the drawings—all are part of their way of life. They sang of honesty:

> Don't try to put the swank on,
> For you know its only sham.
> Think of where you used to be,
> Down in Pinks's factory,
> All amongst the marmalade and jam.

Mr Keeping states in his preface that "the sing songs were never common, rude or vulgar", by which he means that they were never indecent. They were common, however, in being the property of all—not merely of the one family. Mr Keeping quotes a parody of "In the Shade of the Old Apple Tree" telling a version of the folktales of the Englishman, Frenchman and Jew, which is also a variation of the old folksong of "The Briery Bush" which in turn links up with the eternal theme of Death and Resurrection, which is related to the seasonal cycle of killing Winter and reviving Spring, and from that to the classical story of Orpheus and Eurydice. The Edwardian music-halls knew it on a form taken from their own experience in the song "If those Lips could only Speak"; printed here in a copyright version of 1975:

> Could I only take your hand,
> As I did when you took my name,
> But it's only a beautiful picture
> In a beautiful golden frame.

The fact that the music-hall comedians never thought of Orpheus is beside the question; they were drawing on a reservoir of popular culture as all-embracing as the air they breathed. The "knees-up" dance routine the Keepings followed after the solo singing was that of the oldest dance in the world—the chain or round dance—"They would form a crocodile and go around the house, up and down the stairs", says the author. "Fall in and follow Me", "Let's all go down the Strand" or "Knees up Mother Brown" with its Cockney speech: "Mince-pies" (Eyes) "Round-the-'Ouses" (Trousers), "Pig's Ear" (Beer), "Ding Dong" itself and "Tit-fer-Tat" (Hat).

I am old enough to be able to recall the original versions of some of these songs. Some, no doubt have been slightly altered in order to avoid copyright; of the others, some of the tunes have altered for the better and some not; it would seem that this family liked simplification. I do not know the version of "Mademoiselle from Armentiers" given in this book, for I was in the army in the First World War

and this is from Civvy Street, but any schoolboy will be able to tell Mr Keeping that "The Moon shines Tonight on Charlie Chaplin" should be "Bright", not "Tonight". It started, to my recollection, as an unpublishable ditty "The Moon shines bright on Mrs. Bentley", before Charlie and before the Dardanelles Campaign.

In keeping with the high standard of the illustrations is the printing of this book—especially the musical illustrations which are clean and accurate.

> *Reginald Nettel, "Keeping up the Traditions,"*
> *in* The Times Literary Supplement, *No. 3847,*
> *December 5, 1975, p. 1456.*

Like the Cockney's, the ancestry of these songs is decidedly mixed: Victorian ballads, Great War songs, a touch of American and more than a spit of Irish. Some are too well known to be London's property any more (Knees Up, Mother Brown, It's a Long Way to Tipperary, Any Old Iron, If It Wasn't for the 'Ouses In Between). But many others are long, colourful, three-quarters forgotten, and it was an admirable idea to set them out at full length, complete with simple score (sadly, no accompaniment). Lovely for singing with children: the rudest verses of Mademoiselle from Armentières do not appear, but Come Inside, Yer Silly Bugger is perhaps not quite the thing for the school concert. Any similarity to a hymn book is further avoided by Mr Keeping's big, bold illustrations.

> *A review of "Cockney Ding Dong," in* The
> Economist, *Vol. 257, No. 6904, December 20,*
> *1975, p. 103.*

Since the review copy arrived I have taken this exciting collection of songs and pictures to a group of London schools and shown it to a host of teachers. The response has been enthusiastic delight all round, not only because Charles Keeping's character pictures are small masterpieces . . . but also for the encouragement it gives to children and teachers to make their own collections. The range and depth of feeling in these popular rhymes is now being noticed by serious students. Charles Keeping calls the social cohesion that they represent 'a great sense of feeling a part of something'. Keeping's devotion to the London of his childhood touches something in everyone. This joky collection, full of vitality and the sound of singing, will become a classic. No doubt about it.

> *Margaret Meek, in a review of "Cockney Ding-*
> *Dong: A Songbook," in* The School Librarian,
> *Vol. 24, No. 1, March, 1976, p. 80.*

---

### Wasteground Circus (1975)

In some ways this book might have been better without the rather halting text, for the illustrations make the point simply through significant colour, as the drab browns and greys of the waste ground where Scott and Wayne play, and the oddly dull back-quarters of the circus, give way to a blaze of light and colour as the performers substitute silk for denim and spring into action. The artist appears himself, richly tattooed, in the ticket office, as though compèring one more splendid show of London-town.

*Margery Fisher, in a review of "Wasteground Circus," in* Growing Point, *Vol. 14, No. 9, April, 1976, pp. 2858-59.*

Two boys play on a bleak wasteground in the middle of a city. One day they find lorries have moved in, and for a brief time the circus takes over. The change is symbolised by a gradual move from drab brown skeletal shapes of fences and skylines to muted colours for the menagerie, fun fair and circus people and then, with the suddenness of Aladdin's cave, all the colours of the rainbow march in their bands across each page as the boys enter the Big Top. Animals and actors are transformed in a wonderland of mystery and excitement, until the circus vanishes and darkness and drabness return. Only for one boy, however; the other retains the magic colours in his memory: the wasteground has become "a place where anything can happen", a subtly-drawn moral, skilfully reinforced by the unforgettable beauty of Charles Keeping's illustrations, which capture on paper the essential romance of a circus.

*M. Hobbs, in a review of "Wasteground Circus," in* The Junior Bookshelf, *Vol. 40, No. 2, April, 1976, p. 82.*

Surely one of the finest picture books of 1975. Charles Keeping never stays still in his picture books; each one has something visually new to offer the reader. In **Wasteground Circus,** he has deliberately used colour to build up the circus atmosphere: At first the wasteground is shown bleak and drab, in grey and sepia; then the circus wagons arrive, with the first touch of dark green colour; The big top is put up, the green shades into mysterious blue. The boys buy their tickets and wander round the fair-ground which has not yet come truly alive, so the colours stay soft and dark until they enter the main tent and suddenly, as the clowns rush on, the pictures break into vivid rainbow colours as the boys watch the performance. Then, as the Grand Finale comes to an end, so does the colour and we are back in the drab grey of the everyday wasteground, but, for one of the boys it will never be the same again, because he will always remember the colour and glamour of the circus, and this is shown in the narrow strips of red and mauve on the last page. An outstanding example of how colour can be used to underline and complement both text and drawings. How dull and unimaginative Brian Wildsmith's *Circus* seems beside this, despite its own brilliant colours.

*Valerie Alderson, in a review of "Wasteground Circus," in* Children's Book Review, *Vol. VI, October, 1976, p. 35.*

---

### The Wildman (1976)

[The Wildman *is written by Kevin Crossley-Holland.*]

A sad little story, told in clotted prose and illustrated by sombre, grey pictures—it's hard to imagine that anything in this book would appeal to most children. Charles Keeping's illustrations, in that swirling, grainy style he reserves for legend and mythology, have their usual high quality, while the story is an old and haunting one, about a merman caught at Orford during the reign of Henry II. But

together the effect is dark and depressing; something that must have been intentional, since ugliness is emphasized in the pictures and underlined in the text, with the merman turning into a Suffolk Caliban, surrounded by rustic Yahoos, mouths agape and in need of urgent dental treatment. The whole thing would have been better as a limited edition aimed at connoisseurs who could appreciate the skill of Keeping's draughtsmanship and the aqueous effects he creates so vividly, although they would have to look harder to find anything in Kevin Crossley-Holland's prosey narration. For children, however, put off by the initial harshness of appearance, I fear the whole effort will be wasted.

*Nicholas Tucker, "A Picture of Ugliness," in* The Times Literary Supplement, *No. 3900, December 10, 1976, p. 1550.*

Kevin Crossley-Holland is well known for his special interest in East Anglian folk tales and Norse literature generally. Yet, whatever marvels he has already found in these, it must have been a moment of extraordinary excitement for him when he came upon the seed of his new tale, **The Wildman,** in Ralph of Coggeshall's *Chronicon Anglicanum.* The details of the entry are summarised on the last page of the present book: 'A merman was caught at Orford in Suffolk during the reign of Henry II (1154-1189). He was imprisoned in the newly-built Castle, did not recognise the Cross, did not talk despite torture, returned voluntarily into captivity having eluded three rows of nets, and then disappeared never to be seen again'.

With this to work on, the author gives us the Wildman's tale in his own words, entering into his consciousness in a very moving way, first in his free life in the deep, then suddenly kicking and flailing in the strange web that has entrapped him. This hauls him up from darkness through indigo, purple, pale blue until, in bright daylight, he first sets eye on man, a creature oddly like himself but with little hair on his body and wearing animal skins and furs. Everything the Wildman sees and everything that happens to him has the sharp strangeness of first knowing, which gives the tale an immediate affinity with children's half-forgotten early experience. They will also be drawn to him because he is rejected and misunderstood. On the other hand he is convincingly monsterish in the way he loves to pounce on small creatures for his food, then suck their blood and chew them afterwards.

As the brief sad tale unfolds, the Wildman senses that in himself he belongs more with men than the fish he has left behind. Yet throughout men hit him and howl at him, especially when he does not recognise the cross they thrust at him. They also recoil particularly when, from a natural instinct to touch in order to know, he moves to embrace them.

In the end he is returned to the sea as alien and unwanted, but he twists and dives his way out from the nets set against him. Why, he wonders, is he only free away from those whom he resembles, why is he only free with those quite unlike himself in the sea? This paradox is never resolved for this time men truss him up and throw him in a dungeon and treat him so cruelly he wants to escape, and so he does, even though this means returning to the sea.

The author writes very simply and vividly throughout. His style is neither modern nor old-fashioned, but what I would call substantial, working through images and the lightness or heaviness of actual sentences. Like Ted Hughes's *The Iron Man,* which it resembles in poetic power, I think *The Wildman* will be enjoyed by children of very varying ages from about seven to eleven or twelve. Unlike Ted Hughes, Kevin-Crossley-Holland does not seek to impose a message on the story, he is content to let its power come from the symbolic nature of the human behaviour involved. The Wildman cannot be explained, but the experience of his tale will certainly be remembered.

This is especially so, perhaps, because the illustrator, Charles Keeping, has been inspired by it to produce pen and ink drawings of remarkable quality, even for him. T S Eliot once said that the artist must have both primitive and civilised instincts in him. These drawings are often very primitive in vision, yet one recognises centuries of civilisation behind their artistry. In Charles Keeping's other books, when he has written the story as well as illustrating it, one often feels the art work is too powerful, the print often becomes hard to read. In this book the division is much more even, with the text on its own in green type on one side of each double-page spread, the drawings on the other. In one or two instances when particularly appropriate, when the monster, for instance, is crawling over the ground, snuffling and grubbing for mice and moles and shrews, the double page is divided horizontally. The most effective drawing of all I found the last, as the Wildman walks away from us into the sea, heavy with sadness yet alive in every nerve and sinew of his body.

> *Marie Peel, "Kevin Crossley-Holland," in* Books and Bookmen, *Vol. 22, No. 8, May, 1977, p. 66.*

The fourth of Kevin Crossley-Holland's East Anglian tales is perhaps the saddest, the more so because it is the sufferer who tells the story. In the twelfth century fishermen caught a man in their net and brought him to Orford Castle. He was naked and covered with hair. They tried to communicate with him, by words and signs, kindly and brutally, all without success. Eventually the sea-man escaped. Seen through the confused mind of the wildman himself the strange and incomplete story is more sad, not less strange. Keeping at his most powerful preserves the enigma, even as he explores the mystery and the cruelty of the tale. A deeply disturbing book.

> *M. Crouch, in a review of "The Wildman," in* The Junior Bookshelf, *Vol. 41, No. 5, October, 1977, pp. 285-86.*

---

## Inter-City (1977)

[*Inter-City*] is a valiant attempt to turn a picture book into a railway carriage. The six passengers who become progressively more relaxed and sleepy as the long journey continues are more interesting than the views from left or right-hand window—but too seldom during the Inter-City journey do we see them occupying a complete opening: left-hand pages are frequently given over to the view from the left window (even if the view is total darkness)—right-

hand to the view from the right. Keeping's observation of character, his painting of brickwork, iron railings, horses, rain splashing against glass, are breathtaking, page by page; and one does share the relief with which the stiff and weary passengers step out on to the platform at the end. But during the journey there are too many unsuccessful pages; strong editorial guidance might have turned this series of pictures (there is no text) into a great picture book.

> *Elaine Moss, "Look before You Leap," in* The Times Literary Supplement, *No. 3931, July 15, 1977, p. 862.*

Children are left to discover for themselves what happens on this train journey. They will need no text to help them to realise that each one of them is to be, as it were, the small boy seen opening the carriage door on the first page. With him they will watch the six people opposite as time goes by, perhaps envying the stout woman her chocolates, certainly upsetting her with a rude face and so establishing a kind of bond with a demure little girl who would never dare to be impolite (but she is, on the last page). With the boy they will look through the window as fields, houses, people and animals flash by. Whether the pages are arresting with violent colour or closely patterned in sepia and grey, each one tells its particular part of the story.

> *Margery Fisher, in a review of "Inter-City," in* Growing Point, *Vol. 16, No. 4, October, 1977, p. 3193.*

The wordless picture-book, which has given us the sweet simplicity of Paddy Porks and others, lends itself well to more sophisticated treatment. Charles Keeping uses it as a vehicle for social comment, or perhaps as an essay in pure observation. *Inter-City* is about a rail journey. Almost all the pictures are a child's-eye view from the train window, of city merging into country and back again. From time to time the view is put into context by a glimpse of the passengers, portrayed with all Keeping's unflattering candour. As the train gathers speed the pictures become confused, the object elongated and the detail lost. Rain splashes the pane, and then sunlight alters the tonal values. A tour de force, beyond question. But who will enjoy it? A book for artists and art students, I fancy.

> *M. Crouch, in a review of "Inter-City," in* The Junior Bookshelf, *Vol. 41, No. 5, October, 1977, p. 279.*

---

## River (1978)

For the documentation of social change Charles Keeping has his own methods, never more successful than in this latest sequence of pictures, in which bricks and hoardings, graffiti and inscriptions and shop-window fascia, people working or idling, tell half a tale; the other half is discerned as, across the river, a hillside and a castle intermittently appear. In this opposition of man and nature the changes on the near side of the river are those of usage (warehouse to mansion, terrace building, windowless wall, office block) while, opposite, nature changes only in season and colour. In these pages paint makes points, sets moods, tells a story and in its intricate control provides refreshment and delight to the eye.

Margery Fisher, in a review of "River," in Growing Point, Vol. 17, No. 2, July, 1978, p. 3370.

[A] journey is recorded in **River,** Charles Keeping's beautiful new book. . . . The journey is not through space, for each page shows the same stretch of land, but through time. A quiet river bank with single pollarded willow set against a hill is suddenly blotted out by the busy wall of a corn merchant, soon to be reduced to skeletal timbers quickly replaced by a rococo edifice with equestrian monument to The Glorious Brave. Bombed magnificence is demolished to form a functional trading bay and then a monolithic wall. Graffiti quickly relieve the monotony and usher in the planned anarchy of a water playground. A giant office building eventually replaces all, its glassy anonymity reflecting faintly the original rural scene. Thankfully Charles Keeping is not pointing the finger at civilization and her ravages; he is not even saying, Look what time has done but simply, that this is what time is. The people in **River** are not like Anno's figures, caught in a moment of living [critic refers to *Anno's Journey* by Mitsumasa Anno, reviewed earlier]: they are slaves to the movement of time, no more or less important than the bricks and mortar that form their environment.

Each of Keeping's pages is dominated by a wall and a varying number of strong vertical lines against which the in-

"Don't Dilly Dally on the Way." From Cockney Ding Dong, edited and illustrated by Charles Keeping.

cidentals, pigeons, horse troughs, graffiti, cars, people, are set on the absolute horizontal. This grid patterning might have been monotonous, but never is, for the colour washing over the lines changes in tone and shade as the mood of the place alters, **River** is a book whose graphic sophistication is seductive, surprisingly, to children as well as adults.

Sarah Hayes, "The Power of Pictures," in The Times Literary Supplement, No. 3979, July 7, 1978, p. 763.

**River** is an astonishing work, certainly the finest yet in Keeping's long line of brilliantly designed picture books—less obsessively introverted and intense than some of them, fresher but also more subtle. In a sequence of twenty detail-packed pictures, without any words, he tells us the history of one place—a short stretch of river bank—over a period of (maybe) a couple of centuries. Commercial buildings are erected on the site, have a brief heyday of busy use, decay, and are replaced by new ones, each symbolising a different stage in our economic and cultural development. All the while, the river and hills beyond retain their dignified unchanging natural condition. One finds oneself turning the pages to and fro in the book, checking back to see how the equestrian statue in the foreground has altered over the decades, following what happens to the birds as their perches get moved around, noticing the shifts of fashion in working men's clothes. . . . The final appalling office block seems almost to obliterate human life, but does succeed in reflecting the sun and hills in its vast plate glass surface. One is continually comparing and evaluating, which is what makes it an intriguing and important book for mature readers as well as younger ones.

A review of "River," in The School Librarian, Vol. 26, No. 3, September, 1978, p. 230.

As Charles Keeping's drawing increases in strength it becomes more difficult. **River** is a wordless book. Here briefly is a vision of a peaceful riverside scene, before man moves in to transform, or to ruin it. The water disappears behind a facade, of granary or hotel or factory, according to the stage of history. Each opening has its carefully balanced colour-scheme, its own humorous or sardonic message. The drawing is as always hugely competent and richly textured. There is much to admire, perhaps less to like. Essentially it is an artist's book and should prove stimulating, especially to those older boys who may miss the book because of its picture-book format. Its natural destination is not the Christmas stocking but the art college library.

M. Crouch, in a review of "River," in The Junior Bookshelf, Vol. 42, No. 5, October, 1978, p. 250.

It's difficult to pinpoint the reasons why such a beautiful book as **The River** fails to be interesting. It gives an historical perspective of a riverside scene with double-spread pictures showing buildings being erected, neglected and falling into decay to be replaced by others.

The central theme that nature endures as a background to the impermanence of men's activities is one that probably means more to adults than to children. This underlying idea is reflected in the impressionistic treatment of the natural background and the detailed foreground of human activity. But this detail is curiously woolly and its interest lessened by being subordinate to the overall composition.

> *Pam Michell, "For Sitting Comfortably," in* The Times Educational Supplement, *No. 3301, October 6, 1978, p. 28.*

---

### Miss Emily and the Bird of Make-Believe (1978)

A lonely old woman puts an end to Jack Ratty's misuse of London sparrows: her courage wins over the local children and shows them (and her) how much they have taken for granted in their surroundings. A fable of streets and old age illustrated with a bold interacting of heavy line and light wash, the colours more limited and dim than is usual with Keeping, so that the book has a gentle, almost dreamlike quality in spite of its decisive story-line.

> *Margery Fisher, in a review of "Miss Emily and the Bird of Make-Believe," in* Growing Point, *Vol. 17, No. 5, January, 1979, p. 3449.*

[Charles Keeping is a] master of story-making. . . . [He] has sometimes neglected this aspect of his work, but he is back in the mainstream in **Miss Emily and the Bird of Make-believe.** The scene is East London. Jack Ratty, one-man band expert and con-man, lives, appropriately, in Cheetham Street. He sells lonely Miss Emily a bird of make-believe, but when the colours rub off only a common sparrow is left. Miss Emily sees—a characteristic Keeping touch—that an ordinary sparrow in his natural colours is beautiful. Then, helped by the local children, she teaches Jack Ratty such a lesson that he gives up his trade in birds of make-believe for good. As always, Mr. Keeping finds beauty in the commonplace and even in ugliness. Brilliant draughtsmanship and fine subdued colouring make this book memorable.

> *M. Crouch, in a review of "Miss Emily and the Bird of Make-Believe," in* The Junior Bookshelf, *Vol. 43, No. 1, February, 1979, p. 15.*

---

### Willie's Fire-Engine (1980)

Charles Keeping is the artist of the inner city, teaching us to see its shapes and patterns, the beauty that lies beside its squalor. Preferably the city in winter; he evokes as no-one else can the dazzle of bright shop-fronts reflected in rainy streets, the glow of curtain coloured windows, the gleam of rain on flat grey cobbles. Most of all he reminds us how in childhood that drabness could be charged with endless possibilities of magic and adventure. His subject this time is Edinburgh, and Willie, a boy with a dream of heroes. The glamour of Willie's dream is immanent in Keeping's vision of the city; on the first page the streets are ranked, heavy straight lines and dull colours, but above them rises the fiery golden haze of the Castle; and opposite, Willie sits outside the solid grey tenement, drawn (the impression is almost of a scribble) with a swift liquid line, looking little more than a sketch against the weight of his background, but rippling with life. These are Keeping's three visual themes; the strong heavy lines, the

fluid lines of the live creatures, the Jambent colour. Willie's imaginary heroes are firemen of the horse-drawn engines; his real-life hero Mick the milkman. When Willie goes on his quest for Mick, braving the dangers of the streets, guided past locked gates by a beautiful maiden, he comes to a stronghold ruled by a giant and the place where life and dreams unite. Heavy lines dissolve into life, the pages are suffused with fiery colour, and out of the drabness of the city Willie's dream flowers in scarlet and gold. Splendid, cathartic, enriching; or in other words, Charles Keeping.

> *Joy Chant, "Attracting the Reader," in* The Times Literary Supplement, *No. 4042, September 19, 1980, p. 1028.*

Am I alone in feeling that, as Charles Keeping grows ever more brilliant, he becomes less likable? Of the brilliance of this latest offering there can be no question. In searching examinations of faces full of character, in the clang of bells and the snorting of horses, above all, perhaps, in the texture of buildings, he reveals his extreme technical mastery and the power of his vision. But to what end? The book is part simple account of Willie's search for Mick the milkman, part dream-cum-nightmare and wish-fantasy. It is all marvellously done, colours blazing, and the artist's intelligence as well as his skill stand out from every page. But I cannot help feeling that Mr. Keeping has lost sight of the audience, and in these remarkable visions he is indulging his personal fancies, perhaps to excess.

> *M. Crouch, in a review of "Willie's Fire-Engine," in* The Junior Bookshelf, *Vol. 44, No. 6, December, 1980, pp. 284-85.*

Marked by an odd shift from present to past tense in the first sentence, this eerie tale of a young boy's longing for release from a dingy daily existence teeters precariously on the edge of reality. The tenements where Willie lives are transformed into castles, the milkman into the fireman/hero of Willie's dream and a neighborhood playmate into a princess who seems to exist only for the purpose of being rescued. Where fact and fantasy merge is moot. The illustrations, done in brown ink with a variety of washes, waver and bleed across the page, and, as the intensity of Willie's dream accelerates, the colors modulate from drab grays to brilliantly insistent reds and oranges. But both text and pictures share such an inescapably ominous quality that the flight from reality, and all its drabness, to the rarefied world of fantasy seems, in the end, no escape at all.

> *Kristi L. Thomas, in a review of "Willie's Fire-Engine," in* School Library Journal, *Vol. 27, No. 5, January, 1981, p. 51.*

Neither prettiness nor merriment characterizes Keeping's unconventional picture books, but behind their somber façades lies a good deal of inner beauty. His squalid cityscape is now Edinburgh, where far beneath the splendid castle on the hill a little boy sits in front of a dingy tenement block. Willie's imaginary heroes are the firemen of old with their horse-drawn engines; his "real-life hero" is Mick the milkman, whom the boy likes to help. One day when Mick fails to turn up as usual, Willie ventures timidly through the dismal rain-drenched streets in search of him. Then, joined by an encouraging little girl, he continues more boldly until reality and fantasy come together in a triumphant adventure. The human figures shown in soft, wavering line contrast with the forbidding impression of gloomy buildings and streets, all depicted in heavy lines and angels; while the washes of color changing from drab to richness as Willie's spirit quickens, explode into brilliant orange and fiery reds as the little boy's everyday world is transformed into a dream.

> *Ethel L. Heins, in a review of "Willie's Fire-Engine," in* The Horn Book Magazine, *Vol. LVII, No. 2, April, 1981, p. 181.*

### The Highwayman (1981)

[The Highwayman *is written by Alfred Noyes.*]

With its strong rhythms and the matter-of-fact acceptance of betrayal and death, this poem belongs to the ballad tradition, to the energy and detachment of that tradition. Keeping's interpretation ignores the plain tone of the poem and concentrates on the horror implicit in the bitter end of love and the brutality of Bess's answer to those who force her to lead her lover into a trap. Mouths gaping in screams of terror, a sprawled body, limp and bleeding, an empty, moonlit avenue—the atmosphere, stark and forbidding, is created in grim tones of sepia, and action is suggested in lines, straight or crooked, tangled or separate, in a book urging the reader to a direct, human reaction to the poem, drawing it out of the adventure-genre to something totally different.

> *Margery Fisher, in a review of "The Highwayman," in* Growing Point, *Vol. 20, No. 3, September, 1981, pp. 3948-49.*

Alfred Noyes's popular narrative poem has a jaunty rhythm which ironically emphasizes the grimness of its romantic story: Bess 'the landlord's black-eyed daughter', a musket tied to her breast, kills herself to warn her true love of the redcoats lying in wait for him. Madness, treachery, love beyond death are the rich ingredients, and Charles Keeping plugs them for all they are worth. His illustrations carry a powerful charge, stressing the erotic undercurrent in the soldiers' binding of Bess, and recording her death in an image all the more horrifying because it is seen in cold middle distance immediately after a tense close-up. Her right hand and left side are dissolving into a black blur; her face is one ragged blot of blood. The pictures are typically bold, employing frames, shadowing one object through another, varying perspective, using a line as nervous yet precise as the mappings of a brain scanner. The switch to negative images for the final five pages is a particularly effective touch. Whether the young adolescents who are the perfect audience for the melodramatic insistence of the text will respond to Keeping's stark interpretation, time will tell.

> *Neil Philip, in a review of "The Highwayman," in* British Book News, *Children's Supplement, Autumn, 1981, pp. 17-18.*

To my taste, this is Charles Keeping's greatest interpreta-

tion of another's imagination to date. Alfred Noyes' poem with its memorable, powerful rhythms has remained a favourite with generations of children. Keeping's treatment gives it greater depth and at the same time lifts it into an entirely different realm as a visual work of art. It is executed in shades of black and sepia against white, allowing the bloodiness and the violence of mood and action to which today's children are hardened to be given full play, for the beauty of line transmutes them in a remarkable way. Tim the mad ostler becomes a marvellously Peake-like creation. The endpapers typify the beautiful shaping of the illustration: at the beginning, the highwayman and his horse gallop at full stretch across both pages, against an economic background of streaming line and sketched-in moon. At the end, the same figure is seen negatived, the ghostly rider—and other earlier pictures are repeated in negative for the last stanzas, when Bess and her lover are ghosts. It is, quite simply, an outstanding book.

> *M. Hobbs, in a review of "The Highwayman," in* The Junior Bookshelf, *Vol. 45, No. 5, October, 1981, p. 189.*

A teacher friend who tried this book out with a class of eight- to nine-year-olds reports that it was a stunning success which was requested over and over again. In particular, the children were attracted by two very violent illustrations depicting the deaths of Bess and the highwayman. Two other children who knew the poem well before seeing this edition were not so enthusiastic. Adult friends have either shuddered at the sadistic realism of the pictures, or have found these literal and lingering images somehow at odds with their idea of the poem. Having established that this is going to be a controversial book which some adults will want to keep away from some children, it is the second of the adult responses which seems to raise broader questions. Should poems be illustrated at all? What happens to the images we have in our heads when they are? I can give only a brief, personal answer.

I see this poem as a stirring, colourful melodrama with some appropriately galloping rhythm. This dashing quality of movement, a stereotype of a highwayman, is beautifully caught in Keeping's endpiece—a fine double-page spread. The picture creates an effect in the poem which is more than the sum of its parts. The preceding verse-by-verse pictures, however, are stark, gruesome, and very static. Perversely perhaps, I persist in not hearing the tragedy Keeping paints. For me, the poem is a good, old-fashioned romance which gallops apace even when the protagonists have expired. Keeping takes it too seriously: I'm not sure I'd want children to. But isn't it always a jarring experience to see illustrations for long-familiar narratives?

> *Carol Fox, in a review of "The Highwayman," in* The School Librarian, *Vol. 30, No. 3, September, 1982, pp. 236, 238.*

### Sammy Streetsinger (1984)

Sammy Streetsinger, a one-man band in a subway at the edge of town, is discovered by Ivor Chance (Ivor Flatvoice is named later) the circus proprietor. Sammy becomes a singing clown, but Ivor has plans for him which involves hoisting him with a hook so that he is tipped out of his trousers onto the sawdust ring and soaked in water. We see his black polka-dot underpants. Mr Biggknob the impresario is sufficiently impressed by Sammy's talent to offer to make him a star. "With his hair ironed and frizzed up, a guitar and a gaudy suit, he was soon singing on stage each night with two gyrating girls." As the clichés warn us, Sammy is due to fall from the dream which becomes loneliness in a mansion where "Even a dog didn't stop." Actually, the dog in the picture does seem to have stopped to use his wall, but this is no doubt appropriate. Pissed on by Micky Raker, critic of the Daily Muck, who has frizzy hair, a flouncing manner, pince-nez, a cigarette holder two feet long and a bunch of keys dangling at his waist, Sammy slides from fame and recovers peace and dignity by returning to the almost monochrome subway. We can find him there "every day", happy among the litter and the pigeons. He is "A truly real entertainer."

I felt some sympathy with Micky Raker, who first praises Sammy because "he had to write something, he'd had a boring day." The picture of Raker belies this, though, as behind him there is a montage of newspaper stories. Raker's own damning headline "What an Idiot!" is outshone by the real stories with which it is juxtaposed, one headlined "Lion licks sex op" (sadly, its text is missing), and another about Victoria Principal's sex-life. The latter is much more fun than anything else in the book, as it gives us one full column which starts by telling us that Ms Principal "grabs" what she wants "with both her strong, muscular hands" and teasingly cuts the second column's lines in half so that we can guess what is missing from "I chose a pair of jeans a buttoned up couldn't see w underneath I wore a camisole so"; just the stuff for bedtime.

> *Lachlan Mackinnon, in a review of "Sammy Streetsinger," in* The Times Literary Supplement, *No. 4261, November 30, 1984, p. 1379.*

As usual Charles Keeping finds his wonder and mystery in the messy back streets of the city. A bypass has created a new no-man's-land where Sammy Streetsinger exercises his talents for his own pleasure and that of the children and grown-ups using the subway. Sammy's innocence and happiness are destroyed when the Big Chance Circus comes to town and Ivor Chance signs him up. From fallguy in the circus he makes his way up to pop star, when he is expertly packaged until he is 'no more than a tiny video pack'. His only way forward is down until he finds himself sitting on a park bench in the rain. The subway is not far away, and so he returns to his old happy life. Mr. Keeping's images of success and failure are brilliantly powerful; the pop scene dazzles out of the page until you can almost hear it. Each of this artist's books is original. He never shows a sign of repeating himself or building on past successes, and this one, with its salutary moral as well as its masterly draughtsmanship, is as memorable as it is disturbing. One for mums and dads, and for big brother too.

> *M. Crouch, in a review of "Sammy Streetsinger," in* The Junior Bookshelf, *Vol. 48, No. 6, December, 1984, p. 245.*

The material rise and fall of an innocent subway busker, who finds it is but a small step from being a pop-star idol to 'yesterday's man'. As his fortune falls, he grows in grace, and the book closes with a wiser and happier Sammy, back busking, knowing when he is well off. Never mind the implausibility, respond to the colour and line. Opening sequences are in monotone, then come circus scenes, caught on pages coloured by simple rainbow stripes. These give way to the record of Sammy's loss of identity at the height of his pop-star career, which is expressed in an explosion of psychedelic colour. In screaming reds, harsh greens, electric blues, and shrieking purples, dribbles of paint pour down, sweat-wet, over fractured and dissolving forms. Exposing the ugliness of exploitation and the crippling isolation of success is the theme at the heart of the story. Keeping's style, with its idiosyncratic colour and his expressionist line and obsessive patterning, is an apt pictorial equivalent for Sammy's world.

> *Jane Doonan, in a review of "Sammy Streetsinger," in* The Signal Selection of Children's Books, 1984, *The Thimble Press, 1985, p. 12.*

---

### The Wedding Ghost (1985)

[The Wedding Ghost *is written by Leon Garfield.*]

Leon Garfield has always enjoyed what Henry James termed "The note of . . . the strange and sinister embroidered on the very type of the normal and easy"; but the problem is to find a suitable occasion and, even more important, a suitable significance for it. For Garfield is essentially a moralist; he cannot be content with terror for its own sake; it must be the means of revealing some inner truth. His latest book, *The Wedding Ghost,* uses elements of the Sleeping Beauty story to embroider the truism that man's love is divided between "the very type of the normal and easy" and, if not the sinister, at least the strange and unattainable.

Jack's love for Jill is firmly embedded in a domestic setting epitomized by their wedding presents—teapots, cream jugs and toast racks. The strange and alien are represented by the fairy-tale bride, the sleeping princes, achieved through a testing ordeal in which success depends on courage: "none but the brave deserves the fair". Returning from his wedding rehearsal, Jack tramps across a foggy Dickensian London to the docks, sails downstream in search of the wood marked on his mysterious map, and finally, after a nightmarish struggle through thickets festooned with dead men's bones, finds the castle and awakens the princess. As their marriage is celebrated in a cathedral, the pillars tremble and collapse, and the scene dissolves to the parish church where Jack has not, after all, betrayed his old love, but is on the point of marrying her.

The book's last page identifies the fairy bride with "restless uncertainty and desire", and, as Jack marries his familiar Jill, he also, in some inexplicable way, marries his fugitive and intangible princes—"a strange wedding with two brides". Many are symbolically wedded to two such contrary and irreconcilable desires, though the outcome, as often as not, is divorce, even if that divorce remains internalized, and the longing for the strange and unknown is exorcized or exiled, sublimated or suppressed. But marriage is Garfield's chosen image here, and the story's dissonant notes—the uninvited nurse, the map with its lines of destiny, the quest and its fulfilment—collapse and merge into the quotidian present as Jack tastes on Jill's lips the toast and honey he found on the sleeping princess's. Perhaps Garfield's point is that sexual desire may allow us to fix our longing for the alien and the other on the familiar and the known. But this "solution", delicately indicated in the text, becomes disturbingly blatant in Charles Keeping's illustrations.

These vary greatly in quality, from the hauntingly beautiful drawings of the village church and the barge in the fog to the slightly vulgarized portrait of the princess, her teeth worryingly in focus, her hair a series of undulating lines. Jack and Jill are the least successful images; in the text they are scarcely described, but Jack's uneasy sense that he looks more like a street-urchin than a prince confers on him a cartoon-like ugliness, while Jill, for no apparent reason, becomes spotty, squinting and overweight. In the final pages, her face and that of the princess alternate and seem to merge, but such a merging overstates exactly what is weakest in the fable: too easy a reconciliation of such fundamentally opposed impulses runs the risk of being reductive and over-simplifying.

> *Julia Briggs, "At the Honeypot," in* The Times Literary Supplement, *No. 4278, March 29, 1985, p. 350.*

Garfield and Keeping's latest collaboration, **The Wedding Ghost** gives both of them plenty to bite on. Leon Garfield has mixed elements of the Sleeping Beauty into the tale of a dull modern wedding between a plain Jill and a pug-faced Jack. At the centre of the book the hero of the modern story enters the traditional story and wakes the Sleeping Beauty in the usual fashion (Keeping's illustration dwells on the explicitly parted lips).

This is a great brew of a book in which the vulgar suburban wedding and the glamour and foreboding of the fairytale are all intercut with a night spent wandering through Dockland and the City in a Dickensian London fog. Over half of the book, in fact, is taken up with Jack's journey to the Sleeping Beauty's palace, which begins on the Victorian platform of a London station, and takes him down river in a sailing barge to the edge of a forest which becomes the briar forest itself. The whole of this is splendidly done in words and pictures, and the settings chosen offer both writer and illustrator opportunities for brilliant display. Keeping's foggy impressions of the crazily derelict dockside pub and of the sailing barge with its one ghostly sail are thick with atmosphere, and there is relish in Garfield's descriptions of the ghastly briar forest with its mementoes of past suitors: "He saw ribs, sometimes three or four together, like toastracks; he saw fingers and toes scattered like pale confetti on the ground." Both of them linger pleasurably on the details of the sleeping palace—Keeping's sleepers wrapped in dust and webs like covered furniture, Garfield's picture of a sleeping cat, "a velvety grey cushion on a chair, rising and falling . . ." .

*Keeping at his desk.*

But, once journey's end is reached and both stories tumble together again, nothing quite matches up to the magic and suspense of the long build-up. Which is perhaps, in this fable about a modern wedding, the point. The story enforces the hard logic of fairytale—none but the good-looking deserve the fair—but also, through the ghost story, offers a consolation prize—ordinary people are, at the extraordinary moments of their lives, transfigured. For Jack, Jill's face will always wear the shadow of the Sleeping Beauty's smile behind it; the two faces flicker in and out of one another eerily in Charles Keeping's final illustration. It's a shame that of all the pictures those of the Sleeping Beauty are the least well done; a sexy pout and excessive use of mascara sometimes make her look like a porno starlet.

> *Myra Barrs, "Super Stars," in* The Times Educational Supplement, *No. 3597, June 7, 1985, p. 55.*

---

### Charles Keeping's Book of Classic Ghost Stories (1986)

Charles Keeping says in his introduction that he has chosen these stories because they 'are particularly well written'. Six are by the classic authors one would expect for this kind of story—Robert Louis Stevenson, Charles Dickens, M. R. James, Oscar Wilde, Washington Irving and Edgar Allan Poe; two by modern authors, Daphne du Maurier and A.M. Burrage.

The selection is an arbitrary one within this pattern as the editor has used a second criteria, selecting only stories he has not illustrated before. Needless to say, the illustrations have a chilling aptness for their subject.

All these tales are of the supernatural, one only is amusing, Oscar Wilde's 'The Canterville Ghost.' The only tale that seems a little uneasy in the collection is Daphne du Maurier's 'Escort' in which Nelson's ship protects a threatened ship of the Second World War. This, the editor admits, was chosen for its personal associations.

Ghost stories are popular with both children and adults. This is not a children's book, as the inclusion of Robert Louis Stevenson's 'The Body Snatchers' and Edgar Allan Poe's particularly horrible story 'The Black Cat' indicates, Adolescents and adults will enjoy such a collection as this with its accompanying illustrations.

> *E. Colwell, in a review of "Book of Classic Ghost Stories," in* The Junior Bookshelf, *Vol. 50, No. 6, December, 1986, p. 235.*

Charles Keeping is one of Britain's foremost book illustrators, and—judging by the quality of his work on this evidence—quite rightly so. However, one wonders whether the stories were chosen because they were interesting to illustrate, or whether they can really lay claim to be classic ghost stories. In his introduction, Charles Keeping expresses concern for the quality of writing as a criterion for selection; but he does also admit that he left out stories because he had illustrated them before. Five of the eight stories were written in the nineteenth century, and the language and syntax of R. L. Stevenson and W. Irving, for example, is certainly not easy. If one were looking for a ghost story to interest and stimulate young teenagers, this collection does not contain many, if any, of the most likely choices.

> *Robin Barlow, in a review of "Charles Keeping's Book of Classic Ghost Stories," in* The School Librarian, *Vol. 35, No. 2, May, 1987, p. 177.*

The short story form works by a series of paradoxes. It must make its effect quickly yet it must not seem to be rushed; its line of action must be simple, and preferably single, and yet it needs supportive detail; it must make its direction clear—even, often, its final end obvious at once—while leaving plenty for the reader to discover for himself. Economy and richness, directness and subtlety, ease and discipline—these are the short story's opposites, particularly clear in that sub-division called for convenience the ghost story, where the irrational must be evoked from the known and the ordinary. Charles Keeping's selection of *Classic Ghost Stories* offers varied examples of craftsmanship from a period of more than a century. These are stories which assault the senses. In M.R. James's 'Wailing Well' we listen to uncanny sound, as in Daphne du Maurier's tale of the sea, 'Escort' we seem to be aware of silence. Sight is paramount in Dickens's matchless evocation of terror, 'The Signalman', and here Charles Keeping's illustration extends the words with his own vision of a terrified face. The fear that can be roused by a texture comes across strongly in Poe's 'The Black

Cat', while in the most recent tale, 'The Sweeper', the visual image of a garden broom and the sounds of sweeping act impressively on the old lady in the centre of the story as on the reader. The illustrations sum up the atmosphere of each tale—for instance, the oddity of Wilde's 'Canterville Ghost' and the implied evil in Stevenson's body-snatchers at their infamous work—and make it clear, as the choice of tales does, that this is a volume to keep for close and frequent scrutiny.

> *Margery Fisher, in a review of "Charles Keeping's Book of Classic Ghost Stories," in* Growing Point, *Vol. 26, No. 2, July, 1987, p. 4830.*

A compilation of eight ghost stories from the masters, deservedly called "classic," are enhanced with wonderful black-and-white depictions by the noted illustrator, Charles Keeping. Included is the gore of Robert Louis Stevenson's "The Body Snatchers", Poe's elusive black cat, Washington Irving's tale of the decapitated mistress, the ghost who could not scare the Otis family at Canterville Chase by Oscar Wilde, Daphne duMaurier's mysterious ghost ship in "Escort", the sinister "Wailing Well" of M.R. James which ensnares the skeptical schoolboy, "The Sweeper" who eventually comes for his victim by A.M. Burrage, and Charles Dickens' precognitive Signalman. The preponderance of British writers might deter some teenagers; however, if directed, many young adults will find these short pieces at once suspense-filled and delightful, an apt representation of the genre. Appended are brief explanatory notes of several chapters and fine biographical information of each author. Cover art is perfect! Recommended.

> *Hilary King, in a review of "Charles Keeping's Book of Classic Ghost Stories," in* Voice of Youth Advocates, *Vol. 11, No. 2, June, 1988, p. 84.*

---

### Charles Keeping's Classic Tales of the Macabre (1987)

This companion to **Charles Keeping's Book of Classic Ghost Stories** is every bit as good as its predecessor. The British illustrator's taste is impeccable, although he might have chosen a less chestnutty piece of Poe than "The Fall of the House of Usher" and of M. R. James than "Oh, Whistle, and I'll Come to You, My Lad." Fine as they are, those two should be given a rest. Of the other six entries, Thomas Hardy's "The Withered Arm," a somber tale of unintended witchcraft, is far and away the finest written. A story by Keeping's apparent pet writer, the obscure A. M. Burrage, called "Between the Minute and the Hour" and dealing with a time-travel curse, is a particularly nice surprise. "The Statement of Randolph Carter" is superior short Lovecraft, but that writer was best at greater length—say, 30 to 80 pages. Bits of Bram Stoker. Conan Doyle, and H. G. Wells fill out the set enjoyably. Keeping's artwork, the raison d'être for the book, seems relatively tame for these tales.

> *Ray Olson, in a review of "Charles Keeping's Classic Tales of the Macabre," in* Booklist, *Vol. 84, No. 6, November 15, 1987, p. 537.*

It's rare enough that a compilation of this nature lives up to the 'classic' of the title, but in this case it is actually true. There are stories in this collection by acknowledged masters of the craft, such as M. R. James's 'Oh Whistle and I'll Come to You, My Lad', H. P. Lovecraft's 'The Statement of Randolph Carter' and Edgar Allan Poe's 'The Fall of the House of Usher' and one or two curiosities, such as Thomas Hardy's 'The Withered Arm' and a fine story by Sir Arthur Conan Doyle, 'Lot no. 249.' Charles Keeping's accompanying illustrations are always appropriate to the story and convey a sense of mystery and menace without going overboard. I can unreservedly recommend this collection as suitable for any teenager with an interest in ghost and horror stories which extends beyond the latest cinematic offering.

> *Maureen Porter, in a review of "Charles Keeping's Classic Tales of the Macabre," in* Children's Book Review, *December, 1987, p. 25.*

Keeping's collection of spine-chillers would be nothing without the compiler's illustrations. His selection is fairly predictable—Poe, Bram Stoker, M. R. James and five others, all good and reasonably frightening. Charles Keeping's drawings are terrifying in a most subtle way. It is not what he draws but what he suggests that is likely to return to haunt the reader in the small hours. With a head-piece to each story and at least one fullpage drawing to each, this is a book for collectors of this most individual of present-day illustrators. It might also prompt a young reader to a realisation of the relationship between writer and artist.

> *Marcus Crouch, in a review of "Charles Keeping's Classic Tales of the Macabre," in* The School Librarian, *Vol. 36, No. 1, February, 1988, pp. 35-6.*

---

### Jack the Treacle Eater (1987)

[Jack the Treacle Eater *is written by Charles Causley.*]

Whatever else his contemporaries may try, Charles Causley preserves, and enriches, a tradition in children's poetry which holds that the world is a place for innocent surprise and wonder.

In part this is a de la Mare world, where nature, the creatures and human beings are real and recognizable and at the same time cryptic and haunted, where adults hint at and yet withhold the ultimate truths about their motives and their mortality. But Causley's is another generation and background: the 1920s child grew up in the small Cornish cottage within sight of the moors and the sea (where the poet saw long wartime service) instead of de la Mare's middle-class Kent mansion of corridors, attics and magisterial mystery. His world and his world-view are his own.

His poems have always subtly changed for his own purposes the atmosphere, the details and the techniques employed by the poets whom one suspects he most admires, and in **Jack the Treacle Eater** he continues to ring the changes with undiminished flair and exuberance. . . .

Jack himself ran messages on foot to and from London for

a Somerset landed family in the late eighteenth century, and kept fit by training on treacle. In Charles Keeping's illustrations he runs vigorously, and yet more stiffly than in Causley's lively verses about him. He is characteristic of too many of the pictures in the book, which frequently fail to relax into an easy compatibility with the poems. Mr Zukovsky ("always so sober and neat") is not sufficiently in contrast with his wildly untidy wife, the Guy Fawkes in "Why" is not top-hatted and seems to scare none of the children (children will want these details because the poem mentions them), and Aesop in "Fable" is ugly without suggesting charisma. But happily, the word-pictures in **Jack the Treacle Eater,** which is much the best volume of poems for children since the same author's *Figgie Hobbin* in 1970, are entertaining, vivid and memorable enough for readers to conjure up the subjects for themselves.

> *Alan Brownjohn, "Traditional Times," in* The Times Literary Supplement, *No. 4416, November 20, 1987, p. 1287.*

'In the days when you called me your own Rich
  Tea
And you were my Custard Cream.'

So sings Charles Causley's lively and still loving centenarian-plus in one of the many delightful, bubbling and exquisitely crafted poems of his new collection. He ranges wide for his subject-matter around the West Country, in legend and history, and in his fertile imagination, creating a string of entrancing eccentrics from Aesop to Aunt Leonora and Maggie Dooley (who feeds stray cats in the park). All these poems show a total mastery of traditional forms and rhythms, but the reader seldom stops to discover how superbly it is all done, being swept along on the flood of the poet's fantasy and humour. It is not all just fun either. There is a rock-hard note in 'The Twelve-o'clock Stone' which treats of a Cornish tradition, a gentle nostalgia in 'Summer was Always Sun', and a spare economy in 'Morwenstow'. Those who tell stories to young (and old) listeners should add 'The Apple-Tree Man' to their repertoire; this is a version of a Somerset folk-tale which, in balance and perfection of timing, is as good in its way as Eleanor Farjeon's 'Mrs. Malone'.

The rhymes are matched with drawings in monochrome and colour by Charles Keeping. I would guess that the artist was particularly happy with this assignment, for his work here has a rare depth and penetration to go with Mr. Keeping's customary technical ease. This is a book which is going to give much pleasure now and for a long time to come. The blend of a fine text, superb illustrations and excellent format also make it an obvious choice for the collector.

> *M. Crouch, in a review of "Jack the Treacle Eater," in* The Junior Bookshelf, *Vol. 52, No. 1, February, 1988, p. 42.*

---

### Adam and Paradise Island (1989)

Paradise Island is a decaying old place set in a muddy creek but loved by the local people. The nincompoop Council decides to build an unnecessary motorway slap across it. At the same time, two old people encourage children to build an adventure playground nearby. The old pair are appointed guardians of the playground and in the end almost everyone is pleased by the outcome. *Adam and Paradise Island* was Charles Keeping's last book before his death last year. As always with Keeping, it is entirely free of that sweetness, prettiness and patronizing "niceness" which frequently bedevils children's book illustration. His work was always more like that of a Fine Art printmaker in its use of surface texture, flattened design and almost abstract colour. But, unlike most printmakers, he could draw with breathtaking ease. The dilute sepia ink streams off the nib and miraculously flows round the smooth shape of a girl's leg or ripples into the wrinkled folds of an old coat, while at the same time locking itself into an intricate surface design on the page. All Charles Keeping's finest qualities are present in *Adam and Paradise Island.* He maintained his own high standards and total individuality to the end. This book is one of his best.

> *Raymond Briggs, in a review of "Adam and Paradise Island," in* The Times Educational Supplement, *No. 3806, June 9, 1989, p. B11.*

Charles Keeping's *Adam and Paradise Island,* published posthumously, offers a caustic tale about change. Local councillors on the nearby mainland decide that the muddle of shops and houses on Paradise Isle must make way for a fast toll road linking either side of the creek. Bulldozers move in, and the shopkeepers move out to jobs in the new Neata supermarket and nearby Neata homes. Meanwhile an army of children salvage materials for an adventure playground. When the road is finished, Gerry Bandynose, a television and radio idol, arrives to cut the tape, bringing in his wake crowds of adoring girls, rival gangs of hooligans and various demonstrators. There is a forthright vigour to Keeping's characterization of types, but it is energy rather than feeling which charges these illustrations.

> *Frances Spalding, "Endangered Types," in* The Times Literary Supplement, *No. 4501, July 7, 1989, p. 757.*

Charles Keeping, whose posthumous picture-book comes from Oxford, made no secret of his devotion to London, especially its seedier lower-Thames aspect. We are given no clues to the location of Paradise Island, but it seems to belong to some muddy creek not far from the Isle of Dogs. Here lives a happy community of shopkeepers going about their respective trades in great contentment and with no sense of frustrated ambitions. Here too live Old Varda and Ma Burley in caravan and barge, seeing out their lives with memories of the past. Paradise indeed! On the mainland the Council have a different view of Paradise Island. They want to clean it up and at the same time 'put lots of money into the coffers'. They build a toll road over the island. The shopkeepers are re-housed and re-employed in a supermarket. Old Varda and Ma Burley's muddy homes have no commercial value, so they are left undisturbed except by the children who make this area their playground. More realistically than most conservation stories, this one offers either no ending or a set of reasonably happy ones. Everyone gets something out of the deal. Keeping fills his

story with digs at bureaucracy, and illuminates it with drawings as full of strength, accuracy and honesty as ever. If this is really his last book—and there have been others—then he goes out on a 'high'.

> *M. Crouch, in a review of "Adam and Paradise Island," in* The Junior Bookshelf, *Vol. 53, No. 4, August, 1989, p. 158.*

The London of Charles Keeping's picture-books is the one only the discerning, and the real Londoners, ever see—fine proportions and beautiful window embrasures in shaky houses, the patterns of warehouse roofs, unexpected riverside paths and above all, families going back for generations and hanging on in spite of gentrification and big business. Books like *Joseph's Yard* and *Through the Window* are valuable archive material with the extra personal warmth and insights essentially absent from photographic records. *Adam and Paradise Island,* sadly Keeping's last picture-book, offers one more of his unique views of the oldest and best London.

The theme is topical and will be applied by his readers very easily to their own experience. Here in the East End by the Thames is one of those enclaves cut off from the mainstream of traffic and still preserving a village atmosphere, with a row of small shops, a patch of marshy waste land where an old travelling man lives with his arched caravan and assorted animals and a dilapidated pier where old Ma Burley likes to sit and reminisce to anyone with time to stop and listen. A Paradise indeed for Adam, though he is too young to have any voice in the public meetings after news gets round that plan-mad local councillors have decided to:

> .. build a fast toll road across the island, linking either side of the creek. This would improve traffic flow north and south and put lots of money into the coffers.

Some of the locals approve the plan but Adam and his cronies find their own solution. While a glaring new bridge leads to 'the new Neata Supermarket' where the shopkeepers find jobs (going home at night 'to their Neata homes near by'), the younger generation, the future of the community, build on the marsh from a random collection of bits and pieces an unorthodox playground, to be administered with panache by Ma Burley and Old Varda; this inspired use of the land preserves a paradisal island for those who can best appreciate it and a defiant look at the urban development, described with an irresistible mixture of irony and common sense.

As one would expect, the illustrations evoke the shabby beauty of brick and timber, riverside 'beaches' and distant roofscapes, meticulous in detail and glowing with subtle, subdued ochre and orange, pinks and browns. And here are the inimitable characters Keeping delighted in, with their comically descriptive names—Sarah Sprout with her greengrocery and Betty Bun 'smiling sweetly behind her cakes, breads and pastries', snooty councillors Lady Primrose and the Hon. Claude Berk (pro-development, naturally) and Gerry Bandynose, 'a current TV and radio idol' who cuts the tape and officially opens the road. Faces, attitudes, clothes are as revealing as their names and as socially pertinent while the children, shown naturally in exuberant movement or concentrated postures, stand for an unsatirised, satisfying emotional base, with Adam the universal boy in the centre. As a fellow Cockney, I salute the memory of a committed and superbly skilled artist. Whatever happens to our city, he has left the most satisfying record of the real, abiding London.

> *Margery Fisher, in a review of "Adam and Paradise Island," in* Growing Point, *Vol. 28, No. 3, September, 1989, pp. 5205-06.*

Though clearly in sympathy with the children and the diversified pre-bridge community (in contrast to the plastic world resulting from "progress"), Keeping's text itself holds no particular brief here; his masterfully limned illustrations, though, are merciless in caricaturing the adults (especially the council, whose members are all unsavory representatives of their respective classes). For the children, equally individual, he has only affection. The powerful message and sophisticated art here commend the book especially for use with older children.

> *A review of "Adam and Paradise Island," in* Kirkus Reviews, *Vol. LVII, No. 16, September 1, 1989, p. 1329.*

Visually the book is a mixed bag of manners and modes: atmospheric dockland vistas butt up against pastiches of estate-agent ephemera; monochrome collides with eye-bruising colour; the councillors are caricatured but the children aestheticised. Despite the panache and assurance of individual pages the book offers a rather bumpy ride. More importantly, I think that in this, his final picture book for OUP, Charles Keeping ducked some important issues to do with winners and losers in the game of 'urban renewal'. I can't help feeling that, despite the caricatures, the nauseating councillors come off fairly lightly.

> *David Lewis, in a review of "Adam and Paradise Island," in* The School Librarian, *Vol. 37, No. 4, November, 1989, pp. 148-49.*

# Maryann Kovalski

## 1951-

American-born Canadian author and illustrator of picture books.

Major works include *Brenda and Edward* (1984), *The Wheels on the Bus* (1987), *Jingle Bells* (1988), *Frank and Zelda* (1990; U.S. edition as *Pizza for Breakfast*), *Take Me Out to the Ballgame* (1993).

## INTRODUCTION

Recognized as one of Canada's most popular contemporary illustrators, Kovalski is best known as the creator of humorous picture books for preschoolers and primary graders that are celebrated for the strength of both their writing and their art. Featuring children, adults, and anthropomorphic animals as her main characters, she frequently bases her works on popular songs and folktales such as "Jingle Bells," "Take Me Out to the Ballgame," and "The Fisherman's Wife." Rather than employing a traditional approach, Kovalski uses her sources in what is considered an especially original manner. For example, her series of picture books inspired by familiar songs—*The Wheels on the Bus*, *Jingle Bells*, and *Take Me Out to the Ballgame*—feature sisters Jenny and Joanna and their high-spirited, energetic Grandma, who leads the girls into a number of exciting, often surprising adventures that are related to the lyrics; the "Grandma" books also include musical notations for the songs as part of their illustrations. Kovalski is particularly esteemed for her watercolor and ink pictures, which are praised for their humor, exuberance, nostalgic details, and rich color. Her art is also featured in several picture books written by other Canadian authors, including Sharon, Lois and Bram's *Mother Goose: Songs, Finger Rhymes, Tickling Verses, Games and More* (1985) and Tim Wynne-Jones's *I'll Make You Small* (1986).

Kovalski grew up in New York City, where she attended the School of Visual Arts. She later moved to Montreal and then Toronto while working first as an art director in advertising and subsequently as a freelance illustrator of children's picture books. Noting that "the urban sprawl I find myself in is endlessly fascinating to me," Kovalski made cityscapes an integral part of her work. Exposure to the literature she was illustrating prompted her to begin writing as well. The first book that she both wrote and illustrated is *Brenda and Edward*, a story about two dogs who live happily behind a French restaurant in Toronto until Brenda loses her way in the city; the pair is eventually reunited by the man who rescues the lost dog. Kovalski's next project, *The Wheels on the Bus*, features Grandma, Jenny, and Joanna as they embark on a downtown shopping excursion. To help pass time at the bus stop, Grandma leads the girls in several verses of the title song; the accompanying illustrations represent both Grandma's London childhood and the vivid imaginations of the char-

acters, who get so carried away that they miss their bus and have to hail a taxi. The trio reappears in Kovalski's *Jingle Bells*, in which a sleigh ride through Central Park becomes especially exciting when Grandma takes the reins, as well as in *Take Me Out to the Ballgame*, in which Grandma helps the home team win the game by catching the final out while attempting to retrieve a lost balloon. Among Kovalski's most popular books is *Frank and Zelda*. Based loosely on the folktale "The Fisherman's Wife," married restauranteurs Frank and Zelda wish for greater success with their pizza parlor. When their wish is granted, the dizzying array of customers and shortage of help that ensue create such chaos that the couple, learning the value of contentment, make a final wish for the restoration of their old business.

(See also *Something about the Author*, Vol. 58.)

## AUTHOR'S COMMENTARY

One of the things that appeals to me most about being a children's book illustrator is the sanity of the life-style. There's a gentleness about illustrating children's books that I find very comforting. It's a Victorian gentlewoman's sort of occupation. When you're doing editorial artwork or advertising, you've got to get it done and get it out, bang, bang. You just don't have time when you're doing an ad to say, 'Isn't that a lovely cornice?' You'd be fired.

But as an illustrator, I go up to the third floor of my house with my coffee about 9 o'clock, and I put on tapes or the radio. If there's a building that I love that reminds me of Edwardian England, for instance, I'll go to the library and do research and read about it. There's a lot of room for depth and personal growth. Each book is a total project; each one requires different research and has a different feeling. That's partly the way I was trained: one of the mandates of the School of Visual Arts in New York City, where I studied, is that you adapt to a project, it doesn't adapt to you. Each book has its own pattern and takes on its own personality.

An editorial illustration has a much shorter appeal and so has to say a lot in the few seconds the person is looking at that page. In books, there's a lot more room for subtlety. You are capturing a person for longer—sometimes a lifetime.

Of the books I have done, my favourite would have to be *Brenda and Edward* because it was my own story. The image started six years ago. I was on the Toronto subway, and a dog was running up and down the car, absolutely panicked. Other passengers told me he had jumped on at Keele, and this was 10 miles away, at Bloor and Yonge. I brought him home and fed him and his owners were found, but that image stayed with me—the idea of walking into a box and walking out 10 miles away and not knowing where you were or why. I pictured that scene long before the book was ever written. I knew that I wanted it to be an old-fashioned love story, and in coloration I wanted it to be like a 1940s movie. The story and words flew out of that feeling.

Illustrating your own book is very different from working on someone else's story. When you are doing your own story, you are almost writing it as you go along. You can edit the story to fit the illustration, and you can incorporate things you're interested in. *Brenda and Edward* has a lot of architectural features and street scenes because those interest me. When you are given someone else's manuscript—three stark sheets of typewritten paper—you have to find your way in the dark. You don't know what the feel of it was or what the writer had in mind.

As an illustrator, I sometimes feel like I'm directing little movies—I'm totally interpreting the story. If you've got a lousy story, an illustrator can't save it, but if it's a good story, the illustration can really make it sing.

I have had to change my style completely to suit the requirements of printing. I used to use many, many different techniques, but now I just use water-colour, gouache, pencil, and ink. The dyes I used to use were a source of constant frustration because they just didn't reproduce well. When I first started, I didn't know enough even to ask questions. Now, I know to ask printers why something didn't work, or why a certain size of book is more cost-efficient.

I think there's a lot of naïveté when it comes to children's books. People don't realize it's a serious discipline, not just a lot of bunnies and silliness. At dinner parties, often someone suggests that you do 20 finished illustrations and then he or she will put a few words underneath. They don't realize it has to flow in 32 pages and has to be paced in a certain way.

My feeling about doing children's books has been changing as I've done more of them. I really love it, but it's very frustrating when you're handed your royalty cheque and you know it represents six months' work but you couldn't possibly live on it, or when people say they'd love to buy your book but they can't find it anywhere. You have to keep telling yourself over and over and over that you're not doing it for the money, but for a deeper personal satisfaction.

I don't think I'd ever be able to give it up. It's just too much of a pleasure. But it might become more of a pastime—something I do once a year. Like quilting. I don't do quilting that much anymore.

*Laurie Bildfell, "Maryann Kovalski," in* Quill and Quire, *Vol. 51, No. 10, October, 1985, pp. 8, 10.*

---

## TITLE COMMENTARY

### *Brenda and Edward* (1984)

[Children] will be delighted by Maryann Kovalski's charming story *Brenda and Edward.* Kovalski is best known as the illustrator of enjoyable volumes such as *Molly and Mr. Maloney* and *Puddleman.* In this new book, she combines her rich illustrations with the classic folk-tale theme of the separation and reunion of two sweethearts.

Brenda and Edward are canines who live a blissful, contented existence in a cozy cardboard box behind a French restaurant. One day, Edward forgets to take his dinner to his job as a night watchdog at a garage on the other side of town. Brenda attempts to catch up with him, only to become hopelessly lost and scared. In her terror, she is hit by a car and ends up being taken away by the driver. Edward searches in vain. Years later, on Edward's last day at the garage, a car with Brenda's scent comes in for repair. Edward jumps in and will not be moved; eventually, the driver takes Edward to her large elegant country home. There, of course, is Brenda, and the two dogs live happily ever after.

Kovalski's soft, sentimental illustrations are a perfect complement to this gentle story. The dogs are wonderfully anthropomorphized, right down to the eyeglasses and bedroom slippers.

*Anne Gilmore, in a review of "Brenda and Edward," in* Quill and Quire, *Vol. 50, No. 11, November, 1984, p. 12.*

*Brenda and Edward* is a touching picture storybook about two dogs who live in a cardboard box behind a French restaurant. One day Edward, who works as a night watchdog, forgets to take his dinner to work with him. The simple storyline logically unfolds as Brenda searches throughout the city, looking for Edward to deliver his dinner, and Edward in turn searches for her over many lonely years. Eventually he finds Brenda, older but as beautiful as ever. Two happy dogs are reunited.

The twenty-one full page colour illustrations, including several double page spreads, appear to be done in mixed media such as combined pen, coloured pencil and watercolour. Illustrations effectively carry the storyline and depict a wide range of events in city scenes and interior views. They skillfully reflect varied moods conveyed by the text.

This is a tender anthropomorphic story about love, caring, responsibility and faithfulness which should be very appealing to pre-school and primary-age children, especially if they themselves have pets. The theme in this book can easily serve as a jump-off point for discussion about the qualities pets have and the relationships people have with animals, in this case their pets.

*Bernard Schwartz, "Reprise: A Select Group," in* Canadian Children's Literature, *No. 60, 1990, pp. 135-37.*

---

### The Wheels on the Bus (1987)

The essence of the traditional children's song is aptly captured in this picture book adaptation that retains the exuberance and rollicking action of the song. Kovalski builds a humorous original story around the traditional verse. A long wait at the bus stop precipitates a suggestion from a grandmother that she and her two grandchildren pass the time by singing "The Wheels on the Bus." When grandma and the girls get carried away with their song, missing their bus, ever-resourceful grandma hails a cab. Kovalski expertly conveys the spirit with which people sing this song; indeed, this grandmother and these children become so involved that bus scenes are vividly recreated in their minds and on the pages of this book. The action of the song is followed through in detail, flowing from page to page with a cast of assorted characters depicted in watercolor with pencil illustrations. Musical notation accompanies the first verse. Good fun for young children and parents.

*Susan Nemeth McCarthy, in a review of "The Wheels on the Bus," in* School Library Journal, *Vol. 34, No. 3, November, 1987, p. 94.*

In Maryann Kovalski's **The Wheels on the Bus,** the basic situation is a very mundane one—two little girls and their grandmother wait on a downtown corner for a bus. As they wait, they decide to fill in the time by singing the traditional action song about the wheels on the bus going round and round. In the following pages, Kovalski creates a wonderful double-decker bus filled with pompous snobs, crying babies, harried parents, and a wonderful, scrawny little English schoolgirl (Grandmother as a child) taking it all in with wide bespectacled eyes.

*Mary Ainslie Smith, in a review of "The*

*Wheels on the Bus," in* Books in Canada, *Vol. 16, No. 9, December, 1987, p. 13.*

I defy you to read this jolly book without: 1) grinning more broadly with every page, 2) turning back now and then to check a detail in a previous illustration, 3) bouncing merrily along just as preschoolers do, 4) humming the irresistible tune all the rest of the day and, in fact, every time you look at the fetching cover! Maryann Kovalski has adapted this favorite traditional song to our advantage.

Grandma took Jenny and Joanna shopping for new winter coats. The excitement of this special excursion is obvious from the start. In the store, the indecision of the girls and Grandma is evidenced by the piles of coats on the floor surrounding them and consternation on the patient saleslady's face. Bright green coats are chosen and the two, absolutely addled with happiness, are bundled and square and look just like all kids in new coats that have a little growing room.

To shorten the long wait for the bus to take them home, Grandma suggests that they sing the song Granny sang to her when she was a little girl. The double-page illustration that follows is a delight: Grandma and the two girls sing merrily lower left; upper left the first verse of the song is scored. Any Anglophile will know instantly that Grandma had a British granny, for remembering transports her (via a cloud-like frame taking up the rest of the space) to Piccadilly Circus complete with statue and fountain, flower stand, double-decker buses circling with the traffic, and violet, rain-laden skies. Succeeding pages alternate the next verse of the song with a single-page illustration like a stop-action frame of a film. Bit players are the passengers. The star is a monocled gentleman carrying flowers (purchased from the flower lady on the previous page) as he struggles to hold umbrella, hat, bouquet, and newspaper in the crowded bus. The starlet is Grandma in miniature with pigtails, sagging knee socks, and the very same glasses sliding down the very same nose.

As the song goes on verse after verse, the drama unfolds; with the ninth verse, the London memory fades. Grandma and the girls have been having such a glorious time that they miss their bus, and so Grandma hails a taxi.

This is a natural for preschool storytime and beyond for more complete appreciation of the illustrations. Bright watercolors emphasize the focal point of each page with the background details muted but clearly part of the action. Sketchy outlines, shadowing, and details in soft pencil frame the colors and provide much of the humor. Have fun with this one—I feel sure that kids will.

*Virginia Opocensky, in a review of "The Wheels on the Bus," in* The Five Owls, *Vol. II, No. 3, January-February, 1988, p. 42.*

Kovalski has been able to translate the excitement of the two heroines as well as the understanding of a grandmother who does not over-react when the two girls decide on similar coats. The passengers on the double-decker bus are cleverly introduced and children will enjoy following them on their trip. Kovalski takes the children through the lyrics of eight verses of the song.

*From* The Wheels on the Bus, *written and illustrated by Maryann Kovalski.*

The illustrations are lively and full of small details that children will discover as they read the story. This is a well-designed book that will be a favourite with children for many years to come.

> *André Gagnon, in a review of "The Wheels on the Bus," in* CM: A Reviewing Journal of Canadian Materials for Young People, *Vol. XVI, No. 2, March, 1988, p. 57.*

**The wheels on the bus,** a large format picture book, is a story about Grandma and her two grandchildren who go shopping for winter coats and then wait for a bus to go home. The wait is so long that Grandma entices them to join her in singing a song from her own childhood. The song continues with a variety of verses that suggest the activity and rhythm of experiences of a typical bus ride. They have so much fun singing that they miss their bus and have to taxi home.

The fifteen full-page colour illustrations, produced mainly in a dry medium such as coloured pencil with some wash, are whimsical in content, well composed in terms of balance, and uncluttered. Colour, skillfully used, runs from fairly solid, intense colours in foregrounds to pale, diluted colours for backgrounds. Facial expressions and other visual details support the text and warrant further examination by young readers.

Primary grade children would especially enjoy singing aloud and swaying along with the rhythmical verse. As well, they will be stimulated to create their own verse guided by the musical notation of the well known song provided in the book. A bus ride in the city can become through this book quite a meaningful experience for young children.

> *Bernard Schwartz, in a review of "The Wheels on the Bus," in* Canadian Children's Literature, *No. 60, 1990, pp. 135-36.*

---

### Jingle Bells (1988)

Maryann Kovalski is one of Canada's most popular children's illustrators. Since the publication of **Brenda and Edward** in 1984, she has also emerged as a storyteller of considerable promise.

In last year's **The Wheels on the Bus** Kovalski—the author and illustrator—wove a delightful tale from the popular children's song. [In **Jingle Bells**] she returns to the realm of traditional children's songs to tell the story of Jenny, Joanna, and their lively grandma's winter visit to New York City.

The trio have barely arrived at their hotel when the girls

persuade Grandma to take them for an evening jaunt in a horse-drawn carriage. As snowflakes begin to fall, what could be a more appropriate song for the three to burst into than Jingle Bells? And what could be more exciting than the drama of a runaway horse in Central Park with Grandma coming to the rescue?

A Scrooge might say that this beautiful picture book is calculatingly aimed at the biggest seasonal market of the year. But as the reader follows the song's words and notes, cynicism melts. The old ditty has rarely been as handsomely mounted; Kovalski's magnificently detailed images are rich with colour. The book's inevitable success will be well deserved.

> *Peter Carver, in a review of "Jingle Bells," in* Books for Young People, *Vol. 2, No. 5, October, 1988, pp. 13-14.*

Eyecatching pastel-and-watercolor illustrations are stronger than the text of this story which incorporates the traditional song, "Jingle Bells." On a visit to New York, Grandma takes Jenny and Joanna on a horse-and-carriage ride through Central Park. The driver happily joins them in singing "Jingle Bells" (melody lines and words to the first verse and refrain are included on the page). But a low-lying branch snatches the driver out of his seat, leaving poor Grandma holding the nag. Off they go, finally ending up tired and worn out going the wrong way on a one-way street. Not to worry, though, for Grandma confers with two truck drivers who load horse, people, and carriage into the back of their red panel truck. In the twinkling of a page turn, the three are in their beds. But what about the horse? And the driver? Children will enjoy chiming in on the familiar holiday song, but the abrupt and inconclusive ending is unsatisfying. Kovalski renders events humorously, breaks the black-line borders just as children like to behave outside the boundaries once in a while, and delightfully depicts the snowy nighttime city.

> *Susan Hepler, in a review of "Jingle Bells," in* School Library Journal, *Vol. 35, No. 2, October, 1988, p. 35.*

Kovalski's city-scapes are drenched with snowy good cheer evinced by softened shapes and the glow of sparkling lights; it's a friendly world apropos of Christmas high spirits. Only the refrain and one verse of the song are provided, so this has limitations as a song book, but the story's effervescence makes it a sure pleaser as an upbeat Christmas tale.

> *Denise M. Wilms, in a review of "Jingle Bells," in* Booklist, *Vol. 85, No. 4, October 15, 1988, pp. 410-11.*

[A] melody line is printed loud and clear in Maryann Kovalski's *Jingle Bells,* a lovely, lively tale based on Pierpont's famous song of 1857. Her illustrations provide a cheerful dimension to the jolliest of winter ditties. This refreshing and unpretentious publication had me reading its breezy story and enjoying its uninhibitedly merry pictures as happily as I read *Rainbow* when I was eight.

> *Charles Causley, "Ringing in the New," in*

The Times Educational Supplement, *No. 3831, December 1, 1989, p. 31.*

"I want to see everything!" says little Jenny on a visit to New York City with her grandmother. Here is another delightful book from Maryann Kovalski, this time featuring the grandmother and two little girls on a flying visit to New York City. When last seen, the trio were belting out the popular children's song in *The Wheels on the Bus.*

Written for children aged three and up, the book includes the words and music to the traditional song "Jingle Bells." The full-page illustrations show the girls getting ready for an exciting plane trip to a big city. On arrival they decide to take a hansom cab ride to the park.

The authentic paintings radiate life and exuberance. The author cast her mind back to the scenes of her childhood in New York City. Her double-page spread of a city square is beautifully done.

How the resourceful and energetic grandmother saves them from peril when the cab driver is swept away by a tree branch is an exciting episode in this vintage Kovalski book—humorous, lively, nostalgic and a pleasure for adults to share with children.

Modestly priced, well bound, beautifully written and illustrated, *Jingle Bells* is one of the best buys in children's books of 1988.

> *Hazel Birt, in a review of "Jingle Bells," in* CM: A Reviewing Journal of Canadian Materials for Young People, *Vol. XVII, No. 2, March, 1989, p. 87.*

---

### Frank and Zelda (1990; U.S. edition as *Pizza for Breakfast*)

Older picture-book readers will enjoy the food and magic themes in Maryann Kovalski's *Frank and Zelda,* the story of a 1920s pizza parlour hit by hard times. In the tradition of such classics as *Too Much Noise* and *It Could Always be Worse,* pizza shop proprietors Frank and Zelda find themselves regretting the wishes that have magically revived their slumping business and end up wishing for a return to peace and quiet. Kovalski, well known for her humorous illustrations, brings an equally droll pen to the writer's desk. When it comes to pizza, Kovalski delivers.

> *Patty Lawlor, "In Search of Picture-Book Perfect," in* Quill and Quire, *Vol. 56, No. 9, September, 1990, p. 19.*

Based technically on "The Fisherman's Wife," *Frank and Zelda* is an exquisitely rendered story about reckless wishing.

Frank and Zelda own a small pizza shop. They lose their customers when the factory next to them closes down. One day a man comes into the restaurant to eat. He has no money but repays them in wishes. Frank wishes for a thousand paying customers "every day and forever."

The wish is granted but Frank and Zelda cannot handle all the customers. Zelda wishes for help. With the arrival of hundreds of waiters, the restaurant is too small, so they

*From* Pizza for Breakfast, *written and illustrated by Maryann Kovalski.*

wish for a larger place. Everything then gets out of hand. Frank and Zelda wish they had never had their wishes. In an instant all is quiet.

Kovalski has effectively set the story in the 1920s. It is "once-upon-a-time" to young readers but iconographically it triggers images of pre-war films. This is a simple tale told in a direct way without the sinister elements that give "The Fisherman's Wife" an ominous edge. It is humorous, and the moral—be happy with what you have—is satisfying. The soft, overflowing illustrations emphasize the story's humour. Frank is an Oliver Hardyish looking character and the waiters resemble all the waiters in all the madcap comedies of the Thirties.

*Frank and Zelda* is a happy story which will be enjoyed by young children.

> *Theo Hersh, in a review of "Frank and Zelda," in* CM: A Reviewing Journal of Canadian Materials for Young People, *Vol. XIX, No. 1, January, 1991, pp. 27-8.*

The text teaches readers to be careful what they wish for as well as age-old lessons about the dangers of ambition and the futility of trying to change one's life through magic rather than through work. It does so with a lot of humor and bounce and with big, sunny pictures in watercolor and ink. Frank and Zelda are an appealing couple, chubby and vaguely ethnic in appearance. Their happy ending is as pleasing as a good pizza.

> *Leone McDermott, in a review of "Pizza for Breakfast," in* Booklist, *Vol. 87, No. 12, February 15, 1991, pp. 1201-02.*

Although there is also a certain cuteness quotient in *Frank and Zelda,* written and illustrated by Maryann Kovalski, on the whole I found it quite appealing. Kovalski's gentle, but lively and delicately coloured drawings aptly accompany her story, an adaptation of the fable of the fisherman's wife. In this version, a couple who operate a pizzeria in the 1930s fall upon hard times and are saved from bankruptcy by a mysterious stranger, who grants their impetuous wishes with unexpected and unwelcome results. With its low-key humour, believable portrayal of human nature, and plot that actually has a beginning, a middle, and a happy ending, *Frank and Zelda* should make a pleasant addition to the bedtime bookshelf.

> *Anne Denoon, in a review of "Frank and*

*Zelda," in* Books in Canada, *Vol. XX, No. 3, April, 1991, p. 37.*

---

### Take Me Out to the Ballgame (1993)

[In **Take Me Out to the Ballgame**] Jenny and Joanna are taken to a ball game by their wacky, fun-loving grandmother. There's an appealing zaniness to these pictures, as Grandma throws herself into the game with gusto, much to the amusement of the kids and the surrounding bleacher bums. Curious as it may seem, though, there's a problem with the plot. Yes, Jack Norworth's original lyrics are pretty straightforward—if the home team doesn't win it's a shame, and "it's one, two, three strikes you're out"—but just who won this particular game? And what's Grandma up to climbing out of the stands to catch a balloon as the last pitch is on its way? And how does her catching the balloon seem to save the game for the home team? There are no discernible answers to these overwhelming questions, a fact that is likely to infuriate parents and be totally ignored by their kids, who'll just go on chuckling at Grandma's goofy antics.

*Bill Ott, "Rooting for the Home Team," in* Booklist, *Vol. 89, No. 10, January 15, 1993, p. 914.*

Kovalski prefaces her lively version of Norwell's familiar refrain with a new verse, that tells the story of two sisters who—like the Katie Casey of the original—are "baseball mad." The story of Jenny and Joanna and their eccentric grandmother parallels the text of the original song as the threesome enjoys a high-powered game at the stadium. When the girls let go of their red balloon, Grandma in her red polka-dotted dress climbs out of the bleachers just in time to catch the winning baseball that (inexplicably) seems to have been hit on the third strike. Kovalski's characters and black outlined cartoons are filled with mirth and action but the awkwardly phrased new verse and the contrived illustrations, which often have little to do with the lyrics, make this a less satisfying songbook than her earlier efforts. Though Kovalski's rendition evinces considerable kid appeal, it nevertheless suffers to some extent by comparison with Alec Gillman's recent more exuberant and inventive version of the classic tune.

*A review of "Take Me Out to the Ballgame," in* Publishers Weekly, *Vol. 240, No. 7, February 15, 1993, p. 238.*

When their grandmother offers to take them on an outing, baseball fans Jenny and Joanna unhesitatingly elect a ball game. Singing the familiar chorus, which provides the text for the rest of the story, they enjoy peanuts and Cracker Jack and root for the home team. Then, when grandma reaches for a flyaway balloon, she blocks the ball and engineers the third strike—and out—"At the old ball game!" Any fans worth their salt will object to a pop fly being called a strike, and will look askance at the woman's obvious interference and infraction of the rules. But Kovalski's tale is not so much about baseball as much as it is about a grandmother who, despite her girth, her high heels, and red polka-dot dress, is a great sport and good companion at the ball park.

*Shirley Wilton, in a review of "Take Me Out to the Ballgame," in* School Library Journal, *Vol. 39, No. 4, April, 1993, p. 112.*

This book will bring particular pleasure to children who have experienced taking the subway to SkyDome to cheer the Toronto Blue Jays, but all children will enjoy its enthusiastic good spirits. Joanna and Jenny are real fans, chewing masses of bubblegum to get more baseball cards, and when Grandma takes them to a game, they enjoy the food and atmosphere with gusto. The text is mostly the lyrics of the title song—an added benefit to readers who like to sing. It is the sort of picture book you can spend some time on pointing out details to your listener, but don't try to explain the rule by which Grandma saves the game!

*Sandy Odegard, "Play Ball," in* Canadian Children's Literature, *No. 70, 1993, p. 94.*

# Carol Lerner

## 1927-

American author and illustrator of nonfiction.

Major works include *Seasons of the Tallgrass Prairie* (1980), *A Biblical Garden* (1982), *Pitcher Plants: The Elegant Insect Traps* (1983), *A Forest Year* (1987), *Dumb Cane and Daffodils: Poisonous Plants in the Home and Garden* (1990).

## INTRODUCTION

Considered one of the leading creators of informational books for children and young adults, Lerner is celebrated for writing and illustrating attractive, accessible introductions to botanical and biological subjects for readers in the middle grades and high school. Acclaimed as an especially talented and sensitive author whose texts and pictures blend the scientific with the aesthetic, she is acknowledged for the accuracy, usefulness, and elegance of her works as well as for their authoritativeness and excellence of design. Lerner is consistently praised for the distinctiveness of her titles, which are often written to fill a niche; several of her books are noted as superior in the genre of nonfiction. Presenting young readers with intimate guides to plant life and its relationship with the environment, she addresses such subjects as woodland wildflowers, North American carnivorous plants and those that cause allergic reactions, and the flora and fauna of a forest and desert. Considering the form and function of her subjects as well as the backgrounds in which they exist, Lerner is credited for providing her audience with a wealth of helpful information in a concise format that reflects both the extent of her research and the balance of her approach. She defines concepts and terms in a fluid, direct prose, and underscores her works with a strong ecological sensibility as well as an appreciation for the beauty of nature. As an illustrator, Lerner is commended for the precision, accuracy, detail, and appeal of her pictures. Her pen-and-ink drawings and watercolor paintings are considered works of art that lend eloquence and grace to her prose. Although Lerner is criticized occasionally for the lack of scientific names and indexes in some of her works, she is usually applauded for both the obvious respect she shows her readers and the satisfying, thought-provoking quality of her books. Barbara C. Scott writes that "Carol Lerner is one of our foremost writers and illustrators on books of botany for children," while Rudolf Schmid notes that Lerner "has developed into one of the leading authors of juvenile literature during the last decade."

After graduating from the University of Chicago, Lerner worked as a social worker before returning for her graduate degree in history. She and her husband, a professor at the university, lived in Europe for several years before returning to Chicago, where they raised two sons. On summer vacations, the family vacationed on the banks of Lake Michigan, where Lerner began to study plant and animal

life. After taking classes in nature study and botanical illustration at the Morton Arboretum in Lisle, Illinois, she began to study the juvenile nonfiction in which her sons were interested and found that the illustrations in these books lacked the quality of their fictional counterparts. Struck also by the scarcity of children's nonfiction on plant life, she began to write and illustrate her own books as well as to illustrate the works of Robert McClung, Glenda Daniel, Anita Holmes, and Millicent E. Selsam. Her first book, *Seasons of the Tallgrass Prairie*, was actually her third to be published. Describing the botany of the American prairie as well as the ebb and flow of the seasons, it is called by David C. Allison "an exceptional children's book, . . . a *must* book for every child who has even a remote interest in natural history." Her first published work, *On the Forest Edge* (1978), focuses on the meeting of forest and field, a subject she found was ignored by other writers for children; she continues to be inspired to write her works by checking existing titles and finding nothing on the subject. Lerner's fourth book, *A Biblical Garden*, is one of her most acclaimed: the first work written by the author without first-hand knowledge, it covers the characteristics, history, and symbolic significance of twenty plants mentioned in the Old Testament such as the palm, olive, and coriander. *A Biblical Garden* is described by Anne F. Pratt as "a unique blend of science and religion" and "an unusual addition for both the botanical and religious book shelf." Among her other works, Lerner has also written and illustrated two sets of related titles. *A Forest Year* and *A Desert Year* (1991) chronicle the adaptations of plants and animals in the eastern United States and the American Southwest in an annual cycle, while *Moonseed and Mistletoe: A Book of Poisonous Wild Plants* (1988) and *Dumb Cane and Daffodils: Poisonous Plants in the House and Garden* profile wild and domestic plants that cause irritation to the skin or illness and death from ingestion. Lerner writes of her vocation, "One of the foremost attractions of this work for me is that it affords me both opportunity and incentive to pursue any likely subject that piques my interest," and she adds, "I hope to continue making books for as long as I can still hike in the woods and hold the watercolor brush with a firm hand." Lerner received an award for special artistic merit from the Friends of American Writers for *On the Forest Edge* in 1979. *Seasons of the Tallgrass Prairie* was an Ambassador Honor Book of the English-speaking Union in 1980, while *Pitcher Plants* won the Carl Sandburg Award for Children's Literature in 1984 and *Plant Families* was named an honor book by the New York Academy of Sciences in 1989. In addition to her other awards, several of Lerner's books were named Outstanding Science Trade Books for Children and ALA Notable Books in their respective years of publication.

(See also *Contemporary Authors*, Vol. 102; *Something about the Author*, Vol. 33; and *Something about the Author Autobiography Series*, Vol. 12.)

---

# GENERAL COMMENTARY

## Rudolf Schmid

[*The following excerpt is from an essay by Schmid, an associate professor of integrative biology at UC, Berkeley, that surveys books on botany for children published mainly in the 1980s. Noting the explosive growth in juvenile literature on plant science since the 1970s, Schmid distinguishes Carol Lerner as one of the leading author/illustrators of the genre. In summarizing the criteria he uses to judge the value of botany texts for young people, Schmid remarks, "From my viewpoint as a professional botanist, I look for several essential features of biological juvenilia, particularly for the higher grades: indices; bibliographies, if only a few references to inspire the reader; glossaries; use of both scientific and common names of organisms, the former at least in the index or appendix; clear writing; accurate scientific text that has been checked by a competent authority; a minimum, preferably absence, of anthropocentrism and especially anthropomorphism, that is, no cute plants with faces." He adds that "[these] traits certainly characterize many of Lerner's most recent contributions" and notes that books such as Lerner's "certainly should be in the library of any botanical garden or herbarium that has a public education program. Professional biologists*

*may even care to purchase books like these to spread the biological word to young friends and relatives."*]

Chicagoan Carol Lerner has developed into one of the leading authors and illustrators of juvenile literature during the past decade. Many of Lerner's well-done efforts have received commendations. Lerner both authored and illustrated the following contributions to botanical juvenilia, which are listed in chronological order:

*On the Forest Edge* is an account of the plants and animals inhabiting the area where the edge of a forest meets an abandoned field. The book does not use scientific names and contains a glossary but no index.

*Flowers of a Woodland Spring* depicts various examples of ephemeral woodland wild flowers. Scientific names of plants are not used in this unindexed work.

*Seasons of the Tallgrass Prairie* presents the seasonal plant life of the American prairie, including the role of wildfire in its ecology. This book, though lacking an index, uses scientific names.

*A Biblical Garden* which has translations from the Hebrew bible by Ralph Lerner, describes and pictures twenty plants mentioned in the Old Testament, including fig, lentil, olive, papyrus, and pomegranate. Scientific names appear in the figure captions. An index is lacking.

*Pitcher Plants: The Elegant Insect Traps* is a superb and handsomely illustrated discussion of nine species (scientific names are given) of American pitcher plants (Sarraceniaceae) and, in its treatment of "plunderers," (that is, insects eating the "eaters") covers a topic not usually treated in books on plant carnivory. The book is indexed and presents a glossary and list of institutions having public displays of carnivorous plants.

*A Forest Year* is a seasonal diorama of the plant, fungal, and, especially, animal life of a temperate, deciduous forest in the eastern United States. The book has a glossary and index but does not use scientific names.

*Moonseed and Mistletoe: A Book of Poisonous Wild Plants* introduces potentially troublesome wild plants that may irritate the skin or cause illness or death from tasting or eating. Indexed, it includes scientific names of plants.

*Plant Families* is a very handsome and most instructive treatment of twelve common families of angiosperms (buttercups, crucifers, mints, legumes, roses, umbels, composites, lilies, grasses, orchids, etc.). It has an introduction, a useful glossary, and fine, full-page illustrations by Lerner, but lacks an index and, surprisingly, scientific plant names.

Lerner has also illustrated various works authored by other persons:

Anita Holmes's *The 100-Year-Old Cactus* depicts the first century of life of a saguaro cactus (Carnegiea gigantea). Scientific names and an index are lacking.

Millicent E. Selsam's *Tree Flowers* follows the growth cycle of twelve common flowering trees (pussy willow, white oak, sugar maple, elm, apple, horse chestnut, flowering dogwood, magnolia, witch hazel, black walnut, black locust, tulip tree). Selsam's descriptions are brief, but excellent, whereas Lerner's twelve color plates are quite fine, yielding "a felicitous union of talents" (Anonymous, *Bull. Cent. Child. Books* 37:212). Scientific names are given, but there is no index.

Lerner's black-and-white zoological drawings appear in Robert M. McClung's zoological juvenilia on, respectively, the biology of the peeper frog, the dragonfly, and the sphinx moth: *Peeper, First Voice of Spring; Green Darner: The Story of a Dragonfly; Sphinx: The Story of a Caterpillar.* The last two are revisions of, respectively, 1956 and 1949 works that had McClung's illustrations.

Of the above I most appreciate *Plant Families, Pitcher Plants, Moonseed and Mistletoe,* and *Tree Flowers.* Lerner's works are lucidly written and are usually enhanced with fine, delicate watercolor paintings. However, many of her works can be faulted for not supplying indices or scientific names of plants.

> *Rudolf Schmid, "Botany Books for Young People: A Retrospective Look by a Botanist at the 1980's and at the Artistry of Carol Lerner and Anne Ophelia Todd Dowden," in* Appraisal: Science Books for Young People, *Vol. 23, No. 2, Spring, 1990, pp. 1-18.*

# TITLE COMMENTARY

## Peeper, First Voice of Spring (1977)

[*Peeper, First Voice of Spring is written by Robert M. McClung.*]

Could we reproduce a sample, Carol Lerner's natural-history illustration would speak directly to the knowing eye: she combines the descriptive exactitude of McClung himself with the detail, timbre, and dramatic design of Peter Parnall; here, indeed, is black-and-white with color. The icky-sticky title notwithstanding, this is the account of a year among the tree frogs and other denizens of a woodland pond—beginning with Hyla, the young male peeper's, embrace of a mate. Soon she begins to lay eggs, Hyla fertilizes them, some are devoured, some develop, and then we have the age-old story of the tadpole's transformation into a frog. Young Hyla has company, he has "many narrow escapes"—before he and other small creatures go into hibernation to await another spring. "Then the chorus of peepers would once again sound its coming." The precise, near-poetic text expands in line drawings that invite discovery.

> *A review of "Peeper, First Voice of Spring," in* Kirkus Reviews, *Vol. XLV, No. 16, August 15, 1977, p. 854.*

Exquisite pen drawings lend elegance to McClung's simple narrative that describes the life cycles of spring peepers. The tiny frogs' mating calls are synonymous with spring; information on their mating, gradual metamorphosis from egg to tadpole to frog, and hibernation for the coming winter is smoothly set forth. Lerner's drawings, spread over double pages or facing a body of text, command the eye with their beauty and precision. They're

memorable, at once scientific and aesthetically complete. The book sets a striking standard for illustration and design in nonfiction.

> *Denise M. Wilms, in a review of "Peeper, First Voice of Spring," in* Booklist, *Vol. 74, No. 5, November 1, 1977, p. 479.*

## On the Forest Edge (1978)

Few laymen grasp the worth of the edge environment, the border territory between forest and non-forest. Carol Lerner displays it for children to comprehend in its varying width, density, and composition: a home, a refuge, and a source of food for the smaller animals. Wisely for the nine- to thirteen-year age group she does not bring up the red or white-tailed deer, a larger inhabitant of a broader forest edge than she describes. Instead she concentrates on the birds and small mammals, more appealing and comprehensible to this age group. In so doing she has written and illustrated most appealingly an introduction to ecology which will be accepted with ease and joy.

> *R. Gregory Belcher, in a review of "On the Forest Edge," in* Appraisal: Children's Science Books, *Vol. 12, No. 2, Spring, 1979, p. 36.*

Here is an example of that all-too-rare combination: a book which painlessly imparts a good deal of interesting information and is a visual and esthetic delight as well. The subject is the fringe area between deep woodland and open fields. This narrow, shifting border, which at first glance appears to be little more than a tangled, weedy thicket, supports an amazingly varied and numerous population of mammals, birds, insects, and plant life. While it is easy to recognize the value of a forest or a rolling meadow, Lerner's book awakens an appreciation for the rough in-between habitat and the abundance of living things that flourish in this environment. The author points out that a similar "edge effect" may appear along unmowed roadsides and railroad rights-of-way in suburbs and cities. Exquisite pen and ink drawings, large, clear print, and an elegant text make an eloquent case for the preservation of these border habitats. A brief glossary is included.

> *Christine E. Rowan, in a review of "On the Forest Edge," in* Appraisal: Children's Science Books, *Vol. 12, No. 2, Spring, 1979, p. 36.*

The overgrown area where woods and field meet is ecologically valuable; Lerner introduces the scientific term for such a meeting place—ecotone—and explores the special features of one field-forest: its changing face as plant forms rise and fall, plus the kinds of mammals, birds, insects, and plants that find life support there. Smoothly written, the book is also impeccably designed. Lerner's pen forms incisive, pristine spreads that give elegant visual definition to the text. Typography is especially complementary; in fact, the only quibble might be with the artist's rabbits, which aren't as anatomically precise as other flora and fauna in the book.

> *Denise M. Wilms, in a review of "On the Forest*

Soon the weasel disappears among the tall plants in the distance. Now the cottontail races for safety. In a few great leaps it reaches a tumbling mass of bushes and plunges into a thicket of blackberries. The rabbit squeezes through a narrow passageway in the brambles. There, in a hollowed-out spot under the thorny bushes, is a safe resting place.

*From* On the Forest Edge, *written and illustrated by Carol Lerner.*

Edge," in Booklist, *Vol. 75, No. 2, September 15, 1978, pp. 221-22.*

A sensitive, ecological portrait of animal and plant life amidst the brambles of the forest-edge. The importance of this fringe area and how its character gradually shifts are explained in a readable manner. Terms like "ecotone," "edge-effect," and "tension zone" are defined in easily understood prose. Large, well-placed pen-and-ink drawings depict a rich variety of flora and fauna. A pleasing addition to ecology collections that sheds light on a little-noticed but significant slice of forest life.

*Anne Boes, in a review of "On the Forest Edge," in* School Library Journal, *Vol. 25, No. 3, November, 1978, p. 65.*

The charming ink drawings on every page make this book a sure delight for children of all ages. The subject is the richness of plant and animal life along the margin between forest and field. Text and illustrations are excellently coordinated and accurately represent the living members of this habitat and the interactions among them. The book should be quite readable and enjoyable for third to sixth graders; I also found it pleasurable to read aloud to my six-year-old while she looked at the pictures. Children will be drawn to this book by the illustrations: in reading it they will likely acquire a surprising amount of information on the ecology of the forest edge.

*B. Dennis Sustare, in a review of "On the Forest Edge," in* Science Books & Films, *Vol. XV, No. 3, December, 1979, p. 165.*

---

***Flowers of a Woodland Spring*** (1979)

As Lerner's ***On the Forest Edge*** dealt with an "in-between" habitat, here she focuses on ephemerals, those temporally in-between blossoms which bloom profusely but briefly in the early spring—only until the shading can-

opy of tree leaves appears—and wait out the rest of the year underground. Lerner's description of the ephemerals' life cycles is sufficiently smooth and informative, as are her strictly informational drawings—of the different types of underground stem, for example; but most of the illustrations do less, while being called upon to do more. Often allotted full-page prominence, they are too weak and inert to fulfill even a decorative function, let alone vitalize the lesson.

*A review of "Flowers of a Woodland Spring," in* Kirkus Reviews, *Vol. XLVII, No. 18, September 15, 1979, p. 1070.*

Woodland spring flowers that blossom forth briefly and refreshingly before fading into the forest floor are termed *ephemerals*, Lerner tells us. She explains how their presence depends on sunlight, which is soon blocked by the bursting canopy of spring tree leaves. Her meticulous, sinewy pen-and-ink drawings detail their rhizomes, tubers, corms, bulbs, and earthy woodland home. Whereas Lerner's previous work ***On the Forest Edge*** was purely black and white, here color spreads are interspersed. They are literal and true, yet lack the razor-sharp precision that distinguishes the black-and-white spreads. The whole is still undeniably attractive and, of course, informative.

*Denise M. Wilms, in a review of "Flowers of a Woodland Spring," in* Booklist, *Vol. 76, No. 3, October 1, 1979, p. 279.*

The delicacy and fidelity of Lerner's exquisite paintings and drawings (some in color, some in black and white) are set off by spacious and dignified page layout. The text describes the ephemeral flowering plants of early springtime, plants like spring beauty or trout lilies, those early bloomers that disappear as soon as the trees above them come into leaf and block the sunlight. Lerner shows, in clear diagrams and equally clear text, how the storage systems of such plants (through rhizomes, corms, bulbs, and tubers) carry through the long months between their short blooming seasons. A good book for budding botanists, and a pleasure to look at.

*Zena Sutherland, in a review of "Flowers of a Woodland Spring," in* Bulletin of the Center for Children's Books, *Vol. 33, No. 2, October, 1979, p. 31.*

Just before the new spring leaves open and form a canopy over the forest floor, certain woodland spring flowers, the ephemerals, bloom profusely. Lerner captures this delicate radiance in her realistic, graceful illustrations of toothworts, Dutchman's-breeches, wild leeks and trout lilies. In a very brief time-span the ephemerals bloom, produce seeds, store food, develop new shoots and disappear. Their complete life cycle plus that of six individual wildflowers are described in simple, direct prose. Illustrated with fine black-and-white line drawings and soft natural watercolors, this is a high quality nature book surpassing most easy wildflower identification guides in content and refinement.

*Barbara Peklo Serling, in a review of "Flowers of a Woodland Spring," in* School Library Journal, *Vol. 26, No. 5, January, 1980, p. 57.*

A talented author illustrator who gave us **On the Forest Edge** last year has again produced a very special book. Here she describes in loving detail the group of wild flowers called woodland spring "ephemerals" which can be found in deciduous forests throughout the eastern United States. This multitude of small fragile flowers carpets the forest floor for just a few weeks in the early spring before the leaf canopy of maples and birches shades the ground completely. The reader learns first about the unusual above and below ground life cycle of these plants, then gets a detailed description of six familiar examples, the spring beauty, toothwort, Dutchman's breeches, squirrel corn, wild leek, and trout lily. An inviting picture book format and large print combine with smooth flowing prose and fine illustrations to make a beautiful book for the six to ten year old naturalist. Impeccable though the delicate but strong black-and-white line drawings are, I wish that more than eight of the full color watercolor illustrations could have been included. Though this is not a book likely to circulate widely, those who glance between its covers will not be disappointed.

*Diane Holzheimer, in a review of "Flowers of a Woodland Spring," in* Appraisal: Children's Science Books, *Vol. 13, No. 2, Spring, 1980, p. 47.*

The title of this book sounds like the title of a delightful piece of music. The similarity is strengthened by the beauty and accuracy of the text, and of the illustrations, which make up a half of the book. Listen to this: "Last year's leaves lie wet and heavy on the ground, soaked by the rain that falls on them. But the forest floor does not seem to belong in the same season with the bare-branched trees above. Here below, the earth has already been changed by spring." I do not know whether this is a book for children or adults. It is too good for anyone to miss.

*R. Gregory Belcher, in a review of "Flowers of a Woodland Spring," in* Appraisal: Children's

Science Books, *Vol. 13, No. 2, Spring, 1980, p. 47.*

---

## Green Darner: The Story of a Dragonfly (1980)

[Green Darner *is written by Robert M. McClung and was originally published in 1956. New illustrations by Carol Lerner were added to the 1980 edition.*]

This newly revised edition of an "old favorite" sports finely detailed, black-and-white drawings that beautifully portray the life cycle of a dragonfly named Green Darner. These drawings are so accurate and follow the text so closely that even a very young child could "read" the story. The text itself is poetic, yet accurate enough in its descriptions of the various animals living in and around a pond. Mr. McClung is successful in emphasizing the beauties of the dragonfly and in dispelling many harmful myths about the insect. Any teacher who takes his/her class on a field trip to a pond or has an aquarium in the classroom will greatly appreciate this book as a reference.

*Martha T. Kane, in a review of "Green Darner: The Story of a Dragonfly," in* Appraisal: Children's Science Books, *Vol. 13, No. 3, Fall, 1980, p. 46.*

A handsome new edition of a book which has been out of print for some time. This one has the same large, clear print of the author's previous titles, but is packaged in the picture-book format recently popularized by Crowell's "Let's Read and Find Out" science series. Carol Lerner's pen and ink drawings are visually dramatic, with details as fine and fragile as the dragonfly itself. It is unfortunate that no color is used, since McClung's text describes a variety of colorful insects. The text describes the complete life cycle of an insect that is both fascinating and fearsome to some youngsters because of the stories told about it (dragonflies will not sew your ears shut!). The format and the fictionalized text will make this more appealing as recreational reading than for school reports. There is no index or table of contents. Children in grades three and up will read this alone; younger children will find it a good lap book to share with a parent. Those writing reports may prefer to use chapters in the author's *Aquatic Insects and How They Live* (Morrow, 1970), or Hilda Simon's *Dragonflies* (Viking, 1972), but libraries will want to own all three of these titles.

*Susanne S. Sullivan, in a review of "Green Darner: The Story of a Dragonfly," in* Appraisal: Children's Science Books, *Vol. 13, No. 3, Fall, 1980, p. 46.*

Simply and authoritatively written, this revision of a 1956 title is improved by the format and the new illustrations; Lerner's drawings are elegant and sophisticated in black and white, yet completely realistic in their details. McClung begins with the ecological system of the pond community in which his individual Green Darner lives; he continues with an anatomical description, discusses courting and mating, moves to the birth and youth of an offspring and to some of its adventures. In the course of this account (narrative but not anthropomorphic) McClung provides additional facts about growth stages and anatomy, and about feeding habits, predators, and locomotion.

> *Zena Sutherland, in a review of "Green Darner: The Story of a Dragonfly," in* Bulletin of the Center for Children's Books, *Vol. 34, No. 2, October, 1980, pp. 36-7.*

---

### Seasons of the Tallgrass Prairie   (1980)

Meticulously detailed fine-line drawings, carefully labelled, illustrate a text that describes the grasses and flowering plants in each of the seasons on the tall-grass prairie. Lerner's distinctive work cries for color, but her drawings are so exact that even the black and white pictures can be used for identifying plants. The text goes beyond mere description, however, since it discusses the ways in which prairie plants, deep-rooted, hold the soil and contribute to its richness, and the seasonal changes that bring new blooms and new colors. A list of plants mentioned or illustrated in the book is appended, arranged by common names but with scientific names provided.

> *Zena Sutherland, in a review of "Seasons of the Tallgrass Prairie," in* Bulletin of the Cen-

ter for Children's Books, *Vol. 34, No. 3, November, 1980, p. 57.*

In a book about prairie plants, most of which Lerner says are "forbs," or prairie wild flowers, the lack of color in illustration is disconcerting, especially after an attractive color cover. On the other hand, the illustrator's meticulous pen drawings are precise and immaculate looking; a full-page cutaway drawing showing the relative lengths and positions of root systems is an especially striking example of her ability to blend the scientific and the aesthetic. The accompanying narrative describing the prairie plants and their interdependent ways is smooth and concise; above all, it's successful at establishing readers' appreciation for the superficially monotonous "sea of swaying grasses" that is true prairie land.

> *Denise M. Wilms, in a review of "Seasons of the Tallgrass Prairie," in* Booklist, *Vol. 77, No. 8, December 15, 1980, p. 575.*

The dandelions and daisies that grow in vacant lots and country roadsides, Lerner informs us, are imports brought over by early settlers; but the tall grasses and wild flowers that grow in our few remaining prairies and prairie patches are "native Americans." Here she takes a prairie community of grasses and wild flowers through the seasons,

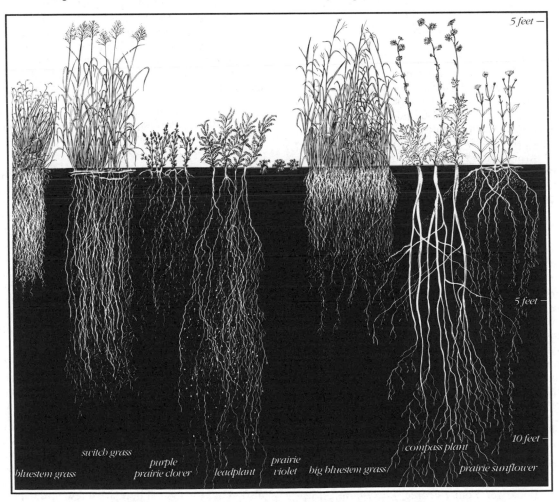

*From* Seasons of the Tallgrass Prairie, *written and illustrated by Carol Lerner.*

noting the underground growth and changing surface, and ends with an explanation of the benefits of fire to the prairie ecology. In prose that is smooth but not sharp, and with fine-line black-and-white drawings that are most successful when least prominently featured, the book reads and looks much like Lerner's *Flowers of a Woodland Spring.*

> *A review of "Seasons of the Tallgrass Prairie," in* Kirkus Reviews, *Vol. XLIX, No. 1, January 1, 1981, p. 1.*

The unique biosphere of the prairie and the seasonal changes it undergoes are well drawn in this carefully planned study, which capitalizes on the mystery and wonder of a special environment while it illuminates the intricate relationships that make the prairie survive and flourish. Following an alluring description of the landscape, we are taken through each season and made aware of the great plant variety and constant change in an equally diverse and changing community. Explanations of legume nitrogen storage and full sun-plant adaptations are clearly and logically presented. The crisp drawings capture the rich textures of each species; however, there are no color photos to document the vivid descriptions of the flowers.

> *Steve Matthews, in a review of "Seasons of the Tallgrass Prairie," in* School Library Journal, *Vol. 27, No. 6, February, 1981, p. 68.*

**Seasons of the Tallgrass Prairie** is an exceptional children's book. It is factual and has outstanding line drawings. It also has the extra dimension of sensitivity to the prairie that the author brings to the book. The book's level of difficulty is such that it could be included in a child's private library, and should definitely be a part of school libraries through the junior high level. While the language and technical information is designed for a young person, the line drawings could also be used by college students and lay botanists for field identification. This is a must book for any child who has even a remote interest in natural history.

> *David C. Allison, in a review of "Seasons of the Tallgrass Prairie," in* Science Books & Films, *Vol. 16, No. 5, May-June, 1981, p. 276.*

Beautifully designed, illustrated, and printed, this is an intimate guide to the seasonal botany of the prairie. Detailed description of the seasons' ebb and flow combine with technical description to create a rhythm that truly suggests the changing of the seasons. Plants are placed in their ecological niches and shown in a cutaway style that juxtaposes them to their neighbors both over and underground. A final chapter discusses the function of fire in maintaining prairie land against the encroachment of forest. Though a list of plants' Latin names is appended, the book is unindexed. An aesthetically pleasing and useful companion to the author's *Flowers of a Woodland Spring.*

> *Carolyn Noah, in a review of "Seasons of the Tallgrass Prairie," in* Appraisal: Science Books for Young People, *Vol. 14, No. 2, September, 1981, p. 26.*

## Sphinx: The Story of a Caterpillar  (1981)

> [Sphinx: The Story of a Caterpillar *is written by Robert M. McClung. The revised 1981 edition has new illustrations by Carol Lerner.*]

First published in 1949, this revised edition of **Sphinx** has been redesigned and now features Lerner's black-and-white line drawings. Her pointillistic style faithfully illustrates what is being discussed; but while her larger illustrations are clear, small details are sometimes lost, as when the caterpillar sheds skin on a leaf. Problematic, too, is the book's narrative tone. Students who like their information straight may not want to dig out the facts from the story format. There is a wealth of information here, however, for those who will take the time to find it.

> *Ilean Cooper, in a review of "Sphinx: The Story of a Caterpillar," in* Booklist, *Vol. 78, No. 8, December 15, 1981, p. 550.*

This short book, originally published in 1949 and reissued this year with new illustrations, is an established classic of its type. The book depicts the life cycle of the Sphinx moth, the insect whose larval form is the familiar tomato hornworm. The text is clear, accurate, and interesting to read. The black-line illustrations, done by artist Carol Lerner, are excellent in every respect. Intended for the six to ten year old reader, **Sphinx** provides a charming and scientifically accurate introduction to insect metamorphosis and balance in nature. The thought occurs that reading the book with a child at the time tomato hornworms appear in the garden would be an outstanding educational experience.

> *A. H. Drummond, Jr., in a review of "Sphinx. The Story of a Caterpillar," in* Appraisal: Science Books for Young People, *Vol. 15, No. 1, Winter, 1982, p. 43.*

The authors present a fascinating look at Sphinx caterpillars, the fat, green caterpillars commonly found on tomato plants. The caterpillar's complete yearly cycle from egg to moth to the next year's egg laying is covered. The line drawings are so explicit and carefully executed that at times they border on fine art. The pictures and text are supportive of each other, with bits of intrigue about what is happening, about the introduction of other animals and about the seasonal changes; there is much to learn as well as much to catch the eye. Body parts are explained and illustrated as the change from fat, green tomato-eating caterpillar to nectar-sucking Sphinx moth is handled delicately and beautifully.

> *Barbara L. Greer, in a review of "Sphinx: The Story of a Caterpillar," in* School Library Journal, *Vol. 28, No. 5, January, 1982, pp. 67-8.*

**Sphinx** is a description of the life-cycle of a tomato hornworm, and each stage of growth is accurately and simply described. The balance of nature is touched on by including the demise of three caterpillars by predation and parasitation as well as by mentioning slugs, birds, and rabbits also vying for food. There are a few minor points of criticism: The term "grub" is usually reserved for beetle larvae and is not applied to the larvae of other orders of insects. Also, the large type size would indicate that the text is intended to be read by young readers, but the words are so closely packed into each line with minimum space between the words that it is difficult to distinguish one word from the next. And finally, "peavine" is written as one word. The precisely drawn black-and-white illustrations appear on every page and are beautiful works of art. This is an interesting, informative book to be read to nursery or primary students and to be followed by appropriate discussion and activities.

> *Sister Edna Demanche, in a review of "Sphinx: The Story of a Caterpillar," in* Science Books & Films, *Vol. 17, No. 4, March-April, 1982, p. 216.*

### A Biblical Garden  (1982)

Handsome botanical drawings are detailed with scrupulous accuracy and are lovely in their shading, grace of line, and—on some pages—subtlety of color; some of the drawings are black and white. Lerner gives a few facts about each plant, usually including information about how it was known, grown, or used in Biblical times and how it may be used today. Each page of text (almost always two brief paragraphs) is preceded by common and scientific names and a Biblical quotation in which the plant is mentioned; each such page faces a full-page painting or drawing. Attractive, with limited reference use.

> *Zena Sutherland, in a review of "A Biblical Garden," in* Bulletin of the Center for Children's Books, *Vol. 35, No. 8, April, 1982, p. 152.*

Only in the very broadest sense can the title-word *Garden* apply here to [the] mention and illustration of 20 plants referred to in the Old Testament and ranging from lentils and barley to date palm and cedar of Lebanon. Pretty is a word for Lerner's illustrations, but disappointing might also be applied. In the ten colored plates the greens are unnaturally light rather than reasonably true (particularly the problem with the fig and the castor bean); and several of the ten black-and-white sketches certainly need some comparison figure to give an idea of size. Lerner notes that, of course, picture cannot substitute for experience with the living plants. For many the references to "the Hebrew Bible" and "the King James version" will be confusing. The brief commentaries on the plants, each about 100 words, make for well-designed pages with lots of white space, but these are informationally scant. The idea for the book is excellent, but text limitations and alternating black-and-white and watercolor plates are not entirely satisfying.

> *George Gleason, in a review of "A Biblical Garden," in* School Library Journal, *Vol. 28, No. 8, April, 1982, p. 83.*

Preceding Carol Lerner's descriptions and exquisite pictures of plants mentioned in the Bible are translations by Ralph Lerner from the Old Testament, his accurate references from the Hebrew and the King James versions

From A Biblical Garden, *written and illustrated by Carol Lerner.*

adding to the book's vitality and interest. The author-illustrator's lovely paintings and drawings begin with the fig tree, mentioned in Genesis, and following are discussions of papyrus (usually translated bulrush in the story in Exodus where Pharaoh's daughter saves Moses), the pomegranate, lentil, coriander, myrtle and other plants that figured prominently in the lives of ancient peoples and still exist, little changed during the long centuries. There should be no age limit on so informative and beautiful a publication.

> *A review of "A Biblical Garden," in* Publishers Weekly, *Vol. 221, No. 15, April 9, 1982, p. 50.*

A sampling of twenty plants mentioned in the Old Testament is presented with full-page illustrations, soft yet luminous color alternating with black and white. The pages facing the pictures list the common name of the plant in English and in Hebrew as well as the scientific Latin name. Beneath this fundamental information is a quotation from a book of the Old Testament in which the name of the plant is found. Thus we are reminded that the dove brought Noah an olive leaf, that manna was like coriander seed, and that a castor bean plant shaded Jonah's head. Finally, there is a short two-paragraph explanation or commentary supplementing the fuller discussion of biblical plant life in the introduction. Attractive and pleasing in itself, the volume helps to illuminate the imagery and symbolism of the Old Testament.

> *Paul Heins, in a review of "A Biblical Gar-*

*den," in* The Horn Book Magazine, *Vol. LVIII, No. 3, June, 1982, pp. 307-08.*

Picture, if you can, the task of trying to untangle the bird-nests of a surf-fisherman's inept casting on a dark and windy beach. It is a simple task compared with that tackled by the author of **A Biblical Garden.** Her birdnest consisted of problems of botanical nomenclature and identification; the sorting of facts, fictions, and fantasies that have grown up around many familiar plants; and the selecting of appropriate examples from a document so old, so much translated, and so variously interpreted as the Bible.

Problems of botanical nomenclature and identification are carefully reviewed in the book's opening pages. The author's reasons for choosing certain plants, deciding what names to use for them and what uses to describe are also explained. In the pages which follow that, descriptive text for each plant is limited to two short paragraphs, neither of which is ever more than four sentences long. Explanations include only simple botanical data along with a description designed to give richer meaning to a biblical verse chosen for its botanical content. Each page of text is faced by an accurate and beautifully executed illustration of the plant concerned.

It all adds up to a botanical book which is simple, beautiful, accurate, and a pleasure to read. **A Biblical Garden** is a tribute to the author's disciplined restraint.

> *William D. Perkins, in a review of "A Biblical Garden," in* Appraisal: Science Books for Young People, *Vol. 16, No. 1, Winter, 1983, p. 42.*

Carol Lerner's **A Biblical Garden,** is a unique blend of science and religion. Many of the plants existing in biblical times have remained unchanged to the present day. References to them are numerous in the bible and it is evident that they played an important role in the lives of the ancient people. In order to give the reader a better understanding of what these plants looked like, where they grew and how they were used, the author has combined full-page watercolors and delicate pen and ink drawings with a simple but adequate text describing the characteristics, history, and symbolic meaning of the plant. For each of twenty species the format is repeated. The left-hand page gives the English, Hebrew and scientific plant name, the biblical quotation where it appears, and the general description. The right-hand page alternates well-detailed color and black and white drawings. Some of the plants described are olive, coriander, papyrus, pomegranate, barley, caper, and date palm. This is an unusual addition for both the botanical and religious book shelf.

> *Ann F. Pratt, in a review of "A Biblical Garden," in* Appraisal: Science Books for Young People, *Vol. 16, No. 1, Winter, 1983, p. 42.*

---

### Pitcher Plants: The Elegant Insect Traps  (1983)

A gracefully detailed, gracefully illustrated report on the carnivorous pitcher plants, which grow in soils that lack certain minerals and thus catch insects to supply the missing nutrients. Lerner interweaves considerations of form,

function, and environment, describing first the pitcher plants' leaves—"elegant, handsome, and deadly"—whose sugary nectar attracts the insects and whose construction propels their victims to the bottom of the "pitcher," to be broken down by the plants' powerful digestive enzymes. Similarly, she notes how the flowers, "also strange and beautiful," have, like other flowering plants, developed structures that "almost guarantee" cross-fertilization; and how, unlike other plants, the pitcher plant species easily interbreed—but taking the train of thought a step further, she then explains why it still makes sense to talk about different species. The final section emphasizes the close relationship between pitcher plants and a variety of insects, some of whom raid the plants' underground "plump storehouse" (the rhizomes filled with starches) while others "invade even the leaves and turn these death traps to their own advantage." "None of these animals is entirely safe from the danger of the trap, and some of them never leave the leaf; but a number of insects spend a large part of their lives within the pitcher leaves without suffering any harm." As a further twist, there are the carrion eaters who enter the leaves in pursuit of decomposing insects and remain to share their fate. An ever-enticing topic, thoughtfully and pleasingly presented.

> *A review of "Pitcher Plants: The Elegant Insect Traps," in* Kirkus Reviews, *Vol. LI, No. 2, January 15, 1983, p. 67.*

Describing eight species of pitcher plant, all indigenous to North America, Lerner discusses the ways in which they trap insects, providing the plant with food and at times with fertilization. She describes the victims and those creatures that prey on the plant; one insect, the Exyra moth, has established a relationship in which its whole life cycle is adjusted to the pitcher leaf as harmless host. The text is direct, authoritative, and logically organized; the illustrations, especially those in color, are both accurate and handsome. In addition to the glossary and index, the book concludes with a list of places where carnivorous plants, including pitcher plants, are on public view.

> *Zena Sutherland, in a review of "Pitcher Plants: The Elegant Insect Traps," in* Bulletin of the Center for Children's Books, *Vol. 36, No. 8, April, 1983, p. 154.*

Pitcher plants, larger cousins of the Venus fly trap, are native to many areas of the United States, and Lerner's elegant presentation should leave readers with respect and curiosity. Handsome colored paintings and informative drawings accompany a carefully developed text. The structure of leaves and flowers, variations among species and the trapping and digesting of insects are described. The book concludes with a list of botanic gardens throughout the country which maintain collections of carnivorous plants. Most likely to serve the serious reader, this is a fine complement to Jerome Wexler's *Secret of the Venus's Fly Trap* (Dodd, 1981) and Annabel Dean's shorter survey *Plants That Eat Insects* (Lerner, 1977).

> *Margaret Bush, in a review of "Pitcher Plants: The Elegant Insect Traps," in* School Library Journal, *Vol. 29, No. 8, April, 1983, p. 115.*

Pitcher plants are carnivorous—and thus of more interest than many other plant species. Lerner offers a good general introduction to these wide-ranging North American plants. Her detailed botanical drawings illustrate their anatomy quite clearly, while the cleanly written text explains which species live in which regions and describes how they operate in their particular ecological niche. Illustrations include both full-color, field-guide-type portraits and airy, precise ink drawings of the plants' parts. Appended are a glossary and list of pitcher-plant collections open to the public. A handsome first look.

> *Denise M. Wilms, in a review of "Pitcher Plants: The Elegant Insect Traps," in* Booklist, *Vol. 79, No. 18, May 15, 1983, p. 1218.*

***Pitcher Plants*** offers a pleasant presentation of the amazing adaptations the plant group has made in order to catch insects and of the even more incredible adaptations of certain insects to living on the plant—despite its offenses. The situation seems like an enactment of the arms race in miniature. If a reader seeks only a description of astonishing adaptations, the book is excellent. But it will be a disappointment if one desires a list of scientific names and identification characteristics, an occasional comparison of insect trapping by other carnivorous plants, information on how the plants can be obtained from propagating nurseries and raised, or comments on possible evolutionary ancestors. One aid in identifying any of the eight pitcher plant species, however, is the presence of exquisite watercolor paintings scattered throughout the text. Since there is only one map, the geographic occurrence of most of the species is explained in words. Several attractive line drawings illustrate the fine points of how a predator attacks and the prey eludes. With a list of gardens and greenhouses open to the public, a glossary, and an index.

> *Sarah Gagne, in a review of "Pitcher Plants: The Elegant Insect Traps," in* The Horn Book Magazine, *Vol. LIX, No. 3, June, 1983, p. 334.*

Once again Lerner presents an outstanding science and botany book for children. The illustrations are excellent, and the technical data are accurate and appropriate. Lerner discusses the eight species of Sarracenia, a group of plants that grows only in North America. She examines the leaf structures that help the plants obtain nutrients that are lacking in their environments, the devices with which they trap their victims, and the special relationships that exist between the Sarracenia and their insect parasites. Although the subject matter is more regional than Lerner's ***Seasons of the Tallgrass Prairie,*** many inquiring children are aware of and interested in carnivorous plants. This book fills their need; each time they read it, they will derive additional knowledge from the text. Lerner demonstrates her acute sensitivity to the world around her as she writes about carnivorous plants and their somewhat perilous future. ***Pitcher Plants*** should be available in school libraries for students from the fourth grade to junior high school. For readers who have an above-average interest in plant science or nature the book is an excellent addition to a personal library. In fact, any general reader will find the book informative.

> *David C. Allison, in a review of "Pitcher*

*Plants: The Elegant Insect Traps," in* Science Books & Films, *Vol. 19, No. 1, September-October, 1983, p. 32.*

Carol Lerner has done it again. She has produced a well-researched, useful book in a clearly-written, beautifully illustrated, high-quality format. Other recent books on insect-eating plants (such as *Carnivorous Plants* by Cynthia Overbeck, Lerner, 1982) include pitchers, but a children's monograph on the subject is unusual and welcome. The author concentrates on the Sarracenia pitchers—their habitat and characteristics, their victims and enemies. There are a glossary, an index, and a special listing of collections of pitcher plants open to the public. Lerner's pen and ink drawings and water color illustrations are the final touch of elegance.

> *Ruth S. Beebe, in a review of "Pitcher Plants: Elegant Insect Traps," in* Appraisal: Science

*Cross section of a pitcher leaf with* Sarracenia *wasp nests. From* Pitcher Plants: The Elegant Insect Traps, *written and illustrated by Carol Lerner.*

*Books for Young People, Vol. 16, No. 3, Fall, 1983, pp. 38-9.*

Plants that "trap" insects are inherently interesting to many children, and perhaps even a little bit mysterious. ***Pitcher Plants: Elegant Insect Traps*** is a book which can satisfy the natural interests of children and also encourage further study about these peculiar plants. The text flows along smoothly, and the illustrations are clear and relevant to the text. Some of the illustrations are in color and others are black and white. I have seen students who are encouraged to draw some of their own plants with pen and ink because they were so inspired by the drawings in this book. Perhaps it is too much to expect any popular writer to avoid completely all hints of personification when writing about plants, but this author does reasonably well. Some of the statements are nevertheless quite misleading. For example, on page 13, the author states, "Their success is linked to the leaf traps that catch insects and use them to feed the plant." Children who read this sentence are given to believe that the leaves somehow lay hold of the insects then feed them to the plant in the manner one might feed an animal. Very little editing would be required to turn this little book into a much more carefully worded book than it is. Overall, however, this is a book of some merit, about a topic of some considerable interest to children. It should make a useful addition to any school library.

*Clarence C. Truesdall, in a review of "Pitcher Plants: Elegant Insect Traps," in* Appraisal: Science Books for Young People, *Vol. 16, No. 3, Fall, 1983, p. 39.*

---

### The 100-Year-Old Cactus (1983)

[The 100-Year-Old Cactus *is written by Anita Holmes.*]

Young naturalists will enjoy this biography of a typical saguaro cactus, followed from its origins as a tiny seed to its towering presence as a 35-foot-high desert skyscraper. Not that this happens quickly. Holmes points out that after five years of growth a cactus stem may only be one inch high. At 15 years, the plant will have attained the impressive height of one foot. Only after a hundred years of growing does it become three feet thick and taller than a telephone pole. At this stage, the cactus functions much like a tree: Gila woodpeckers will methodically nose their way in by digging a deep nest in the main stem; birds and other animals will drink the nectar of the flowers that blossom; desert mice and other animals will thrive in its shady presence.

Holmes tells her story well—it divides neatly into a concentration first on the cactus and then on the woodpeckers who nest inside it—and Carol Lerner's illustrations are both informative and dramatic. Lerner takes the reader in for close-ups of ants next to the minuscule seedling and of the woodpecker chicks at the bottom of their burrow-like nest. She achieves fine dramatic effect when, after pages of light illustrations against bright white background, she unexpectedly plunges her desert into dark tonalities for the night scenes. The only drawback to this otherwise excellent book is the failure to identify all of the desert crea-

tures that scurry about the saguaro. Young readers will certainly wonder what the little kangaroo-like mouse is called.

*Michael Dirda, in a review of "The 100-Year-Old Cactus," in* Book World—The Washington Post, *August 14, 1983, p. 6.*

In her informative book for younger readers, Holmes explains the long growth of the giant saguaro cactus. Readers are shown a simple view of the development of this cactus from the time of the seed to the time it produces flowers and fruit. Some of the desert animals who depend on the cactus and a few other animals that live in the rocky Arizona desert are briefly introduced: particular attention is paid to the Gila woodpecker, who builds its nest inside the saguaro. Lerner's black, green and gold watercolors, soft and appealing to a younger audience, are realistic and fortify the text; she truly captures the spirit of desert life. This book, a brief introduction, should stimulate curiosity, interest and enthusiasm among readers.

*Lisa Brooks Williams, in a review of "The 100-Year-Old Cactus," in* School Library Journal, *Vol. 30, No. 3, November, 1983, pp. 64-5.*

[This] book on cactus is one of the most engaging books on desert ecology that I have encountered. Even children who have not seen a desert should enjoy it, for the text quickly comes alive with illustrations that frequently show full-page close-ups of an animal in its setting. The theme of the book is that a single cactus plant, seemingly alone in its area of the desert, by dint of offering food, water, and shelter, supports a great many species of life—from ants to woodpeckers. We are shown—all by day—ants with seeds; Gila woodpeckers nesting in a trunk; gilded flickers, hummingbirds, a butterfly, beetles, and a hawk's nest. At night there are moths, a bat, a Gila monster, a screech owl, and others. The three-color illustrations themselves are delightful and invite study. Unfortunately, the animals illustrated are seldom named specifically in the text; a list placed discreetly in a corner of each illustration would have made the book more informative.

*A review of "The 100-Year-Old Cactus," in* The Horn Book Magazine, *Vol. LX, No. 1, February, 1984, pp. 88-9.*

---

### Tree Flowers (1984)

[Tree Flowers *is written by Millicent E. Selsam.*]

Carol Lerner's full color paintings are beautiful and make this thin book more than just another description of how flowers are pollinated and develop into seeds as a means of reproduction. A three page introduction by the author explaining the basic theory is followed by a double page spread on each of ten common flowering trees. The text is minimal but full of special interesting facts about each tree and the facing pages include full color paintings of the blossom and its subsequent stages to the mature fruit, nut, or seed. If your budget allows for an extra purchase, this is a worthy addition of a somewhat limited scope.

*Sallie Hope Erhard, in a review of "Tree Flow-*

ers," in Appraisal: Science Books for Young People, *Vol. 17, No. 3, Fall, 1984, p. 37.*

Selsam has chosen twelve trees as examples of specimens bearing different kinds of flowers, so that the highly visible blossoms of the apple or magnolia are included, as well as the small flowers of the white oak or sugar maple. A page of concise, clear descriptive text faces each recto page that includes several detailed illustrations in scale, accurate, beautiful, and carefully labelled. This is easily assimilable botanical information, a felicitous union of talents.

> *Zena Sutherland, in a review of "Tree Flowers," in* Bulletin of the Center for Children's Books, *Vol. 37, No. 11, July-August, 1984, p. 212.*

By focusing on 12 common trees and using concise texts and detailed color drawings, Selsam and Lerner illustrate the different types of flowers and pollination methods by which trees reproduce. The introduction states the general principles of pollination and shows a clear, black-and-white schematic drawing of a representative flower and its parts. Selsam describes each tree, and in addition to botanical information she includes historical facts and folklore. The differences between wind- and insect-pollinated flowers are shown clearly in Lerner's beautiful color drawings of each tree's flower. Comparable to Dowden's *The Blossom on the Bough* (Harper, 1975) in its high quality, **Tree Flowers** will still fill a collection gap as it is more appropriate for younger children. The drawings are beautiful enough, the text interesting enough and the trees common enough to inspire many a springtime nature walk.

> *Frances E. Millhouser, in a review of "Tree Flowers," in* School Library Journal, *Vol. 31, No. 1, September, 1984, p. 123.*

---

**A Forest Year** (1987)

Arranged by season, this book provides 16 glimpses of the plants and animals that might live in a typical forest in the eastern half of the United States. For every season there are four full-page water-color illustrations, each facing a page of descriptive text and each highlighting a set of wildlife: mammals, birds, reptiles and amphibians, or insects. Lerner's precise, colorful illustrations even show what's happening underground and inside trees and old logs through cutaway drawings, which are also used to explain how trees' water and food distribution systems work. A few lines tell about each of the many animals and suggest which is which (most drawings are unlabeled, requiring a little knowledge and deduction to tell one from another). Probably the most interesting pages are those showing the woods in snowy winter. Scenes of animals curled up underground or tunneling through dirt, logs, and snow show that even in relatively quiet times, the woods are full of hidden life. An attractive introduction to the cycle of seasons.

> *Carolyn Phelan, in a review of "A Forest Year," in* Booklist, *Vol. 83, No. 15, April 1, 1987, p. 1207.*

Botanical illustrator Carol Lerner has compiled a catalogue of seasonal characteristics typical of Eastern U.S. deciduous forest creatures. Each page focuses on mammals, birds, reptiles, amphibians, insects, or plants as changes occur in their habitat during the annual cycle. After an initial paragraph generally describing mammals in winter, for instance, there are several sentences devoted to woodchucks, shrews, white-footed mice, and deer, with the text faced by a full-page watercolor illustration of their activities in a snowy scene. The writing is competent and the art attractive (though more static than the artist's black-and-white work) as well as informative, but the explanatory text is somewhat fragmented; the details have a scientific framework but no direction or dominant principle to give the book momentum.

> *Betsy Hearne, in a review of "A Forest Year," in* Bulletin of the Center for Children's Books, *Vol. 40, No. 9, May, 1987, p. 172.*

All woodland life in much of the United States is profoundly influenced by the changing of the seasons. Lerner's attractive paintings, each accompanying a single page of text, observe groups of mammals, birds, reptiles and amphibians, insects, and plants during each season. Winter feeding birds, hibernating mammals, the spring growth of plants and egg-laying of reptiles, and insects feasting on the decaying leaves of fall are a few of the many topics sketched in this pleasant examination of the yearly cycle. As in earlier works—**A Biblical Garden, Flowers of a Woodland Spring, On the Forest Edge**—the author-artist creates pretty views of the natural world in a well-designed volume. In this book the pages of text are framed in blue, while the pictures fill whole pages and some double-spread half-pages with beautifully composed detail; circled insets showing selected magnified items are included for closer viewing in some scenes. Lerner's plants and birds tend to be most precise and realistic, with mammals and other animals sometimes less accurately replicated. This does not detract from an inviting album of forest life. Glossary, index.

> *Margaret A. Bush, in a review of "A Forest Year," in* The Horn Book Magazine, *Vol. LXIII, No. 3, May-June, 1987, pp. 357-8.*

This slim, well-designed volume introduces selected flora and fauna of the four seasons as found in a forest in the Eastern half of the United States. The section for each season is divided into mammals, birds, reptiles and amphibians, insects, and plant life, with a double-page spread for each group. The gracefully-written text discusses four or five examples of that group, giving details that relate to the particular season. An illustration on the facing page or across the bottom half of the pages shows a woodland scene that contains each creature or plant mentioned. The sparsity of labels in the pictures makes readers use content from the text to identify the creatures and plants, although the tiniest of them are enlarged and labeled in insets. While not as elegant as some of Lerner's earlier books such as **Pitcher Plants,** in which an abundance of white space enhances the drawings, the attractive full-color paintings here do convey a different sense for each season, and the charming cover will draw in readers.

> *Kathleen Odean, in a review of "A Forest*

*Year," in* School Library Journal, *Vol. 33, No. 11, August, 1987, p. 86.*

This is a difficult book to review for *Science Books & Films* because there is no science in it. It is a well-done, beautifully illustrated children's nature book, but it doesn't do the things a science book does. It presents facts, but it involves none of the processes of science. What it does, it does very well, however. This book provides a broad picture through words and excellent illustrations of a few of the changes in the life of the forest through the four seasons. What can be shown of the tremendously varied life of the forest in 48 pages? Obviously not much, but the selection here seems appropriate and quite representative. Discussions of the broad range of activities of life of the animals are presented with appropriate examples. The major vertebrate groups plus insects and other invertebrates are represented, primarily. Clearly aimed at a general but young audience; this book might best serve as a "coffee-table" book for 10—12-year-olds.

*Richard J. Seltin, in a review of "A Forest Year," in* Science Books & Films, *Vol. 23, No. 2, November-December, 1987, p. 104.*

*A Forest Year* is a beautifully written and illustrated look at the plant and animal life of the forest through the four seasons of the year. Beginning with winter, each season is divided into five segments, mammals, birds, reptiles and amphibians, insects, and plants, each segment portrayed

*From* A Forest Year, *written and illustrated by Carol Lerner.*

on a double page spread, one page of text facing a page of illustration. The text is divided into two parts, the upper half in italics offers generalizations about the plants or animals during a particular season and the bottom half comments specifically on the plants and animals pictured.

The watercolor illustrations are lively yet at the same time convey the muted tones and mood of the forest. The language is often poetic, as in the concluding sentence which gives a sense of the cycle of the seasons: "Some of the fruits that the animals miss and some of the seeds buried by them will put down roots in some future spring and start new plants."

A glossary and index are included.

*Sarah Lamstein, in a review of "A Forest Year," in* Appraisal: Science Books for Young People, *Vol. 21, No. 1, Winter, 1988, pp. 42-3.*

This book describes the four seasons in a deciduous forest. The text consists of an introductory paragraph which gives general information, followed by short paragraphs about a few specific animals or plants, which are illustrated on the facing page. The writing style is matter-of-fact and the content of the text is accurate and well-balanced between detail and generality. The reading level seems suitable for the middle elementary grades and most of the language is non-technical. A glossary explains the scientific vocabulary.

The illustrations are beautiful, but some of the relative sizes of animals are misleading (e. g. brown creeper, nuthatches, and cardinals all appear to be the same size). Some pictures are in small white circles to indicate that they are magnifications but there is no indication of the power of magnification.

*Gwyneth E. Loud, in a review of "A Forest Year," in* Appraisal: Science Books for Young People, *Vol. 21, No. 1, Winter, 1988, p. 43.*

*Moonseed and Mistletoe: A Book of Poisonous Wild Plants* (1988)

A book that will intrigue children as well as benefit them, this describes and illustrates various types of poisonous plants: those poisonous to the skin; others with poisonous berries, leaves, flowers, or roots; some poisonous bushes and trees. The text is an interesting mixture of description, instruction, and commentary. The gummy juice of poison ivy, for instance, "is so strong that the amount on a pinhead can give a rash to five hundred people. And it has a long life: scientists got skin rashes from touching a dry plant sample that was one hundred years old." The book is handsomely formatted, with each page framed in a green design and illustrated with either black-and-white detail drawings or meticulous full-page paintings of the specimens discussed, which include hemlock, mountain laurel, mistletoe, and many others.

*Betsy Hearne, in a review of "Moonseed and Mistletoe: A Book of Poisonous Wild Plants," in* Bulletin of the Center for Children's Books, *Vol. 41, No. 7, March, 1988, pp. 140-41.*

Thirty of the more than 700 poisonous plant species found in the US and Canada are presented here with brief descriptions, including indications of the poisonous parts and comparisons with similar-appearing, nonpoisonous plants. Lerner warns that this is not intended as a nature guide, but the reader should glean enough information to become wary of strange plants—plus a host of lurid tidbits: children have been poisoned while using peashooters made from water hemlock; become ill from eating honey made from trumpet creeper flowers; and died from eating Virginia creeper berries.

The full-color illustrations are attractive, but dimensions are provided inconsistently: e. g., blue cohosh is described as one to three feet high, but for bittersweet nightshade only the leaf size is given—and no distinction is made between leaf and leaflet. The index gives both common and scientific names but has some anomalies: e. g., poison oak under "p," poison sumac under "s." Readers interested in poisonous plants would do better to look elsewhere.

> *A review of "Moonseed and Mistletoe: A Book of Poisonous Wild Plants," in* Kirkus Reviews, *Vol. LVI, No. 7, April 1, 1988, p. 540.*

With an attractive cover and catchy title Carol Lerner draws the reader into a well-designed and well-written book on poisonous plants. She features those plants which are truly poisonous, causing severe illness and possible death, and those which are labeled poisonous but cause rashes anywhere from bothersome to debilitating. She has chosen only the most widely known flowering plants, including those which resemble harmless species.

The text is divided into five chapters and covers plants which make one itch, harmful berries, leaves, stems and roots of wild flowers, poisonous parts of bushes and trees, and plants used for holiday decorations. Some are more familiar, such as poison ivy and skunk cabbage, but all of these plants grow in fields and woods. Some are indigenous to America, some were brought by explorers and early settlers and some began as garden plants and have spread to uncultivated areas. The clear, well-focused text is interspersed with numerous black and white pencil drawings and is extended and enhanced by six full page color plates. Names of plants in the color illustrations appear in capital letters in the text, some with pronunciations. There is an index with the scientific names in italics and illustrations in boldface. *Moonseed and Mistletoe* is a must for an elementary school library. It will be valuable for pleasure reading and for research.

> *Nancy R. Spence, in a review of "Moonseed and Mistletoe: A Book of Poisonous Wild Plants," in* Appraisal: Science Books for Young People, *Vol. 22, Nos. 1-2, Winter-Spring, 1989, pp. 47-8.*

Carol Lerner's lovely botanical paintings and drawings are always appealing, and the subject is intriguing to both children and adults. The discussion features selected flowering plants common in many parts of the United States and Canada that "are actually on record as causing people to become sick." Beginning with the ubiquitous poison ivy and poison oak and other species that irritate the skin, five

groups of plants are considered in brief chapters. Varieties of berries, wildflowers, bushes, and trees that are poisonous if eaten are discussed, and the final chapter, "Deck the Halls," is devoted to holly, mistletoe, and bittersweet. One full-page color painting in each chapter groups the plants discussed, and small sketches of some leaves, fruit, or roots are set into the text. In addition to describing the appearance and growth patterns of the plants, Lerner explains their troublesome qualities and sometimes provides a bit of information about their history in this country. Some of the plants continue to be used as food or for medicinal purposes, and the reader is cautioned that this practice is unsafe without very specific instructions for identifying and preparing particular plants. The text is informative without being overly detailed, and though it tends to leave the reader wanting to know more, it also encourages observation of these beautifully rendered and widely encountered plants. Index.

> *Margaret A. Bush, in a review of "Moonseed and Mistletoe: A Book of Poisonous Wild Plants," in* The Horn Book Magazine, *Vol. LXIV, No. 3, May-June, 1988, p. 372.*

This exquisite volume outlines several examples of potentially poisonous plants. Through detailed and precise color drawings, Lerner delineates five different cautionary areas—plants that sting and cause rashes, harmful berries, deadly flowers, dangerous trees and shrubs, and deceiving decorations. The text is clear and well-focused on the topic. The color illustrations are graceful and accurate, providing a beautiful complement to the text. While Peter Limburg's *Poisonous Plants* (Messner, 1976; o. p.) covers similar ground, Lerner's book serves as a marvelous introduction to or a concise attractive review of the subject. Only wild plants are covered here. An accessible beginning book on an eternally popular topic.

> *Steve Matthews, in a review of "Moonseed and Mistletoe: A Book of Poisonous Wild Plants," in* School Library Journal, *Vol. 35, No. 9, June-July, 1988, p. 111.*

It must be difficult to decide which poisonous plants to include in a small book for young readers. This one appropriately focuses on some of the widely known flowering ones of temperate North America. The information seems to be accurate, and a professional taxonomist is listed as a consultant reviewer. The text is lucid and interesting. There are only six color pages of 29 plant drawings, but these are augmented by numerous smaller black-and-white illustrations inserted in the text for details; all indicate size and scale. Lower plants, such as mushrooms and ferns, are not included. There are warnings not to use the book as a definitive identification guide and not to taste any wild plant unless it is positively known to be safe. Some look-alikes are differentiated, such as poison ivy from the common three-leaved wild strawberry, raspberry, and fragrant sumac. Plants are grouped as touch-me-nots, berries, wildflowers, bushes and trees, and holiday decorations (holly, bittersweet, mistletoe). Some common wild plants were missed, such as buttercup and elderberry. An index gives scientific names for most, although too many have genus only. There is cross-referencing, and pages with illustrations are identified. References are not given; one that should have been included for general reading is *Dangerous Plants,* by John Tampion (NY: Universe Books, 1977). All in all, this book is appropriate for upper-elementary and junior-high students and general adults. I recommend it as a library reader and for reference, especially for outdoor enthusiasts and teachers of outdoor education.

> *John R. Pancella, in a review of "Moonseed and Mistletoe: A Book of Poisonous Wild Plants," in* Science Books & Films, *Vol. 24, No. 2, November-December, 1988, p. 98.*

It is exciting to find a book that is both attractive and well written directed at the intermediate audience. This book is an excellent addition to the nature library, introducing readers to some of North America's common poisonous plants. Without alarming readers, Lerner cautions them as to the dangers of these plants, designating identifying characteristics, and comparing them with look-alikes. The text is fluidly written, informative, and is well organized.

Those readers familiar with other books illustrated by Carol Lerner will not be disappointed. Lerner's use of warm illustrations and attention to detail once again portrays the beauty of the natural world. (Could it be that her underlying message here is the environmental adage, "Look, but don't touch?") I strongly recommend this book.

> *Lynne Carol Krueger, in a review of "Moonseed and Mistletoe: A Book of Poisonous Wild Plants," in* Appraisal: Science Books for Young People, *Vol. 22, Nos. 1-2, Winter-Spring, 1989, p. 48.*

---

### Plant Families (1989)

A brief, attractive look at 12 common plant families, with full-color illustrations of representative species drawn to scale. Lerner describes the characteristics of leaf, flower, fruit, and seed, with botanical terms appearing in italics and defined in a glossary. While the text is too technical for the novice, and the lack of botanical names will limit usefulness for serious study, the lovely, precise illustrations of common garden and wayside plants (including the arum, buttercup, composite, grass, lily, mint, mustard, orchid, parsley, pea, pink, and rose families) make this an appealing browsing title.

> *A review of "Plant Families," in* Kirkus Reviews, *Vol. LVII, No. 3, February 1, 1989, p. 211.*

With beautiful, scientifically accurate illustrations, *Plant Families* introduces students to the botanical grouping of plants. Twelve of the largest and most familiar families are examined. Representative species are drawn in life-size watercolors with exquisite attention to detail. Parts of the flowers are enlarged and clearly labeled. The text provides a simple description and helpful clues for identification of family membership. Botanical terminology is printed in italics and defined in a glossary. Left-hand pages are solid text, facing illustrations; this format may be intimidating

to some readers. However, the book is informative and attractive. *Flowers and Flowering Plants* by Arthur Aldrich (Watts, 1976; o. p.) only briefly mentions plant families.

> *Barbara B. Murphy, in a review of "Plant Families," in* School Library Journal, *Vol. 35, No. 9, May, 1989, p. 120.*

This handsome botanical guide with its delicate, precise renderings of wildflowers is a perfect complement to the author-illustrator's *Moonseed and Mistletoe.* An extensive introduction gives a brief overview of the development of botanical organization, the parts of the flower, and the reasons for using this particular component of the plant for identification purposes. Some further suggestions for plant identification are also mentioned. The body of the book covers twelve of the largest and most common plant families found in North America. In a clean, well-designed format each double-page spread covers one plant family, with the text on the left and an illustration of a representative plant within that family on the right. The common name of the family is given in the chapter headings, with the Latin name and a pronunciation guide appearing below it. The text offers some indication of where the plants might be found; provides information about different species within the family; and takes note of distinguishing features in the leaves or the stems—though the emphasis is always on the flower itself. The illustrations on the right-hand page include one full-size painting of the plant, with important details drawn in enlargements. One minor quibble is that the name of the representative plant chosen for each illustration doesn't appear with the drawing but occurs somewhere within the text in small capital letters. Since there is no index, this beautiful book might, therefore, be difficult to use as a quick reference source. Glossary.

> *Nancy Vasilakis, in a review of "Plant Families," in* The Horn Book Magazine, *Vol. LXV, No. 3, May-June, 1989, p. 387.*

*Plant Families* provides a concise introduction to taxonomic principles of plant identification through examination of 12 of the largest and most common plant families: buttercup, mustard, pink, mint, pea, rose, parsley, composite, lily, arum, grass, and orchid. Each group is discussed in simplified, accurate terms, complete with pronunciation keys within the text and a brief, appended glossary. Latin names are made memorable with lively imagery. Descriptions and comparisons of basic floral parts are included, as well as examples of species found in various natural and domestic habitats. A representative individual is illustrated in full color for each family, with clear labeling and painstaking detail not often found in many of the more exhaustive "adult" field guides. Meant primarily as a study guide for young adults, this book can be appreciated and enjoyed by all ages.

> *Susan Mirando, in a review of "Plant Families," in* Science Books & Films, *Vol. 25, No. 1, September-October, 1989, p. 37.*

*Plant Families* is another winner from artist Carol Lerner. Her previous books about plants have been characterized by beauty and accuracy, and this is no exception. Lerner begins this book with an essay on plant classification. She starts with the various attempts that have been made to classify plants, talks about how it is still done according to a "natural system," and tells readers how to look at plants in order to classify them themselves. The rest of the book examines twelve plant families, which are common in the fields and along the roadsides of North America. The characteristics of each family are described, and colorful illustrations of the plant, its flowers, fruit and other important parts, are shown. This sounds as if it would be dry reading, but Lerner's style—and her facts—are interesting. Did you know that cabbage, turnips and broccoli are all mustard plants? Can you imagine that the beautiful and delicate Queen Anne's Lace is probably the wild ancestor of the homely carrot? Were you aware that all of our grains, as well as sugarcane, are in the grass family? *Plant Families* will be popular with students studying plant classification, but it will also attract anyone with an interest in the natural world.

> *Barbara C. Scotto, in a review of "Plant Families," in* Appraisal: Science Books for Young People, *Vol. 22, No. 4, Autumn, 1989, pp. 38-9.*

The author/illustrator has created an intelligent, informative botanical guide and a work of art at the same time. While the common name appears at the top of the page introducing each family, the scientific name and its proper pronunciation are located just below the heading. The beautiful color illustrations are placed to the right of the text so that the illustrated plant parts are side by side with the written explanation. The author encourages young botanists to take flowers apart to examine their construction. Let us hope each reader will pay attention to her cautionary notes on rare orchid species and not subject them to that kind of hands-on scrutiny. However most of her choices are common roadside plants better known as "weeds." There is a helpful glossary in the back.

> *JoEllen Broome, in a review of "Plant Families," in* Voice of Youth Advocates, *Vol. 12, No. 4, October, 1989, p. 236.*

---

### Dumb Cane and Daffodils: Poisonous Plants in the House and Garden   (1990)

Common house and garden plants can be quite poisonous, as Lerner makes clear in this instructive and handsomely designed companion to *Moonseed and Mistletoe: A Book of Poisonous Wild Plants.* While there are many poisonous domestic plants, Lerner selects those that grow over wide areas of North America and those that have a history of poisoning humans. Among the entries are bulbs of the narcissus genus (daffodils, snowdrops, and hyacinths among them); flower garden staples such as four-o'clocks, delphiniums, and poppies; and shrubs such as yew, hydrangea, and wisteria. The artist's elegant, captioned botanical drawings (most in color, a few in black and white) of the flowers, leaves, seeds, and internal parts grace the pages, while the text discusses the plants and their poison potential. Researchers will have to use the index for access to particular species; the text is like a leisurely lecture to

be best enjoyed by browsers or plant fanciers, though everyone would be well advised to familiarize themselves with the dangers from these familiar species. An eye-opener.

> *Denise Wilms, in a review of "Dumb Cane and Daffodils: Poisonous Plants in the House and Garden," in* Booklist, *Vol. 86, No. 12, February 15, 1990, p. 1167.*

Like her companion volume **Moonseed and Mistletoe: A Book of Poisonous Plants,** this overview of common shrubs, climbers, vegetables, and decorative plants with poisonous properties is handsomely illustrated. Lerner's detailed botanical drawings and paintings are the real highlight of the book, though descriptions of the plants and explanations of their effects on humans, especially children and house pets, are capably written. Young readers will be surprised to find some of our most attractive garden flowers—narcissus and lily-of-the-valley among them—included as troublemakers, along with common house plants such as philodendron: "Their leaves—and sometimes other plant parts as well—contain sharp crystals. If the plant is chewed or eaten, these crystals cut into the mouth and throat like hundreds of burning spears. The tongue, mouth, and throat swell, sometimes so badly that it becomes impossible to breathe." This will leave kids with a healthy respect for knowing what flora to look at and leave alone.

> *Betsy Hearne, in a review of "Dumb Cane and Daffodils: Poisonous Plants in the House and Garden," in* Bulletin of the Center for Children's Books, *Vol. 43, No. 7, March, 1990, p. 168.*

Pets, young children, and unwise adults may nibble to their peril on the seeds, berries, leaves, or flowers of a host of common plants described in this elegant, slim survey. As members of the nightshade family, for instance, potatoes and tomatoes carry toxic substances in many parts despite their edible products. Plant poisons may irritate the skin and eyes as well as the digestive system, and in some few instances the perfume of flowers is detrimental to the heart and lungs. The general nature of poisonous effects and the physical characteristics of several plants are briefly described in each of the four chapters, which cover garden flowers, shrubs and vines, vegetables, and house plants. Though scientific terminology is supplied for the names and parts of plants, the brevity of discussion precludes in-depth explanations of the poisonous substances and their functions in the plants, leaving the reader to wonder about some tantalizing phenomena. However, the gaps are balanced by other interesting bits of material, such as the historical uses of some plants in healing and witchcraft, particular instances of poisoning, and the tendency of some cut flowers to poison the water in which they stand. As always, Carol Lerner's lovely illustrations—small drawings of seeds, fruits, and flowers set into pages of text as well as six full-page paintings in color—are very appealing. Useful as a sensible, cautionary introduction and interesting in concept and content, the book includes a short bibliography and an index.

> *Margaret A. Bush, in a review of "Dumb Cane*

*and Daffodils: Poisonous Plants in the House and Garden," in* The Horn Book Magazine, *Vol. LXVI, No. 2, March-April, 1990, p. 221.*

Following her beautiful and informative **Moonseed and Mistletoe: A Book of Poisonous Wild Plants,** Lerner now directs readers' attention to the deadly qualities of hyacinths and dieffenbachia. She begins her book by warning that small children and many of the plants commonly found around the home are not a good combination. However, she also says that most just require some common sense and care to be sure that plant parts are not mistakenly ingested. Readers are warned to watch out for crocuses, snowdrops, delphiniums, and foxgloves among others. All this potential danger is offered with exquisite full-color drawings. While this book performs a service to inform home gardeners of possible dangers, its greatest help is in reaffirming a love for the beautiful creations of nature with the full knowledge that readers can protect themselves from danger and enjoy most of the plants discussed.

*Steve Matthews, in a review of "Dumb Cane and Daffodils: Poisonous Plants in the House and Garden," in* School Library Journal, *Vol. 36, No. 9, September, 1990, pp. 242-43.*

Carol Lerner is one of our foremost writers and illustrators of books on botany for children, and she has produced another outstanding volume. **Dumb Cane and Daffodils** is actually a companion work to an earlier Lerner title, **Moonseed and Mistletoe: A Book of Poisonous Wild Plants.** This current work extends the coverage of Lerner's earlier book to those plants planted in our gardens or brought into our homes. Some of the plants, such as the Deadly Nightshade or the Common Privet, can also be found in the wild because the seeds have been carried there from cultivated areas. The book covers four types of common plants: garden plants, shrubs and vines, vegetables and houseplants. Each plant is described, its toxic parts listed and its effects given. Some very interesting historical material is also included. Did you know, for example, that, early in this century, delphinium seeds were ground up and used to kill body and head lice? Also, during World War II, farmers in Holland inadvertently made their livestock ill by feeding them narcissus bulbs when there was a shortage of animal feed. In discussing her subject, Lerner is never hysterical. Instead, she advises readers to be knowledgeable and cautious about the plants in and around their homes.

Lerner's writing is clear and graceful. She conveys a great deal of information, but does it so smoothly and at such a reasonable pace that the reader never feels overwhelmed. Plant names are given initially in capitals and pronunciations are included where appropriate. There is both an index and a bibliography.

This book is not only useful and well written, but beautiful. The colors of the endpapers, of the lines that border the pages, and of the lettering on the title page are restrained and elegant. Lerner's illustrations are, as always, beautifully done, full of detail, and scientifically accurate. This volume is a welcome addition to Lerner's growing list of botany books, and because of its useful subject matter, most libraries will want it in their collection.

*Barbara C. Scotto, in a review of "Dumb Cane and Daffodils," in* Appraisal: Science Books for Young People, *Vol. 23, No. 4, Autumn, 1990, pp. 26-8.*

## *A Desert Year* (1991)

A handsome introduction to desert animals and plants. On a typical two-page spread depicting summer birds, four species are shown with a page of descriptive text and a full-color drawing. Size and scale are not given; scientific names appear only in the index. Since illustrations are not captioned, the viewer is lured into some minor detective work in order to distinguish the ash-throated flycatcher from the black-throated sparrow. Other illustrations combine above- and below-ground views with inserts showing enlargements. There are interesting bits of nature lore here: the road runner has a patch of black on his back to absorb additional heat; the Texas horned lizard squirts a thin stream of blood from its eyes to irritate its predators; eggs of a Couch's spadefoot toad hatch in a single day. Still, less successful in capturing the panorama of desert life than Bash's *Desert Giant: The World of the Saguaro Cactus* (1989). Index.

*A review of "A Desert Year," in* Kirkus Reviews, *Vol. LIX, No. 13, July, 1991, p. 858.*

Lerner's exploration of the North American desert is logi-

*From* A Desert Year, *written and illustrated by Carol Lerner.*

cally organized into four sections, one for each season; the units are further subdivided to allow for the examination of five aspects of life: mammals, birds, reptiles and amphibians, arthropods, and plants. Lerner concentrates on the adaptations each must make to the desert's great variations in daily temperature and to the arid nature of the landscape. The double-page spreads feature well-designed watercolor paintings, which realistically illustrate facts about the eighty species discussed. Insets offer closer views of some of the smaller creatures and plants, adding to the book's usefulness. While researchers seeking in-depth information about a specific animal or plant will need to supplement this book with other sources, this companion to *A Forest Year* will be especially welcome in classrooms studying the desert biome. An intelligently and attractively designed introduction to the ecology of the southwestern United States. Glossary, bibliography, and index.

> *Ellen Fader, in a review of "A Desert Year,"*
> *in* The Horn Book Magazine, *Vol. LXVII, No.*
> *5, September-October, 1991, p. 612.*

Carol Lerner follows seasonal changes in the desert from winter to winter, describing the behavior of animals and alterations in plants throughout the year. Lovely illustrations provide enough detail to identify the creatures, and descriptions provide interesting details about each of the animals, as well as about conditions such as aestivation and hibernation. This attractive book will help third through fifth graders who need information for reports or who simply wish to familiarize themselves with creatures they may see where they live if they are desert dwellers. *A Desert Year* is certainly a worthwhile addition for any elementary school or public library collection.

> *Sarah Berman, in a review of "A Desert Year,"*
> *in* Science Books & Films, *Vol. 27, No. 7, October, 1991, p. 210.*

This attractive introduction to plant and animal life in the deserts of the southwestern United States is arranged by seasons, winter to fall. For every season, there is a page of text opposite a colorful desert scene for each of five topics: mammals, birds, reptiles and amphibians, arthropods (spiders, insects, scorpions), and plants. Three or four different examples of plants and animals are given in each period, making for broader coverage, although allowing only a brief paragraph for any one creature. Text is bordered by a brown line, and the slightly stylized paintings, which are full-page for the most part, run to page edge, and include cut-aways showing burrows or close-ups of the creatures or floral detail. While there are descriptive clues in the text to help identify the examples shown in these scenes, there are no number locations to lessen confusion created by unfamiliar or look-alike groups. Text indicates pronunciation; the index includes scientific names. A useful survey that can also serve as a discussion starter on the other intriguing topics it mentions.

> *Ruth M. McConnell, in a review of "A Desert Year," in* School Library Journal, *Vol. 37, No. 11, November, 1991, p. 130.*

Youngsters seldom realize that a fascinating variety of living things can survive in a climate where lack of water and 80-degree swings in daily temperatures are the norm. In a companion volume to *A Forest Year* this veteran science author-artist introduces readers to plants and animals of the North American desert. Each page of text describes mammals, birds, reptiles and amphibians, arthropods, or the plants of each season, giving general background information as well as shorter entries about specific examples. On the opposing page is a delicate color illustration of a desert scene, in shades of brown, green, and gray. Many of these are well-done cutaways, showing life both above and below ground. Although few labels are included, the straightforward text makes each example obvious. Tidbits to ponder: the desert tortoise can store a cup of water in its bladder for use when the need arises. The Mojave ground squirrel estivates (a type of summer hibernation) for the seven hottest months of the year, neither eating nor drinking during that time. Lerner's illustrations effortlessly and authentically transport the reader to the hot, dry, sandy environment. This book, with its solid science base, will draw science buffs and browsers alike. Glossary; bibliography.

> *Deborah Abbott, in a review of "A Desert Year," in* Booklist, *Vol. 88, No. 5, November 1, 1991, p. 514.*

Although it may appear to the casual observer that not much of anything lives in a desert, this is most certainly not true. Carol Lerner's *A Desert Year* does an excellent job of illustrating the harsh beauty of the desert. Starting with the winter season, she chronicles the adaptations of mammals, birds, reptiles and amphibians, arthropods and plants throughout the entire year. This informative, very readable and well illustrated book includes facts and information that may not normally be found in a children's book. A pronunciation guide for a number of unfamiliar words is included in the narrative. A glossary, index and short bibliography are found at the end of this book.

> *S. Angela Hoffman, in a review of "A Desert Year," in* Appraisal: Science Books for Young People, *Vol. 25, No. 2, Spring, 1992, p. 38.*

Students whose school curriculum includes a study of the deserts of the southwestern United States will find Carol Lerner's *A Desert Year* a valuable resource. . . . Throughout the text and within the illustrations the interrelationship of food, shelter, and protection is stressed. The layout of the text, which is bordered by a brown line, appears clean and crisp.

The illustrations, which cover the entire opposing page much like a painting, depict animals and plants in natural habitats: for example, a Little Pocket Mouse is shown hibernating in its underground burrow, a Gila Woodpecker nesting in a giant cactus, and termites building intricate tunnels. For variety and unity, three illustrations showing arthropods and reptiles extend across the bottom of their text-related pages. The illustrations are not captioned but can be identified from the descriptions of appearance or shelter in the text. Occasional cutaways further one's understanding of size or detail.

There is a short (11 words) Glossary of general terms (unfamiliar words are defined and pronunciations given within the text), an Index with scientific names in italics, and a short Bibliography of mostly nature guides.

*A Desert Year* would be a useful companion to Lerner's previously published *A Forest Year* and an excellent addition to a school or public library.

> *Nancy R. Spence, in a review of "A Desert Year," in* Appraisal: Science Books for Young People, *Vol. 25, No. 2, Spring, 1992, pp. 36-7.*

---

### Cactus (1992)

A clear, visually attractive introduction by the author of several fine nature titles. Carefully describing the special features that help the cacti survive dry environments (e. g., accordion-pleated skin that expands without splitting), Lerner makes a strong plea for conservation and notes that there is at least one species native to every state except Maine, New Hampshire, and Vermont. Her illustrations are detailed and carefully drawn, though scale is not given; scientific names appear in the back. Useful and unusually well written. Glossary; limited index (omitting some species, e. g., night-blooming cereus, described at length in the text).

> *A review of "Cactus," in* Kirkus Reviews, *Vol. LX, No. 15, August 1, 1992, p. 992.*

Lerner's clear prose and precise botanical drawings in color and black and white enhance this presentation of a plant family that is inherently interesting for its adaptation to arid conditions. The book opens with a description of succulents' mechanism for storing water and proceeds to elaborate on the development of cacti, their differences from other plants, and the environments in which they manage to survive. The contrasts speak impressively: "A medium-sized elm tree, for example, may give off a ton of water in a single summer day" while "a column-shaped cactus standing twelve feet high loses only a little over a tablespoon of water." Carefully labeled diagrams clarify the explanations, as in the cross section of a ribbed cactus stem before and after rainfall. With a glossary and index that increase the book's usefulness for reports, this is a practical and appealing choice for the science shelf.

> *Betsy Hearne, in a review of "Cactus," in* Bulletin of the Center for Children's Books, *Vol. 46, No. 2, October, 1992, p. 48.*

An interesting discussion of the cactus stem—the food-producing, water-storing heart of the cactus—explains how the plant has adapted to dry desert climates; a look at the subfamilies of the cactus, however, reveals that some cacti actually grow in tropical habitats. Many more well-researched facts about the structure, location, and means of survival of these intriguing plants are presented in this brief yet fact-filled study. Lerner's exquisitely crafted black-and-white botanical prints realistically detail specific points as needed throughout the text, and her delicately colored full-page illustrations enrich a winner for the science shelves.

> *Ellen Mandel, in a review of "Cactus," in*

Booklist, *Vol. 89, No. 4, October 15, 1992, p. 426.*

This is a straightforward and beautifully illustrated explanation of a plant family that many people see in indoor gardens rather than in the wild. The book shines with full-color drawings and simple but technically accurate text. Cacti rely on their adapted stems for survival. Starting with this all-important characteristic, Lerner explains the adaptation for dry environments, reveals the nature of the cactus family, and shows how a plant works to gather and save precious water. In the final brief chapter, the author talks about the range of cactus and the unchecked gathering of desert plants that is causing some species to become threatened or even extinct. Schools and public libraries will welcome this succinct and lovely volume. A more detailed treatment for a slightly older audience can be found in *Cactus* (Four Winds, 1982) by Anita Holmes.

> *Steve Matthews, in a review of "Cactus," in* School Library Journal, *Vol. 38, No. 12, December, 1992, p. 123.*

A combination of brilliant scientific drawings and clear, well-organized text makes this a useful and attractive book for both researchers and browsers. Four chapters illuminate the unique features of cacti and the mechanics of cactus growth and survival in the desert. As in her previous volumes, Lerner demonstrates a respect for her audience and knowledge of the subject matter. Index.

> *Maeve Visser Knoth, in a review of "Cactus," in* The Horn Book Magazine, *Vol. LXIX, No. 1, January-February, 1993, p. 104.*

---

### Plants That Make You Sniffle and Sneeze (1993)

The author of several fine natural history books describes the pollens responsible for "hay fever." It's not hay but trees, bushes, grasses, and weeds that produce the airborne pollen that causes sufferers to cough, wheeze, and exhibit cold symptoms. Softly colored, meticulous botanical drawings, in color or b&w, show the enlarged pollen grains and the leaves, flowers, and other parts of common culprits. Not as showy as Lerner titles like *Cactus,* but the drawings are still lovely, as well as precise enough for identification. The text describes the seasonal waves of pollen, the species (both native and introduced) causing allergic reactions, and conditions that increase or decrease pollen production, and adds tips for hay fever sufferers. The index lists plants by common name, and gives scientific classifications of species. Attractive and useful.

> *A review of "Plants That Make You Sniffle and Sneeze," in* Kirkus Reviews, *Vol. LXI, No. 14, July 15, 1993, p. 936.*

Like all of Lerner's plant books . . . , this one is clean, clear, and well organized, with beautifully rendered full-color or black-and-white botanical drawings balancing a somewhat dry text. The integrating theme here will prove particularly important to students afflicted with or researching allergies, as Lerner explains the role of plant pollens in hay fever, shows the functions of pollens in plant reproduction, and describes pollen sources—

including various trees, bushes, grasses, and weeds—and the conditions that trigger pollen release. Some tips on avoiding hay fever pollen, annotations for two books on hay fever plants, and an index conclude the book, which will prove to be first-class preparation for field trips and science projects.

> *Betsy Hearne, in a review of "Plants That Make You Sniffle and Sneeze," in* Bulletin of the Center for Children's Books, *Vol. 47, No. 2, October, 1993, p. 50.*

# John Marsden

## 1950-

Australian author of fiction.

Major works include *So Much to Tell You . . .* (1988), *The Journey* (1988), *Letters from the Inside* (1991), *Take My Word for It* (1992).

## INTRODUCTION

Described by Robert Cormier as "a major writer who deserves worldwide acclaim," Marsden is among Australia's most highly regarded creators of literature for young adults and middle graders. The author of powerful, moving novels and stories in a variety of genres, Marsden imbues his fiction with his belief that young readers should be challenged to question their values and actions; of primary concern to him are the ways in which young people regard the world around them and the lessons they acquire through experience. His works, therefore, are generally regarded as insightful and compassionate explorations of the emotional and intellectual lives of his male and female protagonists. Marsden's thematic emphasis is self-discovery through communication: his characters come to terms with their parents, their schoolmates, and their own feelings through vehicles of self-expression such as journals, diaries, letters, stories, and poems. Although he includes graphic scenes of teenage sexuality and domestic violence in his books, some of which are also noted for their grim tone, Marsden balances these aspects with humor and optimism. He is especially commended for the strength of his characterizations and the depth with which he explores the inner lives of his protagonists. Called "a master storyteller" by Libby K. White, Marsden is acknowledged for expanding the boundaries of traditional genres like the school story and the *Bildungsroman* as well as for his skill as a literary stylist and craftsman.

Marsden graduated from Mitchell College and the University of New England. After holding a variety of jobs for short periods of time, he settled on a career in education, becoming an English teacher at the Geelong Grammar School in Victoria, Australia. Marsden began writing during his school vacations. His first novel, *So Much to Tell You . . .*, relates in diary form the experiences of a fourteen-year-old girl who stops speaking after her father disfigures her face with acid intended for his unfaithful wife. By keeping a diary, an assignment for her English teacher in the boarding school to which she has been sent after unsuccessful psychiatric treatment, she is gradually able to reveal the circumstances surrounding her silent unhappiness and begins to heal emotionally; at the end of the novel, she identifies herself as Marina, reconciles with her father, and begins to speak again. Based on a true incident, *So Much to Tell You . . .* is often celebrated as a unique and effective work: for example, J. V. Hansen calls it "a remarkable achievement," while Karen Jameyson notes that "*So Much to Tell You . . .* stands apart." Marsden's

next book, *The Journey*, is a fantasy set in a land where young people must embark alone on long treks to bring back stories that enable the teens to be accepted as adults. The novel centers on Argus, a boy whose rite of passage leads him through a variety of experiences, both pleasant and frightening, that allow him to bring back seven stories praised for providing insight into the human condition. Called by Margot Nelmes "a rare book, fortifying to the spirit," *The Journey* was inspired by Marsden's experience as an instructor at Timbertop, a rural branch of the Geelong School where he became acquainted with the local practice of sending youths into the bush for a year, where they learn to rely largely on themselves. Marsden's other works for young adults include a school story about a fast-talking, talented teenage antihero, a fantasy that describes how a boy who lives in a mysterious research center acquires a hand-held time machine, a horror story consisting entirely of letters between two fifteen-year-old girls, one of whom has a terrible secret, and a companion volume to *So Much to Tell You . . .* that uses the diary motif to reveal the insecurities of a seemingly popular girl who fears that she is responsible for the breakup of her parents. In addition, Marsden is the author of a humorous fantasy for middle graders about a descendant of Merlin who teaches at a contemporary primary school as well as an informational book that blends his own writing experience with advice for aspiring young writers. *So Much to Tell You . . .* received the Book of the Year Award for Older Readers in 1988 from the Children's Book Council of Australia. The novel was also awarded the first Diabetes Australia Alan Marshall Prize for Children's Literature in 1988 and received the Christopher Award in 1990.

(See also *Contemporary Authors*, Vol. 135 and *Something about the Author*, Vol. 66.)

---

## AUTHOR'S COMMENTARY

*[The following excerpt is from an interview with Margot Nelmes.]*

[Nelmes]: Was *So much to tell you* your first novel?

[Marsden]: I've lost track of the chronology; *So much to tell you* actually started as a film script, which I sent to places like the ABC. They responded quite warmly, but not warmly enough to use it. But I kept being haunted by the story. When I next sat down to write something it was still the same story. Somehow, using a diary format seemed to make it all flow much more naturally. I still think it would be interesting to do it as a stage play.

[Nelmes]: For a teenage audience?

[Marsden]: Yes, although it's had an extraordinary effect on adults—I've had extraordinary feedback from them.

[Nelmes]: And from teenagers?

[Marsden]: A lot of letters, which is surprising. There have been all kinds of surprises in this whole thing, really, and that was one of them. I probably get about a letter a day. And they're very nice—very warm. Also some teachers send in assignments that the kids have done, which is good except it's an odd feeling seeing someone talking about your book, and saying what I used to say about books when I was at school . . . The other thing that surprised me was that a lot of the letters come from quite young people. I didn't think anyone under about twelve or thirteen would read it when I wrote it, but I've had letters from kids nine or ten.

[Nelmes]: Your characters are mainly around fourteen years old; is that because you teach children of that age?

[Marsden]: I think partly that, and partly because it's such a pivotal age. But there's a book coming out in July which has year five kids as the characters, called *Staying alive in Year Five.* And Gatenby is probably about sixteen; year ten, although I imagine him being a fairly mature year ten. He seems to be such a man of the world. I didn't like him at first—I used to be writing about him thinking "This guy's repulsive", but gradually I felt affection for him and now I really like him. But I think he's one of those people who you like in a book, but if you had to share a desk with him for a whole year, or even worse live in a dormitory with him, I think he'd probably drive you crazy. He's always got an answer for everything . . . he's a Motormouth, the kind of kid who'd be popular with other kids.

They like naughty kids. Sometimes it's quite obvious that they get a kick out of a kid who's smart and cheeky with teachers. They find it very entertaining.

[Nelmes]: Was Gatenby based on someone you knew?

[Marsden]: He was an amalgam of three kids who were in a school where I was teaching. They were quite different to the other kids, and quite obviously so—they dressed differently, they just came from a different culture. And the thing that I admired about them was that they persisted in sticking to their cultures, despite a lot of pressure from the school to change. They kept wearing their eccentric clothing and listening to their own music and so on, despite a lot of pressure. The pressures that schools can bring to bear on students can be pretty powerful.

[Nelmes]: Is *Staying alive in Year Five* another funny one?

[Marsden]: It's light—it's got funny moments, but there's a serious side to it. The main character's grandfather has a heart attack at one stage, and a couple of his friends are a bit lost. But it's not tragic or over-dramatic or anything. It's a nice light book.

[Nelmes]: It strikes me that the first three have been incredibly different from each other, almost as if you've deliberately set about doing something completely different each time.

[Marsden]: I don't know how deliberate or conscious it is. I equate it with the fact that I've worked in a lot of jobs and the main reason I've kept changing jobs is that as soon as I feel I get on top of a job then it's lost all interest. So for example, working in a meatworks, for about three or four weeks was great. But once I had the routines figured out it all became unthinking, then it was no longer any challenge or anything else. And so I left—and that's the pattern of my working life. I guess the only reason I've stayed in teaching is because you don't ever get on top of it, because every day you come across a situation which you've never struck before. Or a student acts in a way you've never seen anyone at before. As soon as you start getting smug in teaching, it's usually only a matter of hours before some catastrophe strikes, and I realise that I've misread the situation. I think with books, although no one can ever master a genre, I like to try one genre and see how well I can do in that and then move onto another one and have a go at that. But it's not very conscious. I've been trying to figure out myself why they're so different, and I get a bit puzzled by it.

[Nelmes]: Do you write other than novels?

[Marsden]: I wrote a play about a year ago, which I've only read again once since I wrote it. I think it's got possibilities. And I started another play the other day but I don't know whether that's working out. So I'm toying around with other ideas. And I've always enjoyed writing poetry.

[Nelmes]: I was surprised not to find any in *The Great Gatenby.*

[Marsden]: Yes I try to sneak it in, whenever I can. But I don't think Gatenby's really a poet, except in the water.

[Nelmes]: Do you think that a lot of boys will read it, given that most teenage books are read by girls?

[Marsden]: I hope so. The two genres that boys seem to enjoy most are horror and comedy—in films especially, and I think the same goes for books. It interests me that it's horror and comedy, but I suspect the two are closely related anyway. There seems to be a growing appetite for comedy—almost an insatiable hunger and TV seems unable to manufacture enough comedy to keep up with the need. I wonder how much this hunger for comedy is a reaction to the horror and the grotesqueness of a lot of the things that are going on in the world. I enjoy writing about Gatenby, and I've started a sequel. Comedy's hard to write, intellectually, but not as emotionally hard. Writing **So much to tell you** was an emotionally draining experience. **Gatenby** takes longer to write, and is as difficult to write, but it's not emotion.

[Nelmes]: My favourite is **The journey;** why do you think it failed to make the Short List?

[Marsden]: I think there's probably two things; I think there's an inability of adults in Australia to come to terms with the sexuality of young people . . . and I think there's also an anti-intellectual feeling in Australia, that any book which is at all cerebral will be disdained as being too difficult or too old for children.

[Nelmes]: What about feedback from the kids who have read it?

[Marsden]: Fantastic. Very supportive, and a lot of kids saying they liked it more than **So much to tell you.** They accepted the fact that it was very different, and they said they had to read it more slowly. And some of the younger ones at this school would come back to me several times during the book and say What's happening?; they wanted some clarification or explanation, but I was impressed and pleased that they were prepared to not only read it but to think deeply about it, because that's exactly what I wanted the book to be like, and I wanted it to achieve.

And Pan's reaction to it was really strong. As soon as I wrote it, within hours they offered me a large sum of money, and they rushed it out. There's always been a strong positive feeling that it was something very special. Of all the books, I feel that that's the one that's got an enduring quality, and that I hope that people will be reading for a while yet. So I was disappointed that it didn't make the Short List . . . And the reviewers—one or two have been a bit reserved and a bit diffident, but overwhelmingly the reviews have been so positive, and almost embarrassing in their praise for it . . . It was ironic, because I didn't expect the first one to get on the Short List even—it didn't even cross my mind—let alone win.

[Nelmes]: You're not tempted to leave sex out of your books?

[Marsden]: No, I think it's always been a function of books—and it should be a function of books—(how to say this without sounding pretentious) to almost lead society in new directions, or to open doors, open up new possibilities. It's not a function of books to follow along tamely behind society, coming twenty years along behind, like a lapdog. Books should be blazing trails.

[Nelmes]: Where did the idea for **The journey** come from?

[Marsden]: From the concept of Timbertop, where I taught for four years. The kids go into the bush for a year, and they are away from their parents for most of that time and it's a journey of discovery for them, and a journey of maturity. It's quite basic living. There's no TV or anything. There's no teacher living in their huts with them, but teachers come around and check on them at regular intervals. It's a pretty primitive lifestyle, compared to most lifestyles in western society. Compared to the way Aborigines or Indians lived, it's still quite dependent, though it's probably the best anyone's likely to achieve in our society for the time being . . . It's that kind of toughness and challenge that I think we're starting to lose. It's becoming a soft society.

I like the idea of a journey where Argus does leave his parents, because parents are increasingly trying to tie their children to them for longer and longer periods, which is unhealthy. Also I like the idea that Argus does something that's individual, that it's up to him whether he makes it or not. And I like the idea that he has to acquire certain

*Marsden as a schoolboy at The King's School, Parramatta, Sydney.*

traits before he can move on to the next stage of life. It sounds very conservative, but I don't think I'm a particularly conservative person . . . I consciously wanted to write a book that would integrate various cultures, and to help young people to realise that things that were fundamental to Indian and Aboriginal cultures were also relevant to our culture.

[Nelmes]: I suppose that most English teachers would love to write a book that kids love to read?

[Marsden]: Yes, I think most English teachers dream of it occasionally.

[Nelmes]: Do you think you'll stay a teacher? It sounds like you could be happily writing full-time.

[Marsden]: I don't think I could. I like teaching a lot. Plus, with something like Gatenby, I figure as long as I stay in it I'll never run out of ideas.

[Nelmes]: Why did you decide to become a writer?

[Marsden]: It wasn't a conscious decision . . . I've always read huge quantities of books—incredible quantities of books, and I've always loved writing. I always knew in the back of my mind that there was a very good chance that I'd eventually write books.

[Nelmes]: What do you see as your responsibility as a children's writer?

[Marsden]: Just to be truthful.

[Nelmes]: Truthful to yourself:

[Marsden]: Yes, and to children—and to everything—just to be true, to write things that are true. I don't think there's any moral responsibility because truth covers morality as well. I don't ban pornography for children on the grounds that it's immoral (I don't ban it for children anyway), but I wouldn't give it to children, not because it's immoral but because it's not true. It's different to sexuality which can be true. I like to think that I've got a chance to blaze a bit of a trail. I mean I deliberately took advantage of the success of *So much to tell you* to write *The journey;* I knew that the first book was succeeding and I knew that I could cash in on that in a sense. Firstly to challenge people intellectually, and also to be more explicit about sexuality. And I thought I'm in a position where people will listen to me for at least one more book. If *The journey* failed completely, then the next book wouldn't be in such a strong position, but I knew I was in a strong position.

[Nelmes]: I suppose it would be nice to please everyone if you could, but it's not possible of course.

[Marsden]: Yes, there'll be people who hate *Gatenby.* It's subversive, really. But I know that for everyone who hates it, there'll be people who love it.

[Nelmes]: So you can't afford to be affected by the bad—just the good.

[Marsden]: Which takes a lot of strength, and I don't have that strength sometimes, and then other days I do.

*John Marsden and Margot Nelmes, in an in-* *terview in* Reading Time, *Vol. XXXIII, No. IV, 1989, pp. 4-6.*

---

# GENERAL COMMENTARY

### Agnes Nieuwenhuizen

It seems that the best writers in Australia today are finding the key to the door between popularity and excellence. Six rejection slips and 40,000 copies later, John Marsden is still remarkably laconic about the critical and commercial success of his first venture into writing for young people. "The rejection I treasure is the one that said, 'This book would have no interest for high school students.'" Ten thousand hardback copies have been followed by 30,000 paperbacks, with a further 10,000 on the way. *So Much to Tell You* is being published in the U.K., Canada and the U.S., and enquiries are still coming in, according to its publisher, Walter McVitty.

"Perhaps the reason I was not so conscious of what was happening was that I'd written the next one and a half books before *So Much* started having an impact. It did astonish me when it got on the short list and then won the Book of the Year Award. For a little while it did change my life. Everything was jumping all around me. I'd come home and find telegrams under the door . . . and flowers. But it all passed . . . only lasted a few minutes."

Home is a flat at Geelong Grammar School within sniffing distance of Corio Bay. There is a line of bobbing boats. Does he use them? "No, you could drown out there," he quips in tones that are reminiscent of fast-talking Erle in the third book, *The Great Gatenby.* Despite this disclaimer, sport, physical activity and closeness to nature are important to most of his characters. "It's a powerful attraction, a big challenge. Perhaps it's part of any Australian male's culture. I was brought up in the blind decades of the fifties and sixties when cricket was more important than foreign policy or economic management."

Most of the time, though, John Marsden talked with a quiet passion about reading, writing and our society: what it expects of its children and how it treats them. He talked as a writer, reader and teacher. He is head of Middle School English, but teaches the subject from year seven to twelve. It soon became apparent that his reading, writing and teaching are inextricable; each nourishes and embellishes the other.

Passion and compassion or their absence or their replacement with "synthetic emotions" are constant preoccupations. *So Much* deals with "very strong passions". Is this what made it so successful—and with adults as well as children? "I think it touched on the loneliness that all people feel at some time—but they often hide it from themselves and others, so anything that can slip through their defences . . . is always likely to get a very strong response. I think that somehow the book managed to touch a chord.

"I also think that one of the most important moments in people's lives comes when they first experience betrayal by their parents. Perhaps the betrayal the girl has suffered touches on another shared and universal experience."

Marina, in the book, is terribly scarred emotionally and physically as a result of a bitter struggle between her parents. She is then sent (virtually exiled) to boarding school to recover, which she does with the help of some compassionate and caring adults, a few sensitive peers and her own inner strength.

"Sometimes when I think about what happened to her, I'm appalled to think I could write about such a horrific event, but the next minute I look in the paper and read about some guy who has killed his children rather than let them live with an estranged wife—it's happened at least twice in the past year—so it's all entirely credible." I wondered whether part of the power of the book was the very measured and controlled path to the dénouement—as in detective stories. "I guess I like that kind of book myself. I like subtlety in every area of life—clothing, poetry, art or music. And I did have a binge on detective stories from about Grade 6 to Year 9. Another book that influenced me was *Daddy-Long-Legs* which has this great dénouement where the identity of the benefactor is revealed. However, most of the book was written by instinct and written very quickly."

After an assortment of jobs, there have been ten years in boarding schools. Did the idea for this story come out of recent experience? "It came out of experiences everywhere." There is no elaboration but a characteristically subtle nudge away from any suspected attempt to probe.

He offers one clue to his writing. "Without being too analytical, I think that being observant is a big part of writing." Then there is an almost despairing edge to his voice: "Sometimes I feel as though all I do is write things down. What people do, the way they speak. I keep a scrap book. I keep clippings, write down anecdotes, stories, phrases and words that I hear people say. I've been doing that for about ten years. It started more for English teaching. I've just started the third volume."

Later we come back to the fear of being too analytical about the writing process. "It's like magic. I don't know how it works and if I analyse it too much perhaps the magic will go and I won't be able to do it any more. Time and time again when I'm writing it astonishes me to find things coming together in a very satisfying unity and I'll think 'My God, that ties all those things together.' So much of it is subconscious."

A love of language, stories and words surfaces again and again. "I was always very precocious with words and I've always written things. I was a compulsive reader and still am. Right now, I'm reading *Crime and Punishment* for the first time. I hate expressing myself if I can't do it with precision. It seems so important because your language is such a powerful statement of who you are and what you are. As a child I was always composing stories in my head and living in a world of stories and dreams." Poems are another love, and the books contain a few. "I'm always a bit diffident about it." Perhaps this is why the poems purport to be written by young people? "Yes, I feel I've given myself a bit of a cop-out doing that."

John Marsden talks about the impact of *The Catcher in the Rye* when it first came out. "It was the first time I realized you could be honest on paper." Erle, in **The Great Gatenby,** is also honest on paper as he swims, talks, loves and suffers his way through a term at boarding school. John laughs at the memory of Erle. "He's quite repellent in some ways," but then there is a retraction with an almost paternally benign smile. "No, I do like him. He's just got too fast a mouth. 'Motor-mouth' the kids here would call him." **Gatenby** ("It's a bad pun") is a breezy book, deemed an "entertainment" in the sense in which Graham Greene used the term.

"I got the taste for writing humorous prose when I wrote a completely flippant annual review for four years at Timbertop (Geelong Grammar's bush extension). I used to enjoy doing it so much, I thought I'd tackle it in a bigger way."

We talk a little about the lack of tradition of boarding school stories in Australia. Half-seriously I wonder if he set out to resurrect boarding school stories single-handedly. "I did want to update these because they've always had a fascination for kids. (I loved those *Fifth Form at St Dominic's* tales.) They have romantic ideas about boarding school life and I wanted to show them what it's really like." Switching abruptly back to **So Much,** he says, "Many people, especially middle aged women, come up to me and say, 'That's exactly what it was like.' I take that as a great compliment. Girls also want to know how I could know so accurately what it is like being a fourteen year old girl."

Why are the protagonists of the two "serious" books fourteen? "It's such a turning point in life. It's an age when people are at the point of balance between childhood and adulthood and that makes it very interesting. Their lives are filled with contradictions, ambiguities and complexities. I suppose most literature is about people at turning points—passing from one stage to another."

Which brought us to Argus in **The Journey** who very deliberately sets out to prepare himself for the transition from childhood to adulthood. My suggestion that it is about self-knowledge and self-reliance is gently but firmly rephrased. "For me, it's a book about maturing and growing, which you do through experience."

On his journey in an unspecified time and place ("sometimes I think time can be just a distraction") Argus, as his very name suggests, strives constantly to "see better". Is this also one of the functions of good writing? "Yes, definitely, to give you new perspectives and to help people see through the bullshit. It seems as though there are a lot of people out there—advertisers, various propaganda merchants and even teachers—who, in their own interest, are trying to obscure people's vision. So to give people the tools to see through that is a very important part of education and writing."

On his travels Argus endeavours to embrace enough experiences, knowledge, wisdom and understanding to enable him to construct and tell seven tales to the elders of his local council. If the tales and his telling are considered satisfactory, Argus will pass into loving, productive, responsible and fully-fledged adulthood.

*Marsden on a lecture tour of Australia.*

Where did the ideas come from? "Part of it was from Hermann Hesse's *Siddhartha* and part from Timbertop where something similar to what happens in *The Journey* takes place. There was also something from *The Hobbit*. The journey as a metaphor for life has been well used through literature.

"One of the things I wanted to do was to use the rites of passage of Aboriginal and North American Indian people and put them in a Western setting so they could be more accessible to kids in our culture. The idea of kids going out in the desert or the bush as part of their maturing was really fundamental to these cultures. The fact that we've stopped doing that is very dangerous; one of the things that's causing sickness in our society."

While recognizing that it is very difficult for young people today (particularly urban ones) to undertake such a journey, John Marsden clearly believes it is necessary and feasible. "Yes, it's tough and one of the things that's stopping us is the fear of being attacked which seems to be the dominant passion in our society, so you get people who are more and more scared to travel or go to alien places. People have always been attacked but now the attacks get so much publicity that people are getting more and more controlled by this fear." Though he hopes to encourage

young people to make such journeys, he adds that inner journeys can also be made—through reading, talking and thinking.

When I reiterate that fourteen seems very young for the range of experiences that Argus encounters with such equanimity, he talks again and with great respect of his students. "Many are so mature and responsible that they can and *do* do everything. Their approach to life is so wise that you forget their age. We're living in a society that apparently values and encourages immaturity, yet a lot of kids are capable of extraordinarily sophisticated thinking and writing if they are given the right encouragement and stimulus."

This leads to a lengthy discussion about current approaches to writing. "I've got strong opinions about this. To overstress that writing should be about personal experience can make kids too egoistical and egotistical. It can also cut them off from the great pleasures of creating totally unrealistic worlds to wander through."

*The Journey* is such a world and a philosophical rather than an action packed book. What kind of effort and involvement is demanded of the reader? "It *is* a book where people have to think more. I was hoping it would act as a kind of bridge from the shallow popcorn literature that kids seem to be reading nowadays. I hope they might read this and acquire a taste for something more profound." Would it make a good classroom novel? "Oh yes, I hope so. It would be great if it were used that way. Kids *should* be doing books like *Lord of the Flies* and the novels of Gillian Rubinstein and Victor Kelleher that work on several levels and where the teacher has some function."

The best books are those that "relate to all people's lives and express and explore universal truths. I am big on Jung and so I really like the idea of myths and legends as a way of transmitting all kinds of unconscious messages or elements of society." He warns of the danger of archetypal stories being "sanitized" and losing their "deep and real meaning", citing the Disney version of Snow White as an example. "Apart from all that, I'm a sucker for a good story and I've always had a weakness for writers like Neville Shute and books like *Black Beauty*."

The next story is called *Staying Alive in Year 5,* and another book is being typed. Each is different, perhaps "because once I've written one type, I want to try something new." At present he is happy with the mixture of teaching and writing. "It means that I'm on the boil all the time," though most of the writing is done during holidays.

In conclusion I quote back at John Marsden four of his aphorisms from *The Journey:*

"The wanderer's danger is to find comfort."

"Take care but take risks too."

"No-one can refuse to be involved."

"Until I know you better, I won't know what you're like inside."

"They sound almost trivial out of context," he worries. Was he trying to write a book on how to lead a better life?

A pause, then, "Yes, it's the way I'd like to lead my life if I had more courage. They're very strong restatements of how I believe life should be lived."

*Agnes Nieuwenhuizen, "Know the Author: John Marsden," in* Magpies, *Vol. 4, No. 2, April, 1989, pp. 20-2.*

# TITLE COMMENTARY

### So Much to Tell You . . . (1988)

A riveting first novel which grips the reader from the start. A girl has not spoken for a year; treatment in a psychiatric hospital has achieved nothing and now she has been placed in a girls' boarding school. As part of English she must keep a journal:

> This journal is starting to scare me already. When Mr Lindell gave them out in class I felt the fear and promised myself that I would not write in it, that it would stay a cold and empty book, with no secrets. Now here I am on the first page saying more than I want to, more than I should.

Slowly as the girl writes she begins to acknowledge her own emotions, particularly the ambivalence she feels about her father, meanwhile observing the life of the school and particularly of her dorm.

I found the observation and the characters authentic, the suspense gripping, and the slow and subtle revelation of the truth both painful and illuminating. This beautifully produced book is impressively well structured and well written, and is not to be missed.

*Jo Goodman, in a review of "So Much to Tell You . . . ," in* Magpies, *Vol. 3, No. 1, March, 1988, p. 30.*

**So much to tell you** is John Marsden's first novel. I found it interesting and enjoyable to read, but I found myself wanting to know more about Marina, the writer of the journal. I wanted to know more about why she couldn't speak, more about her family, and more about what happens to her after she starts to speak again.

The story is written as an English class journal and because diary writing is so often used in English classes to encourage self expression, it is very appealing to adolescents to read because they are so familiar with it. This book is a little different to the numbers of diaries/journals that have been published for the adolescent market in recent years. Most are about fairly normal adolescents, their peer groups, families and schools. **So much to tell you** is about a girl who, because of severe psychological trauma cannot speak. She has withdrawn completely and it is through being forced to write a journal for English in her new boarding school that she starts to slowly communicate with others. The book is very worthwhile adolescent reading.

*Elizabeth Dam, in a review of "So Much to Tell You," in* Reading Time, *Vol. XXXII, No. III, 1988, p. 56.*

The diarist of this problem novel is a new student at boarding school, and she doesn't talk. Ever. Through her diary entries we gradually learn that her father is in prison, and there has been some terrible trauma that has left her speechless and facially disfigured. We don't learn her name or hear her speak until the last page. The voice is believably that of a fourteen-year-old, and the diary device has the familiar pleasures and pitfalls of that subgenre: the allure of the secret and private, and the frustration of the claustrophobic perspective and insignificant detail. Teens enjoy the illusion of reading over someone's shoulder; they will also enjoy the suspenseful melodrama at the base of the girl's despair. It's ironic how old-fashioned the "new realism" is looking.

*Roger Sutton, in a review of "So Much to Tell You . . . ," in* Bulletin of the Center for Children's Books, *Vol. 42, No. 8, April, 1989, p. 201.*

Marsden is a master storyteller. His characterizations—especially of young people—are interesting and believable. The descriptions of the girls' relationships are humorous and moving. There are faint echoes here of Richard D'Ambrosio's *No Language But a Cry*, a popular nonfiction YA title. This is an intelligent work of literature which is satisfying both intellectually and emotionally.

*Libby K. White, in a review of "So Much to Tell You . . . ," in* School Library Journal, *Vol. 35, No. 9, May, 1989, p. 127.*

Marsden artfully contrives Marina's narrative to maintain suspense as her story emerges. Ultimately, as Marina begins to reach out, acceptance by others gives her the strength to begin the healing process by reaching toward reconciliation with her father—whose crime is finally known to the reader. A moving story, effectively demonstrating that language is a powerful symbol of emotions flowing between people.

*A review of "So Much to Tell You . . . ," in* Kirkus Reviews, *Vol. LVII, No. 10, May 15, 1989, p. 766.*

Based on a true incident, the story is gripping; it also describes a natural evolution of Marina's coming to terms with her life and her relationships. Slightly less believable is the support she gets from the girls at her school. Maybe in Australia (where the story is set) children are more compassionate than in America, but it is difficult to believe that no one ever makes fun of Marina, either for her scars or her self-imposed silence. Nevertheless, this first novel is unique and affecting.

*Ilene Cooper, in a review of "So Much to Tell You . . . ", in* Booklist, *Vol. 85, No. 21, July, 1989, pp. 1904-05.*

**So Much to Tell You . . .** is a remarkable achievement. It is presented in the form of six months of diary entries by a fourteen-year-old girl. We never learn her name until the last page: it is Marina. Just a pretty name? Or is she Pericles' daughter? Marina is in a girls' boarding school, Warrington, and her English teacher, Mr. Lindell, has given his charges journals, in which they are to write every night, "during Homework (except that Homework here is called Prep)." Marina has lost the power of speech and one side of her face has been disfigured. "The Hospital" believes that in the company of other girls she will learn to talk again, but she talks freely to her diary and even in the second entry her father appears. As in a carefully plotted mystery story, John Marsden little by little reveals the cause of Marina's loss of speech, an appalling trauma, finally, but the reader has been waiting for so long that when the revelation comes, he or she (more likely she) is prepared for anything.

The diary entries are sometimes funny, sometimes sad:

> The last time I gave [Grandma] a card I was about 6 or 7 and I made it myself. Not knowing what to put on it, I went into the newsagent and memorised a message that was on a card in there. I can't remember now exactly what it was, but there was a chicken and an egg and some message about 'your birthday being a good time to get laid.' It didn't make much sense to me but I figured the adults would work it out. They did. That was the last time I made my birthday cards.

John Marsden has known three boarding schools at firsthand and his account of Warrington is vividly accurate: the fluctuations in friendships, the weekend boredom, the bitchiness of the girls in Marina's dormitory, sports afternoons, the School Dance (" . . . despite all the teachers there was still quite a lot of grog around, and some boys got busted in the car park selling Southern Comfort"). But this is not at all a mainstream school story. In a mainstream school story the protagonist would be rebellious and bring difficulties on her own head, finally rehabilitating herself within the school community. Marina is none, does none of these things. She is already a victim when she arrives at Warrington, her problems are not of her own making, and she is in the end saved outside the school as institution.

Marina is befriended by Cathy, who will become unwittingly the catalyst for Marina's resurrection, and in second term, things are getting better, although the diary entries still have a sad pathos about them:

> This term's got a different feel to it; I don't know why. I've trapped myself a bit, because I said I wanted to come back, so now, when I get sick of the place and start hating it, I have to remind myself that it was my choice to be here. I think I set myself up a bit. People are accepting me better though. And I walk along pretty normally now, not shrinking into the walls. And I hand some work in to be marked, when I can do it inconspicuously.

By the time Marina writes her last entry, for 11 July, we have learned the whole sorry tale of the abuses she has suffered and endured, and we catch a glimpse of new possibilities. One may hear, if one listens carefully enough, though they are not quoted in the novel, lines from T.S. Eliot's "Marina":

> Resign life for this life, my speech for that unspoken,

> The awakened, lips parted, the hope, the new ships.

***So Much to Tell You . . .*** is a moving story, tragic, simple, generous, tender. It is the kind of novel that seems to come from nowhere, yet we know it has been with us all the time.

> *I. V. Hansen, "In Context: Some Recent Australian Writing for Adolescents," in* Children's literature in education, *Vol. 20, No. 3, September, 1989, pp. 151-63.*

Like a skilled craftsman painstakingly reassembling the fragments of a shattered vase, the author has delicately put together the pieces of a broken life. With control, sensitivity, and respect, he allows his fourteen-year-old narrator to convey her story through the pages of a journal being kept for an English class. "I don't know what I am doing here," Marina begins. *Here,* we quickly learn, is a girls' boarding school, where she has been sent with "anorexia of speech" since her mother "can't stand my silent presence at home. Sent here because of my face, I suppose." With this enigmatic introduction we begin our painful journey with the silent, observant recluse. As we meet her teachers and classmates and sense her reactions toward them and toward herself, we feel her struggles to come to terms with the tragic event that caused her physical and emotional disfigurement. Although many recent young adult novels have successfully incorporated the journal into their narratives, ***So Much to Tell You . . .*** stands apart. So deftly has the author used the journal that not only do we feel the stab of Marina's conflicting emotions but we also come to understand the frustrations of those around her, many of whom long to help her, and see them as vivid, real characters themselves. While the depression so prevalent in young adult literature definitely exists in Marsden's novel, the power and poignancy of the final scene leaves readers with a sense of quiet exaltation and hope.

> *Karen Jameyson, in a review of "So Much to Tell You . . . ," in* The Horn Book Magazine, *Vol. LXV, No. 5, September-October, 1989, p. 630.*

***So Much to Tell You . . .*** by the Australian writer John Marsden is something of a gem. Its accessible diary format makes it a riveting read, likely to convert even confirmed tele-addicts. Our initially un-named diarist suffers from 'anorexia of speech' and this private relationship with pen and paper is at first all she will risk. As her story unfolds, we piece together the appalling though never sensationalised circumstances which have led to this self-imposed silence and understand that she moves in a world fragmented but one still beautifully observed.

Her writing reflects her inner confusion: she describes an elaborate bedcover with a jigsaw pattern of broken stars, and says she likes the school swimming-pool when it is 'clear and undisturbed'—when peopled, it 'cracks' and 'shatters'. In an early entry she herself is 'a shattered shocked heap . . . trying to put myself and everything back together' and it is intriguing to be party to the reconstruction process.

Schoolmates are, unwittingly, an enormous help, and she is quick to tune into the comfort of their trivia if slow to indicate she has registered their existence. Then come the first cautious nods and shrugs and, in time, the first illicit, triumphant note penned in prep. But for the first spoken words we have to wait for her reunion and reconciliation with her father. In his presence she ceases to be 'the phantom', 'the ghost', and becomes, again, Marina with 'so much to tell . . .'

Like her Shakespearean counterpart, she weathers turbulent seas before coming to port. And all without a tacky teen romance to see her through the hard times.

Joanna Porter, "Acne Isn't the Half of It," in The Listener, Vol. 122, No. 3143, December 7, 1989, pp. 28-9.

**So Much to Tell You** is a discreet novel that never burdens the reader with too much material. Very slowly a few facts emerge from the diary: the girl's parents are divorced, her mother has remarried, her father is in prison, the girl's facial injury was caused by acid thrown at her mother by her father.

This fine novel is a slow, careful journey for diarist and reader out of a prison of silence and toward a reconciliation of sorts with the girl's father and with the trauma that has been inflicted on her. **So Much to Tell You** is highly recommended because it charts so well the inner life of a troubled, thoughtful teenager.

*Marsden at home.*

Susan Perren, in a review of "So Much to Tell You," in Quill and Quire, Vol. 56, No. 1, January, 1990, p. 18.

The Australian novel **So Much To Tell You . . .** by John Marsden is an interesting intermediate example of the realistic genre. Small details of vocabulary and geography give the novel its Australian flavor. In a way this tale is as simple as *Cinderella,* but it is also a complex contemporary story with a strand of horror.

Fourteen-year-old Marina tells her story through a diary a teacher encourages her to write. Her father, mistaking Marina for his estranged wife, threw a vial of acid in his daughter's face. The disfigured Marina was sent to a private girls' boarding school, where she speaks to no one, only writing in her diary, which her teacher occasionally reads.

One difficulty, especially for younger readers, might be that this powerful book has almost no plot. What happened to Marina is revealed only two-thirds of the way through, and some readers will be put off by the puzzling, private meandering of Marina's reflections, though others will be drawn in by curiosity and compassion.

What makes the novel so moving is Marina's gradual recognition that she is bound to her father by suffering and love, and that by forgiving him she can begin to heal part of herself. At the end what she says to him is an act of closure for her period of silence and a poignant beginning: "So much to tell you . . .".

J. D. Stahl, in a review of "So Much to Tell You . . . ," in Journal of Reading, Vol. 34, No. 6, March, 1991, p. 496.

### The Journey (1988)

This is a splendid second novel by the author of last year's award winning **So much to tell you.** It shares with its predecessor an intensity of feeling and clarity of expression, here perfectly blended to form a tale with true legendary qualities. The story and setting are timeless, containing elements of past and future alike. It is a world where people travel by foot or by horse, suggesting the past, while names like Mayon and Temora have a futuristic ring to them. But the story itself is universal.

It is the custom, although apparently a dying one, for youths to set out alone on a long journey, the purpose being to return with seven stories for judging by the district Council. A favourable response would enable the youth to be accepted immediately as an adult, and later as a respected elder. And so Argus embarks on his journey, which takes him through a wide range of human experience, teaching him wisdom every step on the way and endowing him with maturity beyond his years. But it is not so much what happens to him, as how he confronts every situation—joyful and frightening—with relish, faith and stamina, that makes his story so memorable. The seven tales he returns to tell are in themselves intriguing parables, adding further dimensions to his adventures. This is a rare book, fortifying to the spirit, gripping, and worthy of reading more than once.

*Margot Nelmes, in a review of "The Journey,"*
*in* Reading Time, *Vol. XXXIII, No. II, 1989,*
*p. 28.*

[Marsden has written] *The Journey* about a world which is not our world, but which resembles a rural pretechnological version of our world, in which the making of stories and poems is a central part of people's lives. It is a utopian vision. As each person approaches adulthood he or she must go on a journey, searching for seven stories that will be uniquely about himself or herself, and yet also be the stories of all people. *The Journey* tells the journey of Argus, who begins writing poems as he searches for his seven stories. Some of these are fragmentary bits of free verse: for example, after meeting a young woman, he writes

> Skin like rain, but more.
> Eyes like clouds, but more.
> Hair like nightfall.
>
> The rest is you.

Argus does not claim to understand the meaning of all of these fragments. But the more polished pieces, which happen to have traditional rhyme and rhythm, are quite clear. For example, another love song, each verse consisting of a triplet, begins like this:

> Loving you is all I want to be,
> There is, you see, no other world but this,
> The one implanted lightly by your kiss.

Very pop-songish, but with more literary flair, less reliance on tune and beat to carry the feelings, more conscious patterning through the verses.

Later, near the end of his journey, after making love on a beach, Argus remembers "a woman he had helped to bury on a beach [and he begins] to form words in his head": the poem starts

> A vessel, fresh-launched, knows nothing
> Of how the sea behaves.
> All that it has and all that it learns
> Comes from the wind and the reef and the
>         waves.
> Fresh-launched, the vessel does not know
> How even a harbour harbours graves.

The dead woman had also written poetry, and one of her poems is quoted earlier. As befits the book, it is about journeying.

By the end, Argus's last poem is also his last story—a Frostian set of quatrains that begins:

> He walked with his feet on a roadway,
> A path that was clearly defined.
> But the journey that really had meaning
> Was the one that took place in his mind
>                 . . . and ends:
> For there's always a road to friendship
> And there's always a road to fame
> And there's always a road to danger
>         —And a road that wants walking again.

Marsden, or his poetry-writing characters may not be writing top quality poetry. But, considering the almost total dearth of any alternative examples of Young Adult

Poetry, we should be grateful for his willingness to give us satisfying pieces that contribute very effectively to the development of and reflection upon the characters and narrative action.

*John Gough, "Young Adult Fiction Rules—*
*O.K.? So Where's the Young Adult Poetry?" in*
Magpies, *Vol. 5, No. 4, September, 1990, pp.*
*5-9.*

---

### The Great Gatenby (1989)

Teenager Erle Gatenby is sent to boarding school away from the "bad" influences of his previous Government school. This is the story of his first term there. He is a bright student and a wonderful addition to the school swimming team but unfortunately he is also insolent, abrasive and on detention most of the time. Erle is saved from disaster by both his intrinsically good nature and his love for Melanie, the school diving champion.

There are some true highs in this short novel. The description of the school hike is very entertaining and rather moving. Our hero's battle with the dreaded tobacco habit is also well-handled with no unnecessary preaching. Erle's steamy love scene in Melanie's bedroom is discreet and just the right amount of naughty bits. The only real drawback is the confusion of overdone metaphors and trendy imagery. The novel is written in the first person, so perhaps Mr Marsden wanted to present Erle as a bit of a pain-in-the-neck poseur. Overall, though, a neat yarn with great interest value for high schoolers.

*Lesley Gruno, in a review of "The Great Gaten-*
*by," in* Reading Time, *Vol. XXXIII, No. IV,*
*1989, p. 28.*

---

### Staying Alive in Year 5 (1989)

The storyteller is a boy called Scott, but the hero really is the teacher, Mr Merlin, who has at least some of the powers of his great predecessor, Merlin. The children in his class think he is wonderful as does Scott's ex-headmaster grandfather, but others find him difficult to appreciate, so he goes and life returns to unimaginative, unstimulating, conservative normality. One child decided: *Staying alive in year five* is great because it turns real life into fantasy. As befits a story written by a teacher of English, this one is well written, with a lot, besides events in the classroom, going on. A really good, humorous story, which I would recommend to any Grade Four or Five.

*Halina Nowicka, in a review of "Staying Alive*
*in Year 5," in* Reading Time, *Vol. XXXIII,*
*No. IV, 1989, p. 24.*

---

### Out of Time (1990)

This is a novel heavy with mystery. Some readers will find it engrossing, while others will be left frustrated and unsatisfied. The story centres on James, a strong, silent teenager, who lives at a mysterious research establishment referred to only as the Centre. James has secretly befriended an elderly and largely forgotten physicist, Mr Woodforde, who has successfully devised a hand held time machine. Woodforde dies in his laboratory before he has revealed his invention to anyone except James, and it is James who finds his body and secretly removes the time machine. Through experimentation James gains some knowledge of and control over the device. The time machine, however, is only one interwoven theme in this complex novel. The story is revealed through a series of frequently disjointed sequences. Gradually the pieces link up. The mood of the novel is sombre, although there is a flash of comic relief in the form of a very Australian joke. The story concludes, however, on a positive note of growing hope for James. An intriguing novel to which many teenagers should relate well.

*Ashley Freeman, in a review of "Out of Time,"
in* Reading Time, *Vol. XXXIV, No. IV, 1990,
p. 31.*

### Letters from the Inside   (1991)

A very powerful and moving novel which consists entirely of the correspondence between two fifteen year old girls. Mandy responds to an ad for a pen pal and finds herself corresponding regularly with Tracy. From their letters both girls appear to come from comfortable middle class homes, but something isn't quite right and Tracy admits that her situation is actually very different. Despite the initial shock, anger and mistrust engendered by this revelation the girls continue to write and develop a very supportive, revealing and important friendship. Amidst growing hope the novel suddenly comes to an abrupt, disturbing end which leaves one with a sense of quiet horror and just a spark of hope. A compelling story, which totally involves the reader. Highly recommended for teenagers. Younger readers may find it distressing.

*Ashley Freeman, in a review of "Letters From
the Inside," in* Reading Time, *Vol. XXXV, No.
IV, 1991, p. 32.*

After his success with the diary format in *So much to tell you,* Marsden turns to the letter format with similar success in his most recent novel. When 16-year-old Mandy answers a request for a pen-friend in a teenage magazine, she establishes a relationship which goes far beyond the usual light-hearted exchange of news about family, friends and school. The revelation of where Mandy's pen-friend lives and why she is there is horrifying enough to ensure that the reader's attention does not waver.

*Anne Hazell, in a review of "Letters from the
Inside," in* Emergency Librarian, *Vol. 19, No.
4, March-April, 1992, p. 22.*

### Take My Word For It   (1992)

John Marsden's **Take My Word For It** is, rather than a sequel, a companion volume to his 1988 award-winning **So Much To Tell You.** Lisa tells this story, in the inevitable Marsden diary-format, set in a parallel time to the period covered by Marina's diary in the earlier book. Lisa is the "dorm leader"—seemingly confident, aloof and in charge of her own life as well as of others, but reveals her insecurity in the face of her parents' marriage break-up, and of her deep-seated fear that she may be responsible. Marsden's style here is relaxed and more assured than in earlier volumes. His "message" is clear—it helps to express yourself. Vocalising and externalising your fears is the first rung on the ladder to self-discovery. The message will prove even stronger for those readers who have read Marina's diary in the earlier novel. For there is real narrative irony in the parallel interplay between the tragically mute Marina, and the ostensibly outgoing Lisa.

The ending of this novel has an element of bathos, however, in that Lisa's secret does not seem at all surprising given the general tempo of this and other Marsden novels. It is difficult to surprise readers. Nevertheless, there is absolutely no reason to suggest that young readers will concur with me in this judgement. Marsden is overwhelmingly popular, and has been critically acclaimed by no less than the great Robert Cormier who has described him as "a major writer who deserves world wide acclaim".

*Robyn Sheahan, in a review of "Take My
Word for It," in* Reading Time, *Vol. XXXVII,
No. II, 1993, pp. 34-5.*

### Everything I Know about Writing   (1993)

John Marsden has achieved considerable success as a writer for young people with award-winning books like **So Much To Tell You** so that no-one could dispute his word craft. The English language, he says, is his number one hobby. As a full-time writer today, with this his ninth book, he is eminently qualified to talk about being a writer. What is more he is an experienced teacher, and he is continually visiting schools, giving lectures to children and teachers and runs workshops on writing. In this new book, he offers a synthesis of his own writing experience with valuable advice for would-be young writers.

He first offers a stimulating collection of examples of what he regards as good English and bad English. Some of the examples come from the pens of his students over the years, but there are many from newspapers and journals, from television, from poetry and from numerous books and even from advertisements and notices. Many of them are hilarious and will inevitably make fun reading for young people as well as vividly making their points.

Next he offers a series of short chapters on how to be a good practitioner of writing with sound advice on themes like avoiding banality, developing imagination, making effective use of imagination, and using plain English. At the end of each chapter, he provides a revisionary set of homilies. He provides plenty of challenges to his readers with well chosen examples, a few from his own works, for emphasis. His fresh approach can be valuable even for the most seasoned author. He concludes with a list of 500 ideas for young adults for writing their own stories and poems. One can only hope that his enthusiastic presentation will inspire many to take up their pens and become themselves literary award winners.

*John D. Adams, in a review of "Everything I Know About Writing," in* Reading Time, *Vol. XXXVIII, No. I, 1994, pp. 36-7.*

# Barbara Park

## 1947-

American author of fiction.

Major works include *Don't Make Me Smile* (1981), *Operation: Dump the Chump* (1982), *Skinnybones* (1982), *Buddies* (1985), *Junie B. Jones and the Stupid Smelly Bus* (1992).

## INTRODUCTION

A popular writer of humorous fiction for young readers in the early and middle grades, Park is praised for creating works that deal skillfully with problems faced by her audience in a manner considered both entertaining and thought-provoking. Favorably compared to such writers as Judy Blume and Paula Danziger, she is commended for her insight, warmth, and understanding of children and their feelings as well as for her facility with dialogue and characterization. Park focuses her works on the relationships of her boy and girl protagonists with family and friends, at home and in school. Admitting a preference for the underdog, she profiles rebellious loners who refuse to adjust to their environments and often feel inadequate because of their height, weight, intelligence, or personalities. Addressing such subjects as adjustment to divorce and remarriage, sibling rivalry, peer pressure, and personal choices, Park presents her readers with a realistic view of life: her books often lack easy answers or happy endings, and her characters do not necessarily solve their problems. However, Park underscores her works with messages about self-knowledge and self-acceptance, and her protagonists find opportunities to grow emotionally and become more mature through their experiences. Park is often acknowledged for using humor in treating her serious topics: called "one of the funniest writers around" by Betsy Hearne, she invests her books—which she usually writes in first person in a fast-paced conversational style—with both light wit and broad humor. Her works derive their comedy from Park's ability to capture the thoughts and speech patterns of young people. In the view of many commentators, her characters are honest to a fault and can be funny without knowing it. For example, in reference to his repeated winning of the most improved player award for his Little League team, Alex, the narrator of *Skinnybones*, cynically comments that he is "the only one to go from stink-o to smelly six years in a row."

The mother of two sons, Park claims that her children have influenced her writing by keeping her attuned to situations that are humorous to her audience. Stating that her books are meant to make children laugh, she notes, "I do like to think that I leave my readers with a sense that the moments of laughter and joy in life more than make up for the sadness. . . . If my books hold any message for the young reader, I hope it is simply that when they see the name Barbara Park, they associate it with fun." Her first book, *Don't Make Me Smile*, is praised by Marsha Hartos

for achieving "a beautiful balance between humor and sadness" as it describes the impact of divorce on an eleven-year-old boy. Refusing to accept the separation of his parents, Charlie reacts in an erratic but often amusing manner—for example, he tells his spelling teacher that "spelling stinks, S-T-I-N-K-S." At the end of the story, Charlie begins to adjust to his situation with the help of a child psychologist and the passage of time. The sequel, *My Mother Got Married (And Other Disasters)* (1989), outlines Charlie's gradual acceptance of his new stepfather, stepbrother, and stepsister. Park is also the creator of two books about Alex "Skinnybones" Frankovitch: in one of Park's most popular works, *Skinnybones*, Alex envies a star player on his baseball team but attains his moment of glory when he wins a commercial contest and begins to dream of being a comedian, while in *Almost Starring Skinnybones* (1988), Alex, cast as Tiny Tim in his school play, plans to steal the show but ends up helping the lead character when he gets stage fright. In addition to writing works for middle graders, Park is the author of three books for slightly younger children that profile what *Kirkus Reviews* calls "as odd a trio as any in middle-grade fiction": a hypochondriac, a tattletale, and a smart-mouthed genius who become friends when they meet in the principal's office. She is also the creator of three chapter books for beginning readers about Junie B. Jones, a spunky kindergartner who makes humorous mistakes with language and is compared to such popular heroines are Beverly Cleary's Ramona and Kay Thompson's Eloise. Park received the Milner Award for her body of work in 1986 and has also won many child-selected awards for her books.

(See also *Contemporary Authors*, Vol. 119 and *Something about the Author*, Vols. 35, 40.)

---

# TITLE COMMENTARY

### *Don't Make Me Smile* (1981)

But the author does make you smile, proving that there is still room for one more middle-grade problem novel on divorce, if it's done well. Here, the quick-witted, first-person narrative of an honest 11-year-old in reaction to his parents' decision exposes the common syndromes of anger and sadness along with some humorous, individualistic quirks of a sensitive survivor. After some attempts to run away from the situation by ducking school and setting up housekeeping in a tree, Charles begins to confront his parents and learns to use a therapist's helpful distinction between yelling and telling his feelings. Scenes and dialogue have a natural bittersweet flavor and move smoothly to the inevitable adjustment.

> *Betsy Hearne, in a review of "Don't Make Me Smile," in* Booklist, *Vol. 78, No. 1, September 1, 1981, p. 50.*

Charlie is the kind of kid who entertains his friends, challenges his teachers and exasperates his parents. Charlie's parents decide to get a divorce and he decides to go nuts. They try to explain how they feel, but he won't listen. He doesn't want to see his father, and his mother gets on his nerves. He wonders, what does she have to cry about? Her parents aren't getting a divorce! Charlie cries, too. He acts rude. He refuses to go to school. He runs away. His father takes him to see Dr. Girard, a child psychiatrist, who helps him; but he still acts rude. He tells his spelling teacher, "Spelling stinks. S-T-I-N-K-S." He persuades his parents to go on a family picnic, and it is a disaster. Dr. Girard helps him again. Nothing dramatic happens. With the passing of time, Charlie grows up a little and starts accepting what is. As he says, "I guess nothing can keep you sad forever. Forever is just too long." Another book with a funny kid, *Something to Count On* by Emily Moore (Dutton, 1980), is set in the real divorce world with real problems (mother's job, father's inattentiveness). In *Don't Make Me Smile,* life is too uncomplicated. Charlie's parents seem to have nothing else to do but help him adjust. Still, this book achieves a beautiful balance between humor and sadness.

> *Marsha Hartos, in a review of "Don't Make Me Smile," in* School Library Journal, *Vol. 28, No. 2, October, 1981, p. 145.*

Charlie, ten, is the narrator and sees himself as a betrayed victim when his parents announce they are separating and will be getting a divorce. He finds a roundabout way to let his classmates know, being too embarrassed to tell them directly; he's determined to bring his parents together and asks for a family picnic for his eleventh birthday. By that time, Charlie has learned to trust the child psychologist he's been seeing, and when the birthday threesome proves to be an uncomfortable occasion, Charlie puts in a quick call to his therapist; he marches back into the room and politely asks his father to leave, a great relief to all three. And for the first time Charlie smiles on his own, not because someone has told him to cheer up and smile. Believable but not unusual, the story is a low-keyed approach to adjustment. It's competently written, a bit slow-moving.

> *Zena Sutherland, in a review of "Don't Make Me Smile," in* Bulletin of the Center for Children's Books, *Vol. 35, No. 3, November, 1981, p. 53.*

Charlie, almost eleven, won't smile because his parents are divorcing, and—in answer to their inquiries—no, he's not okay and never will be. Charlie takes the situation pretty hard, with shouting fits and poor schoolwork and general rudeness; but time and a sympathetic child psychologist do their bit, so that two months later (on the last page) "I think I've come a long way. . . . I don't go around singing all the time, but I don't cry as much either." Meanwhile his refusal to accept what is happening lands him in some mildly amusing situations—as when he runs away to hide in a tree, with three changes of underwear but no blanket. Charlie's behavior is likely enough, and he could serve as an object lesson/companion in misery for others in the same boat. Beyond that, it's a pretty routine and one-dimensional story.

> *A review of "Don't Make Me Smile," in* Kirkus Reviews, *Vol. XLIX, No. 24, December 15, 1981, p. 1520.*

Nearly eleven years old, Charlie Hickle had developed a number of theories about adult-child relationships, such as "anytime you're upset, you're supposed to yell at your mother. They expect it. It's part of their job." But when his parents tell him that they are getting a divorce, Charlie's world view is skewed. Confusion and anger are manifested as uncharacteristic rebellion and gloom as he sets out to thwart his parents' efforts to create a facade of humor and good fellowship. From the description of his attempt to become a tree dweller to an account of a far-from-cheery family picnic, Charlie's story of his gradual acceptance of the shattering change in his life rings true without being deadly serious. The perspective is consistent with the personality of a bright, articulate preadolescent, yet the parents are not unsympathetic foils for his frustration. And while divorce is certainly not a humorous subject, the topic is handled in a way which reminds one that tears and laughter are the warp and woof of the human comedy. Written with warmth and insight in an unhackneyed style, the book is not simply an earnest tract on problem solving but a readable story of a likeable youngster.

> *Mary M. Burns, in a review of "Don't Make*

Me Smile," *in* The Horn Book Magazine, *Vol. LVIII, No. 1, February, 1982, p. 46.*

## Operation: Dump the Chump (1982)

Most children will understand, and many will sympathize with ten-year-old Oscar's story of how irritating he found his brother Robert, age seven. It seems unlikely that many of them will find the story convincing, although they may find it amusing. In a breezy first-person text, Oscar describes his detailed plan for getting rid of Robert by convincing their parents that some elderly neighbors need a boy to live with them and also convincing the neighbors that the family is in financial trouble and must get rid of Robert because he eats so much. That Oscar's lies would be believed—up to a point—is credible; that any normally intelligent child of ten would believe his scheme would work is not credible. It doesn't work; Oscar is told that he will have to spend the summer with the neighbors at their beach cottage. (That's punishment?)

*Zena Sutherland, in a review of "Operation: Dump the Chump," in* Bulletin of the Center for Children's Books, *Vol. 35, No. 7, March, 1982, p. 136.*

Sure to delight kids in the same way as *Tales of a Fourth Grade Nothing* or *How to Eat Fried Worms,* this is the story of 10-year-old Oscar Winkle and his malevolent plan to get rid of his pesky younger brother Robert. From Oscar's description of "the chump," it's easy to sympathize with him. For instance, the first year Oscar was allowed to send out Christmas cards he chose ones with fat, jolly Santas that said "Merry Christmas, _____." Robert fills in all the blanks, "Poopoo Hed." Oscar's ingenious eight-step plan involves an elderly neighbor couple who ostensibly need a boy, and Oscar's supposedly destitute father, too poor to feed his children. Kids might see the punch line coming, but they'll be laughing out loud all the way there.

*Ilene Cooper, in a review of "Operation: Dump the Chump," in* Booklist, *Vol. 78, No. 13, March 1, 1982, pp. 899-900.*

This present-day novel of sibling rivalry has as antagonists two smart-aleck brothers, Oscar Winkle, about 11, and 7 1/2-year-old Robert. Determined to live a Robertless summer, Oscar concocts a decidedly ridiculous and unrealistic scheme, *Operation: Dump the Chump.* He tells the elderly Hensons down the street that his father has lost his job for clowning around and can no longer afford to feed all four members of his family. He tells his parents that Mr. Henson's health is failing and could use a young boy as a live-in helper. Sure that his fake newspaper ads and letters will result in Robert living with the Hensons for the summer, Oscar is crushed when his plan backfires and results in a summer for him with the Hensons. This episodic story closes with Oscar's new plan for Robert: boarding school. This is humorous light reading with a minimum of characterization and suspense. If they can accept the extreme contention between the two brothers (amusing examples are provided), children may find Oscar's efforts justified and entertaining.

*Ellen Fader, in a review of "Operation: Dump the Chump," in* School Library Journal, *Vol. 28, No. 9, May, 1982, pp. 64-5.*

[*Operation: Dump the Chump* belongs] to the Firefly series [published by Macmillan]. Series books don't make me entirely happy. Their formula presumably makes life easier for the publisher; an *en bloc* order does likewise for the teacher; the fairly rigid format provides the writer with a framework; tough bindings ensure the book's longevity. But who are they for? The bright and able readers—do they need a series? The wide vocabulary of the books appears to be quite hard for the reader with difficulties. And what young readers seeking a book for pleasure will make a bee-line for a series book? Someone, please explain.

That said I found *Operation: Dump the Chump* quite entertaining, despite the touch of American "twee" (as opposed to British "twee") in its humour. I cared for the beginning: "I've never liked my brother. Never. And it's silly to pretend I do," with its follow-up: "I was watching my favourite cartoon show when my mother walked through the front door. She was carrying a big bundle of blue blankets". So we know where we are as *Operation: Dump the Chump* moves into action with Oscar, the narrator, trying maniacally to dispose of brother Robert, now aged almost eight. There's a happy twist in this well-constructed story. . . .

*Gene Kemp, in a review of "Operation: Dump the Chump," in* The Times Educational Supplement, *No. 3798, April 14, 1989, p. B8.*

This title in the 'Firefly' series, which bridges the gap between easy readers and longer fiction for children of seven to eleven, was first published in the US, and there are a number of Americanisms, though nothing that makes the text inaccessible. Eleven-year-old Oscar thinks up a brilliant plan to get rid of his younger brother Robert, whom he finds intolerable, for a whole summer. It involves dumping him on some elderly neighbours, by spinning them a hard-luck story about his own family, and by telling his parents that the frail Hensons need a boy about the house to help them. He is utterly convincing, but the plan does go a little—and satisfyingly—wrong. The story is broken up into parts that correspond with each stage of his operation; it is direct, funny, and fluent, and the family atmosphere with squabbling siblings (Robert *is* a terrible tease) comes over well.

*Jennifer Taylor, in a review of "Operation: Dump the Chump," in* The School Librarian, *Vol. 37, No. 3, August, 1989, p. 106.*

*Operation: Dump the Chump* is a classic! The opening line states it all. We feel so sorry for Oscar having to tolerate the exuberant humanity of his younger brother Robert. Not sorry enough though to condone his sophisticated, dishonest plan to burden two charming, elderly neighbours with Robert all summer long. I was really excited when things began to go awry and it looked as though his comeuppance was going to last. Hooray for author intervention and Oscar's demise!

*Pam Harwood, in a review of "Operation:*

*Dump the Chump,"* in Books for Keeps, *No. 63, July, 1990, p. 11.*

---

### Skinnybones (1982)

Park is one of the funniest new writers around; this time out she tackles Little League baseball. Her hero, Alex Frankovitch (short, thin "Skinnybones"), is a realist who knows that winning the Most Improved Player awards for six years only means that each year he has started out "stink-o" and gone to "smelly." His particular nemesis this year is T. J. Stoner; T. J.'s brother plays for the Chicago Cubs, and T. J.'s so good he could be suiting up with them momentarily himself. At least that's the way it seems to Alex, who always manages to be on T. J.' s wrong side and in the middle of a disaster because of it. Alex finally comes into his own when he wins the Kitty Fritters TV Contest and thus gets his own taste of what being a celebrity is like. The ending is improbable (Alex's letter wasn't all that good), but otherwise **Skinnybones** equals tickled funny bones.

> *Ilene Cooper, in a review of "Skinnybones," in* Booklist, *Vol. 79, No. 2, September 15, 1982, p. 118.*

This opens with sixth-grader Alex sending off a smart-alec entry to a Kitty Fritters commercial contest, but it soon settles into his problem as the smallest, poorest, most humiliated player in the local Little League—as he puts it, referring to his repeated winning of the "most improved player" award, "the only one to go from stinko to smelly six years in a row." Alex's response to embarrassment is show-off quipping and clowning, and even if you can't accept the motivation—Alex says he goes through all this for the caps, which make him look like a real ballplayer—you're bound to give in to a few laughs at his retorts. Alex's chief bane is T. J. Stoner, whose older brother is a major leaguer and who, himself, is the best Little Leaguer any coach has laid eyes on. Because Alex can't keep from heckling T.J., T.J. delights in challenging Alex to contests, and consistently shows him up. But on the day that T.J. becomes National Little League Champion, Alex shares a bit of the glory—winning the Kitty Fritters contest he had entered as a joke. Whereas T.J. will get into the *Guinness Book of World Records,* Alex will go on TV. He's already off and dreaming about his future as a comic. It's a neat enough outcome for this sort of easy walk.

> *A review of "Skinnybones," in* Kirkus Reviews, *Vol. L, No. 14, July 15, 1982, p. 799.*

**Skinnybones** is a slim story that attempts to deal with a boy's complex about his small size. Supposedly, the solution to his problem is his fine sense of humor. However, Alex never cements any real friendships, has no confidence in his ability to play Little League baseball, and bemoans the fact that he wins the Most Improved Player trophy. He is so down on himself that it is difficult to sympathize with him. He needs help—as does the novel.

> *Joe McKenzie, in a review of "Skinnybones," in* School Library Journal, *Vol. 29, No. 4, December, 1982, p. 84.*

We've all known an Alex Frankovitch (Skinnybones)—an undersized kid who attempts to compensate for a small stature with a big mouth and a debatable sense of humor. A funny, irreverent story for every child who has ever been an underdog—and for parents and teachers who sometimes forget it isn't easy to be a kid. This book is fun, don't miss it. Highly recommended for grade.

> *Lena Denham Smith, in a review of "Skinnybones," in* Catholic Library World, *Vol. 54, No. 11, May-June, 1983, p. 425.*

---

### Beanpole (1983)

Lillian begins her plaintive, often funny, story just as she turns thirteen; five feet six, she's called "Beanpole" by her classmates in seventh grade. She has a three-part birthday wish: to get a bra, to dance with a boy, to become a member of the Pom Squad. Her wishes are granted, to an extent: Mom buys the bras Lillian doesn't really need, she does dance with a boy but learns he's been paid to do it, and her strenuous efforts at Pom Squad try-outs fail. However, she has a supportive family and two good friends, and by the time the story ends Lillian has learned to laugh about her problems. Light, amusing, adequately written, this deals with a situation (usually temporary) that can cause real pain to sensitive adolescents; it's pleasant reading but is marred by being just a bit too cute, with some stereotyping of minor characters.

> *Zena Sutherland, in a review of "Beanpole," in* Bulletin of the Center for Children's Books, *Vol. 37, No. 2, October, 1983, p. 35.*

Park continues to depict, amusingly, the imperfection of preteen life. For seventh-grader Lillian Pinkerton, adversity is spelled *h-e-i-g-h-t*. The butt of many jokes (when she's asked to turn sideways and stick out her tongue, her nemesis notes how much she looks like a zipper), Lillian nevertheless has some hopes for her seventh-grade year. Dancing with a boy, wearing a bra, and making the Pom Squad are her birthday wishes, which, though they partially come true, do not always bring with them the hoped-for happiness. While this situation is less fresh than *Operation: Dump the Chump,* Park will win readers with her light, bright comedic style. The cover, which depicts Lillian towering over her dancing partner, will be an immediate drawing card for browsers.

> *Ilene Cooper, in a review of "Beanpole," in* Booklist, *Vol. 80, No. 3, October 1, 1983, p. 300.*

Being the tallest girl in seventh grade isn't the easiest thing in the world. But not only is Lillian Iris Pinkerton 5 feet, 6 inches tall, she's as skinny as a beanpole. This is a fact that her class won't let her forget!

One of her best friends, Drew, is short and pudgy, but she's smart. Her other good friend, Belinda, isn't very bright, but she's pretty. As far as Lillian is concerned, she's nothing but a loser, the biggest loser in the seventh grade.

For her 13th birthday, Lillian makes three wishes which

she is convinced will make her a winner: "I want to dance with a boy; I want to wear a bra; I want to make the pompom squad." One by one, it looks like each of her wishes is going to come true.

But things don't always work out the way Lillian wants them to. Instead of becoming a "winner" in her prescribed way, Lillian learns to laugh at herself; she also learns that she really *is* a winner already, in spite of her build. She even learns that there are many times when it helps to be tall.

But Lillian not only learns this for herself, she helps her two friends learn that what they think about themselves is more important than what others think.

Barbara Park is offering her readers encouragement. In this perceptive novel about growing up, she captures the feeling of what it is like to be a seventh-grade "loser" and shows that a place on the pom-pom squad or dancing with a boy isn't necessarily the way to success.

> *Lisa Lane, "7th Grader becomes a Winner," in* The Christian Science Monitor, *October 7, 1983, p. B3.*

Lillian Pinkerton, victim of every label that a tall, skinny frame can suggest, knows names *can* hurt. She expects the big event, turning 13, will transform her right away if her three birthday wishes materialize. She wants to get a bra, dance with a boy and make Pom Squad. Her locker room status secure once she has the bra, Lillian chairs the decorations committee for a penguin theme dance where wish two comes true. Humiliated to learn that the boy won a five dollar dare for asking her to dance, Lillian backs away from Pom tryouts. Through Granddad's applied psychology, she practices, survives the first cut and builds self-confidence that helps her survive losing in the final selection. That Lillian can investigate alternative ways to express herself, joke about her height and value both of her friends, brainy Drew and fashion-fixated Belinda, is proof of progress made. Told in a first-person rambling style, **Beanpole** features common sense outlined in humor with a three-dimensional supporting cast of relatives and friends. Park clearly depicts Lillian's need to stretch toward maturity while at the same time fearing to let go of a child's faith in magic wishes.

> *Pat Harrington, in a review of "Beanpole," in* School Library Journal, *Vol. 30, No. 3, November, 1983, p. 81.*

Growing up isn't easy for Lillian Pinkerton, who stands 5 feet 6 inches tall in the seventh grade. On her birthday, she wishes for the three things that she thinks will make her life bearable: to wear a bra, to dance with a boy, and to make the school pom squad. Her mother can't understand her desire for a bra, because she certainly doesn't need one. When she does get to dance with a boy, he's the shortest one in school. Her closest friends have too many problems of their own to be very sympathetic. Only her grandfather can convince a discouraged Lillian to change her mind and try out for the pom squad.

At first, **Beanpole** seems like just another of the growing-up genre which appeals to the girl who perceives herself

as too short, tall, thin or fat. But under examination it is so much more. The story moves quickly but not predictably as Lillian's problems are solved. Even the cover illustration is attractive and inviting. Those who enjoyed Park's **Skinnybones** will not be disappointed in **Beanpole.**

> *Pat Nutt, in a review of "Beanpole," in* The Book Report, *Vol. 2, No. 4, January-February, 1984, p. 37.*

---

### Buddies (1985)

Park pulls off a neat trick here. She has written an absolutely hysterical novel that incorporates a poignant message. One reason that 13-year-old Dinah Feeney wants to go to camp is to find out what it's like to be popular. Her best friend at home is a nice enough girl, but Wanda does not have that "it" quality that draws kids, and Dinah's own appeal suffers by association. She vows that things will be different at Camp Miniwawa, yet before her bus has even pulled out of the parking lot, unattractive, inarticulate Fern Wadely has latched on to her with a vengeance. Two of Dinah's cabin mates, Cass and Marilyn, are just the sort she has been hoping to make friends with, but while they are willing to chum around with Dinah, Fern is not part of the package. Though she is given a number of opportunities to break Fern's stranglehold on her, Dinah cannot bring herself to be deliberately cruel to the pathetic Fern. It is not until Dinah sees Cass and Marilyn slipping away that she decides to rid herself of Fern, and she does so in a particularly harsh manner—she pushes her out of a canoe in which the four of them are riding. Fern finally gets the message. Instead of freeing Dinah, however, this incident binds her to the girl even more strongly. She cannot believe she would hurt another person so deliberately, and the memory of her cruelty stays with her long after camp is over. Park has done a shrewd job of drawing her characters. Fern is so lumpish, so unappealing that even the most kindhearted reader will understand Dinah's frustration. Yet enough about Fern's family life is disclosed to gain her a good deal of sympathy. On the other hand, Cass and Marilyn are not depicted as typically snobbish kids. They are worth knowing, funny, and bright, if considerably less thoughtful than Dinah. By not making her characters caricatures, Park fleshes out a dilemma that many preteens and teenagers have to face. The humor that has glimmered in Park's previous novels shines here, and she uses the first-person narrative to the best possible advantage, putting her on a par with (and sometimes above) writers such as Blume and Danziger.

> *Ilene Cooper, in a review of "Buddies," in* Booklist, *Vol. 81, No. 16, April 15, 1985, p. 1198.*

Dinah tells the story of her two weeks at a girls' camp, and this is not a formula camp story in which a reluctant camper adjusts. Dinah, thirteen, really wants to go to Camp Miniwawa, and she especially wants to make a fresh start there, to create a new image and be popular. She hasn't anticipated the possibility that a frightened, uncouth girl who happened to get on the bus at the same time will cling to her like a starving leech. Fern is a dolt, and

Dinah isn't the only one who thinks so. It's up to Dinah, however, to tell Fern that her cabinmates don't want her with them. Stalling, Dinah is finally driven to impulsive violence; she pushes Fern out of a canoe. There's no sweetened ending: Fern is adamantly resentful and Dinah unhappily guilt-burdened. The story is painfully believable, although the characters (Fern and the cabin counselor, particularly) tend to be overdrawn, but they are well-suited to their roles; the writing style is capable, the only weakness of the story being that it seems overextended, like a short story that grew beyond control. But it's a rather trenchant short story.

> *Zena Sutherland, in a review of "Buddies," in* Bulletin of the Center for Children's Books, *Vol. 38, No. 9, May, 1985, pp. 173-74.*

Written in Park's familiar, humorous and easy-to-read style, this book is similar to her earlier novel, **Operation: Dump the Chump,** in theme, but it is not as successful. Thirteen-year-old Dinah Feeney decides that she is going to be popular at Camp Miniwawa. A new place and new friends seem to offer her the chance to concentrate on being "in," but on the way to the two-week camp she meets Fern Wadley. Fern tags along with Dinah and wants to be her buddy—much to Dinah's distress. Cassandra and Marilyn, two cabin mates, decide that Fern, the camp klutz, must be dumped. Dinah ends up volunteering to tell Fern to get lost because she feels that she could do it in a nice way. Instead she pushes Fern into the lake when she becomes exasperated with Fern's gaucherie and her own inability to get rid of Fern. The holiday is ruined, and both girls sadly return home on the same bus. The portrayal of Fern as a nerd is so stereotyped (from her name to her uncouth habits, like picking her feet) that this first-person narrative becomes a casebook collection of repulsive behaviors. *Don't Ask Miranda* (Clarion, 1979) by Lila Perl is a far more sensitive look at peer pressure and unpopularity, while O'Connor's *Yours Till Niagara Falls, Abby* (Hastings, 1979) is a much gentler treatment of personality conflicts at camp.

> *Lorraine Douglas, in a review of "Buddies," in* School Library Journal, *Vol. 31, No. 9, May, 1985, p. 94.*

Barbara Park has written a breezy, upbeat novel about teenage popularity in a summer camp. She manages to capture the feelings of helplessness, fate, hilarity, and pathos that face the average girl who wants everyone to like her. Dinah Feeney ("the kind one"), thirteen, goes to camp and sees it as an even chance to achieve a popularity that she doesn't enjoy at home. She is saddled with Fern almost immediately—a girl who lacks good looks, common manners, and the ability to socialize. Dinah fears that she will forfeit any chances of joining the "in" group with Fern as a liability. She tries to ignore the girl, but Fern dogs every footstep. Her cabinmates—the beautiful one, the funny one, and the tough one—find it easy to be cruel, but Dinah feels sorry for Fern. Urged by her cabinmates to dump Fern, Dinah finally does near the end of the two-week vacation. But she is sorry and feels guilty. She tries to apologize, but fails. Dinah resolves to treat her unpopular school friend Wanda with the same enthusiasm and re-spect that she gave her new, popular camp friends. An age-old message is given a new look here. It's refreshing to see that peer pressure doesn't always prevail.

> *Rita M. Fontinha, in a review of "Buddies," in* Kliatt Young Adult Paperback Book Guide, *Vol. XX, No. 3, Spring, 1986, p. 12.*

Some battles at camp are personal ones, waged when a camper is faced with difficult choices. **Buddies** by Barbara Park relates Dinah Feeney's stay at Camp Miniwawa. She decides that for the first time in her life she is going to be one of the Popular Ones, not just her old, kind "pushover self." When a total nerd at camp, Fern Wadley, wants to be her best friend, Dinah has a tough decision to make. She can be mean to Fern and be part of the popular crowd, or she can be kind and kiss her plans for herself good-bye. This well-written, thought-provoking novel provides no easy answers. Because Dinah's predicament is dealt with realistically, it is an excellent choice for the mature reader.

> *Lynne T. Burke, in a review of "Buddies," in* The Five Owls, *Vol. 4, No. 5, May-June, 1990, p. 94.*

---

## The Kid in the Red Jacket (1987)

A boy learns to adapt to his new environment in this realistic story.

Howard, 10, is miserable when his family moves from Arizona to Massachusetts in the middle of the school year. His first days in a new school are as bad as he expects—and, worse, the 7-year-old next door, Molly, decides Howard is her new best friend. After some trial and error, Howard extricates himself from Molly's enthusiasm, and makes some friends his own age.

The tone of this first-person narrative is rather unpleasant—Howard's complaints and self-pity get stale long before he stops feeling sorry for himself. The plot seems to be constructed simply as a story about moving, and the writing is undistinguished. There are some strong flashes of humor, however, especially in the interchanges between Howard and Molly. The story's voice usually sounds like that of a real 10-year-old; it might serve to remind a reader in the throes of change that things do get better.

> *A review of "The Kid in the Red Jacket," in* Kirkus Reviews, *Vol. LV, No. 1, January 1, 1987, p. 59.*

Park, who has turned out some laugh-filled junior novels, continues that string with this amusing story of 10-year-old Howard Jeeter, who is having trouble with his family's move from Arizona to Massachusetts. The story has some pathos as well when six-year-old Molly Vera Thompson, a child of divorce living with her grandmother, takes an immediate shine to her new neighbor Howard. Molly's continual presence embarrasses Howard both in the school yard and at his house during a visit from Pete and Ollie, two new friends. In a realistic scene, Howard chooses the approval of the two boys over Molly's feelings and even joins in when Ollie grabs her doll and begins throwing it around the room. Not until Pete stands up for

Molly does Howard realize that his desire to be a part of the gang has crowded out some of his decency. Although the plot is predictable, Park's shrewdly drawn characters carry the day. Howard and Molly are funny but not in ways inappropriate for their ages. For instance, middle graders will certainly appreciate why Howard has a paroxysm of embarrassment when he finds out his new street is named Chester Pewe.

> *Ilene Cooper, in a review of "The Kid in the Red Jacket," in* Booklist, *Vol. 83, No. 12, February 15, 1987, p. 902.*

With her usual humor and child's-eye perspective, Park tackles a 10-year-old's adjustment to his family's move from Arizona to Massachusetts. Howard Jeeter hates leaving his friends more than any other aspects of moving, *all* of which he hates. His adjustment to the new school is complicated by a first-grade girl across the street. She follows him around adoringly until he deliberately hurts her to impress a couple of sixth-graders who have invited him to play football with them. Although the focus is ostensibly on adjustment, the real theme here is self-confidence and self-knowledge, as Howard sorts out the complexities of friendship. The first-person narrative never gets heavy, however, and readers will appreciate the easy dialogue and sympathize with Howard's difficulties, as when his overactive imagination keeps him up during his first night in the 200-year-old house his parents have bought: "What would I do if some dead colonist came back for his pillow or something?" The sensitive characterizations keep this from being either a flip or formulaic treatment of a common problem.

> *Betsy Hearne, in a review of "The Kid in the Red Jacket," in* Bulletin of the Center for Children's Books, *Vol. 40, No. 7, March, 1987, p. 133.*

Park commiserates with the problems of pre-adolescence in this first-person narrative of ten-year-old Howard Jeeter, whose life is temporarily destroyed by a cross-country move to a new family home. Howard knows what awaits him as he drives east from Arizona with his insensitive parents, bawling baby brother, and smelly basset hound to a historic house in Massachusetts: he will be a vulnerable and possibly despised "new kid." His first contact on Chester Pewe St. is Molly, an intrusive first-grader with red hair "styled kind of like Bozo's." Her desperate attempts to be friendly drive Howard to distraction and also make him anxious that his new classmates won't accept him if he hangs around a first grader. Howard's coming to terms with Molly's need for friendship is a particularly well-done part of the novel. As in **Operation: Dump the Chump** and **Beanpole**, Park writes in a witty and bittersweet style about the awkward, super-sensitive age of early adolescence; her humor both reflects and sharpens the sensibilities of her readers in the areas of family and friend relationships. Another first-rate addition by this author to the middle-grade popular reading shelf.

> *Linda Wicher, in a review of "The Kid in the Red Jacket," in* School Library Journal, *Vol. 33, No. 7, March, 1987, p. 164.*

## *Almost Starring Skinnybones* (1988)

In response to popular demand, Alex Frankovitch is back, fighting the same old classmates with a new weapon: he's going to be a Star.

When his satirical letter for the National Kitty Fritters Cat Food Contest earns him a role in a commercial, Alex begins signing autographs, even though no one wants them. But the commercial is disappointing: he plays an embarrassingly small, inept boy running away with a very large cat; and the fan club he starts consists only of his grandparents, his dog, and a neighborhood three-year-old. His classmates remain unimpressed—even derisive. Undaunted, Alex tries out for Scrooge in a school play, but he's cast as Tiny Tim. Now slightly daunted, he plans to steal the show—until he's made painfully aware that he may have gone too far. His reactions surprise even himself.

Much of the humor here lies in narrator Alex's total self-involvement and lack of awareness of his effect on other people: paradoxically, this gives the book's closing pages a somber edge. Park risks undercutting her own protagonist, but her gamble pays off with a wiser story; middle graders will continue to ask for more.

> *A review of "Almost Starring Skinnybones," in* Kirkus Reviews, *Vol. LVI, No. 4, February 15, 1988, p. 281.*

A sequel to **Skinnybones** finds Alexander Bell Frankovitch starring in a cat commercial after winning a contest with his honest essay about Kitty Fritters cat food. This taste of glory leads him to grab the limelight in an assembly program and try out for the school play. He only gets a bit part but is pivotal in forcing the lead actor past terminal stage fright so the show can go on. Like Park's other books, this is funny and reflective of young readers' insecurities, but it's more frenetic than usual, with Alex's craving and smart-mouth bids for attention a source of irritation in an unrelenting first-person narrative. The ending, in which another junior high student confronts Alex with his obnoxiousness, is a welcome dramatic pause—better late than never.

> *Betsy Hearne, in a review of "Almost Starring Skinnybones," in* Bulletin of the Center for Children's Books, *Vol. 41, No. 7, March, 1988, p. 143.*

Alex "Skinnybones" Frankovitch is back, this time starring in a national TV commercial after sending a prizewinning letter to the Kitty Fritters cat food company. Alex wears sunglasses and is signing autographs (mostly for people who don't want them) in preparation for his newfound celebrity, but things don't quite work out the way he hoped. Onscreen, he plays a sniveling six-year-old running away from home with a cat and pulling a bag of cat food in his little red wagon—quite an insult for a 12-year-old. The kids at school think the whole thing is a hoot, and the fan club he starts for himself consists of his cat and a neighbor so young he has to bring his potty seat with him to the meetings. Alex has one more chance at fame when he wins a role in *A Christmas Carol,* but it's as Tiny Tim, not the more irascible Scrooge as Alex would have liked. When Scrooge gets stage fright, Alex has an opportunity to take over the role, but finally putting someone else first, he gives Scrooge the encouragement he needs to go on with the show. As always, Park is laugh-out-loud funny and kids will have a wonderful time with this story. Teachers, too, should try it as a read-aloud, though getting the class settled down after a few chapters might be a chore.

*Ilene Cooper, in a review of "Almost Starring Skinnybones," in* Booklist, *Vol. 84, No. 13, March 1, 1988, p. 1185.*

Alex Frankovitch figures that he has finally made it. Having won the National Kitty Fritters Commercial Contest, he hopes to impress the folks back home. At last, he thinks, he will shed his humiliating nickname "Skinnybones" and develop a new, more powerful persona through a successful TV career. There is just one hitch: Alex's big break into commercials is as a wimpy, six-year-old weakling, wearing a Davy Crockett cap and pulling a red wagon. To further compound his problems, his nemesis Annabelle Posey is enjoying his discomfort, and Alex can't even land the lead in the Christmas play. This lively sequel to *Skinnybones* won't disappoint readers; once again, Alex's struggles to reconcile his dreams with the rough realities of middle school are related in a humorous, fast-moving style.

*A review of "Almost Starring Skinnybones," in* Publishers Weekly, *Vol. 233, No. 11, March 18, 1988, pp. 87-8.*

Alex "Skinnybones" Frankovitch returns as a media star—in his own mind, at least. Fans of *Skinnybones* will remember that Alex, the winner of a cat food contest, was slated to star in a TV commercial. Here Alex prepares for stardom by signing autographs for his highly reluctant public and by trying to drum up a fan club. Unfortunately, the commercial brings ridicule rather than fame; but is Alex daunted? Not he—he only tries harder to impress, with predictably disastrous results, including a not-so-starring role in the Christmas play. Through it all, he remains a cheerfully unfazed, obnoxious braggart; and what is particularly astonishing is that Park has made Alex a likable character in spite of himself. Once again demonstrating her remarkable ear for dialogue, she also shows a good sense of timing in this fast-paced outing. Every child knows an Alex Frankovitch, so this is sure to be as popular as its predecessor.

*Kathleen Brachmann, in a review of "Almost Starring Skinnybones," in* School Library Journal, *Vol. 34, No. 8, April, 1988, pp. 103-04.*

Alex Frankovitch is back in a lively sequel to *Skinnybones* that is ripe with opportunity for Alex to become a star and thereby shed his "wimp" image. He has an attitude problem even his best friend has difficulty accepting; Alex is brash and precocious and never lets well enough alone. He is, however, as real in all his bravado and desire for charisma as the next seventh-grade boy. The outcome of Alex's bid for the glitter of stardom is also realistic and not all that he expected. Readers will respond to the hilarious di-

alogue, realistic situations, and even to Alex's brief moments of humanity. With plenty of action and characters that are predictable but never flat, the book is a good choice for that next request for a short, funny book.

*Elizabeth S. Watson, in a review of "Almost Starring Skinnybones," in* The Horn Book Magazine, *Vol. LXIV, No. 5, September-October, 1988, p. 627.*

---

### My Mother Got Married (And Other Disasters) (1989)

This refreshing book about parents' remarriage picks up where Park's *Don't Make Me Smile* left off. It is already difficult for Charlie, 11, to accept his parents' divorce, but then his mother starts dating Ben Russo, one of those guys "you see in commercials walking through the woods swinging an ax and eating acorns and wild berries." Ben's wife died five years ago, forcing him to raise their two children alone, but that doesn't mean Charlie "automatically [has] to like him." When Charlie's mother and Ben marry and the Russos move into Charlie's house, life becomes disastrous. Thomas, five, follows Charlie everywhere; Ben's daughter Lydia monopolizes the bathroom and the phone; Ben doesn't seem to like Charlie; and his mother has no time for him anymore. Charlie's honesty and sensitivity is as hilarious as it is touching; his reflections are unique and his realizations are meaningful. This book is a delight for all readers, but will be especially appreciated by those in Charlie's situation.

*A review of "My Mother Got Married (And Other Disasters)," in* Publishers Weekly, *Vol. 235, No. 3, January 20, 1989, p. 148.*

Park has consistently shown an ability to shed humorous light on potentially dreary situations. In this sequel to *Don't Make Me Smile,* Charles' unhappiness about his parents' divorce and about being "displaced" by stepfather Ben (and Ben's teenage daughter and preschool son) makes him a prime candidate for a surprisingly fresh treatment of a common theme. Although the protagonist's first-person voice is entertaining, his selfishness is candidly realistic. At one point he ruminates about having to share a room with five-year-old Thomas: "Sharing is not normal. . . . The only time lions like to share is when they're already finished eating. And to me, that's not sharing. That's full." Later he refuses to feel flattered that Thomas follows him around: "It would be like wading through a swamp and coming out with a leech on your leg. You would never really feel proud that you're the one it picked." The author has a way of introducing information naturally. In describing his best friend, Charles talks about how his "mother says it's getting hard to tell us apart. This is funny only if you know Martin is black." The plot is hardly noticeable among the family interactions. Charles denies adjusting to the new situation even after Ben's quiet understanding brings them closer. But he does accept it, and comes close to admonishing readers (many of whom will have known similar situations) to do the same.

*Betsy Hearne, in a review of "My Mother Got Married (And Other Disasters)," in* Bulletin of the Center for Children's Books, *Vol. 42, No. 6, February, 1989, p. 154.*

Stepfamilies, reflects 11-year-old Charles, mean "stepping aside so that a man who's not your father can hold your mother's hand." Having divorced parents was bad enough, but then Charles' mother marries Ben, "one of those nature guys . . . you see in commercials walking through the woods . . . eating acorns and wild berries." Ben's two children move in, and Charles has to share his bedroom with five-year-old Thomas. Charles' reflections on his new situation, told in perceptive contemporary language, are laced with humor and emotion. At times both funny and touching, this sequel to **Don't Make Me Smile** paints a realistic picture of life in a blended family.

*Elaine E. Knight, in a review of "My Mother Got Married (And Other Disasters)," in* School Library Journal, *Vol. 35, No. 7, March, 1989, p. 178.*

When readers last met Charlie Hickle in **Don't Make Me Smile,** he was railing over his parents' divorce. Now, some months have passed and to Charlie's dismay, there is a new complication—his mother's suitor, Ben Russo, and Ben's two children. Teenage Lydia is a pain, but it is adoring five-year-old Thomas who really grates on Charlie. When Ben and Mrs. Hickle marry, things are even worse, with Thomas now sharing Charlie's small room. Stories about divorce are nothing new, but Park does a superb job of giving this one a fresh feel. Charlie's first-person dialogue is humorous but also realistically bitter. In too many problem novels, the protagonist sees the error of his ways and drops previously unsympathetic behavior. Not Charlie. This kid is mad, and he is not willing to give up his anger until a near tragedy tempers his feelings. While the accident that befalls Thomas is somewhat contrived, Charlie's reactions to it are subtle, reinforcing the hints that Charlie's situation will change, but slowly. A story of surprising depth.

*Ilene Cooper, in a review of "My Mother Got Married (And Other Disasters)," in* Booklist, *Vol. 85, No. 13, March 1, 1989, p. 1195.*

A year after his parents' divorce (**Don't Make Me Smile,** 1981), Charlie Hickle has another shock: his mother marries Ben, a quiet man who is "as different from my dad as you can get," a widower with two children who seem to take over Charlie's house.

Thomas, five, is delighted to share Charlie's small room, his worship of his new stepbrother making him a real pest; teen-age Lydia is always on the phone—except when she's locked in the only bathroom. Meanwhile, Charlie, a self-centered only child who is used to his mother's full attention, has a predictably tough time adjusting and spends most of the book sulking, feeling sorry for himself, or being rude; only after he is inadvertently responsible for Thomas falling from the roof does he take a hard look at himself and start to meet his nice new family half way.

Nothing extraordinary here, but Charlie's narration is an engagingly deft blend of humor and honest self-appraisal. Having thrown a tantrum when his mother offers her new mother-in-law his bed for the night, he observes, "I don't

usually explode like that in front of strangers. Normally I save the worst behavior for those I love." He also realizes that the bickering that follows his withdrawal from his new siblings is a step in the right direction. Not deep, then, but right on target; kids who love *Superfudge* will love this too.

*A review of "My Mother Got Married (And Other Disasters)," in* Kirkus Reviews, *Vol. LVII, No. 8, April 15, 1989, p. 629.*

Barbara Park's third book [to be published in England] is a contemporary tale of relationships as seen through the eyes of a child, Charlie. An original publication in America the book endlessly betrays its New World origins. The first-person spinner of this tale is well into "Geez", "Ohmigod", meatballs, Dunkin' Donuts, waffles, honey (term of endearment), and "What d'ya know". We are well used to Americanisms and to colloquial American but this particular book does seem over the top: small town America writ large.

The story itself starts off as it means to go on—'My parents are divorced'. Thereafter we are into a joint custody situation, and learn all about Charlie's mother falling for the tree-planting Ben Russo. Charlie didn't dig Mr. Russo at all. In the end love triumphs and Charlie learns how to live in changed circumstances.

There is plenty of incident in the book, lots of domestic ups and downs to keep the story buzzing happily along yet I found much of it rather ordinary, somewhat wordy and over-written. **My Mother Got Married** is the latest in Macmillan's 'Firefly' series; a valuable series possibly losing its way a little with this new addition.

*W. M., in a review of "My Mother Got Married (And Other Disasters)," in* The Junior Bookshelf, *Vol. 54, No. 4, August, 1990, p. 191.*

Eleven year old Charlie tells us in first person narrative and naturalistic dialogue his own account of household life after his parents' divorce. The settlement has arranged for him to live mostly at his mother's house, and at first this makes him entirely happy. But troubles come thick and fast when she takes up a relationship with a widower with two off-putting children who eventually move in to share every aspect of his own personal life.

In the twelve short chapters Barbara Park brings, with exemplary objectivity, insights into an area of pained relationships as compassionate as they are entertaining—in the best Judy Blume tradition. The background and overtones of dialogue are very American, but the situations of privacy invaded, parent-child bonding fractured and self-centred conniving are all very recognisable.

This will provide a thoughtful yet entertaining read for grade 5 and 6 children, especially among those who have experienced family break ups.

*Bernice Eastman, in a review of "My Mother Got Married (And Other Disasters)," in* Reading Time, *Vol. XXXV, No. IV, 1991, p. 27.*

### *Maxie, Rosie, and Earl—Partners in Grime* (1990)

Park does it again. Here's a book so funny, readers can't help but laugh out loud. Three misfits come together in the principal's office. Earl Wilber is a new boy, a hypochondriac, who makes a fatal mistake when he is reading aloud. Instead of saying "John sailed, himself," it comes out "John soiled himself." The next time he's asked to read aloud, Earl refuses, and is sent to Mr. Shivers' office. Rosie is a tattletale, whose teacher is fed up with her, and Maxie, a wiseguy, has cut a hole in Daniel W.'s shirt. When Mr. Shivers doesn't have time for them, the unlikely trio decide to cut the rest of their classes—and then worry for the rest of the weekend they will be found out. While the story sounds straightforward enough, Park's characters are so real, yet so wild, the actual plot hardly matters. The incredibly fast pacing, the one liners, and the weird twists (at one point the kids end up in a dumpster—a scene portrayed on the dust jacket) make this irresistible. A good readaloud, too, if librarians and teachers don't mind giving their students a few ideas.

> *Ilene Cooper, in a review of "Maxie, Rosie and Earl—Partners in Grime," in* Booklist, *Vol. 86, No. 13, March 1, 1990, p. 1348.*

Three justifiably friendless fourth graders are sent to see the principal, who can't talk to them just then and sends them back to class; in a moment of ill-considered panic, they run out the door together and hide in a dumpster during a fire drill. Since they know the janitor saw them leaving, they pass an anxious weekend plotting and worrying about what will happen on Monday. The punishments are minimal—the janitor hasn't reported them—but the experience enables them to change their behavior; best, they become friends.

Park's use of funny-sounding, probably unfamiliar words will elicit belly laughs, as will her characters' outrageous predicaments. The nervous new kid who says and does the wrong thing, the officious tattler, and the puny genius who invites teasing—all are familiar types; but as drawn here, they'll win empathy as well as laughter. A minor demerit: crawling into dumpsters is dangerous. Sure to be a hit.

> *A review of "Maxie, Rosie, and Earl—Partners in Grime," in* Kirkus Reviews, *Vol. 58, No. 6, March 15, 1990, p. 428.*

Maxie Zuckerman, age 10, is resented by his classmates for receiving top grades, and Maxie resents their resentment. Earl Wilber, new in town, is a lonely, nervous fourth-grader. In another classroom is a habitual tattler, Rosie Swanson. The three meet outside the principal's office (Maxie's guilty of cutting a hole in a bully's T-shirt, Earl is there for refusing to read aloud and Rosie's tattling is rattling her teacher) and embark on an escapade, thus forging a friendship that injects each with a dose of self-confidence. It's evident why these youngsters dislike school (their unreasonable teachers aren't much help), but they get away with some deceptive behavior. A promising premise is almost totally sidetracked here by a threadbare plot, trite dialogue—the author feels that a brief glossary is needed to explain the obscure vocabulary that comprises Maxie's insults—and less-than-appealing characters.

While a subtle theme exists about the joys of friendship, any other pluses in this book are difficult to find.

> *A review of "Maxie, Rosie and Earl—Partners in Grime," in* Publishers Weekly, *Vol. 237, No. 15, April 13, 1990, p. 66.*

Three elementary school misfits, thrown together by chance, find friendship and a bit of maturity in Park's latest effort. Rosie is a chronic tattletale, Maxie is the class brain (and therefore the butt of jokes), while Earl is the nervous newcomer who can't help getting silly in tight spots. All three find themselves waiting on the bench in the principal's office one Friday afternoon and end up cutting school together. A chance fire drill just as they are making their escape forces them to take refuge in the school dumpster (hence the grime), when they are finally able to flee, Earl realizes that the notorious kid-hating janitor has seen them. A weekend of worry and plotting follows, as they try to figure out how to silence Mr. Jim, or perhaps come up with a reasonable explanation to offer the principal on Monday. By the time things are sorted out, the three have become friends, and they have learned a bit about controlling themselves in situations that would formerly have led to trouble. The promising beginning, with a chapter devoted to the events leading up to the meeting in the office, should hook readers, but the story as a whole never quite takes off. The teachers and parents are not terribly understanding—indeed, they often seem a bit dense—but neither are they uncaring. None are fleshed out enough to seem real, however. Maxie, Rosie, and Earl do show some growth, but the process seems forced, and their actions over the weekend of worry even silly. The story is not told with the same skill found in Park's previous novels for a slightly older audience. The basic ingredients are here, but the end product is less than the expected sum of the parts.

> *Elaine Fort Weischedel, in a review of "Maxie, Rosie, and Earl—Partners in Grime," in* School Library Journal, *Vol. 36, No. 8, August, 1990, p. 149.*

---

### *Rosie Swanson—Fourth-Grade Geek for President* (1991)

Following a wonderful debut (*Maxie, Rosie, and Earl*) that left readers wanting more, Rosie Swanson is back, still funny, "still bossy and overbearing," still buddies with fellow misfits Maxie and Earl, and still a stickler for the truth. This time, she's had it with being picked on and, with Maxie and Earl cheering her on, decides to run for president of her fourth-grade class. But who will vote for "average" when perky, pretty, and popular all want to be elected? As it turns out, the political arena is no place for truth-telling Rosie, who discovers that she has to "smile at kids who make me puke" ("Maxie said it's called 'sucking up' "); that people can steal campaign ideas; and that there's a lot of difference between telling the truth to be mean and telling the truth to be honest. Park, as usual, is right on target with kids' problems, and Rosie learns some pretty tough things about friendship and popularity. With thoroughly believable characters and plenty of laugh-out-loud lines, her experience makes for a very good read.

*Stephanie Zvirin, in a review of "Rosie Swanson: Fourth-Grade Geek for President," in Booklist, Vol. 87, No. 22, August, 1991, pp. 2147-48.*

In this sequel to **Maxie, Rosie and Earl—Partners in Grime,** Rosie runs for fourth-grade president in an attempt to gain more clout at school. Using Maxie's advice about choosing a platform that will distinguish her from other candidates, Rosie focuses on the abysmal cafeteria lunches. But her two popular competitors wrangle strategic information out of the easily intimidated Maxie. Seeking revenge, Rosie spreads a secret to besmirch the reputation of one of her opponents. Her plan backfires, but she learns from the experience. Park's characters are no more likable this time around: Rosie fully deserves the "snitch" moniker, and isn't remorseful until it is she who suffers. Further, the comedy is strained and the dialogue corny. Still, Rosie's first-person narrative offers an inside look at school elections and the ramifications of resorting to smear tactics.

*A review of "Rosie Swanson: Fourth-Grade Geek for President," in Publishers Weekly, Vol. 238, No. 39, August 30, 1991, p. 83.*

The stars of **Maxie, Rosie, and Earl: Partners in Grime** return, as odd a trio as any in middle-grade fiction. Narrator Rosie is running for president of her class; if she can't win, she'll at least take her opponents down with her. With an uncle in law enforcement, Rosie believes it's her duty to inform on wrongdoers: when she's the victim of sabotage by another candidate (cute soccer star Alan Allen), her retaliation is a "secret" note to her classmates alerting them to Alan's past—shoplifting as a first grader. Her tale is as bright and funny as they come, especially when plumpish Earl and too-smart Maxie are on the scene as reasonably loyal allies. Rosie loses the election—but somehow, readers will want to cheer her on to further adventures.

*A review of "Rosie Swanson: Fourth-Grade Geek for President," in Kirkus Reviews, Vol. LIX, No. 17, September 1, 1991, pp. 1168-69.*

In a runaway sequel to **Maxie, Rosie, and Earl,** Rosie recounts her bid to outstrip pretty Summer Lynne Jones and popular Alan Allen in a race for fourth-grade president. She's determined that somebody average (with glasses) should stand a chance, and she campaigns on the issue of improving cafeteria food, which of course gives Park plenty of room to exercise the humor of disgust so appealing to this age group. There's no stinting on the meanness to which kids can stoop, including Rosie, who learns unequivocally that stooping can backfire. Rosie's best friends, Maxie and Earl, maintain sidekick status, and there are minor quickstudy characters as well, especially the nasty girl who delights in downgrading Rosie's chances ("YOU'RE GONNA LUUUU-OOOOZE. YOU'RE GONNA LUUU-OOOOZE"). While the third-person narration in the previous book was from Earl's point of view, here the first-person narration is by Rosie,

who has a glibness that is natural but results in an offhand, sometimes choppy style. The peer group dynamics are almost uncomfortably lifelike, the tone frenetic, and the readership assured.

*Betsy Hearne, in a review of "Rosie Swanson: Fourth-Grade Geek for President," in Bulletin of the Center for Children's Books, Vol. 45, No. 2, October, 1991, p. 46.*

In this sequel to **Maxie, Rosie, and Earl—Partners in Grime,** the same three losers team up to help Rosie challenge the school jock and the class cutie pie for 4th-grade president. It is a funny story with plenty of lively action and humor, but in Park's inimitable fashion she interjects a serious note. Rosie oversteps the bounds of propriety, accepts her comeuppance and, in the end, becomes once again her indomitable self.

*P. G. S., in a review of "Rosie Swanson: Fourth-Grade Geek for President," in Childhood Education, Vol. 68, No. 2, Winter, 1991, p. 108.*

---

### Junie B. Jones and the Stupid Smelly Bus (1992)

One of the initial titles released under [Random House's] First Stepping Stone imprint, chapter books aimed at newly independent readers and arranged in series, Park's (**Skinnybones**) jolly caper is the first installment to feature Junie B., a feisty almost-six-year-old who is not at all happy about riding the bus on the first day of kindergarten. In fact, she doesn't like a single thing about this vehicle: not the kids who get on it ("Loud kids. And some of them were the kind who look like meanies"); not the door ("If it closes on you by accident, it will cut you in half, and you will make a squishy sound"); and not the black smoke it emits ("It's called bus breath, I think"). Other equally candid, on-target perceptions fill Junie B.'s first-person narrative, which is peppered with reader-involving questions ("Only guess what?"; " 'Cause guess why?") that help to propel the story at a whiz-bang pace. When a classmate tells Junie B. that kids will pour chocolate milk on her head on the way home, the spunky child finds a way to avoid the dreaded bus. Park convinces beginning readers that Junie B.—*and* reading—are lots of fun.

*A review of "Junie B. Jones and the Stupid Smelly Bus," in Publishers Weekly, Vol. 239, Nos. 32-3, July 20-1, 1992, p. 250.*

In the "First Stepping Stone" series, a genuinely funny, easily read story. Junie didn't like riding the bus to her first day of kindergarten, so when it's time to go home she hides in a supply closet until everyone but the janitor has left. She has a fine time exploring the contents of her teacher's desk, the school library, and the nurse's office—until she has to go to the bathroom and finds it locked. Only when Junie calls 911 to report this emergency is she located by the frantic adults who've been searching for her. Junie's abrupt, ungrammatical narration sounds just like the feisty young lady seen in the b&w drawings [by Denise Brunkus], with droopy socks, wispy hair, and spit-shined (literally—she licks them) shoes. Kids may need some persuading to read about a younger child, but they're sure to enjoy the understated humor.

> *A review of "Junie B. Jones and the Stupid Smelly Bus," in* Kirkus Reviews, *Vol. LX, No. 15, August 1, 1992, p. 993.*

Park is truly a funny writer. Although Junie B. is a kindergartner, she's sure to make middle graders laugh out loud when they read about her adventures on the first day of school. Even the most insecure readers will feel superior because they know so much more than she does. Brunkus's occasional black-and-white pencil illustrations are appealing and reinforce the mood of the text. Junie B. is a real character; she talks a lot, is funny without knowing it, and honest to a fault. This book will get lots of peer recommendations, and younger kids will enjoy listening to it when read aloud. It's a real hoot!

> *Gale W. Sherman, in a review of "Junie B. Jones and the Stupid Smelly Bus," in* School Library Journal, *Vol. 38, No. 11, November, 1992, p. 75.*

Park, one of the funniest writers around, usually reserves her talent for middle-graders. Now she brings her refreshing humor to the beginning chapter-book set. The perennial question, Will kids read about those younger than themselves? is enthusiastically answered in the affirmative in this case. It's hard for anyone to resist Junie B. A cross between Lily Tomlin's Edith Ann and Eloise, Junie B. (she insists on the B.) is on her way to kindergarten, but that doesn't mean she has to go gently into that abyss. In riotous first-person she describes how she learns the concept of school busing ("WHERE'S THE STUPID SMELLY BUS GOING TO?"), meets her new teacher and the principal ("The principal is a baldy"), and makes new friends ("That Jim, I hate"). To avoid riding the bus home on her first day, Junie B. hides out under the teacher's desk and has a very enjoyable time sticking gold stars on her forehead and writing with "Brand-new chalk that's not even out of its little box yet!" Fortunately for readers, Junie B. is found, paving the way for another book in the series. Pencil illustrations by Denise Brunkus add to the fun.

> *Ilene Cooper, in a review of "Junie B. Jones and the Stupid Smelly Bus," in* Booklist, *Vol. 89, No. 7, December 1, 1992, p. 671.*

### Junie B. Jones and a Little Monkey Business  (1993)

The fractious kindergartner of *Junie B. Jones and the Stupid Smelly Bus* has a new baby brother her grandma calls "the cutest little monkey!" Junie hasn't seen him yet, but she *has* told the kids in her class that he's "A REAL, ALIVE, BABY MONKEY," and she's taking bids from her "bestest" friends for the first look. So far she's got Lucille's locket, Grace's ring, Lucille's red sweater, Grace's hightops, and Lucille's red chair. But when Junie tries to turn in the extra snack tickets that she's also extorted, she finds herself in the principal's office. Kids who like literal-minded Amelia Bedelia's linguistic misadventures will probably enjoy Junie's. Occasional sophisticated words ("confiscate"; "beauteous") and Junie's nongrammatical

speech may challenge new readers; if so, this may work best as a readaloud for Junie's contemporaries.

> *A review of "Junie B. Jones and a Little Monkey Business," in* Kirkus Reviews, *Vol. LXI, No. 1, January 1, 1993, p. 67.*

Welcome back, Junie B. Jones—precocious heroine, a cross between Ramona and Eloise. Junie B.'s new news is that her mom's having a baby. To Junie's delight, what comes out is a baby monkey—at least that's what Junie assumes when her grandmother tells her, "Your brother is the cutest little monkey I've ever seen." The kids at school are duly impressed, all eager to be the first to see him. It takes a visit to the principal and a call to Grandma to straighten things out. Chapter book readers will be laughing at Junie's antics as well as her way with words. For instance, she calls her teacher, "Mrs.": "She has another name, too. But I just like Mrs. and that's all."

> *Ilene Cooper, in a review of "Junie B. Jones and a Little Monkey Business," in* Booklist, *Vol. 89, No. 13, March 1, 1993, p. 1230.*

### Dear God, Help!!! Love, Earl  (1993)

Earl is a fat wimp, Rosie a know-it-all, and Maxie a brain. The trio met in the popular *Maxie, Rosie and Earl—Partners in Grime;* here, the focus is on Earl and his major-league problems with school bully Eddie McFee. Told in the first person, Park's story doesn't cover much new ground in the bully department. Earl is forced to pay protection money to Eddie for the pleasure of not being beaten up. But Earl has a secret weapon on his side. Once he confesses to his friends, Maxie and Rosie come up with a plan that puts Eddie in his place. The plan, an elaborate scheme to make Eddie think he has killed Earl, is only marginally believable; but fans of Earl and his pals may not notice details when the story's broad humor is so amusing. A quick read with an enticing cover—chubby Earl pleading for God's help, a dukes-up Eddie in the background.

> *Ilene Cooper, in a review of "Dear God, Help!!! Love, Earl," in* Booklist, *Vol. 89, No. 15, April 1, 1993, p. 1434.*

Earl brings his skewed self-esteem and scathingly funny lowdown to this continuing saga of three oddball friends—Earl, obsessively honest Rosie Swanson, and Max, master of the coined word ("The guy's pewage, Earl"). Each week, fist-wielding bully Eddie extorts money from timid, overweight Earl, whose impending poverty drives the friends to extremes. Rosie and Max convince Eddie that he has, in a recent attack, actually killed Earl. Posed photos and cemetery shots buoy their case, but it's Earl's mother who nails down the plot with some well-timed (if innocent) remarks. Eddie cries and is told the truth, but a little more extortion is in order: the threesome won't tell about Eddie's tears if he promises to pick Earl and Max first for teams in gym class. With loads of comic moments, Park's book will crack readers up with its morbidly funny plans and guffaw-inducing repartee.

> *A review of "Dear God, Help!!! Love, Earl,"*

*in* Kirkus Reviews, *Vol. LXI, No. 10, May 15, 1993, p. 667.*

---

### *Junie B. Jones and Her Big Fat Mouth*   (1993)

In another hilarious, easy chapter book about Junie B. Jones, the irrepressible kindergartner veers from catastrophe to rapture and back again. This time she has trouble deciding what to be on Job Day. Older kids will laugh at Junie's mistakes and misunderstandings, especially with language, and they'll remember their own bewilderment and bloopers. She gets punished for shooting off her big fat mouth ("Punishment is the school word for sitting at a big table all by yourself"). She's frank that the Pledge of Allegiance is a jumble for her ("I don't know what that dumb story is even talking about"). She's heartbroken to discover that Mickey Mouse isn't real. When she hates, she hates (even her "bestest" friend); when she's humiliated, she can't bear it ("I hided my head"). [Denise] Brunkus' energetic drawings pick up the slapstick action and the spunky comic hero.

*Hazel Rochman, in a review of "Junie B. Jones and Her Big Fat Mouth," in* Booklist, *Vol. 90, No. 5, November 15, 1993, p. 626.*

# John Shearer

## 1947-

African-American author and illustrator of fiction and nonfiction.

Major works include *I Wish I Had an Afro* (1970), *Little Man in the Family* (1972), and the *Billy Jo Jive* series (1976-1982).

## INTRODUCTION

Shearer is the author of a popular five-book series of detective stories for primary graders featuring exuberant urban sleuth Billy Jo Jive as well as two photographic essays that profile New York schoolchildren and their surroundings. Shearer's fiction is distinguished by his characterization of Billy Jo Jive, a self-confident little boy who acts as a private eye in solving neighborhood mysteries. Narrated by Billy Jo, the series is noted for its energetic, fast-paced quality as well as for the appeal of its main character, described by Karel Rose as "a juvenile John Shaft" and by *Kirkus Reviews* as "the inner city's answer to [Marjorie Weinman Sharmat's] Nate the Great"; these works also feature Billy Jo's sidekick Susie Sunset, an admiring friend who is central to the solving of the mysteries. By using language familiar to African-American children in urban areas, Shearer initially sought to appeal to "the little guys who didn't like to read much, who like to play basketball." Although some critics found his later plots repetitive and his use of slang potentially confusing to young audiences, Shearer is praised for filling a niche with his entertaining mysteries for beginning readers. The series is illustrated by the author's father, well-known cartoonist Ted Shearer, who provides lively pictures in marker, pencil, and watercolor that add conceptual clues to the stories. The two men produced an animated film based on the first book in the series in 1978; further short films based on the characters were featured regularly on the children's television program "Sesame Street."

Shearer was raised in New York City, the setting of his Billy Jo Jive stories. An award-winning photographer for national magazines who also taught photojournalism at Columbia University, Shearer first entered the field of children's literature with the stream-of-consciousness essays *I Wish I Had an Afro* and *Little Man in the Family*. The former features photographs and text that reflect the challenges faced by a black child in an impoverished family in Westchester, New York. The black-and-white photos are credited with enhancing the authenticity and impact of the portrayal. Zena Sutherland writes, "[Here] the quality of the photography and the candor and pathos of the text are uncommon." The photographs in Shearer's next book, *Little Man in the Family*, contrast the lifestyles of two boys, one being raised by his Puerto Rican mother and five sisters in an urban apartment, the other the son of a white suburban dentist. Described by *Publishers Weekly* as "visually stunning and revealing," the book portrays the sim-

ilarities and differences of the boys through their own views as well as those of their parents, teachers, and friends. Shearer's remaining books for children, the Billy Jo Jive series, were inspired by his childhood as well as by his desire, as he says, "to really write." Referring to his target audience, Shearer notes: "The books are written in street language the way [these children] really speak, and the characters talk about things they're familiar with. One thing I don't want to lose is that feeling." Shearer's first work of fiction for children was *Billy Jo Jive, Super Private Eye: The Case of the Missing Ten Speed Bike* (1976), in which Jive is introduced to Susie Sunset, whose brother's bike has been stolen. After solving the case, Jive and Susie decide to become partners in the private eye business. In *Billy Jo Jive and the Case of the Sneaker Snatcher* (1977), Jive and Susie expose the thief responsible for taking the lucky basketball shoes of a local team's star player, while in the most recent title, *Billy Jo Jive and the Case of the Midnight Voices* (1982), the duo discover the source of some strange noises that are frightening their fellow campers.

(See also *Contemporary Authors*, Vol. 125 and *Something about the Author*, Vol. 43.)

## TITLE COMMENTARY

### *I Wish I Had an Afro* (1970)

*I Wish I Had an Afro* is a stream of consciousness essay by John Shearer about the problems of raising a boy in the midst of poverty. The author's photographs of dilapidated buildings, run-down backyards and a poorly furnished apartment contribute to this poignant depiction of the struggle against ignorance, gangs, and drugs. The struggle, successful thus far, continues.

> *Michael J. Bandler, "Tales from the Ghetto," in* The Christian Science Monitor, *May 7, 1970, p. B5.*

Some of his sister's friends, says Little John, argue with his father. "I wonder, though, if he agrees with them, why don't he go along with them an' why don't he let me grow my hair like theirs. They sure do dig bein' black. . . . I wish I had an Afro." Big John replies: "I'm not sayin' black power is a bad thing. I'm just sayin' long hair don't make you any blacker than someone with short hair." Big John and his wife are hard-working and conservative, poor and ambitious. They live in a shabby house in Westchester, hoping for some measure of ease, and are adamant about their children's upbringing. The text moves back and forth as Big John, his wife, and their son soliloquize about their lives, evoking a sharp and candid picture of poverty in the midst of plenty, of the rift between the generations and the love that binds them.

> *Zena Sutherland, in a review of "I Wish I Had an Afro," in* Saturday Review, *Vol. LIII, No. 19, May 9, 1970, p. 46.*

Many fine photographs by the author augment the authentic atmosphere of this story of a black family's day-to-day struggle to survive. Ironically, the author's honesty in refusing to manufacture sensation results in a book that is almost too low key. To the question, "What's happenin', baby?" the answer, unfortunately, has to be, "Not too much." On the other hand, the black reader has a character in Little John with whom he can identify.

> *Margaret Berkvist, in a review of "I Wish I Had an Afro," in* The New York Times Book Review, *May 24, 1970, p. 28.*

Books of running first-person commentary combined with photographs have become fairly common; here the quality of the photography and the candor and pathos of the text are uncommon. It is a verbal collage: Little John comments, his mother speaks, his father ponders. The parents are hard-working and conservative, the boy (age eleven) is swayed by what he sees around him: yearning for an Afro (". . . long hair don't make you any blacker . . ." says Big John) and impressed by the militancy of his sister's friends, horrified by drugs and what they have done to the people around him, and imbued with his parents' high ethical standards.

> *Zena Sutherland, in a review of "I Wish I Had an Afro," in* Bulletin of the Center for Children's Books, *Vol. 24, No. 3, November, 1970, p. 48.*

### *Little Man in the Family* (1972)

The author, a *Life* photographer, relies mostly on his vivid pictures to portray the similarities and differences in the lives of two boys. The text is primarily dialogue, views of the boys expressed by their parents, teachers, friends. One boy is a New York City ghetto child; the other is the son of a comparatively affluent suburban dentist. A visually stunning and revealing book.

> *A review of "Little Man in the Family," in* Publishers Weekly, *Vol. 202, No. 25, December 18, 1972, p. 40.*

A double photographic essay about two boys is interesting both in the depiction of their lives and their positions in the family, and in the contrast between the two boys' lives, but this lacks the focus and impact of the author-photographer's *I Wish I Had An Afro.* The essays are based on interviews with the boys and their families and friends; although the jacket picture shows the boys together, and the author's appended note describes the one meeting between them, they do not meet in the textual descriptions. Louis (Lilo) Berrios is his mother's "little man," helping with his five sisters, dreaming of seeing his real father, still in Puerto Rico, wistfully remembering his one sailing experience on an outing arranged by a teen center. David Roth is the youngest of three sons, his parents white, middle-class, and financially comfortable. He excels at sports, his mother worries about his wanting to be best at everything, his father is proud of his son's prowess. The book is convincing—but not cohesive.

> *Zena Sutherland, in a review of "Little Man in the Family," in* Bulletin of the Center for Children's Books, *Vol. 26, No. 6, February, 1973, p. 97.*

### *Billy Jo Jive, Super Private Eye: The Case of the Missing Ten Speed Bike* (1976)

"My name is Billy Jo Jive . . . I'm the best, the bravest, the smartest Private Eye in the world." With that for openers, younger readers won't be hard-pressed to go on and learn how Billy Jo manages to ferret out friend Susie Sunset's brother's stolen 10-speed bicycle. Billy Jo acts as leader all the way, though it's Sunset who comes up with the key clue. By the end, she's sensibly upped to partner status, but feminists will chafe at her whispered "You're a great Private Eye, Jive." However, the snappy first-person story whizzes exuberantly along, and Jive's soaring ego manages to be beguiling instead of abrasive. Charcoal and watercolor—with some thin yellow to relieve the predominant grays and blacks—are as energetic as Jive. An entertainer.

> *Denise M. Wilms, in a review of "Billy Jo Jive, Super Private Eye: The Case of the Missing Ten Speed Bike," in* Booklist, *Vol. 73, No. 12, February 15, 1977, p. 899.*

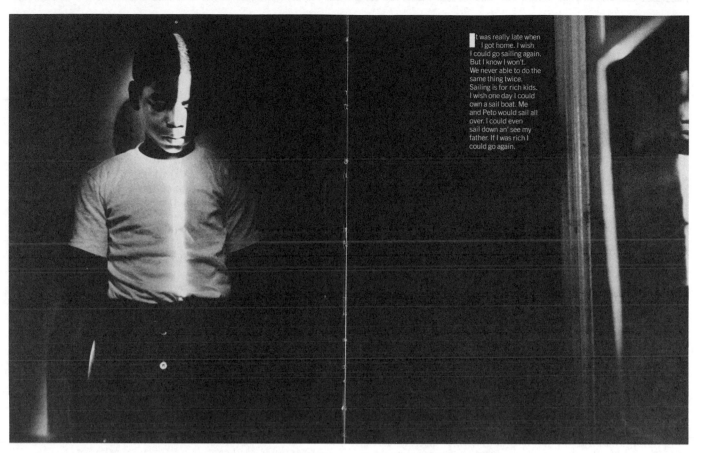

It was really late when I got home. I wish I could go sailing again. But I know I won't. We never able to do the same thing twice. Sailing is for rich kids. I wish one day I could own a sail boat. Me and Peto would sail all over. I could even sail down an' see my father. If I was rich I could go again.

*From* Little Man in the Family, *written and illustrated by John Shearer.*

Some inner-city children will be able to relate to the characters and the fast-paced plot may fulfill their own need for excitement. Others will have to do much detective work to decode the jargon: all words ending in "ing" eliminate the final letter (e. g., cruisin') and other language liberties are taken in a strained attempt to provide a "with-it" atmosphere. As a result, the book departs from standard English to such an extent that it might well confuse children who are still developing their reading abilities.

> *Karel Rose, in a review of "Billy Jo Jive, Super Private Eye: The Case of the Missing Ten Speed Bike," in* School Library Journal, *Vol. 23, No. 7, March, 1977, p. 137.*

---

### Billy Jo Jive and the Case of the Sneaker Snatcher (1977)

Watch out, Nate the Great—here comes ba-ad little Billy Jo Jive, who made his rep with . . . *The Case of the Missing Ten Speed Bike* and now holds his own when asked to track the ripped-off lucky sneakers of basketball ace Sneakers Jones, the 100th Street Jets' main man and chief hope against the Bugaloo Smackers. Smackers heavy Steam Boat Louis, whom Sneakers has just burned off the court, is the obvious suspect—but, pressured by Jets and tipped off by a Dick Tracy comic ("Look for left-handed clues"), Billy Jo and silent partner Sunset put the finger

on Rug Cutter, a jealous Jet, and retrieve the sneakers in time for the game. Dig it.

> *A review of "Billy Jo Jive: The Case of the Sneaker Snatcher," in* Kirkus Reviews, *Vol. XLV, No. 13, July 1, 1977, p. 670.*

John Shearer's *Case of the Sneaker Snatcher* is not only slim but it's something of a retread of boy detective Billy Jo Jive's previous *Case of the Missing Ten Speed Bike.* There the culprit was a rival in an upcoming cycle race; here it's a benchwarmer on the 100th Street Jets who steals the sneakers of the team's ace before a big game. Ted Shearer's cartoons are good-natured but average.

> *Andrew K. Stevenson, in a review of "Case of the Sneaker Snatcher," in* School Library Journal, *Vol. 24, No. 4, December, 1977, p. 61.*

---

### Billy Jo Jive and the Case of the Missing Pigeons (1978)

Zooming along on his Crime Fighter Skateboard with partner Susie Sunset, the inner city's answer to Nate the Great tails big, bad Snake Hips Roberts, likely villain in the case of friend Flip's missing pigeons. But Sunset's closer look at Jive's photos turns up another suspect— straight dude Sugar Brown—and the two detectives not only retrieve Flip's birds but also help Sugar realize that "stealin' ain't what's happenin'." But Jive's readers are likely to realize that what's happenin' here is essentially a replay of what went down in . . . ***The Case of the Sneaker Snatcher.***

> *A review of "Billy Jo Jive and the Case of the Missing Pigeons," in* Kirkus Reviews, *Vol. XLVII, No. 3, February 1, 1979, p. 123.*

---

### Billy Jo Jive and the Walkie Talkie Caper   (1981)

Jive and Sunset, last seen in ***The Case of the Missing Pigeons,*** here help their friend Steam Boat recover his stolen walkie-talkies. He needs them to complete the communications system his Bugaloo Smackers club has already paid him for. This fits the mold of its predecessor, with brisk pace and snappy dialogue; the upbeat cartoon drawings match the story's energy.

> *Denise M. Wilms, in a review of "Billy Jo Jive and the Walkie-Talkie Caper," in* Booklist, *Vol. 77, No. 19, June 1, 1981, p. 1301.*

Billy Jo Jive, the inner-city entry among easy-reading kid-detective series, bops his way through another mystery when Steam Boat Lewis, a Bugaloo Smacker, reports a missing walkie talkie. Billy Jo and female sidekick Sunset arrive at Steam Boat's fix-it shop to find the second walkie talkie missing and Steam Boat's pesty little girl cousins hanging round. Once more, the kids follow a false suspect . . . but instead of . . . ***Sneaker Snatcher*** Rug Cutter, the finger finally falls on the little girls, who haven't been getting enough attention from Steam Boat. Shearer keeps things moving briskly, but his plotting formula has become as tired as Ted Shearer's stock whoosh and speed lines. (And there are other problems with the pictures: the artist, less alert than Billy Jo, draws Steam Boat in sneakers though a key point in the story has him booted.)

> *A review of "Billy Jo Jive and the Walkie Talkie Caper," in* Kirkus Reviews, *Vol. XLIX, No. 12, June 15, 1981, p. 738.*

This fourth entry in the Jive series concerns a pair of walkie-talkies mysteriously "ripped off" from Steam Boat Louis by "some low-down robber" and recovered by Billy Jo Jive and his stalwart companion, Susie Sunset. The overuse of slang, the abundance of clichés and the transparent plot are major disappointments. However, the gray-and-black pencil drawings with red accents are humorous and full of action. The story is an easy-read mystery, a type of book that is popular but undersupplied. The fact that BJJ is a visitor on *Sesame Street* and that the books are likely to be popular doesn't hurt either. Still, this is not an essential purchase—unless y'all got the bread, baby!

> *Holly Sanhuber, in a review of "Billy Jo Jive and the Walkie-Talkie Caper," in* School Library Journal, *Vol. 28, No. 2, October, 1981, p. 136.*

---

### Billy Jo Jive and the Case of the Midnight Voices   (1982)

Again, it's the boy detective who tells the story; this time the mystery is the source of the eerie sounds that frighten the campers. Many of the children are convinced it's a ghost; the crabby counselor orders Billy Joe and his pal Susie Sunset to stop investigating. Undaunted, they continue and discover that one of the boys has put a "Boom Box" in the woods so that the camp will lose campers to a rival camp owned by his uncle. Readers in the primary grades are avid consumers of mystery stories, but neither the concocted text nor the slapdash illustrations in comic strip style offers much substance.

> *Zena Sutherland, in a review of "Billy Jo Jive and the Case of the Midnight Voices," in* Bulletin of the Center for Children's Books, *Vol. 35, No. 11, July-August, 1982, pp. 215-16.*

Scary noises in the night, the "midnight voices" of the title and disappearing campers set the stage for another Billy Jo Jive/Susie Sunset investigative collaboration at Camp Mountain Lake. When counselor "Hammering Hank" fails to solve the problem, BJJ and SS put their heads together and, with more than a little luck, quickly get to the bottom of the mystery. The culprit turns out to be the nephew of a rival camp's owner, who attempts to scare off Mountain Lake campers and, in turn, convince them to attend their own Smoky Camp. The setting, full of campfires, ghost stories, cabin high jinks and unfamiliar sounds and places, all help to create an appealingly spooky atmosphere. While the plot holds few surprises, the hard-to-find, short, easy-to-read format will catch the eye of every young mystery fan. The added attraction of popular Sesame Street characters makes this worthy of consideration.

> *Michelle Quinones, in a review of "Billy Jo Jive and the Case of the Midnight Voices," in* School Library Journal, *Vol. 29, No. 2, October, 1982, p. 146.*

Jive's first-person narration of events has the same self-assured spark as other books in the series. The art is slapdash but energetic as it sketches out a stream of typical camp scenes. This has a formula feel to it by now, but fans won't mind.

> *Denise M. Wilms, in a review of "Billy Jo Jive and the Case of the Midnight Voices," in* Booklist, *Vol. 79, No. 3, October 1, 1982, p. 249.*

# Jean Ure

## 1943-

English author of fiction and editor.

Major works include *See You Thursday* (1981), *The Other Side of the Fence* (1986), *One Green Leaf* (1987), *Plague 99* (1989; U.S. edition as *Plague*), *Come Lucky April* (1992).

## INTRODUCTION

A writer of introspective fiction for readers in the middle grades and high school, Ure is considered a sensitive and perceptive author of distinctive works that address a variety of subjects in a manner both serious and humorous. Called by Peter Hollindale "a gifted writer whose novels for teenagers are at once both relevant and original," she is celebrated for her understanding of and respect for her audience as well as for expanding the boundaries of teenage fiction with several of her books. In her works, Ure's adolescent characters take decisive steps to repel or embrace the norms of their society. Through this process they reach a new level of self-awareness and maturity, often gaining a heightened sense of gender identity as well. Of this latter insight, Robert Leeson has written that Ure "is at her best in illuminating the frontier zone between boys and girls, where independence in girls and tenderness in boys struggles to express itself." Writing books that draw on her love both for animals and for the performing arts, Ure has been praised for her humor, swift-moving plots, credible characters, and true-to-life endings that are often left dangling and unresolved. She is especially commended for her effective depiction of adolescent thoughts and speech, which she expresses through her characters' journal entries and in dialogue peppered with slang and dialectic idiosyncrasies. Although she is credited for her accuracy in relating what Margery Fisher has called "the vital trivialities of school days," Ure is more widely appreciated for her focus on such weighty issues as suicide, homelessness, class distinctions, sexual freedom and orientation, and the complexity of love; she insists that "if there is one main aim I have in my writings, it is to make my readers question received prejudices, question accepted values—above all, to *think*." Commending Ure's skill in addressing these topics, Audrey Laski has written: "Jean Ure has never been afraid of a challenging subject, to which she always seems able to bring a light but sure touch."

Ure began her career as a writer at age seventeen with the publication of *Dance for Two* (1960; U.S. edition as *Ballet Dance for Two*), a story for young adults in which two teenage dancers aspire to be professionals despite their parents' objections. More than two decades later, after working as a translator, attending drama school, and enjoying some success as a writer of romance novels and Georgian romances for adults, Ure once again turned to writing for young readers, primarily because she disliked

the restrictions placed on the writer of adult formula fiction. Marking her return to this audience, *See You Thursday* (1981) is the story of 16-year-old Marianne, whose fondness for 24-year-old Abe, who is blind, affords her a new appreciation for feelings commonly shared among handicapped persons. This book was followed by *A Proper Little Nooryeff* (1982; U.S. edition as *What If They Saw Me Now?*), in which Jamie, an athletic cricket player, joins a ballet company and is torn between his newly-discovered love of ballet and the scorn of his macho friends, and *If It Weren't for Sebastian* (1982), in which indecisive Maggie finds herself attracted to Sebastian, a determined but mentally unstable advocate of animal rights and vegetarianism. Ure's distinctive themes are evident in these works, which deal with universal problems like Sebastian's instability and Abe's blindness, and very adolescent concerns like Jamie's insecurity about his masculinity. Ure has also written highly-regarded stories for middle graders that address sympathetically such sensitive matters as class distinctions (*The Other Side of the Fence*) and terminal illness (*One Green Leaf*). Several of her works have sequels. *See You Thursday* is followed by two other books about Marianne and Abe which follow their relationship through separations, sexual involvement, and Marianne's growing awareness of Abe's need for self-sufficiency. *You Win Some, You Lose Some* (1984) traces Jamie's budding career in ballet, his quest to lose his virginity, and relationships with both his homosexual roommate and his first love, Anita. Margery Fisher has commented: "To write about the young in love, with all that the phrase implies about sexual desire, tenderness, and curiosity, is far from easy. Jean Ure mixes comedy and genuine feeling with candour and without a hint of condescension."

Ure has also written futuristic fiction. *Plague 99* is set in the year 1999, just after London has been destroyed by a disease which is presumed to have been caused by bacteriological warfare. Three teenagers who have returned after an absence which spared them from death now must cope with the loss of their parents and concerns about their own susceptibility. The novel's sequel, *Come Lucky April*, takes place one hundred years later in a society which has become matriarchal in order to avoid the mistakes of the aggressive males of the past. In a world where young men are castrated and the species propagates by artificial insemination, two young people attempt to establish a traditional love relationship. Elizabeth Finlayson, praising the depth of the work, writes: "Very much a novel of ideas, this book is for the mature reflective reader. Plot and characterization take second place to the exploration of numerous interesting themes, ranging over forms of political organization and relationships between the sexes." In addition to her works for an older audience, Ure has written several books for younger readers: her series of "Woodside School Stories" relate everyday events at a school for primary graders, and her fantasies *Wizard in the Woods* (1990) and *Wizard in Wonderland* (1991) introduce twins who befriend a rather incompetent wizard and muddle through several adventures with him.

(See also *Contemporary Authors*, Vol. 125; *Something about the Author*, Vol. 48; and *Something about the Author Autobiography Series*, Vol. 14.)

---

# GENERAL COMMENTARY

## Peter Hollindale

Jean Ure is [a] gifted writer whose novels for teenagers are at once relevant and original. *A Proper Little Nooryeff* takes the theme of balletomania and the crude social prejudice against ballet for boys. Jamie is a real boys' boy, chiefly interested in cricket and discos. One of his chores, however, is to collect his young sister from her ballet class. Then one evening, he finds himself lured into reluctant, embarrassed substitution for an injured male dancer. He proves to have a remarkable natural ability. The book explores the tension between Jamie's social embarrassment and his mounting delight in the realization of his gift. This book is outstanding for its humour, warmth and sympathy, its insights into adolescent uncertainties, and its stirring evocation of the magic of ballet.

The same author's *See You Thursday* is another excellent story of adolescent growth. Marianne is the rebellious teenage daughter of a one-parent family, and the story follows the tribulations of her relationship with the blind music teacher whom her mother has taken as a lodger. The prickly, wild, impulsive Marianne (not unlike Bilgie in Jane Gardam's *Bilgewater*) gradually comes to terms with her tempestuous loyalties and selfishness, but the book is especially remarkable for its sensitive depiction of severe handicap: the story could stumble so easily into mawkishness on one side or didactic, socializing comment on the other, but steers clear of both. Each of these books touches bravely and successfully on tender nerves of adolescent experience.

> *Peter Hollindale, in a review of "A Proper Little Nooryeff" and "See You Thursday," in* British Book News, *Children's Supplement, Autumn, 1982, pp. 7-8.*

---

# TITLE COMMENTARY

### *Dance for Two* (1960; U.S. edition as *Ballet Dance for Two*)

This is an ordinary little story that will inevitably appeal to and momentarily satisfy the young ballet fan. The author is obviously well informed about the subject and manages to convey some of her own enthusiasm, but the vehicle of transference is the same old and by now rather decrepit theme which arouses little fresh inspiration. An English girl and a French boy, both Ballet trainees and enthusiasts, meet in England and thereafter pursue their ambitions together. There are too many coincidences in the story and too many clichés of both plot and characterisation. The illustrations by Richard Kennedy are probably the best part of the book and help to augment that element of healthy enthusiasm and interest which is at times conveyed by the text but so often spoiled by the general stereotyped treatment.

> *A review of "Dance for Two," in* The Junior Bookshelf, *Vol. 24, No. 3, July, 1960, pp. 167-68.*

Two children, a Belgian boy and an English girl, yearn—from the time they are young children—to be dancers. When the two meet, they support each other's ambition in face of the parental opposition which threatens to deprive them of their goals. Together they study, attend ballets, and plan to take their place on the ballet stage. And ultimately they succeed, dancing triumphantly as partners in *Copelia*. The world of ballet enthralls a great many readers who would take eagerly to any work on the subject. This text, beside the vivid insight it gives into the field of the dance is also vigorously supported by characterization, plot, and atmosphere. An old fashioned story.

> *A review of "Ballet Dance for Two," in* Virginia Kirkus' Service, *Vol. XXVIII, No. 16, August 15, 1960, p. 683.*

You'll find many fiction books with a ballet motif. Of those we've read, Jean Ure's *Ballet Dance for Two* is most enjoyable. This is a tasteful story dealing with the relationship between a British girl and a thirteen-year-old Belgian boy, both aspiring to be ballet dancers. Love of dance, not eagerness for fame, is the motivation here. It's gratifying to find a book that includes acceptance of males in ballet.

> *Sam Leaton Sebesta and William J. Iverson, "Nonfiction in the Curriculum: 'Ballet Dance for Two',"* in their Literature for Thursday's Child, *Science Research Associates, Inc., 1975, pp. 396-97.*

---

**Pacala and Tandala, and Other Rumanian Folk-Tales (1960; U.S. edition as *Rumanian Folk Tales*)**

[Pacala and Tandala, and Other Rumanian Folk-Tales *is edited by Ure.*]

The Rumanian stories in **Pacala and Tandala** have [a] full folk-tale flavour and are excellently retold by Jean Ure in a simple, matter-of-fact style that suits them admirably. Some are not far distant from the Grimm tradition, but others, like **"The Man with the Book of Spells"** and **"The Giant and the Rumanian,"** seem to be purely local, and have a pleasant and convincing novelty of their own.

> *"Enchanting Realms," in* The Times Literary Supplement, *November 25, 1960, p. 414.*

This is a collection of Rumanian folk tales, translated as directly as possible from the versions first written down from the story-tellers. A number of the tales have their counterparts in other folk lore, but many are original, though most of them exhibit the well-known type of peasant wit, cunning or moralising. The compiler has done a very satisfactory work, which she rounds off by a chapter giving more information about the stories and an appendix detailing their more immediate origins.

> *A review of "Pacala and Tandala," in* The Junior Bookshelf, *Vol. 24, No. 6, December, 1960, p. 375.*

". . . that's how it was in the old days; there weren't any schools like there are today. We had to learn things by listening to what the old folk said." A final chapter gives the very interesting backgrounds for these stories told when "the women met to get on with their spinning, in the fields while the men were resting or on a winter's evening while the family was gathered indoors." Peasants, gypsies, wealthy boyars, rascals, wise maidens, and kings people these old tales. There is little magic in them, only the magic of wit and cleverness; but the rewards of kindness are shown, and humor lights them all. Many of the stories are variants of familiar themes, but all have the special flavor of their origins for they have been told as nearly as possible in the words of the village storytellers.

> *Ruth Hill Viguers, in a review of "Rumanian Folk Tales," in* The Horn Book Magazine, *Vol. XXXVII, No. 5, October, 1961, p. 444.*

---

**See You Thursday (1981)**

Jean Ure's first novel for teenagers is well constructed and well written, but alas, it lacks that vital spark which sets fire to the imagination. Marianne, sixteen and greatly lacking in self-confidence, grows to an understanding of the problems of Abe, a blind music teacher who comes as a lodger to the house she shares with her mother. Abe is only eight years Marianne's senior, and love inevitably grows, as does opposition to that love. The best part of the book is its description of the problems of the blind, but the story teeters too close to cloying melodrama for today's tastes, and eventually plunges (literally) over the precipice. Other problems are the characters (Abe is such a goody-goody, especially in his punctilious respect for Marianne's chastity, that readers may feel like throttling him, blind or not) and the dialogue, which even for the fee-paying school depicted is far too polished, knowledgeable and sometimes downright unbelievable. Well intentioned, yes; but only the most dedicated reader will reach the (inconclusive) end.

> *Tony Bradman, in a review of "See You Thursday," in* The School Librarian, *Vol. 29, No. 3, September, 1981, p. 257.*

This is a sensitive study of the common problem of a relationship between two young people, intensified in this case by Abe's blindness. It is treated here perceptively and with common sense. It could have developed into the usual 'permissive' situation with its consequent problems, but it is not as commonplace as this. Abe's problems because of his blindness are made clear—how far can he be independent, has he any right to burden someone else with his permanent disability? Abe and Marianne—Abe is the older—are interesting people and Marianne's mother's dilemma is very real. The author has shown that there can be a potentially happy ending.

> *E. Colwell, in a review of "See You Thursday," in* The Junior Bookshelf, *Vol. 45, No. 5, October, 1981, p. 219.*

Ure's principal characters are finely drawn—Abe's sensitivity, his high principles, and his struggle to get along amidst the sighted are especially memorable and never melodramatic. Marianne has obviously matured by the novel's close, and the author's cleverly unresolved ending provides readers with plenty of grist for their romantic imaginings. A quality romance head and shoulders above the new-wave paperback variety.

> *Stephanie Zvirin, in a review of "See You Thursday," in* Booklist, *Vol. 80, No. 3, October 1, 1983, p. 235.*

There are many books about a shy, lonely adolescent who falls in love, but none quite like this. . . . A perceptive book, this explores interreligious understanding and the adolescent's need for independence; it has depth and sensitivity in its depiction of characters and relationships, and a fluent style; it deals with many of the problems common to young adults with conviction and compassion.

> *Zena Sutherland, in a review of "See You Thursday," in* Bulletin of the Center for Children's Books, *Vol. 37, No. 4, December, 1983, p. 79.*

Ill at ease with herself at home and at school, 16-year-old Marianne feels a lodger will be the last straw. When Abe Shonfield arrives, he is young and really quite attractive but blind, and Marianne does not know how to react. What follows is a delicate juggling act, not only two young people learning how to approach each other, but also an active, independent blind person and an inexperienced but open-minded sighted person trying to work out what is best for each other. And what is best is that they finally treat each other as human beings and individuals.

One way in which books come to life in the classroom is that they open up topics for discussion safely at one remove. This seems to be an especially suitable text for this purpose. There is a great deal of practical information as well as an exposure of Marianne's uncertainties and Abe's sensitivities. It would inform both sighted and blind people and may provide an opportunity to air points otherwise left unspoken. The story is, of course, deliciously romantic. (Where were all these humorous, sensitive young men when I needed them?) It is far from soggy, however, and includes other themes of interest to teenagers. Perhaps its most attractive aspect for this list is that the two main characters, one blind, the other sighted, have equal importance. One speculates on what opportunities might be available for blind and sighted teenagers to discuss this one together.

> *Pat Thomson, in a review of "See You Thursday," in* Books for Keeps, *No. 75, July, 1992, p. 26.*

---

*A Proper Little Nooryeff* (1982; U.S. edition as *What If They Saw Me Now?*)

## AUTHOR'S COMMENTARY

*[The first excerpt in this section is from a review written by Michael E. Grafton for* Interracial Books for Children Bulletin; *the second excerpt is taken from Ure's addendum to Robert Leeson's article in which he outlines "Ten Golden Rules" for critics of children's books. After assessing Leeson's rules, Ure comments on Grafton's review as well as her reaction to other critical commentary on her work.]*

Every Friday Jamie escorts his sister Kim home from her ballet lessons at Thea Tucker's studio. Arriving early one evening, Jamie stays to watch the rehearsal. Lo and behold, a replacement is needed for a show. After testing Jamie, Thea Tucker and student Anita Cairncross convince him to assist with the upcoming benefit show. Jamie, forced by the "habit of obedience" to help a charitable cause, unenthusiastically agrees to perform in the show. The remainder of the book describes Jamie's increasing respect for ballet, his admiration for Anita, and his constant obsession with keeping secret his participation in a ballet performance. The show is a success, but who actually succeeds is unclear.

Although the author tried to create an individual who overcomes rigid gender roles, the story is merely another case of potential-gone-sour. Indeed, instances of subtle bigotry are hidden with what appears to be a moderately liberal plot. For instance, Jamie is convinced to help not because of the artistic value of ballet, nor even because of

the exercise he would get, but because the show's proceeds will go to persons with disabilities. More specifically, the money will go to Fairfield, a segregated institution where his cousin (who is never described in detail) resides. "But, Jamie, it's for the handicapped!" rings oppressively loud at key points throughout the narrative. (It is never mentioned that the money would be more appropriately raised for a program which encourages mainstreaming, employment, accessible recreation or independent living.)

Handicapism is matched by the book's classism. The rich are portrayed as genteel, cultured, intelligent and clean ("He marveled at [their weedless flowerbeds]: not an empty Coca-Cola can or cigarette pack in sight."), while the poor are depicted as brazen, uneducated toughs.

And then there's the sexism. Anita's reasoning for wishing that Jamie perform with her rather than be the star attraction herself boggles the mind. She argues:

> "If we *don't* do it I'll be the star attraction because then I'll have to fill in with the Sugar Plum Fairy, which I already did last year. . . . It's the *show* I'm thinking of—that and giving other people a chance. It's a man's thing, not a girl's: I'd only be playing second fiddle."

Perhaps the greatest failure of the book is the finale: That Jamie is a star, that Anita is finally "going potty" over

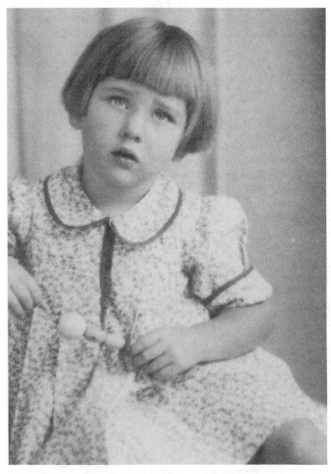

*Ure as a small child with, she notes, "a stomachache."*

him, that he has survived the ridicule of ruffians (the tough guys attend remedial classes, thus reinforcing the myth that bigotry is limited to those with "low" intelligence) does not convince him to pursue his talent openly and with pride. In the end, Jamie worries only about how he will face his "sex-polluted slob" of a best friend, Doug. (Does Jamie fear that Doug will think him a sissy or, perhaps worse, gay?) This is just a cutesy tale with a very *un*cutesy message.

> *Michael E. Grafton, in a review of "What If They Saw Me Now?" in* Interracial Books for Children Bulletin, *Vol. 17, No. 2, 1986, p. 17.*

When writing books I do not consciously consider that I must take care not to offend any of the currently accepted canons. I am, after all, writing novels, not polemics. My own philosophy of life will inescapably come across, and this, I believe, is as it should be.

I recently learnt, however, from the US *Interracial Bulletin,* that my philosophy as perceived in a light-hearted book called **A Proper Little Nooryeff,** is shot through with *'subtle bigotry'*. . . *'For instance, Jamie is convinced to help with the ballet show not because of the artistic value of ballet* (oh, boy!) *nor even because of the exercise he would get* (But, Jamie, think of the exercise!) *but because the show's proceeds will go to persons with disabilities.* (Bad, bad, bad!) *More specifically, the money will go to Fairfield, a segregated* (no, they don't mean racially) *institution where his cousin resides . . . it is never mentioned that the money would be more appropriately raised for a program which encourages mainstreaming, employment, accessible recreation or independent living.'*

Along the way, with almost total disregard for any other qualities the book may have, I'm also taken to task for classism, sexism, remedialism and sissyism . . . *'The greatest failure of the book is its finale. The fact that Jamie has survived the ridicule of ruffians doesn't convince him to pursue his talent openly and with pride. In the end, he worries only about how he will face his sex-polluted slob of a best-friend, Doug. Does Jamie fear that Doug will think him a sissy, or perhaps worse, gay?'*

Yes! Yes! Yes! He does! *Imagine* . . . the horror of it!

We come here to the age-old question . . . is one delivering political messages or is one writing books about people living in the real world? The standard retort, of course, is that OK, in the real world people *might* be classist, sexist, racist, genderist, sissyist, homophobe, but we, the right-minded ones, are trying to change all that. Should we therefore be including such wrong-thinking characters in our books?

My answer is a very firm yes, we should—but not without making it very clear where we personally stand on such issues, which is precisely what I did in **Nooryeff.** Unfortunately, the most well-meaning and high-minded of people, such as I'd suppose the reviewer for *Interracial Bulletin* to be, can be as raddled with prejudice as any blimp. If I had space I could refute every one of the charges made against **Nooryeff** save for the handicapism, to which I

plead guilty. But let us think . . . how could I have handled it?

> Anita: But, Jamie, it's for charity! It's for *Fairfield.*
>
> Jamie: Sod Fairfield. The money would be more appropriately raised for a program to encourage mainstreaming, employment, accessible recreation or independent living.
>
> Anita: Oh, Jamie, you're so right! We should not be supporting these segregated institutions for people suffering from cerebral palsy.
>
> Jamie: Now that you've seen the light, I will dance for you.
>
> Anita: Oh, *Jamie!*

See what I mean?

The question inevitably arises: how much notice should a writer take of reviews?

I don't feel inclined to lay down rules about this. There are writers who claim—indeed, I know one personally—to be totally incurious about their reviews and pretty well impervious to either praise or criticism. I find this difficult to comprehend, but who shall doubt that this is their right? For myself I readily confess to being made of weaker stuff. After twenty-odd years as a professional writer I still remain naively eager to hear other people's opinions of my work. I *care* what my readers think—and my readers include my reviewers. I am made happy by good reviews, cast down by bad ones; not, after all these years, to any incapacitating degree, but sufficient for me to take note of what reviewers say . . . usually.

For instance, I largely (largely but not *entirely*) dismissed the abovementioned **Nooryeff** review on the grounds that it came from the standpoint of ideology rather than literature.

On the one occasion when I did take criticism to heart, it rather rebounded on me. This was when I allowed myself to be riled by a scathing review of **Nooryeff** in the then *Gay News* (ideology again) in which it was somewhat irritably suggested that the book would have been far more interesting had I made my *'butch, attractive, muscly, fantastically gifted, sexy ballet dancer'* gay. Now, I had originally toyed with this idea, but dismissed it as being too much of a stereotype: *Gay News* made me wonder whether perhaps a straight ballet dancer was a stereotype? Thus, in the original draft of the sequel, I did the next best thing and made my fantastic, etc., hero bi-sexual. Unfortunately, there was such an outcry at my publishers—'Not *Jamie!*' they wailed—that I was forced to listen to editorial pleadings and have a re-think: my hero reverted to being madly butch.

*Gay News* had, I think, folded by this time, so I never got a second scathing review, which I should have enjoyed; instead I received a panic-stricken letter from my US editor saying that the ending of the book would have to be changed or they would be inundated with hate mail from the gay lobby. (The sequel, by the by, was rather aptly named **You Win Some, You Lose Some . . .**)

*Jean Ure, "Some More Golden Rules," in* Books for Keeps, *No. 66, January, 1991, pp. 4-5.*

Social strata have considerable importance in *A Proper Little Nooryeff* in providing general as well as personal reasons for the way two young people get to know one another. Jamie's ambitions centre on the cricket field, with some of his energies reserved for scoring off unpopular Mr. Hubbard in the classroom: he enters the close world of ballet only when he collects his young sister from her class on Fridays. When Miss Tucker seizes on him as a partner for Anita in a practice session, he accepts it as a mildly amusing incident. To Miss Tucker, though, he is the perfect substitute for her annual display, not only for certain spectacular lifts designed to show the traditional basis of her school but also in his own right, filling the gap with a gymnastic Russian dance. Never mind the fact that the reluctant, embarrassed Jamie is brought to performance standard in a remarkably short time. What matters in this sparkling tale is the relationship of two young people. Jean Ure uses their different social background and temperaments capably as part of her character—drawing, cutting more deeply through their conversations together in which dislike, attraction, resentment, egotism are unerringly expressed. Serious but never solemn, amusing but never farcical, this is a rare example of a balanced, unostentatious and veracious novel for the 'teens.

*Margery Fisher, in a review of "A Proper Little Nooryeff," in* Growing Point, *Vol. 21, No. 1, May, 1982, p. 3892.*

Male ballet dancing lends itself well to the author's theme of masculine self-image. Modest, likable and a bit bumbling, Jamie has an unformed concept of himself. Despite his grudging employment of his dancing talent, he is concerned about his masculinity. What would his friends think of him prancing about in tights? Eventually Jamie learns to trust his own instincts as Ure adeptly portrays his growing self-awareness and Jamie's point of view is conveyed with lively humor and warmth. Even the most minor characters are people one seems to know or would like to meet. Britishisms are not intrusive; rather, the situations are universal. Though the point is made with a light touch, the book will easily spark self-analysis among teenagers concerned with their images. That doesn't leave out many of them.

*Cathi Edgerton, in a review of "What If They Saw Me Now," in* Voice of Youth Advocates, *Vol. 7, No. 2, June, 1984, p. 98.*

[This] novel is not just another story of teenage romance; it looks at the limitations of traditional male roles. Sixteen-year-old Jamie Carr, an English lad who dreams of emigrating to the United States to play ball for the Yankees, inadvertently becomes the male star of a ballet school's charity show. One afternoon while watching his sister rehearse, Jamie is talked into replacing an injured dancer. Thea Tucker, the grand old dame who runs the school, and Anita Cairncross, the school's prima ballerina, immediately see that Jamie is a "natural," a born dancer. He en-

joys dancing as long as he believes that his friends will never find out and will never see him on stage—in tights. His problems begin when he cannot juggle both dance rehearsals and baseball practice.

Will Jamie be able to hide his secret life from his friends? Will Reggie Jackson be replaced by Rudolph Nureyev as Jamie's idol? Will the cold, ambitious Anita fall in love with Jamie? These questions add to the story's suspense and will occur to young readers. Older readers will want to discover how Jamie resolves his dilemma between wanting social approval and wanting to excel in something athletic—ballet being one of the most strenuous and exacting of the athletic arts.

In this novel, Jean Ure introduces a social issue that is just beginning to receive media attention—men's liberation from degrading stereotypes. And she has fun doing it.

*Jane Yarbrough, in a review of "What If They Saw Me Now?" in* The ALAN Review, *Vol. 13, No. 2, Winter, 1986, p. 41.*

### *If It Weren't for Sebastian* (1982)

Maggie belongs to a serious version of the Bagthorpe family. They are all very superior intellects, and they do not take kindly to the news that Maggie, with three A-levels, proposes to pass up her chance of university in favour of a secretarial course. She is doomed to finish up playing 'wet nurse to some half-witted businessman'. After a grand family row Maggie enrols at the Tech with her friend, the glamorous Val. She joins the ranks of the bed-sitters and so meets Sebastian, who has dropped out—or been thrown out?—of Cambridge. From him Maggie learns to fight the Establishment and embrace vegetarianism, as well as to look after Sunday, the stray cat. The relationship has its ups and downs and then one last nearly catastrophic down. The story closes as Maggie finds a purpose towards which she can direct her energies.

In a story where nothing very much happens everything depends on character. Maggie is nicely done, a not-too-clever girl, outclassed physically by her friend, and groping her way in a puzzling world. I don't feel that the reader identifies with her very closely, but it is a competent piece of character-sketching. The book really hinges on Sebastian, and he does not come off well. After the build-up, in which his erstwhile schoolmates describe him as 'nutty as a fruit cake', he seems just a little too ordinary; a young man with a social conscience, certainly, and rather too sensitive for a hard world, but really, one might think, a representative, rather than an exceptional, member of his generation. Because he fails to make a strong impact on the reader, the action, and the reactions of Maggie, are insufficiently convincing. I am inclined to think that Sunday the cat is the most crisply drawn actor in this modest drama.

*M. Crouch, in a review of "If It Weren't for Sebastian," in* The Junior Bookshelf, *Vol. 46, No. 6, December, 1982, p. 236.*

Maggie had an outstanding academic record, and her family (all high-achieving professional people) was horrified that she wanted to drop college plans and take secretarial training. That's how she happened to leave home, that's how she met Sebastian, who lived in the same rooming house. Although his morbidity and his devotion to causes often irked Maggie, she became increasingly fond of Sebastian. Most of her friends, even her brother who had gone to school with him, dismissed Sebastian as daft, bats, bonkers. It is when Sebastian actually does lose touch with reality that Maggie realizes how much she cares; she decides to go to college after all, then to become a psychiatrist so that she can help people like Sebastian. Ure, a rapidly rising British author, here explores the borderline psychotic and his relationships with great sensitivity and understanding. There are times when the pace of the book slows, but never so much as to lose the feeling of inevitable crisis looming.

> *Zena Sutherland, in a review of "If It Weren't for Sebastian," in* Bulletin of the Center for Children's Books, *Vol. 38, No. 10, June, 1985, p. 197.*

Sebastian's vocal protests against oppression or fascism or cruelty towards animals have not only gotten him labeled crazy but have also gotten him suspended from school. Yet Maggie finds herself drawn to this sensitive, often depressing, generally strange young man. She admires his strong convictions and valiently copes with his suicidal discussions and emotional insecurities, in particular, his fear of hurting the stray cat he befriends. One night when Sebastian is particularly insecure, she tells him to leave. The next day, Sebastian is nowhere to be found. His unconcerned parents tell Maggie that they will call the clinic where he's supposed to be an out-patient and have them find and care for him. The callous attitude of all the characters except Maggie is a little overwhelming. Sebastian's harmless idiosyncrasies do not merit the belittling attitude of his peers nor his parent's cruel disregard. Although the theme is belabored and the minor characters are one dimensional, Maggie and Sebastian are interesting and sympathetic characters. This book will attract readers who enjoy emotional problem novels.

> *Karen K. Radtke, in a review of "If It Weren't for Sebastian," in* School Library Journal, *Vol. 31, No. 10, August, 1985, p. 82.*

---

### Hi, There, Supermouse! (1983; U.S. edition as Supermouse)

Jean Ure's alert prose refreshes familiar domestic situations with pertinent detail and apt expressions. *Hi There, Supermouse!* concerns the rivalry between two sisters, between Nicola who at eleven is tall and gangling, glowering behind her thick dark fringe, and pretty blonde Rose, who has learned early in life how to charm everyone for her own ends. Ambitious to be a dancer in spite of her awkwardness, Nicola is astonished and delighted when a local ballet teacher, catching sight of her dancing alone on a waste site, invites her to understudy Rose. Disastrously, her interpretation of the part pleases everyone and Rose is asked to accept a different role: her tantrums force Nicola to back out of the show but all comes right in the end,

as Rose wins a part in a Christmas show and Nicola is offered ballet lessons by her apologetic, enlightened parents. A happy ending, but not a contrived one, for Nicola's talents are convincingly described and the shifting pattern of family life, with parental blindness and the love-hate attachment of the sisters, is woven through the story in incisive, natural dialogue and well-chosen scenes of anger and reconciliation.

> *Margery Fisher, in a review of "Hi, There, Supermouse," in* Growing Point, *Vol. 22, No. 4, November, 1983, pp. 4163-64.*

The Bruce family is utterly taken aback when Mrs. French, a former ballerina who lives nearby, wants gangling Nicola to appear in her mime show. It is pert and pretty Rose who has the talent, and Mrs. Bruce uses emotional pressure to induce Nicola to resign her part in favour of her sister. Then a practical joke misfires, Nicola takes Rose's place at rehearsal, and proves much better in the role.

The shoplifting expedition which acts as a catalyst in this story seems artificially introduced, and the unpleasant mother's eventual change of heart is not entirely convincing. Nevertheless, Jean Ure is to be congratulated on dealing boldly with the difficult subject of parental favouritism and the distress it can cause.

> *R. Baines, in a review of "Hi There, Supermouse!" in* The Junior Bookshelf, *Vol. 47, No. 6, December, 1983, p. 265.*

Many a young reader will sympathize wholeheartedly with Nicola Bruce's agonizing plight: her younger sister Rose is blonde, petite, talented, and a charmer, while Nicola is trouble-prone, gawky, and completely lacking in self-confidence. . . . Nicola's mother's persistent downgrading of her sensitive older daughter is related with excruciating directness, as are the effects of Nicola's pent-up misery when she's deprived, not just once but twice, of the mime part that earns her the nickname, "Supermouse." Happily, Mrs. French's encouragement helps Nicola to recognize her own talent, a revelation that makes it easier for Nicola to take her prima donna sister in stride. Though slightly contrived, this mildly British novel has a refreshing, head-on honesty (especially in its depiction of parental shortcomings), while the underlying theater and ballet themes can be counted on to attract a popular audience.

> *Karen Stang Hanley, in a review of "Supermouse," in* Booklist, *Vol. 80, No. 17, May 1, 1984, p. 1255.*

Because the story is told from Nicola's point of view, the portrayal of the characters is limited to an eleven-year-old perspective. Yet the author has managed to suggest subtle emotions which underlie the family's values and actions. The theme—that swans are not always recognized as such—is developed logically; Nicola achieves her triumph not at Rose's expense but by learning to appreciate her own unique qualities.

> *Mary M. Burns, in a review of "Supermouse," in* The Horn Book Magazine, *Vol. LX, No. 3, June, 1984, p. 334.*

*You Win Some, You Lose Some*   (1984)

Jamie, the hero of **You Win Some, You Lose Some,** is a seventeen-year-old ballet dancer and a virgin, curious to know what he is missing. Jean Ure is in no doubt that he has no hint of ambivalence in his make up (nor is there any ambiguity in his direct and specific vocabulary). He is determined, in a scientific way, to fill the gaps in his knowledge. The accessibility of the girls in his class is analysed with great attention. Twice he draws up seduction plans, and twice he is thwarted—once by a girl who has emotional hang-ups and once by a girl who reads an invitation to spend a night in a hotel as an offer of marriage. A third opportunity fails through his own inadequacy in the face of the uninhibited and voracious offer from another girl. Neatly counterpointing these reverses are his own rejections of the sexual overtures of his male flat-mate, which are couched in much the same terms as Jamie's overtures to his unwilling female partners. Throughout his surprisingly unobjectionable and amusing adventures he shares a dedication to dancing with Anita, a supportive friend of many years' standing; and it is of course with her that in the end he realizes that for him sex makes sense only in a context of affection. Awkwardness and anxiety vanish. Love sets the rules. Jean Ure is an experienced and accomplished writer and she handles plot with élan, character with understanding and dialogue with realism. What could be laboured and condescending is deft, amusing, even enlightening.

> *Jennifer Moody, "Ready for Action," in* The Times Literary Supplement, *No. 4228, April 13, 1984, p. 414.*

In **What If They Saw Me Now?** a British adolescent, to help an aquaintance, had filled in as a ballet partner and discovered that—to his surprise—he enjoyed dancing even more than the sports at which he was proficient. In this sequel, Jamie transfers to ballet school; much of the story is about his practice and his prowess, but that theme is nicely and realistically balanced by his first awkward efforts at being a suave Lothario, his surprise when he learns that his flat-mate is gay, his happy discovery that the first girl he's ever loved also loves him, and his gradual achievement of self-confidence and independence. All this happens in a book with a brisk pace, empathetic insight, and a light, witty style that is a good foil for the seriousness of many of the issues and problems of the mid-teen years.

> *A review of "You Win Some, You Lose Some," in* Bulletin of the Center for Children's Books, *Vol. 39, No. 8, April, 1986, p. 160.*

Persuaded by his wealthy ballet partner Anita that he really could make it in the world of dance, Jamie quits school to prepare for auditions at Kendra Hall, a premier ballet school. But he must prove himself not only as a dancer, but also as a man.

Preoccupied, like any adolescent, with sex, he finds it tougher and tougher to meet a girl who will respond to him. And all the issues of sexual ambiguity come crashing into his life when the first real "pass" made at him at school is made by another male student.

How the very heterosexual Jamie deals with his image problems, and his girl problems, is a touching story. Adult readers will be pleased to find the sound values of love and friendship in sexual relationships very much in evidence. The world of the British "lower crust" may be somewhat alien, but Ure deals admirably with ambition, hard work, and the more immediate issues of teenage romance as well.

> *Cynthia Samuels, "Wishing That Life Were Different," in* Book World—The Washington Post, *May 11, 1986, p. 17.*

A story about a teenage English boy who decides to leave regular school to enter ballet school does not seem, at first glance, a likely proposition for handing out to YAs. Nevertheless, this book works, in an amusing and unassuming way. Jamie thinks about his life, but he doesn't ponder or agonize, except over scoring with girls, which he consistently does not do. He takes things as they come. He likes Anita, but is positive she considers him only a friend. He has a macho, cynical roommate who turns out to be a gay who wants to seduce him. Throughout all, the ballet aspect is an integral part of the story without ever outweighing the rest. Ballet is what Jamie does, but it's tied in with all the other important things about growing up: making decisions, choosing friends and setting personal values. Jamie is a very likable character in this matter-of-fact snippet of changing youth. **You Win Some, You Lose Some** should have general appeal to boys and girls.

> *Dolores Maminski, in a review of "You Win Some, You Lose Some," in* Voice of Youth Advocates, *Vol. 9, Nos. 3-4, August-October, 1986, p. 152.*

*The You-Two*   (1984; also published as *You Two*)

I read **The You-Two** at a single sitting, completely held by Jean Ure's story of Elizabeth, a bright girl dragged away from Lady Margaret Foster's College (her father is made redundant and can no longer afford the fees) and deposited among the remedials, the cheap exercise books and the rudeness of a Croydon comprehensive. Against all the odds she pals up and becomes a "you-two" with Paddy whose father is away a lot. She says he's in America making films, but then Elizabeth is told that he's in prison. From that moment things do not go smoothly; mother does not approve and Elizabeth endures a period of isolation at school. An honest, provocative novel which gets it right.

> *Hugh David, "Class of '84," in* The Times Educational Supplement, *No. 3545, June 8, 1984, p. 49.*

If readers are going to stay with the story they must share the author's sensitivity to class differences. Even then it is by no means clear whether sympathy is being sought for Elizabeth's plight or one is expected to frown upon her reluctance to come to terms with the outlook of her new chums who are really the salt of the earth, rough diamonds but hearts of gold etc. Life in school provides mate-

*Ure's parents, William and Vera Ure.*

rial for drama which is not difficult to shape into a story but reliance upon contrasting social mores as a dominant theme may not commend itself to some. I can well imagine that in certain egalitarian circles it might be dismissed as too trivial—even anti-social.

> *D. A. Young, in a review of "The You-Two," in* The Junior Bookshelf, *Vol. 48, No. 4, August, 1984, p. 181.*

The setting is an English school, but the group dynamics and the individual relationships should have a universal appeal. Characters and writing style are equally strong, and the author is most perceptive in depicting the loneliness of a child who is rejected by her peers and the contrasting joy and security when she has a friend.

> *Zena Sutherland, in a review of "You Two," in* Bulletin of the Center for Children's Books, *Vol. 38, No. 2, October, 1984, p. 36.*

Elizabeth's character is fully realized, and her fears are well described, but Paddy's motivations are not as clear. The plot hinges on the popular Paddy choosing, on first sight, a shy newcomer as "best friend," and this choice is not convincingly motivated. Overall, **You Two** is a solid new-kid-in-school story, but it is decidedly British, and the heavy emphasis on class distinctions and snobby private schools will put off or puzzle many American readers.

> *Kathy Fitts, in a review of "You Two," in* School Library Journal, *Vol. 31, No. 2, October, 1984, p. 163.*

I'm not sure that the reader should look too closely at the very stereotyped pictures that the author presents concerning the teachers, parents and the children of private and comprehensive state education. That aside this is a very honest and satisfying story about Elizabeth who eventually finds her level in a large comprehensive school after the security of a small private establishment. Her genuine excitement in a new friend and her parents' reservations are very naturally drawn. The depth of Elizabeth's loneliness and the tremendous efforts that her friend Paddy makes to cover up for her shabby family are certainly feelings that children will recognise. Girl readers, in particular, will identify with the ups and downs of school friendships, and find this an absorbing read.

> *Cathy Lister, in a review of "You Two," in* Books for Keeps, *No. 36, January, 1986, p. 16.*

## *Megastar* (1985)

Classroom acting provides plot and momentum for *Megastar,* with sharp details fixing the scene in a North London suburb and placing two tiresome and reluctant pupils at the centre. Jason, whose peers call him Megastar (not altogether derisively), desperately wants the part of the King's Jester in the scenes from *Richard III* which an ambitious and trendy temporary teacher is planning; when he is cast merely as a villager, he and his West Indian crony Mark get ready to protest but are forestalled by a local actor who decides to make a film of the borough with children in the forefront. Noting Jason's talent for mimicry, Dave casts him as the bureaucratic Man from the Council; sundry comical episodes spring from this, with a good-luck climax (Jason applies for a place in an acting school, on Dave's advice) which might have seemed hackneyed if it were not for the breadth of social reference in the book and the rapid, sharp establishing of simple but telling traits of character in adults and young alike.

> *Margery Fisher, in a review of "Megastar," in* Growing Point, *Vol. 24, No. 2, July, 1985, p. 4461.*

Stories for children are beginning to include information about the teaching of reading, class management, and the inability of some middle-class teachers to understand their working-class pupils. No reason why not—as long as the story comes first and we believe in and enjoy the children and their teachers, as we do here.

Mark and Jason, in 4R at Beasleigh Junior School, and with reading ages of nine, are natural outsiders. Mark knows that in the school pageant of Richard II a black boy cannot possibly play the King, and Jason knows that in spite of his very evident talent as a comedian he has not been chosen as Court Jester because his teacher would rather choose any other boy. They can be villagers though, and rehearsals for the pageant move alongside a parallel production organised by a resting actor as a contribution to the local Arts Festival, 'A day in the life of Shrublands Estate'. As the story unfolds, we find out some of the reasons for Jason's low reading age, but he is not a tragic figure; a tough, resilient little comic, he'll make his way to drama school. It's easy to recognise Shrublands Estate with its unnaturally cropped trees, and Jason who longs for a smile from his teacher, a smile that goes regularly to Piers and Deborah. But don't get the impression that this is a sour tale. It's very funny, and certainly not 'teacher's choice'.

> *Dorothy Atkinson, in a review of "Megastar," in* The School Librarian, *Vol. 33, No. 3, September, 1985, p. 243.*

---

## *Nicola Mimosa* (1985; U.S. edition as *The Most Important Thing*)

Nicola's mother is the type of person who satisfies her own ambitions vicariously through the successes of her children—and never ceases to boast about them! The dreadful 13-year-old Rose, already established at stage school and with various appearances to her credit is happy to oblige (and capitalize) upon her mother's senseless pride. Nicola, talented but much more confused about her future, is less sure. When she auditions successfully for a rare place at one of the country's most prestigious ballet schools it never occurs to her mother to even consider any of the alternatives. How Nicola finally resolves the varying pressures from her mother, her school, her boyfriend and her own confusion has been sensitively described by Jean Ure. We may wonder if Rose could really be quite as insensitive as she appears, but a good story helps us to accept it and concentrate on the real dilemma of Nicola, which is convincingly and sympathetically portrayed. An excellent read for a young teenager.

> *J. Nicholls, in a review of "Nicola Mimosa," in* The Junior Bookshelf, *Vol. 49, No. 4, August, 1985, p. 191.*

Ure is skillful at creating colorful characters, and her fans will welcome the return of the Bruce sisters. The dialogue between Nicola and her peers in the opening chapters is sometimes jerky and unnatural, but Ure deftly describes important incidents, and her characters execute their roles perfectly. Although the plot is not unique, aspiring young ballerinas will be enthralled with Nicola's chance for ballet fame and the many dance-related details from darning pointe shoes to dieting.

> *Cynthia K. Leibold, in a review of "The Most Important Thing," in* School Library Journal, *Vol. 32, No. 9, May, 1986, p. 110.*

In a sequel to *Supermouse,* Ure continues the story of two sisters who are proficient in the performing arts: smug and cloying little Rose (who loves to watch her own TV commercials) and Nicola, who is daring to hope that her proficiency at ballet will enable her to enter a fine (mythical) ballet school. Everybody thinks Nicola should seize her chance when it comes except her boyfriend Denny, who would miss her; her science teacher, who thinks Nicola would be a fine doctor; and her father, who fears she is losing the chance to choose a lifelong profession to pursue a beloved but impermanent avocation. Anxious as she has been to get into the ballet school, Nicola finds that she really would prefer a science program, and she courageously faces the dismay of her friends and the wrath of her mother. The latter is Ure's best portrayal, an archetypical but highly individual dragon of a stage mother. This isn't strong in plot, but it has excellent characterization, with interesting relationships (Nicola's love/hate feelings about her simpering sister, or her feelings about Denny, who is black) and a smooth writing style that has dialogue and that falls naturally on the ear.

> *A review of "The Most Important Thing," in* Bulletin of the Center for Children's Books, *Vol. 39, No. 10, June, 1986, p. 198.*

---

## *After Thursday* (1985)

Seventeen year old Marianne is in love with 25 year old Abe, a blind teacher who used to rent a room from Marianne's mother. Marianne willingly gives up other activities to spend time with Abe, but, when he gets a chance to accompany a singer on a tour, Marianne feels lonely and jealous. During his absence she spends some time with Peter, a younger man, but can't shake Abe from her thoughts.

A sequel to *See You Thursday,* the book may appeal to fans of the previous book or those lured by the attractive cover art. Most American readers, however, will find it difficult to relate to the British vocabulary, the low-key plot, the underdeveloped characters, and the slow pace. The climax is so subtle as to make one question whether he/she missed something. The ending is left open—will Abe and Marianne's relationship survive? Perhaps Ure is hoping to write an "After" *After Thursday* book. Unfortunately, this book is a disappointment.

> *Brooke Selby Dillon, in a review of "After Thursday," in* Voice of Youth Advocates, *Vol. 10, No. 2, June, 1987, p. 84.*

A purposefully visual opening sequence sets the stage nicely for more changes in Marianne Fenton's life and serves to remind *See You Thursday* readers of Abe Shonfield's blindness. At 25, Abe is still considerate, gentle, and practical. He has taken to heart lessons learned in the past, which he now begins to apply more assiduously, realizing that he must loosen his dependency on Marianne or stifle her. For her part, 17-year-old Marianne is "no longer awkward and solitary"; yet she is not secure enough to accept separation from Abe, despite touches of resentment she feels when her weekend commitments to him interfere with invitations to participate in activities she would enjoy. When Abe mentions acquiring a guide dog and takes advantage of an opportunity to establish himself as a professional musician, Marianne's jealousy and fear overrule common sense and affection enough to drive her into a relationship with Peter, an attractive young man closer to her own age, who offers her a kind of excitement she has never experienced. Though dependent on its predecessor, this is still a pleasing, well-written, at times humorous novel that authentically explores the give and take of maturing relationships while it conveys the importance of establishing a niche of one's own.

> *Stephanie Zvirin, in a review of "After Thursday," in* Booklist, *Vol. 83, No. 19, June 1, 1987, p. 1517.*

Marianne, in love with Abe, a blind musician several years her senior, suffers pangs of jealousy when he's invited to accompany a rising soprano who is attractive, an old friend of Abe's, and, like him, Jewish.

Marianne, 17, is proud of encouraging Abe's independence; he used to board with her and her mother, but now lives on his own with a friend. Still, she is fiercely protective and dedicates her free time to helping him and to doing things he can share, giving up activities that she would enjoy—sports, dancing, and a coveted part in the school play. It's obvious to the reader long before it is to Marianne that Abe wishes no such sacrifice and is in fact beginning to chafe at the intensity of her well-meaning attention: when he suggests getting a guide dog to increase his independence, Marianne feels hurt and doesn't under-

stand the need. Yet their love is real, even though the reader may suspect that their interests are so divergent and Marianne still so immature that they may not be destined for a permanent relationship.

Though Abe is less fully developed than Marianne, readers will be interested in his self-sufficiency; other characters, including the boozing would-be other man, are succinctly evoked. The British setting makes little difference; these young people are universal enough. Ure belabors her point about Abe's independence, and the loose ends in Abe and Marianne's relationship are more characteristic of life than of art, but, still, this should interest readers as an unusual love story.

> *A review of "After Thursday," in* Kirkus Reviews, *Vol. LV, No. 11, June 15, 1987, pp. 931-32.*

Marianne is an appealing character, full of talent, energy, and unselfish love. When she gives up new friends and extracurricular activities to be with Abe, her mother questions both Marianne's intentions and the nature of the relationship, creating a believable conflict between mother and daughter. This portrayal of a group of teens, meeting together for companionship and the joy of music, and Ure's gentle exploration of Marianne's emotions raise this novel above the level of the formula romances. References to rather obscure musical works may put off a few readers, but most, especially those with more eclectic musical tastes, will eagerly read to the end of this unusual and compelling romance.

> *Phyllis Graves, in a review of "After Thursday," in* School Library Journal, *Vol. 34, No. 1, September, 1987, p. 198.*

---

## The Other Side of the Fence (1986)

Bonny and Richard meet mid-flight at the roadside on a wet March morning. Richard has left home after a traumatic row, and Bonny has been deserted by her faithless boyfriend. After some hesitation he gives her a lift and as the journey progresses, so their personalities emerge. Bonny is a gregarious fantasist with an endless supply of outrageous anecdotes, who comes from a background of abandoned childhood and foster homes. In sharp contrast, Richard is reticent and bears all the hallmarks of a comfortable middle-class upbringing. Their travels eventually take them to London where they find work and a place to live.

In this memorable and humorous adventure, the two come to terms with each other and more importantly themselves, and although shortlived, their relationship has profound repercussions. During some expertly crafted sequences personalities clash dramatically and some widely held assumptions on such significant issues as class and sexual orientation are held up for close examination. This is a challenging and thought-provoking book with a tense and fast-moving plot, strong characterization and worthy content and it will be an important addition to any collection for readers of fourteen and above.

> *Julie Blaisdale, in a review of "The Other Side*

of the Fence," in British Book News Children's Books, *Summer, 1986, p. 31.*

A sad funny tale of innocents abroad in a modern world.

Richard has a row with his reactionary father—it is all about Jan who insisted that the truth should be told—and leaves his comfortable middle-class home for the hazards of the road. Bonny walks out of her squat when she is abandoned by Jake, that experienced lover, chauvinistic pig and louse. It is not too surprising that they should meet, she trying in vain to hitch a ride, he searching for the nearest garage for petrol for his stranded car. They could hardly be less alike, except in the extremity of their dilemmas, but misery makes strange bedfellows—not literally—and Richard and Bonny team up in Vic's squat in London. Here, despite Bonny's chronic inability to tell the truth and Richard's complex and orderly mind—he is reading medieval history—they might have made a go of it. Richard learns something about life from Bonny, she finds with his help that she has a mind. Alas, Jake comes back and Bonny jumps to his call. It is a mistake. She has found a different objective, and Jake is no help to her. So

*Ure's younger brother John. She writes, "[As] children we fought almost continuously while remaining the best of friends . . . [It] is possible that had I not had a brother I should find it difficult to get under the skin of my male characters and write with any degree of insight about them. As it is, my brother appears in many of my books under various guises, though generally, it has to be said, as a rather revolting small boy."*

Bonny takes the road again, feeling her way towards Richard and meeting on the way his sad and puzzled mother. When she finally finds Richard she discovers his secret and the reason why there is no place for her in his life. By now she is a stronger girl. She has learnt to read Orwell and trust her own judgement. She can even leave Richard one priceless gift, her copy of *Forever Amber;* after all he is doing medieval hist'ry!

Perhaps Bodley Head are right in putting this straight into paperback. It is not a long-lasting book. But it speaks directly to today's teenager in accents that she (probably) will recognise and respond to. The portraits are sketchy and recognisable, their setting a familiar land for all its initial strangeness. And how many girls will welcome Bonny, so vulnerable and tough, so lacking in conventional glamour, so good a survivor. A very nice read.

> *M. Crouch, in a review of "The Other Side of the Fence," in* The Junior Bookshelf, *Vol. 50, No. 4, August, 1986, p. 161.*

In another mature and sensitive novel, Ure begins with the older of two adolescents, Richard, who has just had a violent quarrel with his father and has been told to get out of the house. Aimlessly drifting about the English countryside, he gives a lift to another teenager, Bonny. Richard's a university student, Bonny a shrewd drifter, uneducated and amoral, whose tough lover, Jake, has left her. This is not a romance; in fact, it becomes increasingly clear as the story goes on that Richard is gay. Bonny does not know until, at the end of the book, he tells her. She's disappointed, but she likes Richard and is aware that he has encouraged her to get an education and have a more satisfying life than that of a grocery clerk. And Bonny has been good for Richard: in the time they have spent together, he has absorbed some of her resiliency and courage. This is a mature and candid story, told with both momentum and nuance; minor as well as major characters have depth, and they are skillfully developed through dialogue as well as exposition.

> *Zena Sutherland, in a review of "The Other Side of the Fence," in* Bulletin of the Center for Children's Books, *Vol. 41, No. 6, February, 1988, p. 127.*

The class differences are pointed, but Ure's touch is light. Bonny's prattle (some of it lies and wish fulfillment) helps free shy, tense Richard from his sense of futility and incompetence, while he helps her see that she's not the "stupid cow" her boyfriend called her and that she should get some education. Some of the minor figures are caricatures (though funny ones), and the survival details aren't always convincing. Most readers will guess long before Bonny does that Richard is gay (the cause of the family furor), but that doesn't detract from the story's enjoyment, which derives mainly from the comic and poignant interaction of the two innocents. Ure's novels always end superbly—no neat solutions, no sudden realizations of profound truth; in this case, just the quiet parting of two friends the reader has come to love, who have helped each other find some self-acceptance and take a few risks.

> *Hazel Rochman, in a review of "The Other*

*Side of the Fence," in* Booklist, *Vol. 84, No. 11, February 1, 1988, p. 926.*

The plot reads like a soap opera. Jake is truly annoying—that Bonny puts up with him stretches credibility. Bonny is worldly-wise, steals like a pro, yet cannot recognize that Jake is a con man or realize that Richard is a homosexual. Teens may harbor secret fantasies about living in garrets and flaunting parental authority, but even they may find Richard's and Bonny's naiveté too much to stomach.

*Karen K. Radtke, in a review of "The Other Side of the Fence," in* School Library Journal, *Vol. 34, No. 8, April, 1988, p. 114.*

## A Bottled Cherry Angel   (1986)

Midge is becoming increasingly isolated. Her mother is much involved with CND; her older sister is antagonistic and her two closest friends are becoming interested in boys. Midge comforts herself by playing schools with her dolls until suddenly, whilst she is reading *Peter Pan,* a boy comes into her own life.

The Peter with whom Midge plays is ragged and mysterious. Gradually it becomes apparent that only Midge can see him. At the same time Midge is changing; she enjoys the friendly interest of a senior girl, and even accepts a gift and proffered companionship from next-door Damian. At their last meeting Peter accuses Midge of growing up, and she accepts that this is the truth.

Jean Ure develops her fantasy with skill, and arouses sympathetic interest in her heroine. However this seems, like Peter Pan itself, more a book about children for adults than a story for children themselves.

*R. Baines, in a review of "A Bottled Cherry Angel," in* The Junior Bookshelf, *Vol. 50, No. 5, October, 1986, pp. 193-94.*

Not everyone becomes interested in boys at the same stage of adolescence, but if all your friends are and you aren't, you can feel quite confused and isolated. Jean Ure's main character, Midge, feels just that even though she finds at least one ally in her class—Pearl. They feel somewhat excluded by their friends, but it is they who are chosen by one of the sixth-formers to pose for a picture she is painting. Hence 'bottled cherry angel', which is actually 'a Botticelli angel', misheard by Midge.

There is another strand in this story, concerning *Peter Pan,* a book that Midge volunteers to read at school as part of a class project. After she starts to read, she keeps meeting a strange, scruffy boy, who later visits her at night, entering through her bedroom window. He is wilful and headstrong, like Peter Pan, and no one else ever seems to see him. But of course, as Midge starts coming to terms with things, he disappears for ever.

This book should go down well with top juniors and lower secondary pupils. The element of fantasy in the story gives it an extra dimension, and puts it into a different category from the average school story. The characters are well observed too.

*Sheila Armstrong, in a review of "A Bottled Cherry Angel," in* The School Librarian, *Vol. 35, No. 1, February, 1987, p. 69.*

Jean Ure uses a typically English version of the junior novel in *A Bottled Cherry Angel,* a story which turns on the way three girls moving into the 'teens influence each other. The 'Three M's' have squabbled their way through primary school together and now find, in their first secondary year, that the long alliance is to be tested as they approach new interests in differing ways. Midge (Flora) is alarmed by the interest which Match (Antonia) and Emma take in boys and bra sizes and insulates herself against growing up with dolls and athletics; the comment passed on to her by Match that she looks like 'a bottled cherry angel' seems less alarming when she discovers that an artistic senior girl wants to use her in a multi-ethnic Nativity play as a typically Caucasian face. But Midge's retreat into childhood is encouraged almost dangerously by the strange, shabby, anarchic boy who climbs into her room at night to play with her dolls and whose total lack of social inhibitions gets her into trouble with her neighbours. Only when she accuses 'Peter' of being a ghost, only when she picks up from a classroom discussion on the subconscious a vague idea of her regression, does Midge manage to make something of that adjustment to reality which her family as well as her long-standing friends have made it hard for her to achieve. With a shifting pattern of scenes and conversations, here is a picture of everyday school and home as shrewd and telling in social detail as it is in character-drawing.

*Margery Fisher, in a review of "A Bottled Cherry Angel," in* Growing Point, *Vol. 25, No. 6, March, 1987, p. 4761.*

## Swings and Roundabouts   (1986)

In this sequel to *Megastar,* Jason Miller is now a pupil at the Allyson Academy of Dance and Drama, whilst Mark and his other friends from Beasleigh Junior School attend the local comprehensive. Jason's attempts to fulfil his dreams at stage school are frequently at odds with the values and experiences of life on the estate, and when he auditions for a TV commercial, Jason cannot resist the temptation to boast. However, the part goes to another boy and Jason finds the disappointment and subsequent persecution difficult to cope with. Through the advice and support of his actor friend and mentor Dave, Jason comes to terms with failure and his credibility and confidence are eventually restored.

Once again Jean Ure describes the trials of this cheeky yet vulnerable hero with sympathy and humour by her superb use of dialogue and characterization, while at the same time embracing with ease such issues as difference in social background. Any child of eight to twelve years should find this book highly entertaining.

*Julie Blaisdale, in a review of "Swings and Roundabouts," in* British Book News Children's Books, *Winter, 1986, p. 28.*

I suppose it makes a change to read about a stage-struck

boy discovering, as they always do, 'it's not always easy . . . it's a tough business, kiddo, and them as can't take it knows what they can do.' Jason Miller longs for his first professional job out of the Allyson Dramatic Academy. His boasts about a commercial contract do not endear him to the real folk back on his London council estate, and even less so when it proves to be all hot air! Fortunately fame and a lesson in professionalism come from a cycling proficiency promotion and the ending is nicely neatened off. The strict adherence to Cockney dialect will put off some readers—most kids I know like talking to be 'written proper' not realistically!

> *David Bennett, in a review of "Swings and Roundabouts," in* Books for Keeps, *No. 53, November, 1988, p. 11.*

---

### One Green Leaf (1987)

It has taken time, but now writing for teenagers is alive and well and living in this country. We no longer have to look to Scandinavia or the United States for the real thing. There is no longer the embarrassment of seeing "teenage lists" padded out with diverted adult novels which no one under 13 could relate to.

We have a growing body of writers who understand and empathise with teenagers, who honestly try to get to grips with how the world looks from their point of view, who do not talk down to them—perhaps from a wry realisation that adults have less to offer by way of example and counsel than they used to claim.

An interesting aspect of the new writing for teenagers is that it is a development of the new school story, that is the story about the real school and the way it links with the wider community. In the new fictional school life is not single sex and does not remain forever just below the age of 14. It is about young people trying to make sense of their feelings about each other and towards the world at large.

Jean Ure is of course an established writer in this age band and has helped bring about these developments. She is at her best in illuminating the frontier zone between boys and girls, where independence in girls and tenderness in boys struggles to express itself. Her characters, David and Abbey, Zoot and Robyn (who tells the story) enjoy a close friendship, though one never free of female exasperation with the brutal/childish behaviour by which lads show they are lads. An accident which puts David's future in danger obliges them all to grow up very rapidly in the course of a school term, to realize that life does not mean an unlimited number of days ahead to spend in total self-preoccupation.

I wonder if Jean Ure, though, was right to give us the story, not in terms of Robyn's inner thoughts, but in terms of her everyday, outward speech. It may of course for some readers highlight Robyn's struggle to express how she feels about life and death. But there's a danger that the "conventional" mode may simply give the whole story a humdrum aspect and reduce the impact of the events it describes. Teenagers' inner thoughts do match the gravity of

a situation where their speech may not—and that goes for all of us.

> *Robert Leeson, in a review of "One Green Leaf," in* The Times Educational Supplement, *No. 3707, July 17, 1987, p. 23.*

David and Abbey, Zoot and Robyn are four close friends at Clareville Comprehensive. They come from normal homes and have normal teenage preoccupations. Abbey is deeply concerned about the Bomb, nuclear waste and radiation, and she press-gangs the others to attend meetings. In their sixth year Abbey and David become very close, although Robyn and Zoot are just good friends. Their relationships are simply but very effectively described and their often amusing conversations have the ring of truth. Even the minor characters, such as Robyn's father, are illuminatingly portrayed in a few, short, effective pieces of dialogue. Jean Ure has a very light, deft touch. The first sign that something is wrong is when David comes into school limping. At first they think nothing of it, but slowly the gravity of the disease becomes apparent and their normal teenage self-absorption is rudely shattered. Each in his own way tries to help, but their well-intentioned efforts do not always have the results they expect. Much is left unsaid, but it may be none the worse for that. The reader will want to think about and discuss the problems raised. David was only seventeen and had every reason to fight for life. Were his parents right to refuse further treatment for him?

Jean Ure has a deservedly high reputation and this book is one of her best and most moving. It is easy to become involved in the story and . . . the book will challenge the reader to think about problems outside his (or more likely her) experience.

> *Ann Ashford, "Outside Experiences," in* The Times Literary Supplement, *No. 4407, September 18-24, 1987, p. 1028.*

Of the many novels that have been published with a focus on a fatal illness, this is one of the most sensitive and most cohesive. Robyn's viewpoint predominates, but through her Ure shows how tragically and poignantly David's illness (cancer, with unsuccessful surgery) affects Abbey, how David's parents react, how classmates and teachers handle seeing David during a period of remission, and how David himself copes physically and emotionally with illness, loss of a limb, and the knowledge that death is inevitable and imminent. The writing style and characterization have polish and depth, and the gravity of the theme is alleviated by a humor that is appropriate because it comes from the resilient young adults drawn by the author with affection and perceptive respect.

> *Zena Sutherland, in a review of "One Green Leaf," in* Bulletin of the Center for Children's Books, *Vol. 42, No. 9, May, 1989, p. 238.*

Before Abbey and David became a couple, Robyn, Abbey, David, and Zoot had all been friends. They were still close, telling silly jokes, fooling around, defending one another whenever Mr. Harris (otherwise known as the "Great Rhetorical Windbag") was too pompous or cruel in class. Then David became ill. Not until much later did anyone admit it was cancer, but things changed anyway. Here, lively, impulsive Robyn recalls what happened and how she felt; her embarrassment at seeing David in his pajamas, her guilt for continuing to enjoy life while Abbey sacrificed and David grew worse, her anger with David for betraying Abbey with another girl, and her coming to terms with the reasons why he did it. Robyn, ingenuous and imperfect, is very real, and her narrative, while not without its emotional moments—as when she smuggles David's beloved dog into the hospital—is an unsentimental one, laced with gentle humor. It deals with how life changes and goes on, not with how or why life ends.

> *Stephanie Zvirin, in a review of "One Green Leaf," in* Booklist, *Vol. 85, No. 21, July, 1989, p. 1895.*

This well-meaning novel has several problems including the lack of character development of Abbey and Zoot (it seems strange that the feelings of these good friends are not revealed) and the abundance of British slang (such as "rounders," "squat," and "pastoral tutor") which interferes with the flow of the novel. It also bothers me that I can't discover the significance of the title despite several rereads of the text! Instead of purchasing this title, I would instead recommend *Sheila's Dying* or *Invincible Summer* which deal with the same topic.

> *Doris Losey, in a review of "One Green Leaf," in* Voice of Youth Advocates, *Vol. 12, No. 4, October, 1989, p. 218.*

---

### Tea-Leaf on the Roof (1987)

The limitations of youthful experience are very marked in **Tea-Leaf on the Roof.** Jean Ure casts a somewhat sardonic eye on the older type of junior adventure through the medium of her hero, William, who is obliged to listen politely while his father reads the first chapter of his new story aloud ('Alistair and Co. were starting to grow restless. It was time they had another mystery to solve! The last one had been the case of the burnt-out car, when Sergeant Trotter had recommended them all for a share in the reward—but that had been weeks ago'). Simulated sick-noises make William's attitude to this kind of story clear enough. All the same, when leaks in the roofs of more than one house in Tettiscombe Terrace reveal the fact that lead has been stripped by someone unknown, he and his friends West Indian Charlotte and Indian Mash can't resist taking on a case which the police seem unable to solve. The children have their own way of judging people; for William, Chalky White with his single ear-ring and his shocking pink jalopy is as obviously a hero as Alex 'Jogger' Masterson, fussy about his new Fiat, seems increasingly suspicious in his behaviour. Not lacking in courage, buoyed up by the prospect of becoming famous, the three children keep watch on streets and roof-tops and, inevitably, reach all the wrong conclusions; far from earning commendations from the police, they are soundly chastised for getting in the way and letting the true tea-leaf slip away in the confusion. Cheerful and active, laced with the Cockney rhyming slang which William is avidly collecting word by word from Chalky, this is a good example of the

'eighties tale of action, fast-moving and dead-pan and substantial in the presentation of adults and children in a particular urban setting.

> *Margery Fisher, in a review of "Tea-Leaf on the Roof," in* Growing Point, *Vol. 26, No. 4, November, 1987, p. 4877.*

William, the hero of **Tea Leaf on the Roof,** is the son of a Justin Case, famous author of mystery stories for children—the kind in which groups of eager youngsters solve crimes which have baffled the finest brains in CID. The stories fill William with scorn. Life after all, he thinks, is simply not like that. Any group of kids really attempting to get to grips with a mystery would surely be met with a cry of: "You shove off you kids or I'll have the law on you!"

You start to get the feeling that Jean Ure is of a similar mind. Her setting, after all, is Tettiscombe Terrace, a place whence black families go to church in a blue Transit bus, and where there is a man called Chalky, the owner of a pink but rusty Ford Thunderbird. Here is an author, you feel, who is trying to be to Blyton and Ransome what Fluck and Law are to Annette Mills. But stay! Read on, and behold she shows you a mystery after all! Some lead is half inched by a tea leaf, and for William and his friends

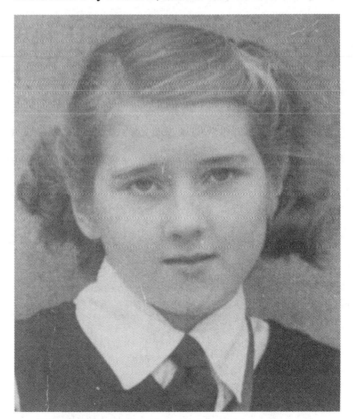

*Ure at eleven. Describing herself as "me, with the hair," she notes that "my main influence [as a writer] was hair . . . I am almost seriously persuaded that had it not been for hair [which wouldn't hold a curl] I would . . . have done what was expected of me and trotted off meekly to read English at university," instead of having her first book,* Dance for Two *(1960), published when she was seventeen.*

the game is suddenly afoot! (Rhyming slang, I should say, is a feature of this book, though Jean Ure eschews the ripest and funniest examples.) This is a good lively read.

*Gerald Haigh, "Round the U Bend," in The Times Educational Supplement, No. 3726, November 27, 1987, p. 45.*

A lively 'Whodunnit' in the East End of London. The setting emphasises the physical deprivation and multi-ethnic culture of the location, and the impact this has on children growing up and living together within it. A cockney slang glossary explains that the 'tea-leaf' of the title means 'thief'. The book opens with the rather pedestrian boredom of the early summer holidays, but once the theft has occurred, the children attempt to track down the culprit, following fictional methods. Adults are rather shadowy stereotypes, but they do not behave predictably and the children's sleuthing is sometimes humorously thwarted. The characters of the children are well drawn, and should be appreciated by readers of this age group.

*Angela Lepper, in a review of "Tea-Leaf on the Roof," in The School Librarian, Vol. 36, No. 2, May, 1988, p. 60.*

---

### The Fright; Who's Talking? (1987)

**The Fright** and **Who's Talking?** deal with themes of friendship, belonging, getting into trouble, coping with the supply teacher and, in Pavindra Patel's case (**Who's Talking?**), the pressure to succeed academically. The stories are mainly concerned (so far anyway) with girls—so for the most part the boys weren't interested. Many were put off by the first chapter of **The Fright**—'too many names, too many characters. I got confused'. They found few points of connection, either, between the style of school organisation and behaviour in the books and what they knew. I thought it more 9+ in 'feel' and will try the books with older children.

*Pat Triggs, in a review of "The Woodside School Stories," in Books for Keeps, No. 48, January, 1988, pp. 8-9.*

**Who's Talking?** is the second of Jean Ure's stories about Woodside School. The two main characters are Sophie and Pavindra, who after a series of misunderstandings become friends. . . . Jean Ure is always good at creating the reality of school classrooms and corridors, and the characters of a group of children who have been together for some time. Sophie is especially well done—her generosity, her meanness, her temper, her embarrassment, all her changes of mood and point of view as she comes to understand herself and Pavindra better. . . . [This] book will show young readers something of the possibilities in stories for considering how we behave and why.

*Donald Fry, in a review of "Who's Talking?" in The School Librarian, Vol. 36, No. 1, February, 1988, p. 21.*

In Jean Ure's **The Fright** in the "Woodside School" series the central character, Catherine, is the loner we all recognize—the girl who let the potted plants die because she did not know how to find a jug to water them. A new girl with problems of her own joins the school, and a complicated and yet very recognizable series of emotional events takes place. Children will find this very telling. Another Woodside School story by Jean Ure in the same series, **Who's Talking?**, deals with tensions and misunderstandings in class, this time about cheating and owning up.

*Gerald Haigh, "Ready to Read," in The Times Educational Supplement, No. 3736, February 5, 1988, p. 54.*

[In **Who's Talking?**] Sophie talks so much that a supply teacher is already aware of her reputation, and ready to pounce when someone speaks during a test. In fact the culprit was a quiet and diligent Indian girl, Pavindra Patel, who seems desperately afraid of making a mistake. Enraged by the false accusation Sophie threatens Pavindra, and is overheard. Next day, when Pavindra has disappeared, Sophie is summoned to the Headmistress' study and confronted by Mr. and Mrs. Patel and a police officer.

Many Asian parents can seem over-demanding in their insistence on academic excellence. This is a useful theme to tackle, and Jean Ure has woven it into her story with experienced skill. It is a pity that, in order to seem authentic, the reported language of the classroom has nowadays to be so ugly and uncouth, but that is less a fault of the author than of our times.

*R. Baines, in a review of "Who's Talking?" in The Junior Bookshelf, Vol. 52, No. 3, June, 1988, p. 144.*

---

### War with Old Mouldy! (1987)

In the close community of school there is something of impermanence yet of intensity in alliances and antagonisms, between pupils and teachers as well as between peers. Age has little to do with the matter; feelings can run as high in primary classes as they do in the adolescent years. **War with Old Mouldy** provides a good example. Moulder Brown's grandiloquent and often sarcastic mode of speech upsets his pupils, though at first none of them agree to help bossy Jody in a campaign against him—not even Simon, though he suffers from the fact that Old Mouldy can even exercise his baneful influence on his home life, because his windows overlook Simon's garden. Eventually the boy does get involved with worms in the teacher's desk and glue on his chair and though their enemy hardly reacts to their tricks as they hoped, he does announce his retirement and this they are satisfied to interpret as victory for their cause. The pattern of classroom behaviour and stratagem is worked out in a neat story in which dialogue and humour refresh the usual interactions of pupils in a middle school.

*Margery Fisher, in a review of "War with Old Mouldy," in Growing Point, Vol. 27, No. 1, May, 1988, pp. 4979-80.*

---

### Frankie's Dad (1988)

Readers deep into this book and anticipating a 'happy'

ending will feel disappointed but not cheated. Brash, athletic, tomboy Frankie, 'all butch and bellicose in her boiler-suit', may have dreamed romantic day-dreams about her absconding West Indian father but when he reappears with a splurge of lavish entertainment she remains level-headed enough to see that after all she *can* adjust to her not altogether favourable circumstances. It was not enough that her deserted mother was to marry a 'pig-eyed slob' called Billy Small but that in addition she must face the traumas of a change of environment, loss of friends *and* the acquisition of a seven-year-old half-brother, Jasper, 'like an under-sized weed that had just struggled up for a bit of air'. Jasper's bed-wetting is the source of endless rows in the new home but Frankie finds some relief in the quirks of patients in a next-door mental home/hospital; Queenie and Mrs. Thatcher are entertaining but not malicious caricatures of well-loved personalities. Much of the time Frankie's reactions are coloured by the indignation inherent in a pre-pubertal junior female who would rather have been born a boy but this particular trauma recedes with time as opportunities to be boyish decline. The novel is thoughtful as well as entertaining but some readers may find its ending disturbingly problematic if not actually sad.

> *A. R. Williams, in a review of "Frankie's Dad," in* The Junior Bookshelf, *Vol. 52, No. 6, December, 1988, p. 311.*

---

### Trouble with Vanessa   (1988)

Two girls of sixteen move from a single sex school to a Sixth Form College. Their expectations of meeting boys, so far a more or less unknown species, are fulfilled to some extent, as the author shows as she describes ruthless Mr. Morrison's Personal Development classes where Kate and Vanessa get to know, if only in a partial and patchy way, the two boys they run into on their first day at college—black Danny, open and clownish, and Ned, who surprisingly plans to join the army. Why, the girls wonder, is Ned taking the Arts and Drama course? And which came first, his idea of a military career or his stiff-upper-lip behaviour which infuriates their tutor? Within the framework of classes, bed-sits., parental adjurations and sexual rivalry Jean Ure invites us to examine the quartet as in dramatic exercises and private meeting they discover what each is prepared to reveal and, in some cases, a little more. A second marriage when Vanessa's father married Kate's mother had bound the girls in an unusual sisterly relationship within which they sometimes enjoy and sometimes resent their differences—for if Vanessa is bossy, as the title *Trouble with Vanessa* suggests, the milder Kate, with a sense of humour, is well able to assert herself when it seems desirable. . . . This is an assured piece of comic writing with a shrewd appraisal of the way young people make friends and rub edges off one another and with at least two characters, Ned and Vanessa, whose motives have the muddled and contradictory origins which require, and are given, a proper novelistic scrutiny.

> *Margery Fisher, in a review of "Trouble with Vanessa," in* Growing Point, *Vol. 27, No. 6, March, 1989, p. 5111-12.*

This is the first in a trilogy about four students embarking on an Arts and Drama course at sixth-form college. Vanessa, Kate, Ned and Danny bring very different experiences and expectations to the new term and one of the book's strengths is its refusal to be overwhelmed by disparity. Instead—largely through the medium of the developing relationship between Ned and Vanessa—the reader is treated to Ure's wryly accurate portrait of student life: uncertainty; precocity, bombast—that fierce energy peculiar to the young. Although there is sufficient to allow the less committed reader to become involved, the language is often pleasingly challenging and likely to positively engage a keen third or fourth-year reader. Put it in the book box and/or library—and wait for the next!

> *Val Randall, in a review of "Trouble with Vanessa," in* Books for Keeps, *No. 56, May, 1989, p. 13.*

---

### There's Always Danny   (1988)

Jean Ure is an assured writer for teenagers and in this second part of a trilogy she has the half-sisters, Kate and Vanessa, continuing their South London College Drama course and coping with the independence of their own flat. A large number of issues are raised—new ones like AIDS and older ones about relationships. It's all done competently and busily and Kate's education, formal and informal, apparently leaves her wiser and maturer. There's a belief in the healthiness of raising issues, of confronting and facing up to them by talking about them (and writing about them) and it's difficult to not to agree, in part anyway.

> *Adrian Jackson, in a review of "There's Always Danny," in* Books for Keeps, *No. 56, May, 1989, p. 13.*

---

### Plague 99   (1989; U.S. edition as Plague)

In **Plague 99** London is wiped out, within little more than a week, by a mysterious new disease. Three sixteen-year-olds from Croydon, Fran Latimer, Harriet Somers and Shahid Khan, set out to walk to Barnet, where Shahid's brother has a wholesale grocery. For a trio of possible survivors, they are desperately mismatched and ill equipped. Shahid is an apathetic television addict, careless about the Bangladeshi culture whose patriarchal habits he proves to have inherited. Harriet, known as Harry, is impulsive, infantile, extravagantly irresponsible. The repressed, bookish and unsociable Fran copes much better than she would ever have expected of herself, largely through dogged middle-class decency. "You couldn't just ignore people," she decides, though for the frightened remnants of a depopulated London, as for a lonely fifth-former, ignoring other people seems to be the rule. For Fran, who perhaps represents Ure's idea of the average reader of "teen fiction", the ordeal is not so much the arduous quest for Barnet as the problems of looking after her companions.

The drama in **Plague 99** is contained within this triangle. Speculation that the plague may be an escaped bacteriological weapon is balanced against hope that, by the end of the book, it may have run its course; but the youngsters do not know. There is no information. The authorities have disappeared, along with everybody else. A few soldiers, a few rioters, are seen from a distance. There don't seem to be many rotting corpses—half a dozen in the Thames—or much of a stench; nor is there any sign of foreign intervention. Literal objections are beside the point, however. What engages Ure is the deserted city as a moral landscape, in which teenage thoughts about social responsibility can be examined in isolation, without adult supervision. "The worst thing is"; Shahid observes, "all the social conventions have gone." He means it sarcastically, but it's true.

*Colin Greenland, "Soul Survivors," in* The Times Literary Supplement, *No. 4509, September 1-7, 1989, p. 957.*

Unlike John Christopher's *Empty World,* which has a similar premise, this focuses more on character than on plot; switching between narrative and diary entries, Ure explores Fran's inner turmoil as she reluctantly changes from dreamy homebody to leader, and Shahid's as he loses some of his adolescent arrogance. Was the plague released deliberately, or accidentally? Neither the characters here nor readers ever find out. After several weeks, Shahid recovers and the two leave London, not knowing how far the devastation has spread. The loose ends make the story all the more chilling.

*A review of "Plague," in* Kirkus Reviews, *Vol. LIX, No. 17, September 1, 1991, p. 1165.*

Gripped by the pall of disease, death and government conspiracy, Ure's tale must work hard to achieve a more hopeful plane. Fran's hard-won, stoic optimism at the book's end seems a faint cheer compared to the thunderous silence of the dead she leaves behind—and is sure to encounter ahead, as Ure suggests a global disaster has occurred. More chilling than thrilling, this frightening, thought-provoking novel grabs the reader's attention and holds tight until the last word.

*A review of "Plague," in* Publishers Weekly, *Vol. 238, No. 43, September 27, 1991, p. 59.*

The desolation of these three adolescents, all high school seniors, is darkly enthralling, but the story isn't up to the atmosphere. Harry wanders off; Shahid catches the disease but doesn't die (why not?); the novel ends with Fran and Shahid on the road to Cornwall, two hundred miles away. Such inconclusiveness may be realistic, but it isn't particularly good storytelling (and/or may indicate plans for a sequel). What works best in this book is its sense of anonymous and deadly menace, and the brave spirits of three teens who face it.

*Roger Sutton, in a review of "Plague," in* Bulletin of the Center for Children's Books, *Vol. 45, No. 2, October, 1991, p. 52.*

Returning from a month-long survival camp to her London home, Fran, 16, finds she must use her new skills to confront a plague that has left her parents and many others dead. With her friends, Harriet and Shahid, Fran embarks on a search for food and shelter through a ravaged present-day London. Fran remains strong as Harriet goes mad and runs away and as Shahid suffers the horrors of the plague. Finding renewed spirit in Shahid's recovery, the pair leave London in search of a new life. The story gets preachy as the teens blame "the government" for the disaster. The writing is awkward in spots, bogged down in a constant "he said," "she said," "I said" rhythm. The beginning chapter intrigues, but the remainder of the book does not live up to its promise. Young readers may identify with Fran's courage, but too many questions are left unanswered.

*Rebecca Neuhedel, in a review of "Plague," in* The Book Report, *Vol. 11, No. 1, May-June, 1992, p. 47.*

---

### Tomorrow Is Also a Day   (1989)

The third of the Abe and Marianne books and to show how they've progressed this opens just after they have given up their virginity. It's part of the style of the book to deal sensibly and calmly with what might be shocking or even erotic. As before the book is full of sensible responses to issues: blindness, being a vegetarian, lesbians, intercourse . . . The major issue is Marianne's mother's affair with a married man and there is at least some toughness in the resolution to that. Jean Ure makes it readable and has a strong following for these and her other novels.

*Adrian Jackson, in a review of "Tomorrow Is Also a Day," in* Books for Keeps, *No. 59, November, 1989, p. 13.*

---

### King of Spuds; Who's for the Zoo?   (1989)

In two new 'Woodside School' stories Jean Ure defines her characters briskly so that their doings are properly motivated. *Who's for the Zoo?* concerns Catherine, a sensitive child who puzzles her friends by refusing to join in a class trip to Regent's Park. Miss Lilly is quick enough to make educational use of Catherine's dislike of caged animals and when the classroom is furnished with chair-cages confining noisy Nicky as a monkey, Shria Shah (suitably) as a panther and outsize Cameron as a yak, children and teacher see the point very clearly. The same quick-witted teacher finds a way to cure Nicky of truanting by setting up a street market as a numbers lesson and using this to convey to the boy that she had spotted him helping his uncle to sell potatoes from his stall, even that she understands his behaviour. The use of colour and emphatic line in the illustrations [by Lynne Willey] extends the sense of place and personality very evident in these easy to read but by no means simple tales in which children find their own level in the world of primary school.

*Margery Fisher, in a review of "Who's for the Zoo?" and "King of Spuds," in* Growing Point, *Vol. 29, No. 1, May, 1990, 5341.*

These books are peopled with highly individualistic children and a wonderfully sympathetic teacher called Miss Lilly. Their adventures together are the basis for the stories. Although they are English, the books will be enjoyed by Australian children as school stories have widespread appeal. There is an interesting multicultural element introduced incidentally in these two books as many of the children at the school are from Pakistani and West Indian backgrounds.

In the first of the books the children have to choose where they will go for the class excursion which is to be the finish to the project work they have been doing on animals. In the other we read about Nick and his problems at school and the ways in which he handles those.

Both have an underlying and thought-provoking message which will give children more than a simple school story. We see Miss Lilly adopt some novel ways to deal with Nick's low self-esteem and we are made to think about our attitudes to caged animals in **Who's for the Zoo?**

> *Margot Tyrrell, in a review of "Who's for the Zoo?" and "King of Spuds," in* Magpies, *Vol. 5, No. 3, July, 1990, p. 30.*

### Jo in the Middle (1990)

Jean Ure's **Jo in the Middle** is another satisfying rite of passage novel. Its theme is the changing, even ephemeral, nature of some friendships and the self-awareness which is required to understand them. In the best traditions of the school story, Jo and Matty arrive apprehensively for the first day of term at their new, large and initially overwhelming secondary school. Friends from primary school days, they seem to drift apart as Matty forms close links with another girl and the gang while Jo, who sees herself as dull and average, doesn't quite fit in. Bemoaning the fact that she is always "Jo-in-the-middle . . . always second fiddle" she falls under the influence of Claire, a self-centred individualist whose passion for ballet inspires Jo to try to be a dancer. Jo's sense of inadequacy is keenly probed, and her struggles to understand herself and to find out what she really wants from life are colourfully conveyed. Jean Ure skilfully captures the quality of adolescent dialogue, of friendships and rivalries. She also tackles the tricky question of attractions and antagonisms between school-mates from different social groups and races.

> *Mary Cadogan, "Dorm Raids," in* The Times Educational Supplement, *No. 3858, June 8, 1990, p. B10.*

Jean Ure's 11 plus protagonists survive their tea-cup storms and are presented vividly enough to enable readers of that age and younger to identify with them. They squabble, name-call and are unkind to each other as the mores of that age-group often demands but no real harm is done. Adolescence beckons with its greater traumas to dim the memory of those childhood years.

> *D. A. Young, in a review of "Jo in the Middle," in* The Junior Bookshelf, *Vol. 54, No. 4, August, 1990, pp. 193-94.*

### Play Nimrod for Him (1990)

[This book] begins uncompromisingly with a solitary

wank. It goes on to explore the world of two introverted (male) sixth-formers who, though they may be trapped in the highly conventional surroundings of Bromley and Chislehurst, are very definitely out of sync with their partying, games-playing contemporaries. Nick and Christopher spend Saturday buying Shostakovich on CD, lapsing into A level French, improvising a future fantasy life and scripting scurrilous sketches for a sixth-form revue.

The (comparative) extraordinariness of the two central characters is utterly convincing and could be very moving to the sort of fifth or sixth former likely to enjoy the book. Nick and (to a lesser extent) Christopher may be unhealthily absorbed in each other: there is nothing rare in such adolescent (chaste) commitment. What I find distinctly unpleasant and very worrying is the ending. Christopher breaks out of the friendship, finds a girl and turns conventional. All right, for many that *is* a happy ending. Nick, however, is left to bear the brunt of accusations of gayness, awkwardness and "not fitting in". When he illegally takes his older brother's Porsche (well, you know what it's like round Chislehurst) and dies in a crash he hoped might be a joint suicide for himself and Christopher, it is seen as a "fitting" ending. "He did it because he couldn't help it . . . he tried to be one of us. He'd come to the party: he just hadn't been able to fit in."

All right, so it's only a book. Teenagers aren't meant to

*Ure's husband, Leonard, about 1973.*

copy all they read in books. But there are plenty of lads like Nick who will identify with the confirmed loner and then find themselves being told it's a matter of either conforming or opting out suicidally. It's a brilliant and powerful book in many ways—but I'm glad it's not my name on it.

*David Self, in a review of "Play Nimrod for Him," in* The Times Educational Supplement, *No. 3859, June 15, 1990, p. B8.*

Jean Ure knows her teenagers. To know them is not necessarily to love them. I found Christopher, the central character—I will not call him the 'hero'—of this clever novel, profoundly unlikable. We meet him first on holiday with mother—it is a single-parent family and nagging old grandmother. The sun is shining but Christopher lies in bed masturbating while the world goes by. His friend Nick, with whom he shares all his fantasies, has gone off to France with his wealthy parents, and Christopher, a scholarship boy at their snob-school, has to make do with Smeaton-on-Sea ('strictly for the wrinklies'). Christopher's trouble is that he despises everyone in the world except Nick. Nick has genius as well as money, while Christopher is just clever. Life changes—he is not sure if it is for the better—when Sal turns up. Sal is 'normal' and downright and attractive. Soon Christopher is absenting himself from his private world with Nick and, alarmingly, enjoying it. The plot seems to be shaping up for a familiar situation of lovers' tiffs and reconciliations, but Ms Ure does not go in for the familiar. She has many unexpected, but psychologically sound, twists to her story before it reaches its tragic yet fairly satisfactory conclusion. There is not a situation cliché in all these 230-odd pages.

As always Ms Ure writes with complete integrity. As always too she is provocative, forcing the reader to react strongly to her creations. She plays a dangerous game. We dislike Christopher so much for most of the time that we come near to losing interest in him. Not quite. As he grows—and no Ure character is ever static—we reluctantly surrender our prejudices and begin to care. My sympathies still stayed mainly with poor bewildered mum—what *has* she produced?—and sensible, humorous Sal. Even disagreeable old grandmother has her points. The reader keeps on thinking and adjusting right to the end. If only Ms Ure had a literary style to match her insight she would be right up in the first rank of writers for the young adult.

*M. Crouch, in a review of "Play Nimrod for Him," in* The Junior Bookshelf, *Vol. 54, No. 4, August, 1990, p. 194.*

Like birds in a courtship display, Christopher and Nick posture and preen to establish their unphysical but intense relationship, using as an indirect way of communicating their feelings an imaginary pair of friends, Guy and Oliver, whose changes of attitude are worked out in a mixture of dialogue and explanation. The friendship not only isolates the youths from their peers but it also exasperates certain teachers who are trying to correct their lack of public spirit. Then a third element appears to alter the pattern, Christopher's cousin Sal whose family comes to live in the suburb, and Sal's cheerful, demanding ways bring trouble.

Jean Ure shrewdly points to the different ways in which the youths and the girl manipulate daily events like discos and parties, school festivals, the claims of siblings and relations, so as to reach some kind of conclusion about their own deepest wishes and needs. The three main characters are revealed to the reader in clues embedded in dialogue and in what is left unsaid; in particular Nick's tormented nature and his unacknowledged dependence on other people are there to be discovered by readers who are prepared to dig more deeply than a casual read requires.

*Margery Fisher, in a review of "Play Nimrod for Him," in* Growing Point, *Vol. 29, No. 3, September, 1990, pp. 5394-95.*

This brilliant novel has received some severe comment—particularly about the starkness of its ending. How can Nick be allowed to die so violently and by his own choosing? What sort of a message is that to give children? Serious criticism indeed—but I am sure it is misplaced. The ending works and is fitting on many levels. The two I would concentrate on are first the formal and aesthetic; second, the psychological. The story has an elegant structure: the patterning of characters with Sal's rise and Nick's decline in relation to Christopher is classical in its intensity. The focus throughout is on Christopher; it's *his* story. He outgrows Nick—the values represented by Sal are his now. On a formal level, then Nick has no place in life, any more than, say, Lear or Othello have a place in life at the end. That may seem crass overstatement. But this book is also a study of different sorts of imaginative life. There is a spectrum here; from constructive role-play to paranoia. Only at the end are we sure that what was pleasant fantasy to Christopher was schizophrenia for Nick. Christopher's attraction to Nick is itself nearly a death wish—but while his attempt at suicide is not really meant and incompetent anyway, Nick's is purposed, effective and designed to take Christopher with him. As a psychological study of a person typifying the terrible logical extremity of the imaginative life, the character of Nick is very effectively realised and seen for what it is: the enemy of life and art. His death is fitting and inevitable and so is the manner of it.

Believe it or not, this is actually a very funny book. The plot moves fast: the setting is authentic: the minor characters drawn crisply and incisively. It ranks as a very fine achievement: there won't be much to better it this year.

*Dennis Hamley, in a review of "Play Nimrod for Him," in* The School Librarian, *Vol. 38, No. 4, November, 1990, p. 161.*

---

### Cool Simon (1990)

Mr. Harris resents being appointed teacher of Class 6: it contains three difficult boys and Samantha Swales, who dislikes being female and is unpopular. He has little time or attention to spare for a new boy, Simon, who is deaf.

However, Samantha proves good at understanding Simon's defective speech, and an unlikely friendship develops. Samantha's energy carries the two of them into involvement with the local newspaper and conflict with a gang of boys more menacing than any of their classroom companions. Whilst rescuing the school rabbit from these louts, Simon proves himself a hero, and attains a position from which he is able to do Samantha a favour.

Jean Ure writes sympathetically about several of the problems which can bedevil contemporary childhood. Her portrayal of Simon, which realistically depicts the speech difficulties caused by his handicap, should help both children and teachers who encounter deaf pupils in the classroom.

> *R. Baines, in a review of "Cool Simon," in* The Junior Bookshelf, *Vol. 55, No. 2, April, 1991, p. 63.*

Simon Ratnayaka has hearing problems and the other children in his new school find it difficult to understand him, except for Sam, an unpopular and aggressive girl whose thwarted desire is to be in the school football team. These two 'outcasts' befriend each other. Then when one of the school's pet rabbits is stolen, they find him in dramatic circumstances . . . and the hero of the hour is 'cool Simon'.

Simon's speech problems are well reproduced, and there is considerable insight into the confused world of the partially hearing and the thoughtlessness which makes life even more difficult. Sam's troubles are also sympathetically handled, though sadly not by her school. Realisation of the school scene and characterisation are both extremely good too.

> *Angela Lepper, in a review of "Cool Simon," in* The School Librarian, *Vol. 39, No. 2, May, 1991, p. 63.*

Some readers may be outraged by the vulgarity of the children at Woodside Primary School and at the impatience and lack of sensitivity among some members of the staff, and they may feel uncomfortable with the portrayal of a child who has partial hearing, Cool Simon, and the comical rendering of his speech—'Dew awway gaw me Goo Dimon'—they always call me Cool Simon. But readers of Jean Ure's other Woodside books will already love and trust their author. They know that she only writes the truth and about things that are real. Moreover, she is a wonderful storyteller. Cool Simon may be deaf and have odd speech, but he is a highly intelligent young man. His only friend, Sam, may be loud-mouthed and ill-mannered but she is fiercely loyal to him. She wants to play in the football team but she can't because she's a girl. He wants to play in the team but he can't because he's deaf. The partnership between the two to combat both sexism and 'deafism' is truly memorable.

> *M. Maran, in a review of "Cool Simon," in* Books for Your Children, *Vol. 26, No. 2, Summer, 1991, p. 17.*

## The Wizard in the Woods (1990)

This story is meshed into a very comprehensive approach to a magical fantasy. From the training of Junior Wizards to the evaporation or strengthening of magic, every possible detail has been changed to meet the rules of the 'Grand Order of Wizards'.

Poor Ben-Muzzy makes a mistake during his examination to become a second-class Junior Wizard. He finds himself in a wood where he meets the twins Gemma and Joel. Together, they are transported to Wishing Land. This is not such a happy place as it might sound. Only their growing friendship, and Ben-Muzzy's rudimentary skills, help them.

By the end of the book, their knowledge of each other, and developing magic, results in a surprise for the twins. It is something they always wanted but as they can never agree its form is surprising. Children of junior age who enjoy fantasy will find much to entertain them.

> *F.B., in a review of "The Wizard in the Woods," in* The Junior Bookshelf, *Vol. 55, No. 2, April, 1991, p. 63.*

Ben-Muzzy, inept apprentice wizard, is hopelessly tangled up by the spell-making words that the Grand High Wizard forces into his head. During an exam to ensure his qualifications as first-class junior wizard, he accidentally sends himself into an ordinary landscape and the care of twins Joel and Gemma. Trying to return him to his own land, all three end up in a strange place that grants visitors three wishes, and then in a country of giants and ogres. Stumbling across a witches' meeting, the wanderers filch a flying broomstick to take them all home. Ure's story—impelled more by high spirits and razzle-dazzle effects than by its arbitrary plot—is as random as the results of Ben-Muzzy's bungled spells. Still, readers who appreciate the loopholes that make magic so difficult may find that humor carries the day. . . .

> *A review of "The Wizard in the Woods," in* Kirkus Reviews, *Vol. LX, No. 17, September 1, 1992, p. 1136.*

None of the main characters are especially memorable, but their escapades are lively and amusing, and the black-and-white drawings [by David Anstey] adequately convey the story's humor. The plot is easy to follow, with the magical elements smoothly interwoven. This appealing light fantasy is a good choice for readers new to the genre, although Yolen's *Wizard's Hall* (HBJ, 1991) and Alexander's *Wizard in the Tree* (Dutton, 1974) are equally accessible and more involving.

> *Steven Engelfried, in a review of "The Wizard in the Woods," in* School Library Journal, *Vol. 38, No. 10, October, 1992, pp. 122-23.*

## Fat Lollipop (1991)

Sympathy is the last thing available to stout, self-satisfied Laurel Bustamente. Nobody likes her very much at school and when the Laing gang (Bozzy, Barge and Fij) decide to get rid of her and adopt Jo Jameson instead, Jo feels only slightly guilty. Gradually she changes her mind and makes a determined effort to help Lol, even though she suspects that the fat girl is cheating over the strict diet which she had agreed to try. Jo has to learn the hard way that you can't force people to change their habits and that she must accept that *Fat Lollipop* is pretty well satisfied as she is, with the usual excuse 'some people are just made big'. This lively tale of 'Peter High' makes good use of the vital trivialities of school days—the agonising over entries for the magazine, the constant shifts of alliances and rivalries in the classroom and on the playing field, the small cruelties and consolations that make each day different in a changeless routine. The peculiar constitution of a gang is analysed, indirectly through Jo's reactions to membership, to the demands made by bossy Barge and lethargic Bozzy, to the comments made by her peers and in her family about her determined experiments in the matter of diet. A brisk idiom, not too fashionably slangy but convincingly casual and judiciously ungrammatical, an observant eye on both crowds and individuals, make this a notable example of the up to date school story genre.

> *Margery Fisher, in a review of "Fat Lollipop," in* Growing Point, *Vol. 30, No. 2, July, 1991, p. 5550.*

*Fat Lollipop* is Jean Ure's second novel for young people featuring Joanne Jameson (Jo, or Jammy) who was the central character in *Jo in the Middle.* Jo has now progressed to the Seniors and finds herself invited to join the Laing gang as replacement for Laurel Bustamente, otherwise known as Lol, or Fat Lollipop. From the start one is hard into a school environment of houses, hockey, fallings-in and fallings-out, friends and enemies . . . and all the detailed paraphernalia of the secret world of adolescent girls. Jean Ure's style is semi-frantic; information and incident bubble and boil throughout the story; there is a whirlwind pace.

Lol has a weight problem—nice, contemporary touch—and Jo becomes involved in a dieting plan. The girls with their plethora of nicknames show boundless talent for rubbing everyone up the wrong way.

Jean Ure is quite excellent with dialogue. The conversations are sharp, the retorts and banter fairly fizz off the page. It is all rather addictive, and I can see readers becoming hooked on the developing series. Bouncy, lively, energy high-octane reading for girls.

> *W. M., in a review of "Fat Lollipop," in* The Junior Bookshelf, *Vol. 55, No. 4, August, 1991, pp. 182-83.*

Ure is a skilful and witty writer and she marvellously captures the flavour of female early adolescence with its intrigues, rivalries, jealousies, friendships, fancies and despairs, the games they play at this twitchily sensitive period. She achieves this through crisp, topical dialogue, sharp and entertaining character sketches and the clever use of nick-names (and names, Laurel Bustamente, Fat Lollipop of the title, is a beauty). At Peter High names matter. "Bozzy, Jammy, Fij and Barge. You must admit," said Barge, "it does *sound* better." So begins the book and bang, we're in the plot. For Bozzy etc are the Laing gang and Jammy is Joanna Jameson, our heroine, a new girl at Peter High whom they've asked to join them, to her delight, for gangs are as important as names, except and on this *"except"* the whole story devolves, that *her* entry

means ousting Laurel Bustamente, Fat Lollipop, and Jammy has qualms about this. Will she be hurt? From then on the unhappiness of Laurel leads Jo into troubles, finally culminating in her joining Fat Lollipop on a slimming campaign, no matter that Jammy is thin to begin with.

There's much food (and food for thought) in this book. Too much perhaps? And was Laurel's obesity really caused only by eating to excess? I wondered. Its liveliness will attract readers, but what about the fat ones? How will they handle this story? But I enjoyed the sports, the Latin (hooray), and the other poems and most of all lovely Nadge, easy, brilliant, laughing, laid-back black Nadge. I wanted more of Nadge, willing to swap the entire Laing gang for her.

> *Gene Kemp, in a review of "Fat Lollipop," in* The Times Educational Supplement, *No. 3930, October 31, 1991, p. 28.*

---

### William in Love (1991)

A writer of Jean Ure's standing is unlikely to let us down. Indeed, *William in Love* does not disappoint and is assured of an appreciative audience of eleven- to twelve-year-olds. Fans of *Tealeaf on the Roof* will be only too pleased to be reacquainted with our young hero. To while away the holidays when his best mate is in hospital, William decides it would be a good idea to fall in love. A series of highly entertaining attempts ensue, with precocious Vicky, voracious Patsy and boisterous, punch-packing Charlotte, helped along by unfortunate coincidences such as a pet dog snatching proffered chocolates and a *billet-doux* getting into the wrong hands. Of course, it is all to no avail and the tables are neatly turned in the last chapter, but I won't spoil your fun by giving the game away. Along the way we are treated to some splendid cameos in a family setting where roles are non-stereotyped. Mother does all the DIY jobs while Father churns out romantic fiction for his publishers. His purple passages feed William's fantasies, but the events on the page do not mirror those in his real life, where the rose-tinted glasses are definitely off.

The tone is nicely ironic, the humour never heavy-handed. It makes a refreshing change to have a young lad dwelling on love and interrogating his parents about the symptoms!

> *Angela Redfern, in a review of "William in Love," in* The School Librarian, *Vol. 40, No. 1, February, 1992, p. 33.*

---

### Dreaming of Larry (1991)

15-year-old Judith falls for an older boy, and from then on the plot hinges on will-they-or-won't-they have sex while Judith is Under Age (they don't, but it's a near thing), and on Judith's discovery of a link between her ancestors and Larry's. The relationship isn't brought to life as successfully as Abe's and Marianne's in Jean Ure's 'Thursday' series, but the realistic portrayal of teenage concerns and conversations will appeal to adolescent girls.

*Linda Newberry, in a review of "Dreaming of Larry," in* Books for Keeps, *No. 73, March, 1992, p. 11.*

Coincidence is sometimes frowned upon as a fictional device but in ***Dreaming of Larry*** it provides an intriguing way of shaping the unlikely and warmly romantic relationship which develops between dreamy Judith, who is fifteen, and Larry (derisively nicknamed Daffy Dreamboat from Down Under by Judith's trenchant best friend), a lordly eighteen and a prefect at the Southampton comprehensive they both attend. Collecting old photographs for a stall at the school fete, Judith is reminded of her great-grandmother, a baker's daughter seduced as a girl by a dashing young squireen. The girl comes to believe, not unreasonably after more old photographs come to light, that it was a forebear of Larry's who was the seducer in question. Judith, an orphan living with an intellectual aunt, and Larry, in a family of accomplished musicians trying to assert his right to be different, are an unlikely item, and their encounters have the charm, for 'teenage readers, of the unexpected, besides a comfortable plausibility because of the author's apt selection of details in a relationship conducted within the constraints and prejudices of village society. In particular her dialogue, free-wheeling with fractured sentences and judicious idiomatic humour, takes one right into the day to day behaviour of the young and their elders, with everyday matters like cooking, cricket practice and coffee shops alternating with passages from Judith's diary and the tantalising emotions sensed in telephone conversations and dreams. To write about the young in love, with all that the phrase implies about sexual desire, tenderness and curiosity, is far from easy. Jean Ure mixes comedy and genuine feeling with candour and without a hint of condescension and after many years of accomplished writing for the young she has reached a new standard of excellence in this new novel.

*Margery Fisher, in a review of "Dreaming of Larry," in* Growing Point, *Vol. 30, No. 6, March, 1992, p. 5661.*

Jean Ure's umpteenth novel is a contemporary love story for teenagers. Fifteen year old Judith ('a dweller in the clouds') is an emerging feminist who falls for Larry Flinders, an older boy at school. Judith records her thoughts in a diary thus bringing variation to the third person narrative. Jean Ure is especially strong on dialogue. There are lengthy conversations, yet the pages seem to flip by easily. It all sounds most natural. Sex plays its part, but rather vapidly and with a touch of teenage prurience . . . 'It was

*Ure's home, a restored house built in 1690 in which she has written several of her works.*

bad enough when a boy kissed you and wanted to put his tongue in your mouth. . . .'

An absorbing and engrossing book; readers will become involved with the wholly believable characters. The author writes truthfully, and with sensitive edge. A 200-plus page book, with big print on big pages, makes for a rewarding literary experience. Quietly memorable in the way it describes the state of growing up in the present day. The battle of the sexes goes on, but entertainingly.

> *W. M., in a review of "Dreaming of Larry," in* Junior Bookshelf, *Vol. 56, No. 2, April, 1992, pp. 82-3.*

Jean Ure has never been afraid of a challenging subject, to which she always seems able to bring a light but sure touch. Here the topic is under-age sexuality. Judith is fifteen, and both she and eighteen-year-old Larry are anxiously conscious of the fact. In London she might well have been more precocious, but she is an orphan living with an academic aunt in a Hampshire village and she and her friend Hatty have thought little about boys before the travelled and dishy Larry enchants her. Jean Ure is very good on the strains put on a friendship when one partner crosses the line into another stage of life before the other, and on all the half-understanding banter of adolescent talk; while Judith's diary record of the evening when she almost makes Larry lose his self-control is powerfully done. There is not very much plot development, though a piece of family history is cleverly used to introduce some mystery and to provide a possible resolution. Some readers may be irritated that so little happens, others will find the pleasures of knowing Judith and Hatty sufficient in themselves. As an unashamed love story, this might be a useful part of a process of weaning from the 'Sweet Valley High' series and its like.

> *Audrey Laski, in a review of "Dreaming of Larry," in* The School Librarian, *Vol. 40, No. 2, May, 1992, p. 74.*

Jean Ure's **Dreaming of Larry** is an account of a 15-year-old girl's first experience of desire. Judith dreams about sex, thinks incessantly about it, and falls in love with Larry, a handsome sixth-former. This love story is given an interesting twist when Judith discovers that her great-grandmother and Larry's great-grandfather had been lovers in 1918. They had an illegitimate child and the mother died in childbirth.

There might have been a powerful story here, in which the young lovers' preconceptions about male seducers and female victims are brought up against Judith's astonishment at her own sexual recklessness. But the possibilities of this story fail to break through the insufferable "adolescent" self-consciousness of the writing. ("All I can think of is that it went to my head, which is hardly to be wondered at since, after all, the first time one has contact with the Male Organ is bound to be traumatic for the girlish system").

This is a story about young passion but there is little passion in it—little sense of the dismay, the urgency, the excitement, the *disruption* of desire. Nor does it provide any detailed sexual practicalities; ("I am going to draw a dis-

creet veil over the details"). Young readers can find, I suspect, more robust accounts elsewhere.

Philip Larkin once explained that he judged a novel by asking four questions: "Can I read it? Can I believe it? Do I care about it? And will my caring last?" **Dreaming of Larry** raises the questions how substantial, how memorable, and how seriously re-readable can a teenage novel be if its narrative is confined to the perceptions and language of "safe" imagined characters.

> *Victor Watson, in a review of "Dreaming of Larry," in* The Times Educational Supplement, *No. 3957, May 1, 1992, p. 12.*

---

### *Wizard in Wonderland* (1991)

In a note that comes down the chimney on a broomstick, junior wizard Ben-Muzzy invites Joel and Gemma to meet him in the woods for more "FUN AND ADVENCHER." The twins, who were lost in many strange places because of the wizard's bumbling magic in *The Wizard in the Woods,* are ready. They take a whirlwind tour of Wonderland and other places populated with strange creatures, both friends and foes. The butterflylike Airy Fairies steal their broomstick; they encounter the absent-minded, big, furry walloper; the evil Paddiwack Gnomes; and the Great Nurdle Bore, who literally bores everyone stiff, before finding their way home. Too many characters and places prevent much development of any one; it's unfortunate because some of them are original and amusing. Fans of rapid plotting will be pleased; the book moves right along. . . . It's busier than the first book, but the light humor remains, and Ben-Muzzy's magical powers improve ever so slightly.

> *Carolyn Jenks, in a review of "Wizard in Wonderland," in* School Library Journal, *Vol. 39, No. 7, July, 1993, p. 87.*

---

### *Come Lucky April* (1992)

**Come Lucky April** is the sequel to the excellent **Plague 99**. A century has passed. Daniel leaves his Cornish community on a quest for Croydon and his great-grandmother's diary. April and Meta from the local community find him injured. Daniel's world is traditional. April's has evolved into a society run by women: their androgynous men are willingly "civilised" to avoid the previous errors of a male-dominated world. So David, embodying rape and murder, is both dangerous and beyond understanding. His effect—on the community and on April—is performed.

It is both strange and significant that children's literature is the main home of the constructive dystopia. This novel is—among other things—a serious debate about society and the nature of history. Two possible futures are projected and opposed—with hooks for a future synthesis between the thesis of **Plague 99** and the clearly-defined antithesis of **Come Lucky April.** The trilogy must be completed: Jean Ure is giving superbly-realised enactments of urgent questions in a riveting and absorbing sequence of novels.

*Dennis Hamley, in a review of "Come Lucky April," in* The Times Educational Supplement, *No. 3962, June 5, 1992, p. 34.*

Members of one of the colonies established after **Plague 99** are taught that the horrors of life before the devastation were the result of aggressive domination by males, and this problem is solved by removing boys from the community during adolescence and returning them only after they have been castrated. Fertilisation of the females is, necessarily, an artificial process.

This well reasoned and very interesting book revolves around the dilemma of April Harriet, who encounters Daniel, an entire male from another settlement. He offers her marriage, with a full sexual relationship: but there is also David, April's childhood friend, whose virility has been taken from him but who retains his spirit and strong intelligence.

Jean Ure, writing with impressive skill, draws interesting parallels between the opinions of some of the eunuchs and the attitudes of women who reject emancipation. Her book retains until the last page its capacity to surprise.

*R. Baines, in a review of "Come Lucky April," in* The Junior Bookshelf, *Vol. 56, No. 4, August, 1992, p. 168.*

Very much a novel of ideas, this book is for the mature reflective reader. Plot and characterisation take second place to the exploration of numerous interesting themes, ranging over forms of political organisation and relationships between the sexes. The nature of the Croydon community may impose a certain strain on the reader's credulity, but undoubtedly this is an ambitious and rewarding book.

*Elizabeth Finlayson, in a review of "Come Lucky April," in* The School Librarian, *Vol. 40, No. 3, August, 1992, p. 115.*

### Always Sebastian  (1993)

This story is a sequel to **If It Weren't for Sebastian** and concerns the efforts of a group of anti-vivisectionists called A.F.F. (Animal Freedom Fighters). A great deal of the story is set in the somewhat untidy home of a family who are very friendly with Sebastian, and who support his views. As the story develops the author is careful to give expression to the many sides of this problem, as well as the views felt by the A.F.F.

As to the family which consists of a mother and her two teenage daughters, they all seem to be in love with Sebastian. Towards the end of the book Maggie, the mother, gives her two children her diary, written when she herself was not much older than they are now. This proves to be partly a very intimate, personal account of her relationship with Sebastian. This story is one for the Intermediate library.

*B. Clark, in a review of "Always Sebastian," in* The Junior Bookshelf, *Vol. 57, No. 4, August, 1993, p. 163.*

### A Place to Scream  (1993)

**A Place to Scream** presents a disturbing picture of the world in the year 2015. It would appear that the grim areas of our present society are to be compounded by added lack of care and concern (for the elderly), unemployment, homelessness and poverty. Not a pleasant picture. Sixteen-year-old Gillian, although one of the more favoured teenagers of her time, still suffers from angst, guilt and depression. Her work with the all-pervading computer is tedious. A meeting with unconventional Rick proves a turning point, and we are into a novel of relationships.

The book, for me, was a painful read. Well-written, pacey and realistic it may be, but the sense of hopelessness in a world gone to the dogs is all-pervasive. Jean Ure writes with strength; the dialogue is punchy; the characters are well and truly alive, yet the tone is one of grimness. Perhaps teenagers will respond differently to the depiction of the future as bad news. If they do, then they will swim avidly through the warts-and-all world in 2015.

*W. M., in a review of "A Place to Scream," in* The Junior Bookshelf, *Vol. 57, No. 4, August, 1993, pp. 163-64.*

# Children's
# Literature
# Review

# How to Use This Index

## The main reference

Baum, L(yman) Frank
1856-1919 .......................... **15**

lists all author entries in this and previous volumes of *Children's Literature Review.*

## The cross-references

See also CA 103; 108; DLB 22; JRDA;
MAICYA; MTCW; SATA 18; TCLC 7

list all author entries in the following Gale biographical and literary sources:

*AAYA = Authors & Artists for Young Adults*
*AITN = Authors in the News*
*BLC = Black Literature Criticism*
*BW = Black Writers*
*CA = Contemporary Authors*
*CAAS = Contemporary Authors Autobiography Series*
*CABS = Contemporary Authors Bibliographical Series*
*CANR = Contemporary Authors New Revision Series*
*CAP = Contemporary Authors Permanent Series*
*CDALB = Concise Dictionary of American Literary Biography*
*CLC = Contemporary Literary Criticism*
*CLR = Children's Literature Review*
*CMLC = Classical and Medieval Literature Criticism*
*DA = DISCovering Authors*
*DC = Drama Criticism*
*DLB = Dictionary of Literary Biography*
*DLBD = Dictionary of Literary Biography Documentary Series*
*DLBY = Dictionary of Literary Biography Yearbook*
*HW = Hispanic Writers*
*JRDA = Junior DISCovering Authors*
*LC = Literature Criticism from 1400 to 1800*
*MAICYA = Major Authors and Illustrators for Children and Young Adults*
*MTCW = Major 20th-Century Writers*
*NCLC = Nineteenth-Century Literature Criticism*
*PC = Poetry Criticism*
*SAAS = Something about the Author Autobiography Series*
*SATA = Something about the Author*
*SSC = Short Story Criticism*
*TCLC = Twentieth-Century Literary Criticism*
*WLC = World Literature Criticism, 1500 to the Present*
*YABC = Yesterday's Authors of Books for Children*

**Author Index**

# CUMULATIVE INDEX TO NATIONALITIES

# CUMULATIVE INDEX TO TITLES

# CUMULATIVE INDEX TO TITLES

Title Index

Title Index

Title Index

Title Index

Title Index

Title Index

Title Index

Title Index

ISBN 0-8103-8473-6

9 780810 384736